Nathan Brown's comprehensive and penetrating account of the development and operation of the courts in the Arab world is based on extensive fieldwork in Egypt and the Gulf. The book addresses several important questions. Why, for example, did Egypt's political leaders construct an independent judicial system which so obviously limited their own authority? And why does a seemingly autonomous and dilatory system recommend itself to Arab states outside Egypt as diverse as Libya, Kuwait, Iraq, and the Gulf? While most accounts stress the role of imperialism or liberal ideology in answering such questions, the author maintains that the primary purpose of the system – certainly in the eyes of the political leaders who have built and sustained it – is to provide support for the officially sanctioned order. In other words, the Egyptian legal and judicial system was constructed as an integral part of an effort to build a stronger, more effective, more centralized, and more intrusive state. The system offers similar attractions for other Arab rulers.

From the theoretical perspective, the book makes a powerful and original contribution to the debates about liberal legality, external and internal sources of political change during and after imperialism, and the relationship between law and society in the developing world. It will be widely read by scholars of the Middle East, law students, and anyone with an interest in the history of law and its evolution.

*Cambridge Middle East Studies*

# The rule of law in the Arab world

*Cambridge Middle East Studies 6*

**Cambridge Middle East Studies** has been established to publish books on the nineteenth- and twentieth-century Middle East and North Africa. The aim of the series is to provide new and original interpretations of aspects of Middle Eastern societies and their histories. To achieve disciplinary diversity, books will be solicited from authors writing in a wide range of fields including history, sociology, anthropology, political science and political economy. The emphasis will be on producing books offering an original approach along theoretical and empirical lines. The series is intended for students and academics, but the more accessible and wide-ranging studies will also appeal to the interested general reader.

# The rule of law in
# the Arab world

*Courts in Egypt and the Gulf*

Nathan J. Brown

*The George Washington University*

CAMBRIDGE
UNIVERSITY PRESS

CAMBRIDGE UNIVERSITY PRESS
Cambridge, New York, Melbourne, Madrid, Cape Town, Singapore, São Paulo

Cambridge University Press
The Edinburgh Building, Cambridge CB2 2RU, UK

Published in the United States of America by Cambridge University Press, New York

www.cambridge.org
Information on this title: www.cambridge.org/9780521590266

First published 1997
This digitally printed first paperback version 2006

*A catalogue record for this publication is available from the British Library*

*Library of Congress Cataloguing in Publication data*
Brown, Nathan J.
The rule of law in the Arab world: courts in Egypt and
the Gulf / Nathan J. Brown.
  p.  cm. – (Cambridge Middle East studies)
Includes bibliographical references and index.
ISBN 0 521 59026 4 (hardback)
1. Courts – Arab countries.  2. Courts – Egypt.
3. Courts – Persian Gulf States.  4. Rule of law – Arab countries.
5. Rule of law – Egypt.  6. Rule of law – Persian Gulf States.
I. Title.  II. Series.
KMC459.B76  1997
347'.1492701–dc21      96–44075  CIP

ISBN-13  978-0-521-59026-6 hardback
ISBN-10  0-521-59026-4 hardback

ISBN-13  978-0-521-03068-7 paperback
ISBN-10  0-521-03068-4 paperback

To Judy

# Contents

# Preface

In 1995, the Palestinian authority in Gaza and Jericho took its first unambiguous step in the direction of statehood by creating State Security Courts for cases of political violence (especially against Israeli targets). At the same time an assortment of Islamist movements in neighboring Egypt were engaged in a violent struggle with state authorities, with the movements claiming that the failure to implement the Islamic *shari'a* rendered the regime illegitimate. The regime responded by using all tools available, including, most controversially, military courts to try civilians.

Courts and legal systems have been the focus of intense political struggles in the Arab world, in some locations for over a century. Legal issues are, as everywhere, technical and arcane at times, but just as often they are closely connected to the definition and operation of political power and political community. Residents of the Arab world encounter courts and the legal system in many of their affairs; in fact, they seek out the courts at surprisingly high rates.

This study concerns the role of courts in social and political life in the Arab world. Egypt receives the major focus, but I have also conducted primary research in the Gulf and have included references to other Arab cases in order to cast the argument as widely as possible.

In transliterating Arabic names and terms, I have endeavored above all to be consistent. In general I follow the system suggested by the *International Journal of Middle East Studies* except that I have not used any diacritical marks. Consistency does have its costs, one of which is that several of the people mentioned may barely recognize their own names.

In the course of carrying out the research for this book over the past six years, I have received much assistance from friends, colleagues, students, and acquaintances. At George Washington University, Jenab Tutunji, Saba Atteyih, Roni Amit, and Jocelyn Aqua provided research assistance. Khalid Bishara not only assisted me with his encyclopedic knowledge of Kuwait; he also arranged many of my interviews in that country. My colleagues Harvey Feigenbaum and Marty Finnemore also read portions of the manuscript, offering expert comments on the theoretical argument. Outside of GWU, I have benefited from the advice and assistance of a number of colleagues, including Lisa Anderson, Elizabeth Burns, Jerry Green, James Rosberg, Armando Salvatore, Ron Shaham, Diane Singerman, Robert Vitalis and John Waterbury. Emad al-Din Shahin read a draft quite carefully, making comments that have helped me improve both accuracy and clarity.

In Cairo, Enid Hill, Nabil 'Abd al-Fattah, Ahmad 'Abd Allah, and Bruce Rutherford, fellow scholars with similar research interests, took time out from their own work to offer their comments and suggestions. I spoke with a number of Egyptian judges over various aspects of this research; I was consistently struck by their openness and hospitality; indeed, I have gained several new friendships as a result of this research. In particular, I would like to thank 'Awad al-Murr, Muhammad Abu al-'Aynayn, 'Abd al-Rahman Nusayr, 'Adil 'Umar Sharif, Najib 'Ulama, and other members of the Supreme Constitutional Court and its Commissioners Body; I am also grateful to Muqbil Shakir, Fathi Jawda, Khalid 'Abd al-Ghaffar, and Bakri 'Abd Allah. Several other individuals with knowledge or experience in the Egyptian legal system were of great assistance in Cairo, including Kamal Abu al-Majd, Rajab al-Banna, Mahmud Riyad, Alex Shalaby, and Yahya Salim. I received invaluable research assistance from Husam Mahmud Muhammad, Muhammad Hanafi, and Sahar Hasan.

In Qatar, I also found an open and friendly research climate. 'Abd Allah al-Marri and Salah Hasan helped me establish many of the contacts necessary for research. Elizabeth Thornhill, Michael Adler, Bushara Bushara, and the staff of the American Cultural Center helped me use my time in Doha as efficiently as possible. Members of the Qatari judiciary were extremely helpful, including Ahmad Fakhru, Thaqil al-Shammari, Yusuf al-Zaman, and 'Abd al-'Aziz al-Khulayfi. Others in Qatar also helped me with their knowledge on the Qatari legal system. In this regard, I thank 'Abd Allah al-Muslimani, 'Abd al-'Aziz Hanifi al-'Usayli, 'Abd al-Rahman Al Mahmud, Fath al-Rahman 'Abd Allah al-Shaykh, and Bihzad Yusuf Bihzad.

The research climate in Kuwait deserves special mention. Although I poked into some of the most sensitive issues in Kuwait (such as the treatment of domestic servants), I found no obstacles in the course of my research. On the contrary, Kuwaitis in official position and in private life talked freely, rarely showing even a trace of inhibition in addressing any topic. To be sure, conducting research as an American in the aftermath of the restoration of Kuwait greatly facilitated matters, but I received the strong impression that many Kuwaitis talked as freely to me as they would to each other. The frankness and freedom of Kuwaiti political discussions may come as a great surprise to those who conducted research elsewhere in the Arab world.

Before I arrived in Kuwait, three colleagues, Jill Crystal, Greg Gause, and Mary-Ann Tetrault, gave me helpful suggestions on whom I should speak with. Several Kuwaitis, most notably 'Abd al-Rahman al-Humaydan, assisted me in establishing contacts with Kuwaiti legal practitioners and experts. The USIS staff in Kuwait, Millie McCoo, Barton Marcois, and Mona Faruqi, were also of great help. In the Ministry of Justice, Jamal Ahmad al-Shihab and Muhammad al-Ansari gave me more time than I had a right to expect. In the Ministry of Interior, 'Adil Ibrahim, Fallah al-'Utaybi, and Muhammad al-Fahd were especially helpful, as was the staff at the Dasma police station and at the Office of Household Labor. In the judiciary, Khalid Faysal al-Hindi and Riyad al-Hajiri provided assistance. Several members of parliament took time out of busy schedules to speak with me about my project; in this regard I would like to thank Nasir al-Sani', Mishari al-'Usaymi, Ya'qub Hayati, and 'Abd Allah Rumi. At the Faculty of Law at Kuwait University, I benefited from the constitutional expertise of 'Adil al-Tabtaba'i and Muhammad al-Muqatti' (who even let me audit his graduate course). Others in Kuwait who were generous with their time and expertise include Bahbahani 'Abd al-Rusul 'Abd al-Rida, and the staff of the Embassy of the Philippines, 'Abd al-'Aziz al-Dukhayl, Muhammad al-Jasim, Khulud al-Fili, Sharon Kenny, Ghanim al-Najjar, Badriya al-'Awadi, Sara al-Du'ayj, Baron Hall, Ernest Alexander, and Mustafa Ayad.

Some of the research for this book was funded by the United States Institute of Peace and by a Fulbright regional research grant. In connection with the latter, I also owe thanks to my sponsors and sponsoring organizations in each country: the binational Fulbright Commission and 'Ali al-Din Hilal of Cairo University in Egypt, USIS and Qatar University in Qatar, and USIS and Ahmad al-Samdan of Kuwait University in Kuwait. Of course, the opinions, findings, and conclusions or recommendations expressed in this book are my own and do not reflect the views of any sponsor or funding organization.

Also in the course of research I was fortunate to be able to present preliminary findings to audiences in the region. In Egypt, my lecture at the Department of Political Science at Cairo University provoked a very lively and interesting discussion. At Qatar University, the Department of Law invited me to give an informal presentation; their comments proved quite helpful. And in Kuwait, the Lawyers' Association sponsored a public lecture and provided a friendly audience for me to explore some of my ideas.

My wife Judy has read all of what I have written, contributing her own knowledge and expertise, restraining some of my more fanciful arguments, and sharpening much of the prose. She accompanied me in visiting the region as well (along with our children, Ariel and Eran). This book would be less well-informed and far more muddled without her help. Whatever training I have as a political scientist does not equip me to do more than acknowledge this assistance in a direct and unadorned fashion. I hope that I may compensate for this by dedicating this book to her.

# Glossary

| | |
|---|---|
| 'Abbas | Egypt's khedive (hereditary governor from 1849 to 1854) |
| *'Adliyya* Courts | The civil courts in Qatar (as opposed to the *shari'a* courts) |
| Arab Socialist Union (ASU) | Egypt's sole political party from 1961 until it was dismantled by Sadat in the mid-1970s |
| capitulations | Agreements by the Ottoman Empire to try subjects of foreign powers by their own laws; continued in Egypt until the Montreux conference of 1937 resulted in an agreement to abolish them |
| *diya* | Indemnity paid for causing death |
| Free Officers | The group of army officers who launched the 1952 coup, overthrowing the monarchy and the parliamentary regime |
| Isma'il | Egypt's khedive (hereditary governor) from 1863 to 1879; during his reign the Mixed Courts were established |
| *mahdar* | A formal statement made to the police |
| *Mahkamat al-Naqd* | Egypt's Court of Cassation; the highest level for civil and criminal cases |
| *mahr* | In most Muslim societies the groom pledges an amount to the bride. There is great variation among (and sometimes within) societies as to who holds the money and the precise form that it takes. In Egypt it is common to pledge one amount (the *mahr muqaddim*) upon marriage and a separate amount (the *mahr mu'akhkhar*) in the event of a divorce or death. |
| *majalla* | A late nineteenth-century Ottoman attempt to codify law on an Islamic basis (the full name was the *majallat al-ahkam al-'adliyya*) |
| *Majlis al-Dawla* | Council of State; in Egypt the structure was |

|  |  |
|---|---|
|  | established in 1946 and comprises administrative courts as well as a body to offer advice to the government on legislation |
| *Milli* Courts | Personal-status courts that operated for different religious communities in Egypt until 1956 |
| Mixed Courts | A court system that operated in Egypt from 1876 until 1949; had jurisdiction in civil cases in which a foreign interest was involved; also given limited criminal jurisdiction |
| National Courts | Established in 1883 with jurisdiction in Egyptian civil and criminal cases (also referred to in English as the Native Courts and in Arabic as *al-mahakim al-ahliyya, al-majalis al-ahliyya,* and *al-mahakim al-wataniyya*); with the abolition of the Mixed Courts in 1949, and of the *Shari'a* and *Milli* Courts in 1956 they were referred to simply as the regular Egyptian courts |
| *niyaba* | An institution based on the French *parquet* system in which judicial personnel have responsibility for investigating and presenting criminal cases to courts; the *niyaba* system was adopted first in Egypt and later emulated in many other Arab countries |
| Nubar | Egyptian political leader of the late nineteenth century; served in various diplomatic and cabinet positions (including prime minister) before and after the British occupation; instrumental in establishing the Mixed Courts and influential in domestic legal reform as well |
| *qadi* | Judge; in Islamic courts the term refers to any judge whereas in civil courts it generally refers to a judge of lower rank (as opposed to a *mustashar* or senior judge) though the plural (*quda*) refers to judges as a body regardless of rank |
| *qanun* | In current usage, positive laws and codes; in the Ottoman Empire *qanun* generally referred to texts that fixed or codified Islamic and imperial law |
| Revolutionary Command Council (RCC) | The body established by the Free Officers after the 1952 coup to exercise executive authority |

| | |
|---|---|
| Riyad | Egyptian political leader of the late nineteenth century; influential in legal and judicial reform |
| al-Sanhuri, 'Abd al-Razzaq | Egyptian jurist of the mid-twentieth century; rewrote Egypt's civil code; served as president of the *Majlis al-Dawla*; assisted other Arab states in writing their civil codes |
| *shari'a* | Generally translated as Islamic law; the *shari'a* covers all areas of religiously-mandated and regulated behavior |
| *siyadat al-qanun* | Sovereignty of law; Arabic equivalent to the phrase "rule of law" |
| Supreme Judicial Council | The Egyptian body responsible for judicial hirings, assignments, and promotions; from 1969 to 1984 the body was replaced by the Supreme Council of Judicial Organizations (this latter body still operates but its role in judicial assignments for the regular judiciary is now a formality) |
| *'urf* | Custom and customary law |
| 'Uthman Khalil 'Uthman | Egyptian legal scholar who drafted Kuwait's constitution |
| Wafd | Nationalist Egyptian political party that emerged out of the 1919 revolt against the British occupation; banned with other parties after the 1952 coup, it resumed activity as a result of political liberalization under Sadat and Mubarak |

# 1 Arab courts in comparative perspective

Modern Egyptian courts would seem to be unattractive both to ruler and ruled. Yet since their establishment over a century ago, they have not only become important parts of the social and political landscape but have been imitated throughout the Arab world.

Why did Egypt's political leaders construct and maintain a system that seems – at least at first glance – to restrict their own authority? Egypt may be the Arab country that has come closest to establishing the strong and autonomous legal institutions necessary for the rule of law. With courts that have freed political extremists and twice brought down the country's parliament, Egypt's judicial system is regarded as possessing remarkable independence and integrity (even while it is often perceived as a European imposition).

Why does an autonomous and dilatory system recommend itself to Arab rulers outside Egypt? Far from filling Arab observers with dismay, Egyptian courts are a model throughout the region, emulated in varying degrees in political systems as diverse as those of Libya, Kuwait, Iraq, and Yemen. Egyptian legal models – along with many Egyptian judicial personnel – have been employed in much of the Arab world.

Why do so many Egyptians choose to bring their disputes to court? The Egyptian legal system is widely held to be confusing, overburdened, and forbidding. Criticized as culturally inappropriate when founded a century ago, lampooned by Tawfiq al-Hakim as overworked and incomprehensible to Egyptians a half-century ago,[1] and constantly described today as slow and strained to the breaking point, Egyptian courts not only survive but are increasingly sought out by Egyptians from all walks of life.

This study will focus primarily on Egypt and more broadly on the Arab world (especially the Arab states of the Gulf). Nevertheless, there will be an effort to cast the answers to these questions in more general terms. Throughout the developing world, legal systems based on

[1] Tawfiq al-Hakim, *Yawmiyyat na'ib fi-l-aryaf* (Diary of a Prosecutor in the Countryside), Cairo: Maktabat al-Adab, n.d., originally published 1937.

Western models are very much the rule rather than the exception. The influence of such models did not die with imperialism. Indeed, in recent years one alternative legal orientation has collapsed with communism, leaving the former Soviet bloc scrambling to undertake reforms quite similar to those begun in Egypt over a century ago. Thus the motivations behind, and the reactions to, legal reform in the Arab world are likely to have global relevance.

In at least one respect, the legal systems of the Arab world are particularly accessible to this sort of study. Unlike Europe and the United States (and parts of the developing world as well), they were consciously created in a relatively short historical period. Those involved in the creation of modern court structures and legal codes are easily identified, and their writings and actions are thus not difficult to uncover.[2] A brief consideration of the history of legal reform in the modern Arab world will assist us in discovering what impelled them to create the system and understanding how their creation has operated.

## The construction of the modern legal system

Most countries in the Arab world share comprehensive legal codes, on the continental model, that combine elements of French and Islamic law. Court systems are similarly based on centralized and hierarchical civil-law models. The origin of the current legal system in most Arab countries can be traced back to the Ottoman reforms of the nineteenth century. Prior to that time, the Ottoman government certainly had a strong interest in the administration of justice, and *qadis* (judges), appointed by the Empire or its local representatives, adjudicated disputes based on a combination of *sharaʿa* (Islamic law) and *qanun* (state law, itself heavily based on the *sharaʿa*).[3] Other localized systems of justice, often informed by custom, operated in specific areas. A series of centralizing reforms throughout the nineteenth century resulted in a more hierarchical system as well as several attempts to codify existing law. The culmination of the Ottoman codification effort, the *majalla*, issued between 1869 and 1877, was intended to be Islamic in content but was based in form on the *Code Napoléon*.[4] Even as domestic legal

---

[2] The use of the term "modern" to refer to the court system (here and throughout the text) simply designates the historical period in which the system was adopted and operates. No necessary connection with other aspects of the modern period is assumed.

[3] Haim Gerber, *State, Society, and Law in Islam: Ottoman Law in Comparative Perspective* (Albany: State University of New York Press, 1994).

[4] June Starr, *Law as Metaphor: From Islamic Courts to the Palace of Justice* (Albany: State University of New York Press, 1992), chapter 1. Brinkley Messick argues that the attempt to codify Islamic law inherently changed its meaning; see Brinkley Messick, *The*

reform progressed, the capitulations, a series of agreements with European powers, generally expanded in their impact until they gave Europeans (and some others) extraterritorial status; this led to a system of consular courts for those who could claim European citizenship.

The effectiveness of the Ottoman reforms varied according to the degree of influence exercised from Istanbul. Egypt, technically an Ottoman province but autonomous throughout the century, generally followed Ottoman developments, though the pace and content of reform sometimes differed.[5] A series of tribunals, consisting of local officials (sometimes supplemented by *shari'a*-trained qadis) was established throughout the nineteenth century that operated alongside the *Shari'a* Courts, ruling on the basis of locally enacted legislation, itself partly based on the *shari'a* and Ottoman legislation.[6] The 1870s saw a protracted (and finally successful) effort to establish Mixed Courts, which had jurisdiction in all civil cases in which a foreign interest was (even remotely) involved. These courts operated according to their own code, drawn heavily from the Code Napoléon.[7] They continued until 1949 when foreign residents became completely subject to the regular Egyptian courts. Following the establishment of the Mixed Courts, Egyptian governments attempted to construct a new, centralized court system, based largely on a French model. Work on the new system and its code was interrupted in 1882 with the British occupation, but was completed in 1883 when the new National Courts began operation. While some effort was made to incorporate Islamic elements, the Egyptian code was far closer to the French than to the Ottoman *majalla*. *Shari'a* Courts continued in operation, though they were much restricted in scope, handling only matters of personal status (chiefly marriage, divorce, and inheritance). In 1956, the work of the *Shari'a* Courts (and of the *Milli* Courts which served Egypt's other religious

*Calligraphic State: Textual Domination and History in a Muslim Society* (Berkeley: University of California Press, 1993), chapter 3. For a different version of the same argument, see Ann Elizabeth Mayer, "The Shari'ah: A Methodology or a Body of Substantive Rules?" in Nicholas Heer (ed.) *Islamic Law and Jurisprudence* (Seattle: University of Washington Press, 1990).

5  The most authoritative works on judicial reform in Egypt are: Byron Cannon, *Politics of Law and the Courts in Nineteenth Century Egypt* (Salt Lake City: University of Utah Press, 1988); and Latifa Muhammad Salim, *Al-nizam al-qada'i al-misri al-hadith*, 2 vols. (The Modern Egyptian Judicial System), (Cairo: Markaz al-Dirasat al-Siyasiyya wa-l-Istratijiyya bi-l-Ahram, 1984).

6  See Rudolph Peters, "The Codification of Criminal Law in Nineteenth Century Egypt: Tradition or Modernization?" in Jamil M. Abun-Nasr, Ulrich Spellenberg, and Ulrike Wanitzek (eds.), *Law, Society, and National Identity in Africa* (Hamburg: Helmut Buske Verlag, 1990).

7  Nathan J. Brown, "The Precarious Life and Slow Death of the Mixed Courts of Egypt," *International Journal of Middle East Studies*, 25 (1), 1993, p. 1.

communities) was folded into the National Court structure. While Egypt's law codes have been updated at several points, they remain linear descendants of those enacted with the construction of the National Courts. The courts themselves, while supplemented at various points (with, for instance, an administrative court system in 1946 and a constitutional court in 1979), have continued to constitute the center-piece of Egypt's judicial system.

In the other Ottoman Arab provinces, the *majalla* was at least theoretically in effect when the Empire collapsed in the wake of the First World War.[8] The mandatory powers – France in Lebanon and Syria; Britain in Jordan, Iraq, and Palestine (as well as Sudan) – attempted in varying degrees to recast the legal system in their own images. Especially in Sudan, Jordan, and Palestine, the British drew on the Indian experience in an attempt to meld the *majalla* or other sources with a common law system. With independence, most countries amended their codes (often with the assistance of Egyptians) and continued or increased the centralization of their court structures.

In most of the Arab Gulf states, the British slowly obtained jurisdiction in cases involving foreigners. British officials therefore attempted to establish their own courts and codify law, drawing principally on their Indian experience. Attempts were made to draw up legal codes (with Indian, Jordanian, Palestinian, and *shariʿa* law informing the efforts to various degrees). Local rulers drew up their own codes, generally with Egyptian (though sometimes with British) assistance. Even before the British withdrawal from the area in 1971, Egyptian influence had increased markedly.

Since Saudi Arabia and Yemen never came under British protection, and since the Ottoman reforms were felt only in certain areas, the preexisting *shariʿa* system was never restricted. Yemen has made efforts to centralize and codify its legal system quite recently. Saudi Arabia has generally avoided the appearance of doing so, and *shariʿa* courts retain general jurisdiction in the kingdom. Alongside *shariʿa* courts, however, a complex system of tribunals enforce commercial, financial, and labor regulations.[9] French influence was paramount in North Africa, although Morocco is notable for the large degree of Islamic influence in its codes.

Turkey and Iran, Muslim neighbors to the Arab world, also

---

[8] For a summary presentation of legal reform in the Arab world, see Farhat J. Ziadeh, "Permanence and Change in Arab Legal Systems," *Arab Studies Quarterly*, 9 (1), 1987, p. 20.

[9] A. Lerrick and Q. J. Mian, *Saudi Business and Labor Law: Its Interpretation and Application* (London: Graham and Trotman, 1982), chapter 6.

centralized and Europeanized their legal systems. Republican Turkey did so by effecting a fairly complete secularization of its law code, even in matters of personal status. Iran under Reza Shah adopted a version of the Swiss law code; this remained in effect until after the Islamic revolution. Even after the revolution, Iran's courts are more hierarchically and formally organized than the preexisting Islamic courts.

## The adoption of the modern legal system

Why should Middle Eastern states turn to centralized, hierarchical, and Western models? The first two questions posed by this study – involving the purpose of legal reform in Egypt and the remainder of the Arab world – require a focus on elite motivations. These motivations, although often taken for granted by students of the area, have rarely been systematically explored. When considering the evolution of legal systems more generally, three orientations have generally suggested themselves. First, a legal system can be imposed by the outside for motives related to the interests of an imperial power. Second, a legal system can emerge along liberal lines in an effort to regularize (and even limit) authority and guarantee property and predictability of economic relations. Third, modern legal systems have been portrayed as emerging out of efforts to centralize authority and secure the domination of specific groups or classes. All three of these explanations have been suggested not simply for Egypt (and the Arab world) but for the non-Western world more broadly. Each grows out of a distinct approach to the question of legal development in non-Western settings.

### Imposed law

Imposition of law by imperial powers has been adduced most frequently to explain why non-Western societies adopted Western legal systems. Such a perspective has implicitly guided many studies of the history of the Egyptian legal system for a century: European states (especially Britain) imposed new standards of justice and new legal procedures on a country that had known only arbitrary government tamed occasionally by Islamic practices.[10]

Most of the world's population which experienced European imperialism now lives under legal systems that have been based, at least

---

[10] See for instance the Earl of Cromer, *Modern Egypt* (London: Macmillan, 1908); and Jasper Yeates Brinton, *The Mixed Courts of Egypt*, revised edition (New Haven: Yale University Press, 1968). Also of interest is Tariq al-Bishri, "Mi'a 'amman 'ala al-qada' al-misri" (One Hundred Years of the Egyptian Judiciary), *al-Quda*, 5/6 1986, p. 28.

partially, on European models. Some tie between imperialism and law has thus been obvious for at least a century.[11] Late nineteenth-century and early twentieth-century European writers understandably adopted such a view because law was often seen as an integral part of (sometimes even a justification for) the imperial mission. A British author who visited Egypt on the eve of the First World War wrote that "We have introduced the principle of English law which requires that a person, even if known to be guilty, shall not be punished unless his guilt can be proved in open court by the evidence of witnesses. This is alien to the Eastern temperament."[12]

More recent writings have actually accentuated rather than undermined this view of the relationship between law and imperialism. While scholars are increasingly open to discovering local resistance and the survival of precolonial law, many still "show how law served the 'civilizing mission' of colonialism – transforming the societies of the Third World into the form of the West."[13] Perhaps because studies of subsaharan Africa have been influential in understanding the relationship between imperialism and law, much current scholarship continues to assert or assume that the basic contours of legal systems were laid by the metropole, local imperial officials, and expatriate populations.[14] Recent studies of the origin of "customary" law have revealed that even when imperial authorities claimed – and indeed sought – to leave law in the hands of traditional authorities, they often ended up creating "traditions" or thoroughly transforming what had existed previously.[15] Attempts to codify and enforce indigenous law often had the paradoxical effect of enshrining anachronistic or particularistic (rather than customa-

---

[11] See Sandra B. Burman and Barbara E. Harrell-Bond, (eds.), *The Imposition of Law* (New York: Academic Press, 1979), and John Schmidhauser, "Power, Legal Imperialism, and Dependency," *Law and Society Review*, 23 (5), 1989. Also of interest is Sally Engle Merry, "Law and Colonialism," *Law and Society Review*, 25 (4), 1991.

[12] Sidney Low, *Egypt in Transition* (New York: Macmillan, 1914), p. 248.

[13] Merry, "Law and Colonialism," p. 894.

[14] Joan Vincent, "Contours of Change: Agrarian Law in Colonial Uganda, 1895–1962," in June Starr and Jane Collier (eds.), *History and Power in the Study of Law* (Ithaca: Cornell University Press, 1989); Richard Roberts and Kristin Mann, "Law in Colonial Africa," in Kristin Mann and Richard Roberts (eds.), *Law in Colonial Africa* (Portsmouth: Heinemann, 1991); Francis Snyder and Douglas Hay, "Comparisons in the Social History of Law: Labour and Crime," and Frederick Cooper, "Contracts, Crime, and Agrarian Conflict: From Slave to Wage Labour on the East African Coast," in Francis Snyder and Douglas Hay (eds.), *Labour, Law and Crime* (London: Tavistock Publications, 1987).

[15] Martin Chanock, "Making Customary Law: Men, Women, and Courts in Colonial Northern Rhodesia," in Margaret Jean Hay and Marcia Wright (eds.), *African Women and the Law*, Boston University Papers on Africa, VII (1982), and Bernard S. Cohn, "Law and the Colonial State in India," in Starr and Collier (eds.), *History and Power in the Study of Law*.

rily accepted) legal texts as national standards.[16] In Burma, J. S. Furnivall describes a British effort to safeguard local custom by providing for the attendance in court of a Burmese "skilled in Burman law and usages." However, "the whole idea of giving judgment in accordance with fixed legal principles was contrary to Burmese customs, and the decisions on this plan were as foreign as the court."[17] Similar transformations in the very meaning of law occurred (though not always so unintentionally) when the legal system was Islamic in nature, even though Europeans recognized Islamic law as sophisticated and highly developed.[18] These experiences indicated that it may have been possible that imperialists determined the structure and workings of the legal system whether they wished to or not.

This view, centered as it is on the motives and actions of the imperial power, should cause some discomfort because it risks writing the population of much of the world out of its own history. It may be such discomfort that has prompted some scholars to investigate ways in which local populations have reacted to legal changes initiated by the imperial power, often in ways European rulers found quite frustrating. Indeed, such an approach was adopted as far back as Lloyd Rudolph's and Susanne Hoeber Rudolph's *The Modernity of Tradition*.[19] More recent writings have focused on the effect dominated populations had on shaping the operation of law in an imperial context.[20] Even with this increasing focus on the subaltern, however, the stress on the actions and intentions of the imperial power is not lessened. The local population emerges subverting imperial goals not so much through overt resistance as through self-interested behavior (which sometimes can also be characterized as resistance) informed by preimperial ideologies and practices. Even in this work, the local population responds to external challenges; historical change is still primarily the turf of imperialism.

---

[16] Lloyd I. Rudolph and Susanne Hoeber Rudolph, *The Modernity of Tradition: Political Development in India* (Chicago: University of Chicago Press, 1967); and Leopold Pospisil, "Legally Induced Culture Change in New Guinea," in Burman and Harrell-Bond (eds.), *The Imposition of Law*.

[17] J. S. Furnivall, *Colonial Policy and Practice: A Comparative Study of Burma and Netherlands India* (Cambridge: Cambridge University Press, 1948).

[18] Allen C. Christelow, *Muslim Law Courts and the French Colonial State in Algeria* (Princeton: Princeton University Press, 1985); and David S. Powers, "Orientalism, Colonialism, and Legal History: The Attack on Muslim Family Endowments in Algeria and India," *Comparative Studies in Society and History*, 31 (3), 1989.

[19] Rudolph and Rudolph, *The Modernity of Tradition*.

[20] Merry, "Law and Colonialism"; Roberts and Mann, "Law in Colonial Africa"; Julia Wells, "Passes and Bypasses: Freedom of Movement for African Women Under the Urban Areas Acts of South Africa," in Hay and Wright, *African Women and the Law*; and Peter Fitzpatrick, "Transformation of Law and Labour in Papua New Guinea," in Snyder and Hay, *Labour, Law and Crime*.

We should be careful before we remove the initiative from the subject population. Since imperialism often worked through, around, or in spite of local elites, we must consider the possibility that those elites may have played an independent role in constructing and maintaining new legal systems. In point of fact, such a role has been noted for rulers and regimes that felt foreign pressure without coming under direct imperial control. David Engel notes such a situation in Japan, Ethiopia, and Turkey; he states that in Thailand "while the end result of judicial centralization . . . was comparable in many ways to the process that took place in her colonized neighbors, a greater flexibility and adaptability in the Thai legal system probably resulted from the fact that it was administered for the most part by the Thais themselves."[21] In order to ascertain the relative role of the imperial power and of local elites in our study of the Arab world, it will be necessary to examine the timing and the nature of legal reform there.

If local elites did play a prominent role in constructing legal systems that at least appeared to limit their authority, what impelled them to do so? Two alternative orientations direct our attention inside rather than outside the country. One is based on liberal legality; the other is based on the idea that law is a tool of domination.

### The emergence of liberal legality

Liberal legality posits the rule of law as the surest guarantee against arbitrary government. A proper legal system must guard against despotic and tyrannical rule and circumscribe the authority of rulers, forcing them to rule in compliance with established procedures and norms. Legal reform in Egypt and the rest of the Arab world would thus be understood as an attempt to restrict – or at least regularize – the unlimited authority that Egyptian rulers possessed at the beginning of the reform period. Few social scientists would employ a liberal perspective uncritically, but the ideas behind it remain powerful in Egypt. Members of the Egyptian legal profession have generally found liberal legality appealing, jealously guarding whatever measures of autonomy they have managed to achieve for the legal system. Indeed, many writings on the Egyptian legal system betray a largely liberal image of law.[22] And international human-rights organizations work hard to measure current practice against largely liberal standards.

---

[21] David M. Engel, *Code and Custom in a Thai Provincial Court* (Tucson: University of Arizona Press, 1978), p. 28.

[22] See, for example, Farhat Ziadeh, *Lawyers, the Rule of Law, and Liberalism in Modern Egypt* (Palo Alto: Stanford, 1968); Donald M. Reid, *Lawyers and Politics in the Arab*

Images of liberal legality tend to be far more prescriptive than descriptive. It is far easier to explain what an ideal system would be than to explain how it might emerge. Unsurprisingly, therefore, academic writings that deal with the social and political origins of legal systems are far less likely to adopt such a liberal perspective that may seem naively idealistic. Central to the liberal perspective is the idea of the "rule of law"; the corresponding Arabic phrase *siyadat al-qanun* occurs in constitutions as well as legal and human-rights writings throughout the Arab world. In the criminal realm, the rule of law would allow no punishment without a clear legal justification. In the civil realm, the rule of law would protect property rights, again allowing no infringements on property that did not have a clear legal basis. Authority operates on the basis of fixed, identifiable, and predictable legal rights rather than unlimited personal discretion. An independent judiciary, free from executive interference, works to apply the law to concrete disputes, and is equally accessible to all. Rulers are fully subject to the text of the law just as ordinary citizens are.

Defenders of the rule of law rarely take the position that it is ever fully realized or that the rule of law alone can guarantee a perfect and just society. Yet they point to real benefits, both moral and material, that accrue from approximating its ideals. Andrew Altman writes, "liberal theory does not promise salvation through legal rules; what it promises is a society that does a better job of protecting people from intolerance, prejudice, and oppression than it would if law was dispensed with."[23] Certainly some conception of the rule of law is necessary for a liberal political system to be maintained; a state that is separate from, and accountable to, the society could not exist if the authority of public officials was arbitrary and unrestricted. Beyond this, some have argued that litigation is itself a form of political participation consistent with and supportive of the goals of democratic theory.[24]

In recent years, a separate argument has been revived: the rule of law is a necessary foundation for market economics and economic development. Hernando de Soto gained great attention for arguing that the unsuitability of the political and legals system of Peru forced would-be entrepreneurs to operate informally, without the protection and predict-

---

*World, 1880–1960* (Minneapolis: Bibliotheca Islamica, 1981); and Salim, *Al-nizam al-qada'i al-misri*, vols. I and II.

[23] Andrew Altman, *Critical Legal Studies: A Liberal Critique* (Princeton: Princeton University Press, 1990), p. 200.

[24] Susan E. Lawrence, "Justice, Democracy, Litigation, and Political Participation," *Social Science Quarterly*, 72 (3), 1991, p. 464; and Frances Kahn Zemans, "Legal Mobilization: The Neglected Role of Law in the Political System," *American Political Science Review*, 77, 1983, p. 690.

ability of the legal system. This, he claimed, discouraged investment, innovation, specialization, and commerce with disastrous results for the Peruvian economy.[25] Douglass North has written in a similar vein, viewing uncertainty concerning property rights as characteristic of Third World legal systems and a major impediment to economic development.[26]

Yet a concentration on the benefits of liberal legality begs some questions. If it provides so many benefits, why is it not universally adopted? Here many of its advocates, including de Soto, point to the entrenched though particular interests that sustain illiberal legality. Yet this leads to a further question: if powerful elites and interest groups profit from illiberal legality, how can its liberal counterpart ever emerge?

Surprisingly, the burgeoning literature on democratization and liberalization gives us little guidance in answering these questions. In the current public policy debates in the United States, democracy, free markets, constitutionalism, and the rule of law are not only seen as linked; the terms are also used almost interchangeably. Such analytical imprecision hardly aids understanding. Yet even in the scholarly literature on democratization and liberalization, courts and the law are rarely mentioned. Given the historic importance of the rule of law in liberal ideologies and political struggles, the short shrift given to law and courts in writings on liberalization is striking indeed. Just as the authoritarian regimes of Latin America and the communist regimes of Eastern Europe were easier to bring down than to replace with stable, free-market democracies, so scholars have had far more success understanding the breakdown of authoritarian regimes than in exploring what replaced them.[27] Even Adam Przeworski, who explicitly addresses himself to democracy and economic liberalization rather than simply the breakdown of old regimes, says little more about law than "we tend to believe that an independent judiciary is an important arbitrating force in the face of conflicts"; this comment occurs in a discussion of how little empirical knowledge exists about institutional design and democratic stability.[28]

[25] Hernando de Soto, *The Other Path: The Invisible Revolution in the Third World* (New York: Harper and Row, 1989); see especially chapter 5.

[26] Douglass C. North, *Institutions, Institutional Change, and Economic Performance* (Cambridge: Cambridge University Press, 1990).

[27] For example, see Nancy Bermeo (ed.), *Liberalization and Democratization: Change in the Soviet Union and Eastern Europe* (Baltimore: Johns Hopkins University Press, 1991); and Guillermo O'Donnell and Philippe C. Schmitter, *Transitions from Authoritarian Rule: Tentative Conclusions about Uncertain Democracies* (Baltimore: Johns Hopkins University Press, 1986).

[28] Adam Przeworski, *Democracy and the Market: Political and Economic Reforms in Eastern Europe and Latin America* (New York: Cambridge University Press, 1991), p. 35.

It might be tempting to dismiss liberal legality at this point as constituting a powerful ideology in Europe and the United States but too vague and prescriptive to inform our understanding of law and courts in the Arab world. Yet even if liberal legality itself is historically grounded in the Western experience, Muslim intellectuals have certainly been friendly to the idea that rulers are subject to (and must enforce) law that is not entirely of their own making. Recent research on specific Islamic settings has revealed that the idea was sometimes put into practice.[29] In many ways, the popularity of calls for the application of the Islamic *shari'a* flows directly from the continuing appeal of this image of law. Thus the adoption of new legal systems took place in a context in which the superiority of law to rulers was often accepted in theory. The great restriction (and sometimes abolition) of the older Islamic courts in the Middle East may have changed rather than removed the local basis for the rule of law.[30]

### Law and domination

Another perspective provides a distinct contrast to liberal legality, emphasizing instead the strong role that a legal system can play in supporting the authority of dominant groups. Scholars studying legal systems elsewhere, writing from a variety of ideological perspectives, have noted that the establishment of an independent judicial system can further rather than circumscribe existing relations of authority.

One of the primary ways law can sustain or bolster existing power relations is through legitimation. Considerable controversy surrounds the ways this can and does operate, and some of the leading proponents of the legitimating features of law have been rightfully criticized as surprisingly vague.[31] In some scholarly writings, law is shown to serve

Interestingly, Przeworski stresses the importance of indeterminacy in the political realm in sustaining democracy; this stands in contrast to (though hardly contradicts) the emphasis of predictability in the economic realm.

[29] Gerber, *State, Society, and Law in Islam*; and Galal H. El-Nahal, *The Judicial Administration of Ottoman Egypt in the Seventeenth Century* (Minneapolis: Bibliotheca Islamica, 1979).

[30] While Lisa Anderson herself sees the restriction of Islamic law in most modern Middle Eastern legal systems as aiding the centralization of authority and undermining possibilities for opposition, her portrait of current Middle Eastern regimes is itself based on a liberal conception of legality; hence her description of current Middle Eastern governments as "lawless." Lisa Anderson, "Lawless Government and Illegal Opposition: Reflections on the Middle East," *Journal of International Affairs*, 40, 1987, p. 219. June Starr acknowledges that the current Turkish legal system was the product of centralizing reforms but also portrays it as based on populism and equality and staffed with compassionate and highly trained judges. Starr, *Law as Metaphor*, p. 169.

[31] One author has gone so far as to attack the entire idea of legitimacy. See Alan Hyde,

dominant groups and classes by obscuring inequality. Douglas Hay casts law in unequal societies as furthering class domination while masking it: "True equality before the law in a society of greatly unequal men is impossible: a truth which is kept decently buried beneath a monument of legislation, judicial ingenuity and cant."[32] In this view, law legitimates by cloaking the interests of specific classes in general language that appears class neutral, and in procedures and rituals designed to inculcate respect and awe.[33] For some, the indeterminacy of legal texts allows them to appear egalitarian even as they prove malleable to class interests.[34] For others, law (at least in capitalist societies) promotes the reproduction of capitalist relations by casting class problems in individual terms; class exploitation becomes a matter between employer and employee.[35]

Perhaps the most controversial idea is that legal orders legitimate political or economic orders not simply by masking the domination of specific groups or classes but also by making concessions – or at least offering opportunities – to subaltern groups. Law thus serves the interests of dominant groups but not by being their mechanical tool. In his study of eighteenth-century England, E. P. Thompson, like Douglas Hay, found law central to the ideology of dominant groups, but he also found that this ideology was taken seriously by its proponents in ways that could result in tactical defeats. In so doing, he combines a Marxist historiography with concessions to liberal conceptions of legality:

For there is a very large difference, which twentieth-century experience ought to have made clear to the most exalted thinker, between arbitrary extra-legal power and the rule of law. And not only were the rulers (indeed, the ruling class as a whole) inhibited by their own rules of law against the exercise of direct unmediated force (arbitrary imprisonment, the employment of troops against the crowd, torture, and those other conveniences of power with which we are all

"The Concept of Legitimation in the Sociology of Law," *Wisconsin Law Review*, 1983, pp. 379–426.

[32] Douglas Hay, "Poaching and the Game Laws on Cannock Chase," in Douglas Hay, Peter Linebaugh, John G. Rule, E. P. Thompson, and Cal Winslow, *Albion's Fatal Tree: Crime and Society in Eighteenth-Century England* (New York: Pantheon Books, 1975), p. 189. Interestingly, Hay immediately goes on in this essay to examine a case in which law served no legitimating function: "when they wrote the laws protecting wild game, the rulers of eighteenth-century England dispensed with such hypocrisies," with the result that notions of ownership and justice differed markedly across class lines.

[33] Douglas Hay, "Property, Authority and the Criminal Law," in Hay *et al.*, *Albion's Fatal Tree*, pp. 62–63.

[34] See, for instance, Karl E. Klare, "Critical Theory and Labor Relations Law," in David Kairys (ed.), *The Politics of Law: A Progressive Critique* (New York: Pantheon Books, 1990).

[35] See, for instance, Sol Picciotto, "The Theory of the State, Class Struggle and the Rule of Law," in Piers Bierne and Richard Quinney (eds.), *Marxism and Law* (New York: John Wiley and Sons, 1982).

conversant), but they also believed enough in these rules, and in their accompanying ideological rhetoric, to allow, in certain limited areas, the law itself to be a genuine forum within which certain kinds of class conflict were fought out.[36]

Having established rules that generally worked in its favor, England's ruling class had to live by them. More striking and perhaps more subtly, Eugene D. Genovese explored the workings of law in the slaveholding states of the American South, finding contradictions both in legal practice and in governing ideology that could be exploited by slaves in limited ways.[37]

What is striking in much of the literature on the legitimating functions of law is the weakness of empirical analysis, especially on the degree to which legalistic ideologies legitimate the prevailing order in the eyes of subaltern groups. Hay, for instance, writes convincingly of the ideology of England's ruling class, but his only sustained examination of non-elite ideologies shows them to be starkly in conflict with the conceptions of the dominant and hardly schooled in justice, terror, and mercy.[38] Indeed, some have questioned more broadly the hegemonic function of dominant ideologies.[39] In general, most authors are far more convincing in arguing that law legitimates a prevailing order in the eyes of a dominant elite; evidence that it does so for subaltern groups is surprisingly sparse. Because our present interest here is precisely in the motives and actions of dominant groups, this distinction seems much less important for present purposes. (Later, when we focus our attention on actual uses of the courts, the views of the subaltern will be considered.)

In the Middle East, observers sometimes do note the economic benefits provided to dominant groups by legal reform.[40] Nevertheless, scholars more frequently emphasize how law serves the political authority rather than the economic interests of rulers and ruling classes. Here the European-style legal reforms of the past century can

---

[36] E. P. Thompson, "The Rule of Law," in Bierne and Quinney, *Marxism and Law*, p. 134.

[37] Eugene D. Genovese, "The Hegemonic Function of the Law," in Bierne and Quinney, *Marxism and Law*.

[38] Hay, "Poaching and the Game Laws."

[39] Nicholas Abercrombie, Stephen Hill, and Bryan S. Turner, *The Dominant Ideology Thesis* (London: Allen and Unwin, 1980).

[40] An argument along this line is made by Hanna Batatu in *The Old Social Classes and the Revolutionary Movements of Iraq: A Study of Iraq's Landed and Commercial Classes and of its Communists, Ba'thists and Free Officers* (Princeton: Princeton University Press, 1978). Michael M. J. Fischer makes the case much more briefly for Iran in "Legal Postulates in Flux: Justice, Wit, and Hierarchy in Iran," in Daisy Hilse Dwyer (ed.), *Law and Islam in the Middle East* (New York: Bergin and Garvey Publishers, 1990).

be recast not as the triumph of liberal legality but as part of the emergence of centralized states. Ann Mayer writes: "The adoption of national law codes in the Middle East signifies the acceptance of the idea that it is rules formulated and enacted by the government that determine what the law should be on the national territory."[41] Similarly, Laura Nader observes: "Scholars who point out the role of national law in governing rights of property may emphasize the continuity between colonial regimes and the new nations – a continuity of increased state power."[42]

The link in the Middle East between centralization and national law codes is certainly not unique. Either on their own or under imperial rule, most countries of the non-European world have adopted national law codes over the past century. And Francis Snyder and Douglas Hay note that "the law which was exported from Europe and received in the Third World was not, however, simply metropolitan law. It comprised the most authoritarian aspects of European law, from which most provisions regarding social welfare, basic rights, and other entitlements largely had been excised."[43] Stephen Holmes makes another argument supporting the link between central authority and aspects of liberal legality, focusing on the "government enabling" nature of the separation of powers: "it disentangles overlapping jurisdictions, sorts out unclear chains of command and helps overcome a paralyzing confusion of functions . . . The earliest justifications of the separation of powers emphasize its power-enhancing functions."[44]

Whatever the historical variations in the attractiveness of centralized legal systems, the interest shown by authoritarian and centralized governments in their codes and courts is striking. Yash Ghai notes that "few rulers have found it possible to govern without the assistance of law

---

[41] Mayer, "The Shari'ah," p. 180.

[42] Laura Nader, "Introduction: Property, Power, and Law in Middle Eastern Societies," in Ann Elizabeth Mayer (ed.), *Property, Social Structure and Law in the Modern Middle East* (Albany: State University of New York Press, 1985), p. 2. Messick, *Calligraphic State*, basically describes the same phenomenon of centralization in Yemen.

[43] Snyder and Hay, "Comparisons in the Social History of Law," p. 12. Nor is this necessarily a Third World phenomenon. Vilhelm Aubert notes that in the nineteenth century, the Norwegian state governed through a fairly harsh legal system, partly for fiscal reasons. The welfare state that emerged in the twentieth century had markedly different features. Vilhelm Aubert, "Law and Social Change in Nineteenth-Century Norway," in Starr and Collier, *History and Power in the Study of Law.*

[44] Stephen Holmes, "Precommitment and the Paradox of Democracy," in Jon Elster and Rune Slagsted (eds.), *Constitutionalism and Democracy* (Cambridge: Cambridge University Press, 1988), pp. 228–29. For a brief survey of some of the functions courts can serve in authoritarian regimes, see C. Neal Tate and Stacia L. Haynie, "Authoritarianism and the Functions of Courts: A Time Series Analysis of the Philippine Supreme Court, 1961–1987," *Law and Society Review*, 27 (4), 1993, p. 707.

and legal institutions."[45] In administering the West Bank and Gaza since 1967, Israeli authorities made extensive use of courts that maintained the form but little of the content of liberal legality.[46] Regimes regarded as harshly oppressive find uses for law codes and judiciaries. Martin Chanock writes of South Africa: "The oppressions of apartheid have, until the beginnings of its disintegration, characteristically been imposed not by the random terror of the death squad, but by the routine and systematic process of courts and bureaucrats."[47] Nazi Germany and Allende's Chile are particularly noteworthy for their ability to combine despotic rule with the maintenance of judicial structures. In the former, judges proved willing participants in the Nazi legal order; in the latter, judges not only failed to obstruct but sometimes facilitated the regime's repressive practices.[48] In both cases, judicial sympathies with the regime were sometimes cloaked in positivist language. There can be no more convincing proof that ruling elites (and not just liberal theorists) can find the law an attractive tool.

*Law and politics: employing the three perspectives*

These perspectives on Western-style legal systems in the developing world – that they are best seen as tools (or at least residues) of imperialism, that they are built to establish the rule of law and circumscribe the authority of rulers, and that they underwrite the positions of elites – stand in sharp contrast to each other. Where the perspectives differ most strongly is precisely over the questions at hand: What is the purpose of a legal system? What motivated those who built the Egyptian and similar systems elsewhere in the Arab world?

The first part of this study (chapters 2, 3, and 4) is concerned with the relationship between the political system and law. How does the form and nature of government explain the nature of the legal system? Is the legal system best understood as an imposition of imperial government, an attempt to regularize political authority, or an element of illiberal political domination?

---

[45] Yash Ghai, "The Rule of Law, Legitimacy and Governance," *International Journal of the Sociology of Law*, 14 (1), 1986, p. 179.

[46] Lisa Hajjar, *Authority, Resistance and the Law: A Study of the Israeli Military Court System in the Occupied Territories*, Ph.D. dissertation, Department of Sociology, The American University, 1995.

[47] Martin Chanock, "Writing South African Legal History: A Prospectus," *Journal of African History*, 30 (2) 1989, p. 265.

[48] On Germany, see Ingo Muller, *Hitler's Justice: The Courts of the Third Reich* (Cambridge: Harvard University Press, 1991). On Chile, see Pamela Constable and Artura Valenzuela, *A Nation of Enemies: Chile under Pinochet* (New York: W. W. Norton and Company, 1991), chapter 5.

Egypt has been selected for detailed consideration for several reasons. First, the past century of Egyptian legal history is very well documented in a wide variety of sources. Thus a focus on Egypt allows for a more sophisticated and nuanced understanding of the relationship between the political and the legal systems. Second, the Egyptian case has been influential throughout the Arab world; Egypt is easily the most important Arab case. Third, modern Egypt has experienced great variation in political systems, specifically in those areas most relevant to explaining its legal system. Imperial rule, liberal forms of governing, and autocratic and authoritarian regimes have risen and declined over the past century. The country provides an excellent opportunity to assess the effects of such political variation on the structure and uses of the legal system.

Why have Egypt's political leaders constructed and maintained an independent and European-style judicial system over the last century? In order to understand, it will be best to turn to the writings and actions of those directly involved in the construction of the judicial system. What were the forces behind judicial reform inside and outside the country? How important was legal reform to them? What did they seek to accomplish with the reform? Were their goals primarily political, relating to the nature of governmental authority in Egypt? Were they anxious to restrict the authority of the state? Or were their goals also social and economic, related to the preservation of prevailing relationships in these spheres? Chapters 2, 3, and 4 will address these questions by a review of the history of the Egyptian legal system over the past century. Chapter 2 concerns the foundation of the system in the late nineteenth century and its initial operation. Chapter 3 considers the further centralization of the system after mid-century and its accommodation with Egypt's post-1952 authoritarian political system with its generally increasing commitment to nationalism and socialism. Chapter 4 concerns the limited but genuine reemergence of liberal legality in Egypt since the 1970s and the relationship between judicial and executive conceptions of the proper role of the legal system.

In general, three sorts of evidence will be brought to bear on the question of motivations for legal reform. First, timing is a critical element of any explanation based on imposed law. If law was imposed by an outside power then we would expect that legal reform would be initiated and sustained under imperial rule. If we find otherwise – that legal reform preceded or came long after imperial rule, or if we find that imperial rule retarded legal reform – then we must look instead to internal explanations.

The second source of evidence will be the nature of the institutions built. Were judiciaries independent and given real opportunities to restrict executive power? If so, liberal legality might be seen to have descriptive and not merely normative power. Or did central and executive authorities (or economic elites) maintain close control over judicial institutions? If so, then the domination-based explanations of legal reform will prove more helpful.

Finally, the writings of those involved in the construction of new legal and judicial orders will be consulted. Did they react primarily to the demands or desires of an imperial power? Did they address a perceived need for stable property rights or regularized and restrained executive authority? Or did they focus on the need for social, political, and economic control and on the legitimation of elite domination?

The second section of this study will shift the focus from Egypt to the Gulf. Gulf states are of great interest because they turned to the same European legal models, despite significant historical, cultural, economic, and political differences from Egypt. This is more than historical coincidence. When the Gulf states embarked on their efforts in the twentieth century, they generally hired Egyptians to advise them, write their codes, and staff their courts. (As will be seen, even the Egyptian-drafted Kuwaiti constitution reflects political concerns of the Egyptian legal community more than it reflects Kuwaiti politics in certain provisions.) In essence, very similar institutions were implanted in different political environments. Studying the operation of similar institutions in different societies will tell us something about the nature of politics in these societies and about the diverse appeal (and, as will be seen, the plasticity) of seemingly liberal legal models.

What did the British and the rulers and elites of the Gulf seek to achieve through legal reform? How has the political history of the Gulf affected its legal development? And why have diverse regimes throughout the Arab world recreated the major features of the Egyptian system? This last question is striking because of sharp differences among the states of the Gulf. Kuwait has had elected parliaments, a strong sense of constitutionalism, and a fluid relationship between government and opposition. Qatar has had neither elections nor a fully implemented constitution, and opposition has been clandestine or non-existent. These two countries will draw particular attention because they closely resemble each other in social and economic terms but have differed in political terms. They should therefore illuminate the relationship between regime type and legal system. Chapter 5 will focus on the construction of new legal systems in the Gulf during the period of British domination; chapter 6 will consider the post-independence era and the relationship between judicial and executive authority in the different political systems of the Gulf.

Chapters 2 through 6 will serve to illustrate that the three perspectives on law and the legal system are not always mutually exclusive. Indeed, this study will show that imperialism was a far weaker force for legal reform than has generally been assumed to be the case but was hardly irrelevant to the process. Liberal legality has informed some of the legal reform effort, particularly in Egypt. Yet this liberal legality is one that has been highly restricted and generally quite consistent with – and even supportive of – executive visions of political authority and community. Domination-based explanations will be seen to have the most relevance to the Arab experience, but the economic and legitimation aspects of these explanations are far less helpful than those that focus specifically on politics and especially on the centralization of authority.

The timing of reform, the structure of the new institutions, and the writings of those involved all will support the idea that the primary roots of legal reform in Egypt and the Gulf have always been domestic and have had more to do with supporting rather than restricting political authority. Yet even if these questions are answered we have not necessarily discovered how these systems actually operate from the perspectives of non-elites.

## The role of legal institutions in Arab societies

Intentions should not be confused with consequences (a point often forgotten in research on legal systems). After we have discovered why the legal system was constructed in its present form we still need to know how it operates in practice. What is the role of legal systems in Arab societies? How have local inhabitants reacted to prevailing systems? In the third section of this study (chapters 7 and 8), the focus will move to the role that courts play in society. As the institutions most immediately involved in the application of law, courts invite special attention in any attempt to discover reactions to, and perceptions of law.

Indeed, different perspectives on law are often most directly expressed in different images of what law courts are. While the three perspectives considered above will not be formally laid against each other in this section, they do serve to highlight some subtle differences in the way that courts are perceived. For those who emphasize imposed law, courts are often seen as cultural expressions; the social and political effects of imposed legal systems are imposed primarily through a culturally inappropriate court system. For those seeking to understand law in liberal terms, courts are neutral structures for dispute resolution. To be sure, their rules and procedures reflect underlying political and legal arrangements, but a court is distinct from other social and political structures (such as bureaucracy) by its autonomy from a particular dispute. Two litigants – even if one is an official actor – approach the court as equals. For those who emphasize the relationship between law and domination, courts are structures for imposing the interests of political or economic elites. They are also sometimes portrayed as devices for obscuring such imposition behind a mask of equality. These images of courts are not mutually exclusive; indeed, all will be seen to reflect the experience of Egyptian (and Gulf) residents to some degree.

It is surprising to find out how little we know about the actual operation of courts and the law, particularly those systems based on Western models. It is often the case that more attention is paid to the restricted and often atrophied Islamic structure than to the more dominant Western-style structures. If we wish to know who goes to court, when they do so, and what they find there, we have only a few ethnographic studies on which to draw.

When legal systems in the Arab world (or the developing world more broadly) do draw attention, they are often portrayed as inaccessible or inappropriate for most of the citizenry. Concerns about the suitability of legal systems based on Western models are as old as the adoption of those systems in non-Western settings. As will be seen in chapter 2, the British occupiers of Egypt expressed grave doubts about the adoption of a French system; Tawfiq al-Hakim's observation quoted earlier echoed many British statements a half-century before. Throughout the developing world, legal systems created in the colonial period (or along Western lines) have been criticized as remote and expensive. For example, in the context of a study of how residents of a Turkish village resolved disputes, June Starr wrote: "National systems of law enforcement may be more professional, but they also are more expensive in terms of time, money, and numbers of employees, and they frequently give less attention to the individual, his family, and his problems. In many countries, furthermore, there appears to be considerable discrimination in national courts against ethnic and religious minorities as well as against the urban and rural poor."[49]

Many scholars interested in the relationship between law and development have come to see legal systems in the developing world as either irrelevant or hostile to the interests of the majority of the population.[50]

[49] June Starr, *Dispute and Settlement in Rural Turkey: An Ethnography of Law* (Leiden: E. J. Brill, 1978), pp. 277–78.
[50] See David M. Trubek and Marc Galanter, "Scholars in Self-Estrangement: Some Reflections on the Crisis in Law and Development Studies in the United States," *Wisconsin Law Review*, 1974, p. 1062. See also James Magavern, John Thomas, and Myra Stuart, "Law, Urban Development, and the Poor in Developing Countries," *Washington University Law Quarterly*, 1975, p. 45.

For some, this argument was simply a continuation of radical critiques of liberal views on law: law is seen as furthering elite domination in class-divided societies and thus it hardly serves as a friendly or fair forum for the subaltern. Arguments that the legal system is expensive, cumbersome, and complicated are hardly restricted to the developing world; they are very familiar to American ears.

The most frequent charge against new legal systems in the developing world, however, is that they are culturally inappropriate. National codes based on Western models, judges trained in European-style law schools, and procedures borrowed from Europe rather than based on indigenous practice could constitute unfamiliar and perhaps even threatening intrusions into the lives of villagers and urban dwellers in the developing world. This forms a particularly strong theme in the writings on law in imperial settings referred to above (although one ethnographic work on working-class uses of courts in a Massachusetts town describes how residents go to court with feelings of legal entitlement and emerge thinking "that the institution is erratic, unreliable, and sometime ineffectual"; it is also "indifferent to the ordinary person's problem").[51]

Thus a variety of authors evoke bleak images of the fate of the subaltern in legal systems throughout the developing world, particularly when the systems' operations betray alien origins. Yet a wide variety of evidence should lead us to question an overly stark portrait. June Starr, in a work on the legal system of Republican Turkey subsequent to the one quoted above, claimed that after a century of attempts to impose increasingly secular law codes and procedures, "popular legal culture was not greatly removed from the official law of the land in western Anatolian villages."[52] Other authors have noted instances in which secular or Western-inspired codes and procedures can be operated in ways more consistent with local practices and values.[53] And even with a culturally inappropriate legal system, the existence of a gap between local, informal mechanisms and dispute resolution, and the formal, state-sponsored system can leave potential litigants multiple options in choosing the forum most favorable to them. Indeed, the frequent frustrations expressed by imperial officials in local abuses of the legal system should lead us to suspect that lawyers and even litigants could be highly creative in their resort to the courts.[54] A switch to a focus on how

[51]  Sally Engle Merry, *Getting Justice and Getting Even: Legal Consciousness among Working-Class Americans* (Chicago: University of Chicago Press, 1990), p. 170.

[52]  Starr, *Law as Metaphor*, p. 175.

[53]  See, for instance, Safia K. Mohsen, "Women and Criminal Justice in Egypt," and Suad Joseph, "Working the Law: A Lebanese Working Class Study," in Dwyer, *Law and Islam.*

[54]  Nathan Brown, "Law and Imperialism: Egypt in Comparative Perspective," *Law and Society Review*, 29 (1), 1995, p. 103.

law actually operates and especially on litigant strategies invites a more nuanced – and possibly more favorable – image of the operation of Western legal systems in non-Western settings.

Indeed, a variety of authors have suggested ways in which the subaltern have been able to mold the legal system in their own image, either by forcing concessions from elites or by using rules and procedures in unintended ways. In South Africa, New Guinea, and Zambia, women and men resisted the policies of colonial elites by exploiting the law or by ignoring it, thus forcing changes in its applications.[55] This activity should not be romanticized or exaggerated; even using the law and forcing changes in it had little effect on overall relations of power and domination. It should be no surprise then that most studies have indicated that Western-style courts are used as a last resort. In highly stratified societies it is unlikely that courts serve as islands of equality, even if they allow for limited resistance to the prevailing order. Indeed, it is precisely the role that courts and the legal system can play in enforcing the prevailing order while allowing for modest and individualized resistance that leads to the argument, alluded to above, that law serves to legitimize (and render hegemonic) prevailing power relations. Such an argument, even if rarely substantiated, would seem plausible given the possibilities for limited resistance discovered in many different settings.

To ascertain the effects of legal reform on the subject population, it is best to consider how the courts are actually used. In chapters 7 and 8 the focus will be first on working- and middle-class involvement in the courts and then on business leaders and litigation. How and under what circumstances do Egyptians go to court? Do they find a court system that is inaccessible and skewed to the rich and powerful? Do their experiences in court affect their general political outlook or serve as a substitute for alternative forms of political action? In fact, the evidence of these two chapters will show that the courts have proven quite friendly territory for many small-scale disputes, and that litigation, while slow and sometimes frustrating, is often anything but a tool of last resort. But because Egyptians resort to the courts with such ease, the connection with political legitimacy is tenuous. Litigation will be shown not to be an alternative to other courses of action but to be part of strategies that include the use of several different tools simultaneously. And the friendliness of Egyptian courts to so many litigants will be shown to

[55] Wells, "Passes and Bypasses"; Sally Engle Merry, "The Articulation of Legal Spheres," in Hay and Wright, *African Women and the Law*; and Peter Fitzpatrick, "Transformation of Law and Labour in Papua New Guinea," in Snyder and Hay, *Labour, Law and Crime*.

make them less friendly to business leaders seeking swift and predictable justice; a major source of inequality will be shown to reside not in a bias of the courts towards the rich but in the ability of the rich to find other fora for resolving their disputes.

For over a century, legal reform and courts have been at the center of domestic Arab politics and often international diplomacy as well. To understand Arab legal history, we begin with Egypt in the nineteenth century.

## 2 The creation and operation of the modern Egyptian legal system, 1876–1937

In the last quarter of the nineteenth century, Egypt's rulers worked to build an independent judiciary and implement codified law. In the process they consciously turned away from Islamic and Ottoman sources and towards continental Europe. How can this change be explained? Was it primarily caused by imperial penetration, a desire to construct a liberal political and economic order, or a state-building and centralization project? A study of the timing and nature of the changes, combined with an analysis of the writings of some of those involved, reveals that the role of imperialism, though significant, at most accentuated and modified already existing trends. Liberalism played a notable role as well, though the nature of that liberalism was hardly inconsistent with the primary factor: the desire to build a strong and centralized state. The imperialist, liberal, and statist pressures for legal reform will each be considered in turn. Yet because the exact nature of the late nineteenth-century reforms have often been miscast (and even overstated), it is necessary to offer an accurate understanding of the changes of that period (along with the continuation of those trends in the early twentieth century).

### The construction of a new legal system in Egypt

The reforms of the late nineteenth century did mark a new departure for Egyptian legal development but also built on some trends that had been evident in earlier reforms. For several decades various efforts had been made to build a more centralized and hierarchical judiciary in addition to accentuating the role for positive legislation (without contradicting or eliminating the influence of the Islamic *shari'a*).

#### *Judicial reform in the nineteenth century*

In the early nineteenth century, Muhammad 'Ali (r. 1805–1848) constructed several judicial structures alongside the *Shari'a* Courts.

Largely staffed by officials, these councils combined judicial with non-judicial functions (including administration and issuing laws and regulations). Specialized commercial tribunals were also established in Cairo and Alexandria. Under Muhammad 'Ali's successors, local councils, similarly staffed by officials (sometimes joined by *shari'a*-trained judges), operated both to decide cases and to prepare them for decisions by superior bodies. In general the councils applied laws and regulations issued by the Egyptian government; since Egypt was an Ottoman province, the influence of imperial *qanun* and legislation was felt at times as well. Under Isma'il (r. 1863–79), the system was expanded to a hierarchy of councils or administrative organs in villages, provincial centers, and Cairo.[1] Alongside these official tribunals, the *Shari'a* Courts continued to operate. In addition, the capitulations, which had the effect of granting extraterritorial status to most Europeans, necessitated that consular courts try most criminal charges and civil suits in which the defendant was non-Ottoman.

The non-*shari'a* judicial structure that existed for Egyptians in the first three-quarters of the nineteenth century thus exhibited three fundamental features. First, it was a centralized system, with officials and bodies in Cairo exercising a great deal of control. When local and village councils were established, their role was generally limited to encouraging conciliation or deciding minor cases; thus, even when the system penetrated the country outside of Cairo it was highly hierarchical in nature. The reliance of these bodies on administrative regulations and legislation issued from the government in Cairo accentuated the centralizing aspects of the system still further, as Kenneth Cuno has shown (especially for issues relating to land tenure).[2] Local officials probably still retained a great deal of discretionary authority (especially because they often staffed the judicial organs), but the groundwork was laid for a centralized and hierarchical judicial system.

Second, the system made no effort to distinguish between adminis-

---

[1] For descriptions of the judicial system of Egypt in the first three-quarters of the nineteenth century, see Byron Cannon, *Politics of Law and the Courts in Nineteenth Century Egypt* (Salt Lake City: University of Utah Press), especially chapter 2 and Latifa Muhammad Salim, *Al-nizam al-qada'i al-misri al-hadith* (The Modern Egyptian Judicial System) vol. I, 1875–1914 (Cairo: Markaz al-Dirasat al-Siyasiyya wa-l-Istratijiyya bi-l-Ahram, 1984). The most comprehensive description of the system as it existed immediately prior to the construction of the National Courts is the memorandum submitted by the minister of justice, Husayn Fakhri, to the Egyptian cabinet on December 2, 1882. It is printed in *Al-kitab al-dhahabi li-l-mahakim al-ahliyya* (The Golden Book of the National Courts), 2 vols., (Cairo: Al-matba'a al-amiriyya bi-bulaq, 1937), vol. I, pp. 107–15. See also Ehud R. Toledano, "Law, Practice, and Social Reality: A Theft Case in Cairo, 1854," *Asian and African Studies*, 17, 1983, p. 153.

[2] Kenneth J. Cuno, *The Pasha's Peasants, Land, Society, and Economy in Lower Egypt, 1740–1858* (Cambridge: Cambridge University Press, 1992), especially chapter 10.

trative and judicial functions. Indeed, there is no reason to believe that the two were regarded as constituting separate functions of the state, at least for the first half of the century. Administration involved drawing up and implementing policies and regulations; the application of criminal and land law, for instance, was very much a proper role for administration. If central authorities felt any concern about the large role that administrative officials played, it was only that the system allowed some to use their authority in ways that violated official policies.[3] The councils and bureaux involved in applying the laws and regulations to concrete cases were never referred to as courts; only at the apex of the system was there reference to anything related to justice (the *Majlis Jama'iyyat al-Haqqaniyya* or Council of the Assembly of Justice, founded under Muhammad 'Ali; later reconstituted as the *Majlis al-Ahkam* or Council of Judgments).

Third, the judicial structures of the first three-quarters of the nineteenth century, while not entirely based on the *shari'a* and Islamic courts, hardly repudiated them and in fact worked alongside them, generally harmoniously. The law applied by the state-operated courts varied, but was generally based on a shifting blend of Ottoman *qanun* and Egyptian regulations and decrees. For the most part, this body of law was either based on the *shari'a* or did not contradict it. In areas where there was no obvious text to apply, judicial bodies had considerable interpretive latitude.[4] While there is little evidence on how this latitude was exercised, it is likely that local custom and the *shari'a* would have informed the work of the courts. Under Isma'il some departures from traditional *shari'a* criminal punishments were implemented, but there is little evidence that this excited controversy, especially because *shari'a* judges continued to sit on some judicial bodies and tried some cases (especially murder) concurrently with the state-sponsored courts (indeed, the concurrence of a *shari'a* judge was required before a murderer could be executed.)[5] The only significant controversy involving the *shari'a* was more political than religious in nature. When 'Abbas (r. 1849–54) claimed the right to order executions, the Ottoman authorities objected on the grounds that this was a violation of *shari'a*-

---

[3] See, for instance, Ehud R. Toledano, *State and Society in Mid-Nineteenth Century Egypt* (Cambridge: Cambridge University Press, 1990), pp. 170–77.

[4] The latitude was especially great in civil disputes. See the memorandum by Husayn Fakhri, *Al-kitab al-dhahabi*, vol. I, p. 109.

[5] Cannon does claim, however, that the village courts constructed under Isma'il did prompt some criticisms: "Conservative defenders of the inviolability of the *qadi*'s traditional jurisdiction naturally criticized the councils for their apparent disregard of the importance of the *shari'a* in the lives of villagers" (*Politics of Law*, p. 34). However, Cannon provides no source or reference for this assertion.

sanctioned procedures (reserving the authority for the sultan and the *shari'a* judge). In essence, the sultan viewed the measure as a step towards Egyptian sovereignty. After a diplomatic crisis, a compromise was adopted under which 'Abbas would refer execution orders to a committee which included the Ottoman-appointed *qadi*.[6] Without adequate documentary evidence, it is difficult to ascertain how the state-sponsored judicial system actually operated. It is likely, however, that even after the construction of village courts, Egyptians at all levels of society continued to bring some cases to *shari'a* judges regardless of official procedures (as will be seen in chapter 6, this is precisely what occurred in Qatar in the 1970s and 1980s). Thus, rulers abrogated the *shari'a* in only a few areas and the net effect of the new judicial structures probably did little to decrease the actual influence of *shari'a*-trained judges.

In the last quarter of the nineteenth century, a new court system emerged that partially evolved from the earlier structures designed to build a centralized and hierarchical judicial structure. Indeed, the new courts were initially called "councils" (*majalis*) as well, rather than courts, in contemporary discussions.[7] Yet an examination of these courts – the Mixed Courts and the National Courts – also shows that there were some important departures from previous efforts, particularly in the degree to which they separated the judiciary from administration (by building an independent and professionalized judiciary) and in their deliberate adoption of European models and codes at the expense of Islamic and Ottoman antecedents.

### The formation of the Mixed Courts

The growing European political and financial presence in Egypt throughout the nineteenth century made the issue of the capitulations and the consular courts increasingly salient in Egyptian politics and economics. In the 1860s and 1870s Egyptian officials grew frustrated at their inability to enforce civil and criminal law against foreigners. European residents of Egypt jealously guarded their privileges, but none could describe the system as clear and rational. In the 1870s a mounting fiscal crisis left European creditors and bondholders worried that official debts would not be repaid, and there was no confidence that the

---

[6] 'Aziz Khanki, "Legislation and the Judiciary before the Construction of the National Courts," in *Al-kitab al-dhahabi*, vol. I, p. 79. See also Salim, *Al-nizam al-qada'i* vol. I, pp. 17–18.

[7] The Mixed Courts and the National Courts were generally referred to as "majalis" rather than "mahakim" in the Arabic press until the middle of the 1880s.

Egyptian judicial system would enforce claims against the government. Egypt's leaders badly needed a system that would protect the country's financial interests without alienating foreign bondholders who could cause a diplomatic crisis and fiscal collapse. And Europeans wished for courts that would not diminish their privileges but whose judgments would be enforced.

Constructing a system that gained the assent of this diverse coalition took great diplomatic effort and considerable time. Nubar Pasha, an ambitious and creative politician who served the Egyptian government in a variety of capacities (including three terms as prime minister) sought to respond to such conflicting pressures. It took nearly a decade for him to assemble an international coalition that acquiesced in the creation of a new judicial system for all civil cases in which a foreign interest was involved. Nubar began pursuing the idea of Mixed Courts in 1867; they did not begin operation until 1876.[8]

Nubar initially proposed a unified judicial system for civil and criminal cases in Egypt, having jurisdiction over cases involving foreigners and later even over cases involving only Egyptians.[9] The courts, to be staffed with a large European contingent, would rule on the basis of a European-derived code. The judicial and administrative functions of the state were to be separated. In the course of negotiations with the capitulatory powers, Nubar was forced to make many concessions before he achieved his objective. France in particular jealously protected its privileges. Egypt had to accept a foreign majority on the bench and a fairly faithful adoption of the Code Napoléon. The scope of the courts narrowed: consular courts would retain criminal jurisdiction in cases involving foreigners; the Mixed Courts were to deal only with civil and commercial cases. Various measures ensured not only the independence of the mixed judiciary but also, in some ways, its predominance.

Two specific concessions merit mention. First, an article added to the mixed codes (and borrowed neither from the Code Napoléon nor from English law) required the government to enforce judgments against itself; that is, if a foreigner brought a suit against the government and won, the government was obligated to carry out the ruling. Second,

---

[8] For more detail on political struggles concerning the Mixed Courts from their creation to their abolition, see Nathan J. Brown, "The Precarious Life and Slow Death of the Mixed Courts of Egypt," *International Journal of Middle East Studies*, 25 (1), 1993, p. 33. See also F. Robert Hunter, *Egypt under the Khedives 1805–1879* (Pittsburgh: University of Pittsburgh Press, 1984), and, more comprehensively, Cannon, *Politics of Law*.

[9] Nubar's initial proposal of 1867 was slightly less ambitious; the proposal was expanded in 1869. See Jasper Yeates Brinton, *The Mixed Courts of Egypt*, revised edition (New Haven: Yale University Press, 1968), chapters 1 and 2, and Cannon, *Politics of Law*, chapter 3.

Egypt agreed to adopt the French *parquet* system which designated officers of the court to investigate and prosecute crimes, advise the court on legal matters, and represent the general interests of the state. The Mixed Court parquet was to be headed by a foreigner and staffed by both foreigners and Egyptians.[10] The construction of the parquet and its removal from Egyptian control limited the degree to which Egypt's rulers could influence the courts. Not all these changes represented concessions for Nubar. His aim in working to establish the courts was not only to secure some relief from the problems engendered by the capitulations; he also sought to restrict the power of the Khedive.[11] The Mixed Courts thus had much to recommend them. On the one hand, the system appeared to offer Egyptian interests greater protection than the system of consular courts. On the other, the operation of the system was safe from – and even circumscribed – the power of the Khedive.

The Mixed Courts were certain to offend some of their creators in operation because they had been founded to meet the needs of antagonistic parties. The coalition that had constructed the Courts broke apart as soon as they began issuing judgments, especially in light of the growing fiscal crisis that intensified the conflict between Isma'il and his creditors. In fact, by the time the Courts began operating in 1876 (for a five-year trial period), Egypt was bankrupt and had accepted foreign oversight of its finances. When the Mixed Courts began to rule favorably on many claims against the Khedive and the Egyptian government, Isma'il began to grow hostile to the new judicial structure.[12] Although Isma'il did not openly challenge the authority of the Courts, he claimed that implementation of the rulings would have to be delayed until Egypt's finances improved. Initially he did so with some European support; Egypt's financial overseers agreed that full compliance would result in fiscal and political upheaval. When Isma'il went farther, however, and attempted to evade foreign financial control as well as the Mixed Courts, he was deposed by the Ottoman sultan under heavy European pressure.[13]

Thus the coalition that had created the Mixed Courts quickly turned

[10] Najib Makhluf, *Nubar basha wama tamma 'ala yadihi* (Nubar Pasha and What He Accomplished) (Cairo: al-Matba'a al-'umumiyya, 1903), p. 96; Cannon, *Politics of Law*, p. 50.
[11] See F. Robert Hunter, "Self-Image and Historical Truth: Nubar Pasha and the Making of Modern Egypt," *Middle Eastern Studies*, 23 (3), 1987, p. 370, and Earl of Cromer, *Modern Egypt* (London: Macmillan, 1908), vol. II, pp. 316–17.
[12] On the contribution of the Mixed Courts to the fiscal crisis, see Cannon, *Politics of Law*.
[13] Salim, *Al-nizam al-qada'i*, vol. II, pp. 75–79, and Cannon, *Politics of Law*, chapters 4 and 5. According to Cannon, Egyptian landowners shared Isma'il's resentment of European control, but also feared that unlimited khedival power would threaten their own economic position and therefore were sometimes protective of the Mixed Courts.

against its own creation. Isma'il and the two most important European actors, Britain and France, were suspicious of the Courts almost from the beginning, both recognizing that their rulings had undermined Egypt's precarious finances and obstructed several attempted solutions. They did not attempt to abolish the Courts outright but did propose reforms. However, after Isma'il's fall in 1879, threats to the Courts came from different sources. Powers such as France came to appreciate the Mixed Courts as a check on Egyptian autonomy and khedival authority. But Egyptian resentment of the Courts spread outside the government to the growing nationalist movement. The British defeat of the nationalists in 1882 and their resulting occupation probably saved the Mixed Courts from fatal attack.

### The creation of the National Courts

Shortly after the establishment of the Mixed Courts in 1876, some of Egypt's leaders began to pursue domestic legal reform. Nubar's original plan to have the Mixed Courts evolve into courts of general jurisdiction for both Egyptians and foreigners had stalled because of Egyptian fears this would aggravate foreign domination and European unwillingness to make concessions that would make the Mixed Courts more attractive to the Egyptian government. In 1880 and 1881 the Egyptian government therefore developed plans for a separate judicial structure (though for most of those involved the goal of unification with the Mixed Courts was hardly forgotten). The new bodies were referred to first as *al-majalis al-mahalliyya*, or local councils (the same term used for their predecessors) and later *al-mahakim al-ahliyya*.[14]

Creating the new structures was seen to involve two separate tasks. First, the structure and composition of the courts had to be determined. This task was completed by May 1881 and a decree to construct the courts was issued in the fall.[15] Second, a code had to be developed for them to enforce. Even though the proposed courts attracted great attention, work proceeded very slowly, and contemporary newspapers frequently urged the committee to speed its efforts. For instance, on April 18, 1882, the daily *al-Ahram* reported: "The council of ministers did not complete yesterday the question of al-majalis al-mahalliyya, and it will consider the matter again. It is to be hoped that it is swift in

---

[14] The contemporary English translation of these terms was generally "Native Courts" or "Native Tribunals." By the 1930s complaints that this was derogatory led to the term "National Courts." I have used the latter term for the sake of consistency.

[15] See *al-Ahram*, May 28 and September 29 1881; the decree itself is covered in the newspaper throughout November and December 1881; more generally, see Cannon, *Politics of Law*, chapter 6.

enacting them as there has been a long delay."[16] When the quasi-parliamentary *Majlis Shura al-Nuwwab* ended its session in the summer of 1882, two years after the cabinet had authorized planning to begin, work was still incomplete. Parts of a draft code had been submitted, but the increasingly assertive Majlis had not made its feelings known in any definitive way. The matter was not easy: while some favored an adoption of the code of the Mixed Courts, others preferred a code more closely based on the *shari'a*. The former would aid the cause of judicial unification; the latter could be argued to be more appropriate to a Muslim society.

The brief war between Egypt and Great Britain in 1882 delayed matters for the rest of the year. By the time that the Egyptian government returned to the question, the country was occupied by the British and the Majlis Shura al-Nuwwab no longer existed. Cabinet ministers were divided on whether or not to implement the previously developed court structure and code immediately (using an adapted mixed code) or to postpone the matter until a better code (presumably based on the *shari'a*, building on the earlier efforts) was completed. The cabinet decided on speed rather than perfection; the argument was explicitly made that any delay would only open Egypt to greater influence. The faster the new courts could be set into operation the less Europeans would be able to guide their development. Ironically, therefore, it was an attempt to contain foreign influence that led to a code more divergent from Islamic sources than most would have liked. The mixed code was adopted with minor modifications.[17] While religion was not irrelevant to the debate over legal reform, more attention was given to the specific relationship between the courts and other official bodies. Perhaps the matter which drew the most controversy was how lawsuits against government officials should be handled. An effort to establish a separate administrative court was abandoned (though, as will be seen, the idea was revived and implemented in 1946); instead it was decided that the National Courts would be competent to rule on infractions committed by government officials in performance of their duties. The final decrees establishing the National Courts and their codes were issued in 1883; they began operating in 1884 in Cairo and Lower Egypt (National Courts were not established in Upper Egypt until the end of the decade). The structure of the National Courts mirrored that of the Mixed Courts fairly closely; the cabinet even decided to cancel earlier plans for a supreme court, termed the *Mahkamat al-Tamyiz*, at the apex

---

[16] For similar comments, see *al-Ahram*, February 12, February 28, and April 27, 1882.

[17] The chief modification involved a more favorable treatment of debtors; the goal was to make the code friendlier to rural landowners. See *al-Ahram*, January 22, 1883.

of the system because it would result in a tier not found in the Mixed Courts. The Egyptian leadership clearly hoped not only to maintain control of the new National Courts but also to merge the National and Mixed Courts (so as to gain control over the latter) at an early date. In other words, establishing independent National Courts was a step towards diminishing the independence (even enmity) of the Mixed Courts as soon as possible. Despite the government's hopes, the Mixed Courts continued their separate existence for sixty-six years rather than six months.[18]

### The nature and impact of the reforms

The judicial reforms adopted in the 1870s and 1880s entailed fundamental changes in the administration of justice in Egypt. Yet they also built upon several decades of reform and experimentation that had the general result of increasing the oversight of the central government over issues of law and justice. The creation of the Mixed Courts and National Courts furthered the process of building a centralized and hierarchical judiciary (though the Mixed Courts in particular can hardly be said to have been controlled by the central government). What separated the new court systems from their predecessors was therefore not their hierarchy and structure (where they simply accentuated previous trends) but three other features – their separation from administration, their use of comprehensive codes, and their abandonment of Islamic and Ottoman for European models.

First, the new judicial bodies were to be staffed by a professionalized judiciary independent from the remainder of the state apparatus. No longer would administrative and judicial position be linked (though low-level local administrative officials did retain some authority over minor infractions and disputes), and judges were to be drawn from those with formal legal training rather than administrative experience. The ideal was immediately put into practice for the Mixed Courts; it took somewhat longer to develop the professionalized judiciary for the National Courts (and some judges from the previous judicial bodies were appointed to positions in the National Courts). Not only were the new courts to be separate from the administrative apparatus, but an effort was also made to meet more ambitious standards of judicial independence. International support for the Mixed Courts and the

---

[18] The information on the construction of the courts between 1882 and 1884 is based on the several memoranda and cabinet minutes published in *Al-kitab al-dhahabi*, vol. I; contemporary press coverage (chiefly in *al-Ahram*); and Cannon, *Politics of Law*, chapter 7.

insistence of various countries of their right to nominate judges to the bench meant that any attempt to establish Egyptian government authority over the Mixed Court judges would have led to diplomatic crisis. Yet even in the National Courts, provisions were made for judicial independence that went beyond simply separating administrative and judicial functions. Judicial appointments were to be made by the Khedive (the hereditary governor) on the recommendation of the minister of justice and the cabinet, but judicial discipline would be solely in judicial hands.[19] Administrative acts were specifically placed within the jurisdiction of the National Courts (though, as mentioned above, the attempt to establish a specialized administrative judiciary proved abortive). When the prime minister informed provincial governors of the creation of the National Courts he specifically admonished them against interfering in judicial affairs.[20]

Second, both the Mixed Courts and the National Courts were based for the first time on comprehensive law codes. The role for positive legislation had increased throughout the nineteenth century in the Ottoman Empire as a whole, and Egypt generally kept pace with Ottoman developments (though without always adopting Ottoman legislation). Thus the idea that courts would rule on the basis of state-legislated or ruler-decreed law had a firm basis by the time of the creation of the Mixed Courts and National Courts. Yet these two systems went much further than their predecessors. The new codes were to cover all civil and criminal cases; they governed both substantive and procedural matters. Of course, subsequent legislation could amend or supplement the codes, but their existence established permanently in Egypt that, except in matters of personal status, law was made by the state and by political authorities. No argument was made that these were simply regulations, carried out within the bounds of – or codification of – the *shari'a*.

Indeed, the third innovation of the late-nineteenth century consisted precisely of a turn away from Islamic and even Ottoman models and legal thought and towards European sources. Throughout Isma'il's reign there had been a definite but limited growth in European (particularly French) legal influence. The Mixed Courts were based on European models so the European powers would cede them jurisdiction. But European models were used even in the National Courts. This did occasion discussion in Egypt, and there were proponents of a greater use of the *shari'a* in the National Court codes. What seems remarkable in

[19] See the provisions of the National Court law published in *al-Ahram*, December 30, 1881.
[20] *Al-Ahram*, 29 September 1881.

retrospect, however, is how little acrimony characterized the debate. The authority of the National Courts to order an execution without the presence or approval of a *shari'a*-trained judge did occasion debate (and it is still the case today in Egypt that executions must be approved by the *mufti*, the official charged with issuing authoritative interpretations of Islamic law).[21] Yet given the current-day strength of *shari'a*-minded critics of the Egyptian legal system, the subdued tone of the debate in the 1880s is striking. The Egyptian government does seem to have lessened the speed of the transition by allowing the *Shari'a* Courts to continue to hear all suits that were brought to them (much as the Qatari political leadership did in the 1970s, as will be seen).[22] And many of the original judges of the National Courts had experience in the preexisting al-majalis al-mahalliyya which had coexisted with the *Shari'a* Courts.[23] In a different way, however, the Egyptian government increased discontinuity by staffing the National Courts with foreign judges. The majority of the judges were Egyptians, and when foreign judges were hired an effort was made to resort to nationals of countries with a lower political and military profile in Egypt (the first judges were drawn from Belgium and the Netherlands).[24] Even though the foreign element was eventually eliminated in the twentieth century, the decision to look almost exclusively to continental Europe in matters of legal reform marked a decisive break from preexisting judicial structures.

### The battle for control of Egyptian justice, 1884–1922

The British did not turn their attention to matters of law and justice until several months after the occupation in 1882. Making use of the delay, Egypt's government rushed to complete the construction of the National Courts in order to keep the courts out of the control of the occupying authorities. Even after this step, the occupiers focused on legal issues only sporadically until the end of the decade. Thus they

---

[21] See *al-Ahram*, March 5, March 10, and April 24, 1883. Some of the controversy may be explained by Ottoman criticisms that failure to consult a *shari'a*-trained judge would be contrary to practices prevailing throughout the Ottoman Empire.

[22] The matter is not completely clear, but the cabinet did decide in December 1882 to allow *shari'a* courts to continue to hear such suits. See *Al-kitab al-dhahabi*, vol. I, pp. 116–18. Fourteen years later, an Egyptian lawyer claimed that when the National Courts were still established, Egyptians would still bring disputes to the *shari'a* courts. See "The Progress of the National Courts," *al-Muqtattaf*, 20, July 1896, pp. 521–22.

[23] See the cabinet decision to create the National Courts issued in December 1882, reprinted in *Al-kitab al-dhahabi*, vol. I, pp. 119–20.

[24] Indeed, the Egyptian government sought Belgian judges months after the occupation, even before the codes for the National Courts were completed. See *al-Ahram*, April 18, 1883.

found themselves confronting two judicial structures not of their making (or even of their liking): the Mixed Courts and the National Courts. For the four decades of the British occupation, these structures remained important (and even grew in significance) despite numerous British attempts to dominate, reshape, or even replace them.

The Mixed Courts represented a particularly complex issue for the occupation because of their international nature and close connection with many aspects of Egyptian government and finances. In the early years of the occupation, the British seemed uncertain as to their purpose in Egypt. The problem was that they had two contradictory commitments: to restore the khedival government and sound finances to the country and to leave it as soon as circumstances warranted. The capitulations blocked both paths. On the one hand, if the British left Egypt with the capitulations intact, the sort of fiscal and political crisis that had led to the occupation might recur. On the other hand, were the British to remain in Egypt, capitulatory privileges would obstruct their control of Egyptian affairs. Already during the first year of the occupation, Lord Dufferin complained "Every day my attention has been attracted by the absolute impossibility of even the most necessary police regulations being carried into effect in consequence of the impotence to which the Egyptian Police officials are reduced by the capitulations, and the facilities afforded to foreigners to escape from the consequences of their illegal acts."[25] The capitulations were an obstacle to reforms that went beyond the suppression of crime. The British sought changes in the state budget, taxation, justice, and a whole host of administrative matters. Such changes inevitably affected foreigners and thus came within the jurisdiction of the Mixed Courts. Indeed, in 1887 the Mixed Court of Appeal ruled that the Egyptian government had no authority to change the codes of the Mixed Courts unilaterally, guaranteeing each capitulatory power the right of veto over legislation.[26]

When it became increasingly apparent that the occupation was not a temporary measure, British resentment of the capitulations only increased. The British came to feel that the capitulations were the largest obstacle to their domination of the country.[27] Yet this resentment only protected the Mixed Courts. While the Courts were often regarded as a

[25] Dufferin to Granville, April 28, 1883, FO 141/168, no. 138A.
[26] For one example of the difficulties this caused in the reform program the British would have liked to carry out, see Nathan Brown, "Who Abolished Corvee Labor in Egypt and Why?" *Past and Present*, 144, August 1994, p. 116.
[27] Lord Lloyd wrote of this period: "The chief problem seemed to have crystallized itself at length into a choice between stagnation – an eternal prolongation of the existing state of affairs – and the extinction by hook or by crook of the Capitulation privileges." *Egypt Since Cromer* (London: Macmillan, 1933), vol. I, p. 27.

nuisance by the British occupation authorities, any diminution of the capitulatory privileges could be accomplished only by either strengthening the Courts or by ignoring the claimed rights of capitulatory powers (which would have precipitated a diplomatic crisis). In general, British officials therefore avoided any direct attack on the Courts themselves (and even worked to strengthen their legislative authority).[28]

Egyptian leaders, too, were ambivalent about the Mixed Courts in the early years of the occupation. On the face of it, a system that limited Egyptian autonomy, especially in areas of great contemporary concern such as public finances and the judicial system, would have little to recommend it. Yet most Egyptian leaders, like the British, found some attractive features in the Courts. Particularly in the first few years of the British occupation, the Egyptian government sought to increase its judicial authority and therefore pursued the idea of amalgamation of the Mixed Courts and the National Courts; this necessitated a respectful attitude to the Mixed Courts in order to make the proposal attractive to capitulatory powers. Later in the occupation, the usefulness of the Mixed Courts increased. Even Egyptian officials who found their own authority limited by the capitulations and the Courts often identified the British occupation as the more significant threat to their power and the country's autonomy. The capitulations and the Courts seemed to be obstacles to annexation or other British efforts to assert greater control.

Thus the Mixed Courts survived: for the British and the Egyptian governments the Courts limited the effects of the capitulations; for Egyptians the Courts also circumscribed the authority of the British (an increasingly attractive feature as the occupation wore on). Of course, for foreigners resident in Egypt and their home governments, the Mixed Courts appeared to offer the surest guarantee of the continuation of their capitulatory privileges.

The National Courts operated on a firmer political foundation than the Mixed Courts but became an early focus of a subtle battle for control between the Egyptian government and the British occupiers. Despite their initial non-involvement with the National Courts themselves, the British moved quickly after the occupation to establish some measure of

---

[28] In general, Cromer, the British Consul-General in Egypt, was more resentful of the Courts than Drummond Wolff, who negotiated Britain's status in Egypt with the Ottomans. Drummond Wolff saw strengthening the Courts as the price of capitulatory reform; Cromer seemed to see the Courts as a significant obstacle in themselves, albeit a lesser one than the capitulations. For the positions of the two men, see Confidential Prints 5531/1(i), 4, and 7 and 9238(i) in *British Documents on Foreign Affairs: Reports and Papers from the Foreign Office Confidential Print*, Part I, Series B, vol. 15 (University Publications of America, 1985). For a comprehensive account of this complex period, see Cannon, *Politics of Law*, Part III.

influence in the Ministries of Interior (where the undersecretary was British and the police were staffed with British officers) and Justice (where a British official headed the *niyaba*, an Egyptian counterpart to the French parquet in which members of the judicial corps supervise the investigation and prosecution of crimes and represent state interest in court). A deliberate decision was made to leave provincial administration free from direct British control. In 1884 Nubar, the architect of the Mixed Courts and a leading proponent of judicial reform, returned to the premiership. He managed to provoke crises that led to the resignations of the senior British officials in the Ministries of Interior and Justice, but the police remained under British control. The National Courts began to attract increasing British attention. In order to avoid the pockets of British control, Nubar argued that a wave of rural criminality required the construction of new, emergency structures. The National Courts, therefore, were deprived of jurisdiction in most provincial criminal matters only one year after their construction. New "Commissions of Brigandage," under the supervision of the provincial governors (and thus independent of the British, the police, and the National Courts) were constructed to investigate and suppress crime throughout the country.[29]

The construction of the Commissions of Brigandage under Nubar constituted an ironic step indeed: forced to choose between judicial reform and Egyptian autonomy, Nubar opted for the latter. The result was that matters of crime and justice were placed again in the hands of administrators, and all scruples about judicial independence (and even torture) were forgotten in the effort to keep matters of law and justice partially free from British hands. The step was also temporary. In 1887 Nubar was compelled to appoint a European to head the *niyaba* (though he managed to select Charles LeGrelle, a Belgian rather than British official). Later he attempted to fill the vacancy created by the death of the British head of the Egyptian police with an Egyptian official. Increasingly suspicious of Nubar, the British pressured the Khedive to dismiss him in 1888.[30] Lord Cromer, the British agent and Consul-General in Egypt, wrote to the British Foreign Office at the time of the unsatisfactory state of Egyptian justice, making clear that a

---

[29] For more detail on this episode, see Nathan Brown, "Brigands and State Building: The Invention of Banditry in Modern Egypt," *Comparative Studies in Society and History*, 32 (2), 1990, p. 258. See also Harold Haakon Tollefson, *Police and Ghaffir Reforms in Egypt, 1882–1914*, Ph.D. dissertation, Department of History, University of California, Santa Barbara, 1987.

[30] The story is recounted in Afaf Lutfi Al-Sayyid, *Egypt and Cromer* (London: Murray, 1968), pp. 72–74.

stronger British hand would be introduced when the timing was propitious.[31]

That moment came the following year in the wake of a report by LeGrelle charging the Commissions of Brigandage with systematic abuses (including the use of torture to extract confessions). Cromer confronted Riyad, Nubar's successor as prime minister, presenting him with only two choices:

One was to abolish the Commissions of Brigandage altogether; the other was to provide that the prisoners should always appear before the Commission of Revision, and that a European member should be appointed to this latter Commission.

Riaz Pasha was evidently much indisposed to abolish the Commissions which he considers necessary for the time being. At the same time, he is so violently prejudiced against the employment of Europeans in the Egyptian service that he preferred complete abolition to the appointment of a European member to the Commission of Revision.[32]

The Commissions were abolished in the May of 1889.

Having reestablished the jurisdiction of the National Courts, the British occupation authorities then began to assert control over the Courts and the administration of justice. As a first step additional European judges were appointed to the Egyptian courts. Then, in 1890, John Scott, a judge in India, was called upon to investigate the Egyptian legal system. He recommended the appointment of a British advisor for the Justice Ministry. This would effectively complete the process of bringing the Ministry under British control. Scott himself was selected to be the first advisor. Riyad had now lost everything Nubar had gained and resigned in the wake of losing this battle in 1891.

Scott's title of "advisor" was misleading: he quickly established his ability to supervise the employment of foreign judges (where he favored British over continental judges). And he charged that shortcomings in the National Courts required that he be consulted in matters of judicial appointment and promotion. Accordingly he chaired a committee of judicial inspection within the Ministry of Justice.[33] While the committee was theoretically only to advise the minister of justice, the step effectively gave the British a supervisory role over the National Courts and established a greater degree of executive authority over the judiciary. After the first decade of the occupation, the British stood clearly in

---

[31] See Baring to Salisbury, February 23, 1888, FO 141/255, no. 88. Evelyn Baring did not become Lord Cromer until 1892; I refer to him as Cromer even before his elevation to the peerage to avoid confusion.

[32] Baring to Salisbury, May 9, 1889, FO 141/266, no. 221.

[33] Muhammad Sami Mazin, "The National Courts after their Construction," *Al-kitab al-dhahabi*, vol. I, p. 179.

control of the National Courts. However, a more ambitious effort to go beyond controlling to reshaping Egyptian justice was indefinitely postponed. The British attitude was clear even before the occupation: French law codes were unsuitable but probably unavoidable in Egypt.[34] The National Courts were flawed in British eyes from the beginning because of the decision to adopt a complex and culturally inappropriate model. After his departure from Egypt, Cromer wrote:

It is true that, prior to 1883, no system of justice existed in Egypt. It is not, however, on that account to be supposed that the English were free to introduce into the country any system which they preferred. Such was far from being the case. French law and procedure had already taken root in Egypt. The codes administered by the Mixed Tribunals were French. All the young Egyptians who had received any legal training had been educated in France. It was, therefore, inevitable that the new Tribunals should be based on a French rather than on an English mode. The necessity was regrettable, for a simple code of law and procedure, somewhat similar to that which was subsequently introduced into the Soudan, would – more especially in criminal matters – have probably been more suited to the requirements of the country than that which was actually adopted.[35]

Indeed, the introduction of British judges who had often served in India insured that periodic proposals would be made to "Indianize" or "Anglicize" Egyptian justice throughout the history of the occupation. In 1883, even before the National Courts began operation, Benson Maxwell, the British official hired to head the *niyaba*, endeavored to convince Egyptian and British officials to change course, complaining that he could not operate with a French-style code of criminal procedure. The Egyptian minister of justice replied that "it is more easy for one legal officer to master the foreign system than for the eighty judges who are to be employed in the new courts to administer a justice the rules of which are foreign to their whole legal education."[36]

While Maxwell's efforts in 1883 met with no success, limited forays in the direction of Anglicizing Egyptian justice were made in following decades. Modifications to Egyptian law codes under the occupation were often based on British expertise and advice, though changes were relatively minor. The *Shari'a* Courts came under frequent criticism from British officials, and Cromer expressed his belief that the only solution was "to abolish [them] as a separate institution altogether, and to transfer their jurisdiction to the ordinary Civil Courts."[37] However,

[34] For an example of such a complaint at the time that the codes were being written in 1881, see Malet to Granville, November 28, 1881, FO 141/144, no. 348.

[35] Earl of Cromer, *Modern Egypt*, vol. II, pp. 516–17.

[36] Malet to Granville, September 1, 1883, FO 141/175, no. 385.

[37] Cromer to Salisbury, November 8, 1896, FO 371/14620, no. 137.

because of the political sensitivity of anything related to the *shariʿa*, this step was not taken until 1955, long after the British had lost their influence over the legal system. Under the occupation, British authorities limited themselves to encouraging the Egyptian government to increase the formalization of the *Shariʿa* Courts and to construct a clear hierarchy of lower-level and appellate courts. The British education advisor also clashed with the French director of the Egyptian law school; in 1907 a British director took his place.[38]

More significant measures were taken at the local level. Convinced that Egyptian justice was remote and procedurally complex, British officials experimented with various systems of circulating courts using simplified procedures and often local notables as well. Based on British experience both in England and in India, these courts focused generally on criminal matters, handling minor cases and issuing verdicts that were difficult (sometimes impossible) to appeal.[39] In 1912 over two hundred "Cantonal Courts" (*mahakim al-akhtat*) were established, using simplified procedures and non-professional judges (generally drawn from the ranks of rural notables).[40] The Cantonal Courts had critics: some thought that they encouraged litigiousness; *ʿumdas* (village mayors) saw them as an encroachment on their authority.[41]

The British had only achieved slight modifications in the Egyptian legal system by the time of the First World War. The Mixed Courts and the National Courts were still very much intact and operating on the same French-inspired basis as they were founded upon. The outbreak of war between Britain and the Ottoman Empire in 1914 finally made it possible for the British to pursue a far more ambitious plan. Britain declared a protectorate over Egypt and considered outright annexation into the British Empire. While that option was rejected (although it was raised periodically throughout the war), Britain made clear its opinion that Ottoman sovereignty over Egypt had ended. The British Foreign Office pushed the matter further, arguing that the end of Ottoman sovereignty also entailed the end of the capitulations, a position imposed on a suspicious Egyptian government with difficulty.[42]

[38] Donald M. Reid, *Lawyers and Politics in the Arab World, 1880–1960* (Minneapolis: Bibliotheca Islamica, 1981).

[39] See Salim, *Al-nizam al-qadaʾi*, vol. I, pp. 133–38.

[40] ʿAbd al-Latif Ghurbal, "Statistics on the National Courts," *Al-kitab al-dhahabi*, vol. II, pp. 239–40; Salim, *Al-Nizam al-qadaʾi*, vol. I, pp. 138–43.

[41] See, for example, the objections of the financial advisor contained in a letter to Kitchener, March 30, 1912 and the 1914 report by the judicial advisor, FO 141/583/9352.

[42] See the Foreign Office minute by C. Hurst, March 11, 1916, FO 371/169181/16. The Egyptian government probably feared that an abolition of the capitulations paved the way for moves tantamount to annexation.

While British officials deliberated on the status of post-war Egypt, the Egyptian government, under British control, appointed a commission to examine capitulatory and mixed-court reform. The commission outlined its proposals in March 1918, suggesting what William Brunyate (a leading member of the commission) later termed "a more or less openly avowed Anglicization of the law and legal institutions of Egypt."[43] Capitulatory privileges of foreign powers were to be abandoned; instead the British would take responsibility for protecting foreign interests in Egypt. The Mixed Courts and the National Courts were to be unified, the number of British judges would be greatly increased, English would become the principal language of the new unified court system, and British jurisprudence would naturally begin to outrank French in influence. The Brunyate proposals excited controversy, but British determination to push forward was clear to all. Egyptian nationalist leaders, fearing correctly that the proposals amounted to a step just short of annexation, protested strongly.[44]

The culmination of decades of far more timorous British proposals, the Brunyate commission's recommendations seemed likely to be implemented until the nationalist uprising of 1919. The nationwide rebellion against the occupation, though eventually suppressed, completely changed the British outlook on their presence in Egypt. Rather than increasing their role, the British were forced to consider ways to guarantee their interests and influence while scaling back their presence. As part of this effort, Great Britain unilaterally declared Egypt independent in 1922. While the British did claim continued privileges in Egypt (including the protection of foreigners and minorities), the Egyptian government finally found itself far more able to pursue its own vision of judicial and legal reform.

### Courts in independent Egypt, 1922–1937

Egyptian independence did not bring immediate changes to the judicial system, but it did ultimately undermine the position of the capitulations and the Mixed Courts and lead to minor structural changes in the National Courts. The Mixed Courts and the capitulations survived for some time because the British held out the issues as a bargaining chip. Britain insisted on retaining the limitations on sovereignty implied in the

---

[43] Brinton, *Mixed Courts*, pp. 186–87. Brinton's quotation is from Brunyate in a lecture at Cambridge in 1924.

[44] The memory of Brunyate's proposals were sufficiently strong that the Foreign Office kept him out of Egypt for months after the eruption of the 1919 uprising; only in 1920 could a visit be discreetly arranged. See the file on Sir William Brunyate, FO 141/686/ 8760.

unilateral declaration of independence and the capitulatory system until a suitable Anglo-Egyptian treaty was negotiated.[45] By 1927, the two governments had agreed on a section of the treaty requiring Britain to help Egypt reform the capitulatory regime, making it conform "with the spirit of the times and with the present state of Egypt."[46] In spite of this agreement on principle, the failure to close negotiations on the treaty as a whole led the British to withhold any diplomatic assistance in securing capitulatory reform.

Opposition to both the capitulations and the Mixed Courts grew markedly in independent Egypt, as those in power often found their plans and objectives blocked by them.[47] Some Egyptian governments began to make limited forays in the direction of reform even without British help. In 1926, the Egyptian ambassador in Washington tried but failed to convince the Secretary of State that the United States should take the lead by unilaterally renouncing its capitulatory privileges.[48] The following year the Egyptian cabinet put forward a proposal to strengthen Egyptian participation in the Mixed Courts. The proposals attracted the attention of Egyptian newspapers, many of which called for modifying or abolishing the capitulations. The Egyptian government even issued invitations for an international congress to discuss capitulatory reform, but eventually dropped the idea.[49] By the 1930s calls for unilateral abrogation of either the capitulations or the Mixed Courts were regularly heard in the Egyptian press.[50]

Yet all of these efforts proved futile; few even drew the sustained attention of the Egyptian government. It was not simply foreign

[45] See, for example, Jardine to Secretary of State, December 28, 1931, USNA 783.003/44. In 1935, J. S. Somers Cocks, a Foreign Office official, wrote: "Ever since 1922 our attitude towards the Capitulations has been to treat them as a bargaining asset when negotiating a treaty with Egypt." See the minute included in FO 371/J852/507/16. Also quoted by Alexander Kitroeff, *The Greeks in Egypt 1917–1937* (London: Ithaca Press, 1989), p. 56. For a slightly less direct but equally frank description of British policy, see the note by G. Arthur W. Booth (then serving in Egypt as judicial advisor), March 5, 1930, FO 141/650/443.

[46] The text of the drafts is included in Great Britain, Foreign Office records, *Egypt No. 1 (1928). Papers Regarding Negotiations for a Treaty of Alliance with Egypt.*

[47] See, for example, Husayn ʿAmir, *al-Ahram*, August 90, 1923.

[48] Memorandum of conversation between Secretary of State Kellogg and Egyptian Minister, Samy Pasha, September 29, 1926, USNA 783.003/4.

[49] Howell to Secretary of State, April 7 and 27, 1927, and Winthrop to Secretary of State, December 23, 1927, USNA 783.003/5; Brinton, *Mixed Courts*, pp. 191–92.

[50] ʿAziz Khanki, a leading lawyer and one of the founders of the Bar Association of the National Courts, was a particularly strong advocate of unilateral action. His articles are collected in *Al-mahakim al-mukhtalita wa-l-mahakim al-ahliyya* (The Mixed Courts and the National Courts) (Cairo: Al-Matabiʿ al-ʿAsriyya, 1939). A slightly more modest proposal that also involved abolition of the Mixed Courts was advanced by ʿAbd al-ʿAziz Fahmi, then president of the *Mahkamat al-Naqd*. See the memorandum by the British judicial advisor, G. Arthur W. Booth, June 9, 1932, FO 371/J1819/32/16.

opposition that blocked these attempts to reform the system. Egyptians did not stand united behind the efforts. In particular the Wafd, representing the majority of Egyptian nationalists, viewed the question as premature. The Wafd ruled for only twenty months during Egypt's first decade of independence, but the pressure it could bring to bear (and the instability caused by attempts to deny it political power) robbed the Egyptian government of the political strength to push for reform during most of the period. The Wafd consistently called for complete independence for Egypt; certainly it found noxious any restrictions on Egyptian sovereignty. However, abolition of the capitulations and the Mixed Courts generally remained a long-term objective.

The more immediate goal of the Wafd was complete independence from Britain. Here the Wafd followed the same reasoning as had pre-war Egyptian nationalists. Britain was the immediate adversary; moving prematurely against the capitulations and the Mixed Courts might actually undermine Egyptian independence. As long as Britain still claimed a role in protecting foreigners and minorities, any move affecting them might strengthen the British rather than the Egyptian government.[51] Thus a premature move against the system might deepen British penetration of the country.[52]

Only after the successful negotiation of a treaty in 1936 did the Wafd's leaders turn to dismantling the capitulations and the Mixed Courts. Egypt secured Britain's pledge in the treaty to work "to bring about speedily the abolition of the capitulations in Egypt" and to have the Mixed Courts take over the work of the consular courts for a transitional period at the end of which "the Egyptian Government will be free to dispense with the Mixed Tribunals." An international conference would be called to negotiate an end to the capitulations and the Courts. An annex to the treaty also implied British acceptance of unilateral abolition

---

[51] Mahmud 'Azmi, *al-Ahram*, April 24, 1923. For a non-Wafdist version of this view, see the reply of 'Adli's delegation to British proposals in 1921, printed in Great Britain, Foreign Office records, *Egypt No. 4 (1921) Papers Respecting Negotiations with the Egyptian Delegation*, p. 9. See also Sprigg to Secretary of State, March 31, 1921, USNA 883.00/339.

[52] For instance, in reply to a question on his views on the Capitulations in a 1923 interview with the *Journal du Caire*, Sa'd Zaghlul, the leader of the Wafd, stated: "It would be premature to reply to that question . . . I have the hope, if not the certainty, once independence has been obtained, that it will be easy to discover a basis of agreement between the capitulatory Powers and ourselves." The interview was printed by the *Egyptian Gazette* on September 26, 1923. It is included in Howell to Secretary of State, September 27, 1923, USNA 883.00/470. In late 1935, only months before assuming the leadership of a Wafdist government that finally negotiated an Anglo-Egyptian treaty, Mustafa al-Nahhas announced that he opposed abolition of the capitulations "so long as the British retained the privileged situation which they had acquired without right in the country." Fish to Secretary of State, November 20, 1935, USNA 783.003/109.

should the conference fail.[53] Before the conference met, the Egyptian government drew up a proposal to eliminate the capitulations, transfer jurisdiction over criminal cases involving foreigners from consular courts to the Mixed Courts, and then, after a short transitional period, transfer all the work of the Mixed Courts to the Egyptian National Courts. The Egyptian government obtained nearly everything it wanted when the conference was held in 1937 in Montreux, Switzerland.[54] At Montreux, the Egyptian delegation was aided openly by the British and covertly by the Americans who were told the Egyptian negotiating position in advance, allowing them to introduce Egyptian ideas, representing them as compromise proposals.[55]

Independence brought few changes in the National Courts. The system was expanded, with an appeals court established at Asyut in 1926 (following through on a decision made, but never implemented, in 1883). This small step brought problems because the existence of multiple appeals courts threatened the uniformity and centralization so central to official Egyptian conceptions of law and judicial affairs. Accordingly, a higher court was constructed at the apex of the Egyptian judiciary, the *Mahkamat al-Naqd*, or Court of Cassation.[56] Independence gave Egypt legislative autonomy for the first time since the British occupation, yet a wholesale revision of the codes did not occur for over two decades (there were some revisions made, particularly in political

---

[53] Brinton, *Mixed Courts*, p. 194. The annex read: "It is understood that in the event of its being found impossible to bring into effect the arrangements referred to in Article 2, the Egyptian Government retains its full rights unimpaired with regard to the capitulatory regime, including the Mixed Tribunals." USNA 783.003/217.

[54] The agreement and negotiating record are contained in USNA 783.003 – Montreux. Almost unnoticed was a provision for the transition period barring the Mixed Courts from reviewing "acts of sovereignty" by the Egyptian government. An American judge on the Mixed Courts advising the American delegation did criticize the text, but the Egyptian wording was adopted with little modification. See Judge Brinton, "Brief comments on the Egyptian note of February 3, 1937," included in Fish to Secretary of State, February 15, 1937, USNA 783.003/174. Had such a position been taken at the construction of the Courts the nature of the political and fiscal crisis of the 1870s and 1880s would have been quite different, because the Egyptian government would have been far more able to rein in the Courts. (Indeed, as will be seen, the doctrine of "acts of sovereignty" has limited the political effectiveness of courts throughout the Arab world.)

[55] The British later thanked the Americans for their "collaboration." See Fish to Secretary of State, May 12, 1937, 783.003/252; and R. C. Lindsey, British Ambassador to the United States to Cordell Hull, Secretary of State, June 4, 1937, USNA 783.003/261. For a recapitulation of the preparations made by the British as well as other parties, see Wallace to Eden, June 11, 1937, FO 371/J2750/13/16.

[56] For an explicit linkage between the existence of multiple appeals courts and the need for a new, supreme level, see the speech by the minister of justice on the opening of the appeals court in Asyut, reprinted in *Al-kitab al-dhahabi*, vol. I, p. 150.

crimes, however[57]). Perhaps most surprising was the small impact of the introduction of written constitutions to Egyptian political life. The constitution of 1923 was twice suspended (and once even temporarily replaced), and, as will be seen, judicial review was not firmly established until the late 1940s. As a result, courts wishing to introduce constitutional jurisprudence did not have a strong basis on which to do so.

Thus, the six decades after the establishment of the Mixed Courts witnessed the construction of a separate National Court system, its maintenance despite British attempts to modify it, and an agreement on its assuming general jurisdiction for all criminal and civil disputes arising on Egyptian territory.

### Motivations guiding the course of legal reform

How can the legal reforms of the nineteenth and early twentieth centuries be best explained? In the remainder of this chapter, we will consider the usefulness of the three approaches adduced in chapter 1. Were they impositions of external powers, steps towards the development of a liberal order, or elements of a state-building centralization project?

#### Imposed law

It is important to note that legal reform was initiated before European penetration was most acutely felt, and the system constructed was maintained under some anti-imperialist regimes. The reforms of the nineteenth century were often more evolutionary rather than revolutionary in nature. There was certainly no sudden break from a system based largely on Islamic jurisprudence to the Code Napoléon; rather there was a gradual emergence of a centralized and hierarchical state-sponsored system. Thus the key periods in legal reform hardly coincide with the height of imperial penetration. The construction of the Mixed Courts and the decision to construct the National Courts both predated the British occupation of 1882; the British were in fact highly critical of both systems from the beginning. It should therefore be no surprise that an examination of the attitudes of the British towards courts and law demonstrates clearly that imperialism did shape legal development in Egypt but to a much lesser extent than is often assumed.[58]

---

[57] Muhammad Labib 'Atiya, "The Development of the Criminal Code in Egypt since the Time of the Construction of the National Courts," *Al-kitab al-dhahabi*, vol. II, p. 5.

[58] For more detail, see Nathan Brown, "Law and Imperialism: Egypt in Comparative Perspective," *Law and Society Review*, 29 (1), 1995, p. 103.

The British occupiers of Egypt never felt comfortable with the National Court system. It had been established in spite of their misgivings; John Scott, a former Mixed Court judge and future advisor to the Egyptian Ministry of Justice, wrote to the British consul-general in Egypt in 1887, attributing the unsatisfactory operation of the Courts to the fact that "they have been left to Egyptian supervision more than other reforms."[59] To be sure, the British did successfully infiltrate the workings of the National Courts as the occupation wore on (indeed, Scott himself had a major role in that process). Yet even when British influence in the National Courts was at its height – from the 1890s until 1922 – British actions made clear that they were frustrated by their inability to exercise greater control.

For instance, the British moved to avoid the National Courts in matters deemed extremely sensitive. This was particularly true with offenses involving British military forces in Egypt. Less than four years after British troops had landed, the British consul-general complained of "the delay which constantly occurs, in the Native Courts, in dealing with cases in which natives are charged with offences against British soldiers."[60] The result was the establishment of special tribunals to deal with such offenses.[61] The most notorious of these tribunals sentenced several residents of the village of Dinshway to hang and several others to flogging after they had clashed with pigeon-hunting British troops in 1906. Lord Cromer expressed directly and publicly at the time that extraordinary measures were necessary because reliance on the regular institutions of justice was sometimes insufficient in a country accustomed, in his eyes, to lawless and despotic government.[62] It was this distrust of the National Court system that led to periodic calls for Anglicization, including the abortive proposals of the Brunyate commission.

Even when appointing foreign judges to the National Courts the Egyptian government made the most of the leeway granted them to limit British influence. The preference for Belgian and Dutch judges has already been noted. The Commissions of Brigandage represented a similar attempt to maintain Egyptian control over matters of law and justice. Even after the collapse of these efforts, Egyptian lawyers, judges, prosecutors, and other court personnel frequently frustrated imperial officials. Allen Christelow, writing on Algeria, notes this phenomenon about colonialism more generally:

[59] Scott to Baring, December 12, 1887, FO 141/246/597.
[60] Baring to Rosebery, March 29, 1886, FO 141/232/103.
[61] Muhammad Jamal al Din al-Masadi, *al-Jumhuriyya*, June 19 to 27, 1969.
[62] Cromer, *Modern Egypt*, vol. II, pp. 32–33.

Colonial administrators tended to see the native lawyer as an unscrupulous opportunist, out to exploit the gullible, and to sow discord where patriarchal peace and harmony had prevailed. They were thus inclined to keep as much of law as possible in the hands of customary sages of the village councils, or in their own presumably equally sage hands. Custom and administration were to be allied against the corrosive, divisive effects of the law and lawyers.[63]

From Algeria to India, imperial officials were as likely to see local lawyers as their adversaries rather than their tools. Over time, the lawyers became a bastion of nationalist opposition as well.[64]

Yet it was not simply lawyers who were suspect to the British. Egyptian judges were generally held excessively inclined towards nationalist sentiment. In 1912, after the alleged attackers of a French engineer were acquitted in an Egyptian court, Lord Kitchener (then the British consul-general in Egypt) wrote:

All legal authorities agree that the case was fully and satisfactorily proved against the two men accused, one of whom had been twice tried for attempted murder in the last four years; yet they were both acquitted by Egyptian judges. These judges were known to be Nationalists, and it is naturally considered that race and religious feeling alone can account for their finding.[65]

Kitchener's complaint was not unique. Throughout the occupation, the British expected unfavorable rulings from Egyptian judges whenever nationalist feelings were involved. Indeed, it was precisely this feeling that led to the establishment of special courts in politically sensitive cases such as those discussed above.

In fact, the British frustration with Egyptian courts and law was directed not only towards lawyers and judges but the population as a whole. The way Egyptians used the legal system helps makes sense of a paradox displayed in British (and frequently Egyptian) writings about Egyptian courts. On the one hand, British officials in Egypt joined their counterparts in India, Burma, and elsewhere in complaining of the litigiousness of the local population.[66] Egyptians were far too willing to bring even the most trivial cases to courts which were slow and inefficient to begin with. As local disputants flocked to courts (at least in civil cases), imperial authorities worried that they were aggravating social

---

[63] Allen C. Christelow, *Muslim Law Courts and the French Colonial State in Algeria* (Princeton: Princeton University Press, 1985), p. 4.

[64] See especially Farhat Ziadeh, *Lawyers, the Rule of Law, and Liberalism in Modern Egypt* (Palo Alto: Stanford 1968), and Reid, *Lawyers and Politics*.

[65] Kitchener to Grey, June 27, 1912, FO 371/27388/27388/16, no. 1363.

[66] On India, see Lloyd Rudolph and Susanne Rudolph, *The Modernity of Tradition: Political Development in India* (Chicago: University of Chicago Press, 1967); on Burma see J. S. Furnivall, *Colonial Policy and Practice: A Comparative Study of Burma and Netherlands India* (Cambridge: Cambridge University Press, 1948).

tensions rather than alleviating them. One British document even cited a lawsuit filed after a guest invited for dinner was not fed by his host.[67]

With respect to criminal courts, on the other hand, the Egyptians (as with other colonized populations) seemed too reticent to cooperate with the new institutions of criminal justice to allow them to work; when they did testify officials complained they took perjury very lightly. Crime was one of the major obsessions of the British occupation, and even those Egyptian officials most committed to European-style legal reform used the crime rate to justify extrajudicial methods of apprehending and punishing suspected criminals (such as the Commissions of Brigandage).

How could the British simultaneously complain that Egyptians went to court too frequently and that they did not cooperate enough with the courts? How could Egyptian governments echo the same complaints before and after independence? Few officials noticed the irony of their own complaints because the contradiction was more apparent than real. In civil disputes, Egyptians proved ready to enlist courts when necessary. By 1920, shortly before the British declared Egypt independent, Egyptians were bringing over half a million civil or *shari'a* cases to court. The inefficiency and frequent postponements associated with the courts did not always discourage potential litigants; indeed, some quickly became adept at using delays as part of their strategy of obtaining a favorable settlement. Involvement in criminal cases, however, could be much less attractive. Charges were difficult to drop once they had been filed, giving the aggrieved party less control over process and outcome. Witnesses to crime often had no incentive to testify. As a result, considerably less than one-half of serious crimes in Egypt were even brought to trial. Reflecting on his experience in Egypt, Cromer wrote:

The protection of the weak against the strong is, however, not the sole function of justice. It should also be able to protect society against evil-doers. That this protection has, of late years, been inadequate in Egypt, can scarcely be doubted. It is easy to indicate the main reason for this state of things. On the one hand, civilisation insists on the cardinal principle that no man is to be punished for any offence unless he is clearly proved to have committed it. On the other hand, the peculiar conditions of Egyptian society render it often a matter of extreme difficulty to obtain evidence of guilt sufficient to warrant a conviction.[68]

---

[67] Hazel to Graham, November 13, 1912, FO 141/583/9352.
[68] Cromer, *Modern Egypt*, vol. II, p. 521. This attitude is a recurring theme in British documents. See, for instance the "Memorandum by Mr. Machell on Crime in Egypt," contained in Cromer's annual report for 1905, pp. 115–17, and Kershaw to Findley, September 23, 1906, FO 371/43853/16, file 68.

Indeed, some British officials held the new legal system responsible for encouraging crime.[69] Egyptians therefore shaped the operation of both civil and criminal courts – the first by their creative uses and the second by their creative avoidance.

If the modern Egyptian legal system was established partly independently of imperialism and partly to restrict imperial influence, then how can the largely European content of the codes (and inspiration for court structure) be explained? Why did Egyptian elites work to build a European-style legal system if European powers did not always force them to do so? While some reasons for turning to France had nothing to do with imperialism (as will be seen), in some other ways use of the French model could actually be a tool of resisting direct European penetration. In this limited sense, legal reform could be an indirect effect of – or more accurately, a preemptive response to – imperialism.

Law constituted the defining difference between European civilization and the despotism of the rest of the world – such was the view of many imperialists. Britain and France were governed by the rule of law; Egypt and the entire Middle East were held to be governed by the will of capricious rulers. The establishment of structures and procedures that Europeans could not help but recognize as law might serve to rob imperialism of its justification. Thus the Mixed Courts were designed not to serve imperialism but to limit the effects of the capitulations.

After the establishment of the Mixed Courts most Egyptian leaders seemed to believe that the only way to regain control over (and perhaps even abolish) them was to build a system as similar as possible in the National Courts. The discussions of the cabinet on this point are quite clear: the code and structure for the National Courts were established precisely to make amalgamation possible.[70]

As the occupation wore on the goal of amalgamation receded. Yet the French system and the Mixed Courts both began to have a different attraction – they obstructed British attempts to assert control over the system and thus helped keep some measure of official power in Egyptian hands. Insisting on following non-British models allowed Egyptian lawyers and judges to follow a path independent of their occupiers. The preference for Belgian judges has already been mentioned, as has Brunyate's proposals to rein in Egyptian autonomy by Anglicizing the legal system. And the continued survival of the Mixed Courts kept an important segment of the legal system out of British hands.

---

[69] See, for instance, Findley to Grey, July 7, 1906, FO 371/24014/16; also Baring (Cromer) to Salisbury, January 3, 1890, FO 141/276/4.

[70] Those discussions are contained in *Al-kitab al-dhahabi*, vol. I.

## Legal reform and liberal legality

If the legal reforms of the late nineteenth and early twentieth centuries cannot be seen as an external imposition, can they be portrayed instead as the beginning of the rule of law in Egypt? The reforms certainly did move in the direction of liberal legality: the judiciary was separated from administration (and given some degree of independence as well), and the law was made more fixed and predictable with the introduction of new codes. Property rights were more securely guaranteed in both the Mixed Courts and the National Courts, and citizens could freely resort to the courts without restriction in civil cases; punishment without trial was greatly diminished. And the institutionalization of liberal legality continued: four decades after the foundation of the National Courts the authors of Egypt's first effective constitution guaranteed equality before the law and judicial independence.

In fact, a specific kind of liberalism did inform the legal reform efforts of the period. The liberal legality of the Egyptian leadership was genuine but was an integral part of the effort to build a stronger, more centralized state; it was also indigenous, restricted in what it could achieve by the British imperial presence. A strong consensus emerged among the Egyptian political leadership during the last quarter of the nineteenth century supporting the establishment of an independent judiciary, checks on executive authority, and stable property rights. A brief historical review of how these three goals emerged and guided Egyptian judicial development helps clarify the meaning of (and limitations to) liberal legality in Egypt.

First, judicial independence was both genuine but circumscribed in practice. The desire to build an independent judiciary was evident in the first Mixed Court proposals in the 1860s.[71] When discussion of the National Courts began they were similarly predicated on the assumption of the necessity to construct an independent judiciary for Egyptians as well as foreigners. Judicial independence clearly meant that administrative and judicial functions would no longer be combined and that a professionalized judiciary would be developed or imported from Europe. The combination of administrative and judicial functions was seen as inefficient and encouraging official abuses.

Yet the precise relationship of the new judges to top political officials

---

[71] It is interesting to note in this regard that Nubar, one of the leading architects of the Mixed Courts (and judicial reform in general) is often not well regarded in Egyptian nationalist historiography because of his close connection with European powers. However, his role in establishing judicial independence leads Egyptian judges to view him in a far more favorable light. See, for instance, Sa'id al-Jamal, "The Rule of Law and the Independence of the Judiciary," al-Wafd, March 27, 1990.

was sometimes ambiguous. In the Mixed Courts there was no question that judges were independent of the Egyptian government. Technically appointed by the Khedive, foreign powers successfully asserted a claim to specific seats on the Mixed Courts bench and to a strong role in selecting judges. Moreover, there is considerable archival evidence to suggest that judges considered themselves representatives of their home governments and not of the Egyptian government and Egyptian interests. Many served informally as legal advisors to diplomats from their home country.[72] And Mixed Court judges had a limited authority to approve the application of Egyptian laws and regulations to foreigners.

The independence of the National Court judges from top political officials was more limited. The head of the *niyaba*, a judicial position, was a highly politicized post from the beginning, with the Egyptian government striving (and ultimately failing) to keep it in Egyptian hands. Positions on the bench could be politicized as well. After 1891 the strong role of a committee headed by the British judicial advisor in appointments and promotions has already been mentioned. This committee established a measure of British political control over the National Courts; it also put in place an institutional mechanism for Egyptian governments to use upon independence. After 1923, it was frequently charged that partisan loyalties more than judicial qualifications determined appointments.[73] Ironically British officials frequently noted and deplored irregularities in appointments, oblivious that their predecessors had established the system precisely to enforce political oversight of the judiciary.[74] In 1936, a transition government created a new body, the Supreme Judicial Council, headed by the minister of justice but with strong judicial representation. The Council was to make recommendations on promotions and transfers to the cabinet, in essence

---

[72] To cite one example, Jasper Brinton, an American judge, advised the American delegation to the Montreux conference on the capitulations and the Mixed Courts.

[73] For examples of such charges of politicization, see Lloyd to Chamberlain, July 2, 1928, FO 371/J2024/2024/16, Hoare to Murray, September 2, 1930, FO 371/J3076/4/16, and Loraine to Henderson, May 13, 1931, FO 371/J1676, 1676/16.

[74] Most ironic in this regard is the activity of J. F. Kershaw during the trial of those accused in the 1924 assassination of Lee Stack, the commander of the Egyptian army and the governor-general of Sudan. Kershaw served simultaneously as a judge and as the acting legal advisor to the British High Commissioner. When most of those accused were acquitted, Kershaw, in violation of Egyptian judicial practice, made public his dissent and resigned from the Egyptian judiciary in protest at the verdict after the British cabinet guaranteed he would not suffer financially. Earlier he had recommended that an Egyptian colleague who sat on the case with him receive an honorary decoration from the British because of his helpful attitude. See Henderson to Chamberlain, June 20, 1925, FO 371/J1817/90/16, and Lloyd to Chamberlain, June 8, 1926, FO 371/J1691/215/16.

reversing the 1891 decision to give executive officials predominance.[75] As will be seen in the next two chapters, judicial appointment and promotion have been at the center of controversy over judicial independence in Egypt up to the present.

Second, judicial checks on executive action, though a goal in the abstract, similarly operated in an ambiguous and controversial matter. Once again, matters were clearer in the Mixed Courts, where the Egyptian government quickly found that judges were quite bold in reversing government decisions, and an early attempt by Isma'il to ignore a court ruling was aborted by his deposition. In fact, the Mixed Courts, by guarding the capitulations so jealously, restricted both executive and legislative authority – the latter by agreeing only to recognize laws that had drawn the assent of the capitulatory powers (a process requiring protracted diplomacy) or the judges of the Courts themselves (in minor matters).

The National Courts never acted as boldly as the Mixed Courts in confronting the Egyptian government, but the clear intention of their architects was to have them review administrative acts by officials. Some unsuccessfully proposed requiring government permission before a lawsuit could be filed against administrative officials; others preferred to establish a special administrative court for such suits. Despite strong sentiment for the latter (in order to strengthen the ability of the judiciary to reverse administrative actions), the cabinet finally approved a proposal to allow administrative lawsuits to fall within the jurisdiction of the National Courts. If an official was acting within his official capacity, the state would be liable for damages; if the official was acting on his own then he would be personally liable.[76]

The National Courts quickly established their willingness to take official abuse seriously by acquitting those whom they suspected were tortured by the police or by other officials (including provincial governors). It was this attitude which helped justify the establishment of the Commissions of Brigandage. But it was not simply the Egyptian government that was frustrated by the fastidious manner of judges in cases where torture was alleged. As British officials increased their control over matters of law enforcement they complained that the guilty were often set free because of "a tendency to adhere too strictly to the methods which obtain in countries where legal procedure is in a more

---

[75] Salim, *Al-nizam al-qada'i*, vol. II, p. 299. On judicial independence more generally, see pp. 292–311. It is possible that the 1936 measure was taken in anticipation of the return of the Wafd, which on previous occasions had moved to promote pro-Wafd judges that it charged had been passed over by non-Wafd governments.

[76] For coverage of the debate, see *al-Ahram*, January 24, January 31, February 1, February 2, and February 5, 1883.

advanced state than in Egypt."[77] An extrajudicial system of administrative surveillance and internal exile was therefore constructed to insure that disreputable characters could be apprehended. Compiling a list of those subject to control based on their reputations was solely an administrative task. Since witnesses were reluctant to testify and confessions obtained under torture were not recognized by the courts, the British helped to establish a tradition – still observed in Egypt today – of special procedures to deal with those whom officials were convinced were guilty but judges might not convict.

Third, legal reform was also motivated by a desire to define and guarantee property rights. But this effort was an integral part of, rather than antithetical to, the effort to build a more effective state apparatus. An emerging and increasingly influential class of landowners was particularly interested in making ownership of their agricultural property as secure as possible. That class had an interest in insuring that transactions involving land be recognized, organized, and enforced by the state. A state that simply deferred to local custom and structures offered fewer benefits. Cuno writes that prior to the land laws of the mid-nineteenth century

the law courts had no supervisory role in peasant land tenure. Their role was passive: a dispute over land could be settled outside the courts as well as within them, and a land transaction could be made and witnessed without the use of a document or its registration in court. Many simple peasants continued to conduct their affairs in the customary way, using verbal agreement, especially when it came to renting land – in the 1960s the government was still trying to curtail this practice. Yet official refusal to recognize transactions unless they were made according to the new procedures would naturally favor the interests of the notables, merchants, Levantine traders, and others who understood how the rules worked and wished to acquire land.[78]

While Cuno shows that landowners were hardly responsible for the legal changes of the mid-nineteenth century, those changes, combined with the continued acquisition of land by high officials, insured that by the last quarter of the nineteenth century rural notables and large landowners had become politically powerful, particularly in the creation of the new legal order.[79]

Yet the new legal order was not simply a creation of self-interested property owners. High officials, while often property owners themselves, had other motives in constructing a legal system that protected property: while state prerogatives might be slightly limited as a result, the overall

---

[77] Baring (Cromer) to Salisbury, May 20, 1890, FO 141/277A/165.
[78] Cuno, *Pasha's Peasants*, p. 203.
[79] This is a consistent theme in Cannon, *Politics of Law*.

result would be a stronger state and more prosperous economy. Nubar was generally explicit on this front. In 1881, at a time when the Mixed Courts had exacerbated a protracted political crisis and the National Courts had yet to be established, he wrote that without a sound legal system it would be impossible to effect administrative reform or attract investment. The Mixed Courts had been able to attract foreign investment and had aided Egyptian progress, even if capitulatory powers had successfully transformed the Courts into an international rather than Egyptian system. To complete the work begun with the construction of the Mixed Courts, a single, unified system of justice would have to be built, enforcing a single law code (though Nubar seemed to be willing to employ foreign judges and have some courts designated for mixed cases). Only then would Egyptians have the same confidence as foreigners in investing their money in productive enterprises. Nubar was only slightly more guarded in expressing the claim that unlimited khedival autocracy would make the development of a sophisticated and complex bureaucracy impossible.[80]

In the late nineteenth century the property generally at issue was agricultural land or loans secured by agricultural land. In the twentieth century Egyptian business interests emerged and began to constitute a new source of pressure for legal reform. The particular targets of their resentment was the Mixed Courts and the capitulations, and they sought to abolish both. Even the exclusively Egyptian group that founded Bank Misr in 1920 (outside the jurisdiction of the Mixed Courts), had neither the ability nor the desire to avoid foreign investment, technology, and business dealings.[81] If they were to deal with foreigners in any way, their Egyptian nationality provided no escape from the capitulations and the Courts. They thus found the system a problem for two reasons. First, Egyptian business leaders who did not have foreign nationality felt that the system of the capitulations and the Mixed Courts placed foreigners in an advantageous position.[82] More precisely, their complaint was that the capitulations barred discrimination against foreigners and that the Mixed Courts tended to interpret "discrimination" fairly broadly. The Courts and the capitulations thus prevented the Egyptian government

[80] The letter by Nubar is printed in Makhluf, *Nubar basha*, pp. 123–35.
[81] For the rise of the Egyptian bourgeoisie, see Tignor, *State, Public Enterprise, and Economic Change in Egypt 1918–1952* (Princeton: Princeton University Press, 1984); Eric Davis, *Challenging Colonialism: Bank Misr and Egyptian Industrialization, 1920–1941* (Princeton: Princeton University Press, 1983); Robert Vitalis, "On the Theory and Practice of Compradors: The Role of 'Abbud Pasha in the Egyptian Political Economy," *International Journal of Middle East Studies*, 22 (2), 1990; and Robert Vitalis, *When Capitalists Collide* (Berkeley: University of California Press, 1995).
[82] See, for example, the note by E. G. Payne, acting judicial adviser, August 4, 1936, FO 371/J6964/190/16; and the article by Muhammad As'ad, *al-Ahram*, January 15, 1937.

from implementing the policies that business interests wanted, such as tariffs and preferential employment.[83]

The second reason Egyptian business groups and pro-business politicians resented the capitulations and the Mixed Courts was that they required international consent before foreigners could be taxed directly.[84] So long as the capitulations remained, and so long as the Mixed Courts enforced them, Egypt could not raise the tax revenue necessary to fund many of the programs desired by pro-business politicians. An income tax was out of the question; a protective tariff was enacted only with difficulty; even a tax on matches provoked a diplomatic dispute between Egypt and the capitulatory powers.[85] Any attempt to launch projects to develop infrastructure or to subsidize Egyptian industrialization would founder without Egyptian fiscal autonomy. Isma'il Sidqi, the political leader most publicly identified with business interests, argued this as early as 1926 in a speech to the Bar Association of the Mixed Courts. Perhaps with unintended irony, Sidqi was able to quote three British imperialists from the era when Britain resented the capitulations – Lord Cromer, Sir William Brunyate, and Viscount Milner – in support of his position.[86]

Thus the struggle to end the capitulations and the Mixed Courts was partly a struggle by Egyptian business leaders to secure a state able to protect their interests. Defense and protection of property rights were tasks only a strong state could undertake. The argument can be made much more generally: in Egypt and the Arab world as a whole, from the nineteenth century until the rise of Arab socialism, the relationship between state and market has been far more symbiotic than antagonistic. Strong states secure property and investment and are able to pursue effective economic policies; market transactions are generally easier to regulate and tax and are thus fiscally vital.

This sort of liberalism, while influential, was also restricted in its implications. An independent judiciary, checks on executive authority,

[83] The Egyptians claimed that tariffs were limited not by the capitulations but by the 1906 Customs Convention with Italy (and with other countries under Most Favored Nation treaties). When the Convention expired in 1930, therefore, the Egyptian government resolved to enact a more protective tariff. The capitulatory powers complained, and a compromise was negotiated. The compromise helped establish a precedent for Egyptian autonomy in the matter of tariffs. See "Memorandum Regarding the Egyptian Customs Tariff and Customs Regulations (*Reglement Douanier*)," December 12, 1936, USNA 783.003/140.

[84] On this point generally, see Booth to High Commissioner, December 7, 1935, FO 371/J3066/190/16.

[85] See the memorandum by Charles W. Yost, then American Vice-Consul in Cairo, "The Taxation of Foreigners in Egypt," June 6, 1931, USNA 783.003/37.

[86] *Egyptian Gazette*, March 30, 1926, contained in Howell to Secretary of State, April 3, 1926, USNA 783.003/3.

and stable property rights all had distinctive meanings; none implied a general egalitarian or democratic spirit. To be sure, demands for legal equality were often made by Egyptian writers and political leaders, but the inequality targeted involved nationality far more than class.[87] Decrying foreign privileges did not always lead to calls for equal treatment among Egyptians. Capitulatory privileges for foreigners rankled many; when Nubar complained about inequality in the 1881 letter mentioned above, he referred to the differing legal status of foreigners and Egyptians.

This is not to say that there was open opposition to legal equality among Egyptians. Distinctions between ruler and ruled were sometimes held to be irrelevant in the application of the law; occasionally a writer might even mention rich and poor. But there was a far more common (though not always explicit) theme in many contemporary writings that equated social equality in Egyptian society with disorder. Timothy Mitchell deals with one work written in such a vein that has been subsequently misinterpreted:

The Tale of Isa ibn Hisham, as the book was called, was described by later writers as the most important work of imaginative literature of its generation. It was very widely read. An expurgated version was later used by the Ministry of Education, as a text in all government secondary schools. It has been interpreted as a work of social criticism that expresses the liberalism which emerged in the political thought of the period. The term liberalism tends to be misleading. The donkey driver's statement about an age of liberty has been cited to illustrate a major theme of the book, that Egyptians must be taught the principle of equality before the law. But these words come from the mouth of an insolent peasant. The concern of the book is not with equality of rights but with social chaos, a chaos suddenly visible in the indiscipline of the city's streets where the peasant behaves as an equal of the Pasha. Indiscipline is not usually considered a central concern of liberal thought, but rather than abandoning the label of liberalism I would prefer to use these writings from Egypt to understand liberalism in its colonial context. Egyptian liberalism spoke about justice and equal rights; but these concerns were contained within a wider problematic. Rights could only be enjoyed within a society of obedient and industrious individuals, and it was these characteristics, as we have seen, that Egyptians now suddenly seemed to lack.[88]

The concern was not unique to the book in question, nor was it a product of the British occupation: over one year prior to the occupation a horrified writer in al-Ahram was provoked to discuss his conception of the true meaning of freedom after a youth had responded to his

---

[87] See, for example, the conclusion of the article on the National Courts in al-Ahram, 5 February, 1883.

[88] Timothy Mitchell, Colonising Egypt (Cambridge: Cambridge University Press, 1988), pp. 115–16.

reprimand with the retort that in the nineteenth century people were free to do as they pleased.[89]

Some pushed the matter even further, arguing that true justice required a sort of inequality. In 1889, a writer in the Cairo daily *al-Muqattam* turned the argument for legal equality on its head by complaining that when rich and poor given the same punishment for the same offense the result was unequal – the rich suffer far more from imprisonment than the poor, for instance. As a further example, the author cited the case of a blind man who insulted the wife of a minister. He was given the same sentence as he would have received had his victim been a trash collector – even though the impudence he displayed might have led him to murder a person of low social standing.[90] In a sense, the Akhtat Courts established in the early twentieth century were based on a similar view. Notables were charged with issuing judgments in small and simple disputes; their social position and prestige were seen to be guarantees of fairness and judicial temperament. And when the Akhtat Courts were abolished, the move was justified by the claim that less influential people had managed to obtain judicial appointments, decreasing the quality of the courts and discouraging people of substance and honor from serving.[91]

The fear of the consequences of equality generally extended to a skeptical view of democracy until the growth of a broad-based nationalist movement in the early twentieth century. Indeed, given the current near-equation of rule of law with democracy (in both Egypt and the United States) the absence of demands for democratic government in late nineteenth-century Egypt is striking. Political participation by notables was sought by some, but a broader popular role in selecting leaders was not part of the agenda of those who built Egypt's legal structures.[92] As will be more fully explored in subsequent chapters, liberal legality may be a necessary condition for sustaining democracy but it is hardly a sufficient condition.

*Centralization and state building*

Given this conception of liberal legality, it should no longer seem paradoxical to claim that the architects of Egypt's legal system were motivated by a desire to build a liberal order and a strong state

[89] *Al-Ahram*, February 12, 1881.
[90] "Revision of Egyptian Law," *al-Muqattam*, March 9, 1889.
[91] Ghurbal, "Statistics on the National Courts," *Al-kitab al-dhahabi*, vol. II, pp. 239–40.
[92] For a discussion of Nubar's thinking on this question, see Hunter, *Egypt under the Khedives*, pp. 171–73.

simultaneously. Those who argue that legal reform in the Middle East has been a tool of state building and centralization will find much support and little surprising in the Egyptian experience.

Perhaps the strongest evidence in this regard are the areas in which legal reform generated little or no controversy among the Egyptian political elite. In the first three-quarters of the nineteenth century, the institution of a hierarchical, state-administered, and centralized judicial system drew no visible opposition. While Ottoman authorities and local leaders in eighteenth-century Egypt had not left judicial and legal matters alone, the various systems employed in the nineteenth century had represented a dramatic increase in the state's role in judicial affairs. In the last quarter of the nineteenth century, of the three innovations in legal reform – a professionalized and independent judiciary, codified law, and a turn towards European rather than Islamic and Ottoman sources – only the last drew any debate. In the contemporary discussions in the press and the cabinet discussed above regarding the construction of the National Courts, the need for a professionalized, independent judiciary was taken for granted. The only question raised was where appropriate personnel could best be found. (It is true that local officials and the police did drag their heels in cooperating with the new structures, but this expressed itself almost exclusively in a rivalry with the *niyaba* rather than the judiciary. In fact, traces of the rivalry between the *niyaba* and the police continue to this day.[93]) Similarly, the need for a comprehensive law code to replace the earlier reliance on a mixture of local legislation, custom, Islamic law, and judicial volition, drew little comment. Only the sources for the code (in particular its relationship with Islamic law) provoked muted controversy.

Indeed, it is possible in this context to make fuller sense of the decision to turn to French law as the primary source for the Egyptian codes. French sources were favored not simply because they were European but also because of their attractiveness to ambitious and centralizing state elites. What attracted such elites was not the Western nature of the legal systems they constructed but the increased control, centralization, and penetration they offered. It is instructive in this regard that Egypt was not alone among Middle Eastern states generally which turned to civil law – most often French – models. Civil law systems were adopted even by non-Arab states, including both Iran and

---

[93] With regard to the attitude of local officials to the new structures, it is notable that daily newspapers regularly recorded cases in which they were disciplined for failing to notify their superiors or the *niyaba* immediately after a crime had occurred. The rivalry between the police and the *niyaba* now has little to do with the former not accepting the latter but with educational and class differences.

the Ottoman Empire. The French system, unlike the British, offered a unified law code and a nation-wide hierarchy of courts to enforce it. While rulers may not have been able to influence individual decisions by courts, they would have tremendous influence over how courts would approach disputes submitted to them – much more influence than Islamic law courts, customary courts, or a common law system would have offered. Indeed, in one important way a civil law system has more to offer central authorities than any alternative. Because judges are to rely on codified law rather than judicial precedent, the role of case law is fairly weak. Judicial interpretation is discouraged (and sometimes denied even when it obviously occurs). This amounts to a strong positivist bias which often makes civil law courts less willing and able to develop a strong outlook that challenges executive and legislative authorities. To be sure, government organs, when subject to the courts, can lose individual cases, but even when they do each individual who is affected by a decision must sue separately. (Not until the establishment of an administrative court system in the mid-twentieth century did the Egyptian judiciary successfully assert the right to strike down or cancel laws and regulations; prior to that point each aggrieved individual would have to file a separate suit.) Thus, the point of turning to French models was hardly to repudiate Islam; it was to have codified law and hierarchical courts operating under the supervision of a centralizing state.[94]

A system based on *shari'a* courts was therefore particularly inappropriate for several reasons. While not immutable, the *shari'a* tended to evolve sometimes according to a logic quite different from that of the rulers. The paucity of clear, authoritative texts led to a widespread image of an incomplete *shari'a* that allowed judges to rule arbitrarily. Leading Egyptians, including many whose piety could not be doubted, shared a common belief with many colonial officials that the *shari'a* in its present form was unsuitable for a modern state. This feeling was general throughout the Ottoman Empire.[95] The *shari'a* was not abandoned, but it was restricted to matters of personal status and to areas where it could be clearly and easily codified.

Indeed, the only serious alternative proposed to a French-inspired law code was one which made a greater effort to draw on Islamic sources

---

[94] James Rosberg, writing on the period since the 1960s, explores the uses of an independent judiciary for top leadership, focusing on the role that they can play in providing information on the actions of subordinates. See *Roads to the Rule of Law: The Emergence of an Independent Judiciary in Contemporary Egypt*, Ph.D. dissertation, Department of Political Science, Massachusetts Institute of Technology, 1995.

[95] Brinkley Messick, *The Calligraphic State: Textual Domination and History in a Muslim Society* (Berkeley: University of California Press, 1993), pp. 54–68.

within a codified framework. The attempt to draw on the *shari'a* as part of codification, begun in the Ottoman Empire, was continued in Egypt by two of the most influential individuals associated with the development of law codes – Muhammad Qadri in the nineteenth century and 'Abd al-Razzaq al-Sanhuri in the twentieth. Yet Qadri's law codes were not adopted and, while al-Sanhuri specifically sought to draw on Islamic jurisprudence in his codifying work, he did so in ways (for example, selecting doctrine from various schools of law and seeking to reconcile the *shari'a* with modern sensibilities) that many Islamic jurists would probably have found overly eclectic at best and incoherent at worst.[96]

What the proponents of legal reform sought, then, was a system consistent with (and occasionally even derived from) principles of the *shari'a* but not a wholly *shari'a*-based system. As noted earlier, what is most striking about the gap between the new codes and the *shari'a* is that however much some (especially radical Islamicists) may view it as unbridgeable, at the time it provoked limited public discussion. Codifying law, even if it meant considerable borrowing from the law of non-Muslim states, was not seen as undermining the *shari'a*; if anything it strengthened Islamic law through clarifying it.

Further evidence of the state-building project of the architects of the modern Egyptian legal system is the nature of their liberalism. As discussed above, the liberal legality current in Egypt in the late nineteenth and early twentieth centuries hardly involved a minimalist state. Where there was a clear conflict between their distinctive brand of liberal legality and the goal of state building – most vividly illustrated in the construction of the Commissions of Brigandage (but also in their later tolerance for extrajudicial suppression of crime) – Egypt's leaders generally preferred the latter.

After Egypt's independence in 1922, the Egyptian government exercised full autonomy in legal matters involving Egyptian citizens for the first time since the 1880s. It is therefore instructive to note that the Egyptian government first exercised this autonomy to increase the statist and centralized nature of the system. Egypt's codes were amended to introduce new kinds of political crimes, including those which were aimed at the king and the political system.[97] In structure, the major change was the creation of a new appeals court and a court of cassation, again justified in the name of uniformity and hierarchy.

---

[96] See Abd al-Razzaq al-Sanhuri, "On What Basis Will the Egyptian Civil Code be Improved," *Al-kitab al-dhahabi*, vol. II, and "Our Legal Duty after the Treaty", *al-Ahram*, January 1, 1937. Also of interest is Enid Hill, "Al-Sanhuri and Islamic Law," *Cairo Papers in Social Science* 10 (1), 1987.

[97] See 'Atiya, "Development of the Criminal Code."

While the courts were to serve the purposes of strengthening the state, they do not seem to have been designed to legitimate it. To be sure, there is every reason to believe that Egypt's leaders viewed the legal system they were building as fair and just, but there was little attention to how the system would be perceived by the majority of the Egyptian population. The system was criticized (generally by the British but occasionally by Egyptian writers) for instilling insufficient fear and therefore for allowing criminal activity to continue, but there is no evidence that the system was intended to render the political, social, or economic order legitimate or inevitable.

In attempting to explain the construction of the modern Egyptian legal system, there are stark differences in the helpfulness of the three approaches. The idea of imposed law does underscore the importance of the international context, but is an inadequate and sometimes misleading approach when applied to Egypt. Imperialism and European penetration certainly shaped the development of the legal system, and the Mixed Courts would not have existed without them. European power and influence also increased the attractiveness of the French law code. Yet even the Mixed Courts were not imposed on Egypt and in fact are better seen as an attempt to contain European influence generally (and at times British influence specifically). Finally, the interest in codified law was domestically generated, and even the attractiveness of the French code had domestic aspects.

The legal system can be seen as an attempt to foster liberal legality in Egypt, but the liberalism of the Egyptian leadership involved regulating state authority to make it more effective (and the economy more productive). Far more prominent in providing the rationale and motivation for the construction of the legal system was a statist outlook and political project.

Courts and law were to render state domination of Egyptian society more effective and efficient. The first half-century of this project took place within the confines of imperialism. After the Montreux conference of 1937, Egypt finally became fully independent in all judicial and legal matters. How did the new generation of Egyptian leaders view, use, and modify the system that they inherited?

# 3 Egyptian courts, 1937–1971: centralization, authoritarianism, and socialism

In the three decades following the Montreux conference the most striking feature of the Egyptian judicial structure was its institutional continuity. The few major changes that were made (with the possible exception of the establishment of the *Majlis al-Dawla*) had the effect of furthering the centralization of the system. What makes this continuity especially noteworthy was that it coincided with tremendous political changes in the country. The battles between the Wafd, the British, and the king, the end of the constitutional monarchy, and the establishment of an authoritarian and socialist regime under Gamal 'Abd al-Nasir caused significant changes in the political role of the judiciary without altering its basic structure. Only in the last few years of 'Abd al-Nasir's rule were more fundamental changes discussed, and only some of these were effected. For the most part, dramatic political changes in the country were accommodated by seemingly minor changes in the judicial structure. The periods both before and after the 1952 coup, which replaced the parliamentary monarchy with rule by army officers, witnessed further centralization of the judicial system. This coincided with an attempt to entrench further liberal legality. The attempt realized some successes, but within a few years after 1952 these successes, though formally institutionalized, were effectively reversed.

## The unification of the judiciary

The agreement at Montreux to end the capitulations and to transfer the work of the Mixed Courts to the National Courts after a twelve-year period finally made possible the unification of the judicial structure anticipated by Nubar and others in the 1870s. With the Mixed Courts seen as an anachronistic limitation on Egyptian sovereignty, they were allowed to disappear completely. While the codes and jurisprudence of the Mixed Courts did inform the efforts of some Egyptian jurists to revise the Egyptian law code, few Egyptians mourned their abolition. The building housing the Mixed Courts in Cairo was transformed into

*Dar al-Qada' al-'Ali* where the *Mahkamat al-Naqd* and eventually other high judicial bodies sat. No attempt was made to retain foreign judges, and, while Mixed Courts lawyers were admitted to the National Bar (as agreed at Montreux), no efforts were made to accommodate those who could not practice in Arabic.[1]

Prior to the Montreux conference, residents of Egypt fell under the jurisdiction of four separate judicial structures; jurisdiction depended on nationality, religion, and the nature of the case. Criminal charges against foreigners (as well as their personal status cases) were tried in consular courts; civil disputes involving foreign interests were tried in the Mixed Courts; civil disputes involving only Egyptians and criminal charges against Egyptians fell under the National Courts; and matters of personal status involving Egyptians were assigned to the *Shari'a* and *Milli* (confessional) Courts according to the religion of the litigants. The first of these structures, the consular court system, was largely dismantled (except for personal status cases) immediately in the wake of the Montreux conference and its work transferred to the Mixed Courts. In 1949 the twelve-year transition mandated at Montreux ended, leaving the National Courts jurisdiction over all cases except matters of personal status involving Egyptian nationals. Thus, the abolition of the Mixed Courts helped force the issue of religious courts on to the agenda.

Criticisms of separate courts of personal status emerged as early as the 1890s and grew steadily from the 1930s on. Three years before the Montreux conference, 'Abd al-'Aziz Fahmi, then president of the *Mahkamat al-Naqd*, called for unification of the judiciary.[2] A similar call was made by 'Abd al-Razzaq al-Sanhuri, hardly an advocate of total secularization, a few months before the beginning of the conference.[3] Proponents of unification advanced several arguments. First, the *Shari'a* and *Milli* Courts were often seen as more susceptible to corruption than the National Courts. Lawyers were seen as poorly trained, and the less lucrative nature of litigation before the courts probably did in fact lead

---

[1] In 1943, Robert L. Henry, an American judge in the Mixed Courts, published a proposal to establish a special French-language section of the National Courts. The idea was subjected to a barrage of criticism, and denunciations were issued by the minister of justice, the dean of the law school at Cairo University, and an Egyptian judge on the Mixed Court of Appeals. The American ambassador felt compelled to disassociate himself from the proposal in private communications with the palace and other diplomats. See Kirk to Secretary of State, September 27, 1943, USNA 883.05/634, and Kirk to Secretary of State, October 5, 1943, USNA 883.05/636. See also the British correspondence on the letter, contained in FO 371/J 4545/1218/16.

[2] *Al-Jumhuriyya*, December 26, 1955, p. 1.

[3] 'Abd al-Razzaq al-Sanhuri, "Our Legal Duty after the Treaty," *al-Ahram*, January 1, 1937.

the country's best legal minds in other directions.[4] Some practices in the *Shari'a* Courts (such as the use of professional witnesses) appeared corrupt or at least undignified to more secular observers.[5] Criticism also centered on the jurisdictional confusion caused by the existence of courts whose competence was not always clearly defined. Instances in which courts issued conflicting judgments in the same case, in which litigants changed their religion in order to move the dispute into a more advantageous forum, or in which judgments could be portrayed as defying common sense, drew frequent criticism from those outside the courts and were often lampooned in the press.[6] The courts of non-Muslim communities also came under attack on nationalist grounds. In 1952, for instance, the secularist weekly *Ruz al-yusuf* criticized *Milli* Court judges claiming that they often held foreign citizenship and knew neither Arabic language nor Egyptian law – yet their rulings governed Egyptian citizens and were issued in the name of the king.[7] Indeed, the 1955 decision to abolish the *Shari'a* and the Milli Courts was partly justified with the argument that "a system of courts which is responsible to foreign organizations and presided over by judges which are not selected by the national government is reminiscent of the capitulations and therefore not appropriate in a modern independent state."[8]

Behind most of these criticisms lay the belief – widespread not only among the personnel of the National Courts but also among the political leadership of the country – that the existence of separate and autonomous personal status courts, with their own laws, procedures, training, and personnel was inconsistent with a unified, centralized, national judiciary. Thus, the dominant attitude towards these courts differed only in degree from nationalist denunciations of the Mixed Courts. Both were seen to limit governmental authority and national sovereignty.[9] In justifying abolition in 1955, the government claimed to be removing "all traces of exceptional judicial systems with their consequential limitations of governmental authority which tended to undermine the national sovereignty of the country."[10] The abolition of *Shari'a* and *Milli* Courts

---

[4] Farhat Ziadeh, *Lawyers the Rule of Law, and Liberalism in Modern Egypt* (Palo Alto: Stanford, 1968), p. 59.
[5] See, for instance, "In front of the *shari'a* courts stand witnesses for sale!" *Akhir Sa'a*, February 1, 1950.
[6] Ziadeh, *Lawyers*, pp. 105–11; *Ruz al-yusuf*, November 1, 1954, p. 24; "Two Jews in front of the *shari'a* court," *Ruz al-yusuf*, October 26, 1953; *Ruz al-yusuf*, October 31, 1955, p. 25.
[7] *Ruz al-Yusuf*, July 21, 1952, p. 20.
[8] Peter R. Chase, "Abolition of the *Shari'a* and Melli Courts Announced," January 4, 1956, USNA 774.31/1–456.
[9] Ziadeh, *Lawyers*, pp. 111–14.
[10] Garvey to Macmillan, November 7, 1955, FO 371/JE 1641, piece 113768.

was therefore seen by both the political and juridical elites as completing the process begun in the 1880s with the creation of the National Courts. Constructing an independent judiciary was an accepted goal, but the idea of that judiciary enforcing laws developed outside of any conception of national progress and advancement was unthinkable. A decentralized system of courts with overlapping jurisdictions and only incompletely organized by Egyptian law had little appeal to reformers of any stripe. Adherents of Islamic modernism, liberalism, nationalism, and socialism (in their various permutations and combinations) all had few objections to bringing the separate religiously based courts into a single unified structure. Yet nearly two decades passed between the Montreux conference and the unification of the Egyptian judiciary. What delayed judicial unification for so long?

First, the question of the unification of the judiciary was complicated by the attitude of the *shari'a* judges that they constituted the legitimate courts of general jurisdiction, not simply for personal status cases involving Muslims, but for all legal disputes in the country. At times, the attitude could take symbolic form, such as when *Shari'a* Court judges boycotted the 1933 ceremony marking the fiftieth anniversary of the foundation of the National Courts.[11] Yet the *Shari'a* Courts could sometimes offer more than symbolic opposition, especially when they interpreted their jurisdiction as ambitiously as the Mixed Courts had before them. In 1953, for instance, a *shari'a* court rejected a claim by the husband in a marital dispute that the court had no jurisdiction because both litigants were Jewish and one held Italian citizenship. The court announced that "if the matter was in our hands then we would rule in all disputes which occur among the people by what God handed down." Further, the court announced its "hope that the day comes when the judgements of the Islamic *shari'a* prevail and are applied to all the people in all inhabited regions of the world."[12] The frequent portrait of the *Shari'a* Court judges as obscurantist, obstructionist, and avaricious is exemplified by Farhat Ziadeh's description: "the defensive position of the *shari'a* advocates can be gleaned from the stand they took against many measures that were considered by secular elements as proper and progressive. A perusal of the minutes of the bar meetings reveals those advocates as thoroughly conservative, especially when conservativism

---

[11] Arthur Yencken to Sir John Simon, January 5, 1934, FO 371/J143/14/16. While the boycott was justified as a protest against the failure to base Egyptian law on the *shari'a*, it is just as likely that the motive was to avoid siding with government against the Wafd, which boycotted the official celebration and held its own. Indeed, the president of the *shari'a* Bar Association attended the Wafd's ceremony.

[12] "Two Jews in front of the *shari'a* court," *Ruz al-yusuf*, October 26, 1953.

preserved their own financial interests."[13] Thus for many the *Shari'a* and the *Milli* Courts subverted the goal of judicial unification. In fact, the attitude of the *Shari'a* Court judges and lawyers probably helped solidify support for judicial unification even as it delayed it.

Yet the attitude of *shari'a* judges was less of an obstacle than the minority and foreign communities. Their opposition to abolition of separate personal status courts became increasingly prominent after Montreux. After some ineffectual efforts in the 1930s, in 1944 the Egyptian government advanced a draft law which would have asserted much more control over the *Milli* Courts without unifying personal status with other courts. The proposals elicited a storm of protest from the leadership of the various Christian communities in Egypt. While a few advanced the position that the Egyptian government had no right to interfere in the internal affairs of their communities, most accepted that the *Milli* Courts could be regulated by Egyptian law. They were disturbed by several provisions in the draft law, however. One would have subjected the judgments of the *Milli* Courts to the approval of National Court judges. (It is likely that the intent of the Egyptian government was to insure that judgments were issued in the name of the National Courts and the king; there is no indication of any intention to have all judgments reviewed by a National Court judge.) Since National Court judges were predominantly (though not exclusively) Muslim, the religious leaders argued that this would have rendered their courts subordinate to "Muslim courts." This fear was aggravated by the requirement that a National Court judge be included in the appeals court for all communities. (The Muslim Brotherhood actually opposed the proposal. Rather than increasing the influence of Islamic law, the law simply represented intervention in the affairs of the religious courts. The Brotherhood, though hardly known as a defender of the prerogatives of foreign communities, clearly feared that a move against the *Shari'a* Courts could follow reform of the *Milli* Courts.[14]) Christian leaders also worried that the law would further encourage conversion for the sake of obtaining an advantageous position in litigation, since it allowed a case to be transferred to the *Shari'a* Courts if one of the litigants converted even after litigation had commenced. After forming a united front, the Christian communities approached the Egyptian government with their objections and began work on their own alternative proposal. Various leaders also approached sympathetic embassies, advancing the argument that the draft law would apply to their nationals when the Mixed Courts

---

[13] Ziadeh, *Lawyers*, p. 58. See also *Ruz al-yusuf*, November 1, 1954, p. 24.

[14] Latifa Salim, *Al-nizam al-qada'i al-misri al-hadith* (Cairo: Markaz al-Dirasat al-Siyasiyya wa-l-Istratijiyya bi-l-Ahram, 1984), vol. II, pp. 575–76.

were abolished in 1949. Although there was no evidence of any intention on the part of the Egyptian government to bring foreign nationals under the *Milli* Courts, the fate of personal status cases involving foreigners, temporarily reserved to the consular courts under Montreux, was unclear. Many embassies therefore showed clear concern with the government's proposals, though some were reluctant to become involved publicly in an argument with strong religious and nationalist overtones. The frequent changes of government in Egypt combined with the sustained opposition of the religious minorities (supported obliquely by some embassies) postponed any decision. Several Egyptian governments revived the older proposals, but only minor changes in the structure of the *Milli* Courts were legislated by the parliament.[15]

When personal status cases involving foreign nationals, the last area of jurisdiction for the consular courts, passed back to Egyptian jurisdiction in 1949, the Egyptian government agreed to apply the national law of the parties. The National Courts, not the *Milli* Courts, would have jurisdiction, however. This measure placated the foreign embassies, especially because they were consulted on the content of the law the National Courts were to apply to their nationals. The effect was to establish the competence of the National Courts to deal with personal status cases involving foreigners. Yet the minority communities still clung to the *Milli* Courts for non-Muslim Egyptians. Increasingly isolated in their opposition to judicial unification, however, they could stave off unification no longer. When the Egyptian government announced the abolition of the *Shari'a* and *Milli* Courts in 1955, the Catholic leadership circulated an announcement that Christmas Eve ceremonies would be cancelled in protest. Because several were briefly arrested for publishing a document not submitted to the censors, the Coptic leadership protested more cautiously, announcing a similar cancellation orally from the pulpit.[16] Various communities complained to foreign embassies in the bitterest possible terms. Yet by this time even the religious communities themselves were no longer united. One of the leaders of the formerly united front, Saba Habashi, a prominent Copt and former minister of justice, endorsed the move in an interview with a Lebanese newspaper (recounted on the front page of the Egyptian

---

[15] For some of the correspondence detailing the suggested changes, the stand of the religious communities, and the reactions of the embassies, see the various documents contained in USNA 883.044 for 1945. Also relevant are the files contained in USNA 883.05 for 1949. See also FO 371/J2594/1037.

[16] Peter R. Chase, "Abolition of the *Shari'a* and Melli Courts Announced," January 4, 1956, USNA 774.31/1–456. See also Chancery to African Department, April 11, 1956, FO 371/JE 1641/3. For the text of the Catholic statement on Christmas Eve services, see Chancery to African Department, December 22, 1955, FO 371/JE 1645/3.

regime's new daily, *al-Jumhuriyya*). Habashi noted that even in predominantly Christian countries civil rather than religious courts applied the law.[17]

Thus the opposition to judicial unification could be portrayed as obscurantist and self-interested; it was hardly united and was in fact increasingly isolated. A determined effort on the part of the Egyptian government to enact unification of the judiciary was bound to be successful if ever it was attempted. It was not attempted for quite some time, not simply because of the opposition it engendered, but because of the complex legal nature of the question and the uncertainty of how to accomplish it. Would a uniform law of personal status be applied to all residents of Egypt? Would foreign nationals be subject to a secular Egyptian law, the law of their religious community, or the law of their own country? Would separate religious courts continue to exist under their own rubric or under the rubric of the National Courts? What would be the fate of the judges and lawyers of the *Shariʿa* and *Milli* Courts? The eventual solutions enacted in 1956 – to abolish the *Shariʿa* and *Milli* Courts and transfer their work to personal-status sections of the National Courts, and to have the sections apply the religious law of the litigants rather than a uniform law of personal status – was only one of several options discussed over the years.

The place of the *Shariʿa* Courts in Egypt's judicial structure was a far older topic of debate than the place of the *Milli* Courts. While the *Shariʿa* and *Milli* Courts were abolished with one stroke, the existence and law of the *Shariʿa* Courts had always posed a different set of issues. In the first third of the twentieth century, would-be reformers of the *Shariʿa* Courts had focused their attention on codification of law. Some even had gone so far as to argue against categorizing personal status as a separate area of law.[18] Yet partly because changes in the law were far more religiously sensitive than changes in the organization of the courts, attention began to shift from rewriting the law to reorganizing the *Shariʿa* Courts. At first, reform rather than unification was mooted. Proposals included adding social workers and others in cases of marital disputes, and organizing the affairs of the various courts more tightly. When the post-1952 regime turned its attention to the matter, it finally settled on a course that was in one sense very radical and in another sense very conservative.

On the one hand, the new regime elected not to reform or regularize the old courts but to abolish them completely. Rather than bringing the

---

[17] *Al-Jumhuriyya*, December 12, 1955.
[18] See Salim, *Al-Nizam al-qadaʾi*, vol. II, pp. 528–30; and Ziadeh, *Lawyers*, pp. 116–26.

*Shari'a* and *Milli* Courts under greater control or placing their work under the supervision of the National Courts, the new leaders folded their work into that of the National Courts. In fact, it was at this time that the term "National Courts" began to fall out of use – with the abolition of both the Mixed Courts in 1949 and the religious courts in 1956, the National Courts and the administrative courts became the only regular elements of the civilian judicial system. From time to time exceptional courts were created, as will be seen, but the goal of Nubar and other reformers at the end of the nineteenth century – to have a single, unified judicial system for Egypt – was largely accomplished.

Yet if there was no compromise over the structure of the courts and the unification of the judiciary, the potential opposition (especially the *Shari'a* Courts themselves) was mollified by two concessions rendering the reforms more conservative. First, the content of the law applied by the courts was not changed. Earlier proposals that centered on reform and even unification of Egypt's personal status law were ignored. Thus objections to the measure on religious grounds were robbed of much of their potency, and had to center not on the law itself but on the judges applying it. With special personal status sections being established within the National Courts, it would now fall to secular judges to apply religious law. Yet even this feature of the unification was made less objectionable to the personnel of the *Shari'a* Courts by the second concession: *shari'a* judges were transferred to the new personal status sections, and the *shari'a* bar was allowed to continue to practice in personal status cases. Government authorities went to great lengths to portray the reform as a matter of administrative rationalization rather than a fundamental change in personal status law.[19] Concerned for years that any reform might abrogate *shari'a* law and simultaneously cost them their jobs, the judges and lawyers of the *Shari'a* Courts were assuaged by both these measures.

With politically weakened foreign communities satisfied by the application of their national law, and the personnel of the *Shari'a* Courts assured that the measure, though noxious, would not greatly affect their ideological and material interests, it was only the various Egyptian Christian communities that were left in ineffectual (if strident) opposition. The new regime had successfully accomplished what several Egyptian governments over the previous two decades had attempted, not by ignoring the opposition but by dividing and outmaneuvering it. It might be noted that despite the stronger opposition of the Christian than

[19] See, for instance, *al-Jumhuriyya*, December 26, 1955, p. 1.

the Muslim authorities, in fact it was the latter who lost more over the long run. Courts did apply Christian law faithfully and no wholesale conversions took place as the Christian leaders had feared. And Muslim Egyptians, after the last generation of *shari'a*-trained judges and lawyers had passed from the scene, found themselves under the jurisdiction of judges familiar at best with the letter of Muslim personal status law, but far less cognizant of the spirit or traditional methods of judicial interpretation. Further, once personal status cases were folded into the National Courts, it became easier for Egyptian governments to regard personal status law as falling under their competence, and amendments to the law became easier to contemplate.

The abolition of the Mixed Courts highlighted not only the existence of separate personal status courts but also the civil code, which many Egyptians considered to be outmoded. By gaining jurisdiction over mixed cases, the National Courts would be ruling on critical economic and business issues that had previously fallen to the Mixed Courts. Reform of the civil code had actually drawn sporadic attention since independence in 1923, but the attainment of full legal autonomy in the wake of the Montreux conference focused the attention of the Egyptian legal community on updating a code that was based fairly faithfully on an early nineteenth-century French model. After some preliminary work, al-Sanhuri (eventually assisted by a committee within the Ministry of Justice) began the process of redrafting, drawing not only on French sources, but also on Egyptian jurisprudence, comparative law, and the Islamic *shari'a*. When adopted, the code was presented as a major step forward in several ways: it closed gaps in the previous law; it resulted in a more culturally appropriate code; and it was based on the most modern principles of legislation.[20]

### The tactical success and strategic failure of liberal legality

Even as centralizing and nationalist forces were completing the unification of the judiciary, many of the same forces were also at work constructing a more liberal political and legal order. In 1943, the judiciary won major concessions increasing its corporate autonomy in the form of a new law amending its organization. Seven years earlier, a law (specifically titled the "Law of the Independence of the Judiciary") had given judges a non-binding voice in hirings, transfers, and promo-

[20] See Salim, *Al-Nizam al-qada'i*, vol. II, pp. 402–409. See also Enid Hill, "Al-Sanhuri and Islamic Law," *Cairo Papers in Social Science*, 10(1), 1987, and Ziadeh, *Lawyers*.

tions. This was greatly strengthened by the Wafd government's 1943
law. While the Wafd was often accused of packing the judiciary, its 1943
law strengthened the authority of the Supreme Judicial Council,
increased the judicial element on the Council, rendered transferring and
dismissal of judges more difficult, and created a judicial panel within the
Ministry of Justice to inspect and evaluate the work of junior judges.[21]
While the new law did not eliminate all suspicion of government
interference in the judiciary, it undeniably furthered the independence
of judges from executive authority.[22] After solidifying the independence
of the judiciary, the effort to foster liberal legality focused on two major
projects: the construction and operation of the *Majlis al-Dawla* (Council
of State), and the writing of a new constitution after 1952. While both
efforts realized some short-term successes, they provoked considerable
controversy, and their liberal accomplishments were reversed during a
marked turn towards authoritarianism in the 1950s. Al-Sanhuri was a
central figure in both efforts. His ultimate failure was both institutional
(the *Majlis al-Dawla* was reined in and the constitution adopted did not
provide strongly for the liberal order he sought) and personal. In 1954
he was forced out of Egyptian political life, although his influence in
broader Arab circles continued.

The *Majlis al-Dawla* was added to the Egyptian legal structure in 1946
and constituted the last direct borrowing from France (though in
conception and especially in operation the Egyptian institution soon
struck out on a different – and in many ways more ambitious –
direction). When the Mixed Courts had been created in the 1870s there
was no move to construct separate administrative courts on the French
model. After the Mixed Courts began operation the addition of a
separate administrative court structure became nearly impossible: any
significant amendments to the Mixed Courts structure involved the
complex process of obtaining the consent of all of the capitulatory
powers, and the Egyptian government (and, after 1882, the British)
would have been highly suspicious of an attempt to give the Courts any
greater jurisdiction over internal administration. There was still some
interest in the idea of a counterpart to the French institution unattached
to the Mixed Courts, however, and attempts were made to establish a
body in 1879 and 1883. The first body, which never began operation
(partly because of fiscal crisis), had largely consultative functions,

---

[21] For a summary of the law and a brief analysis of its political background, see Killearn to
Eden, August 5, 1943, FO 371/J 3515/1218/16. For the historical background to the
1936 and 1943 laws, see Salim, *Al-nizam al-qada'i*, vol. II, pp. 292–313.

[22] On a controversy over court appointments in 1944 – immediately after the new judicial
bodies were created – see the correspondence in FO 141/945/120/3/44.

though it did have some limited judicial authority. The second body actually operated for one year, though it was limited to the consultative function. As discussed in chapter 2, some Egyptians favored transforming this into a permanent and distinct administrative court system, but in the end the decision was made to place administrative disputes under the jurisdiction of the National Courts. After 1884, the British discouraged any further efforts, especially because a consultative and adjudicative body would have encroached on the position of the judicial adviser (a British official within the Ministry of Justice who theoretically served the Egyptian government but reported directly to the British consul-general).[23]

The post of judicial adviser was abolished after the Anglo-Egyptian treaty of 1936, and the Montreux conference removed the worry that the construction of the *Majlis al-Dawla* would lead to the demand that a similar body be established within the Mixed Courts. Accordingly the issue was again raised, though it was still controversial. The *Majlis al-Dawla* finally constructed was to be an independent, quasi-judicial body with the twin tasks of reviewing draft legislation submitted by the government and adjudicating disputes over administrative actions. The former function was attractive to the legal elite because it would have mandated that jurists be consulted about legislation before it was enacted, but it was the latter function that especially attracted its proponents. They argued that such a body was necessary to give citizens the right to appeal to a neutral authority in cases of illegitimate administrative actions.[24] While the National Courts were, at the time, increasingly bold in the matter (they had begun to go beyond ordering compensation to those harmed by administrative action to actually ordering the cancellation of regulations that exceeded the authority of the issuing agency), the creation of a specialized body with a mandate in such disputes was seen by many as adding a strong guarantee to the rights of citizens.[25] The reasons for the parliament's acceptance of the legislation creating the *Majlis al-Dawla* remain unclear, although some far from liberal motives have been mentioned (including the frustration

---

[23] For the history of the abortive efforts to construct the *Majlis al-Dawla*, see the paper by the US legal attaché (Judge Brinton), "Review of History, Organization and Work of the Egyptian Council of State," transmitted in Caffery to Department of State, March 31, 1951, USNA 774.3/3–3151. See also Hill, "Al-Sanhuri," pp. 92–95. See also the comments of Sulayman Hafiz, then vice-president of the *Majlis al-Dawla* reported in "The Palace of Justice Which is Transformed into A Battlefield" *Akhir sa'a*, February 8, 1950.

[24] Personal interview with Mahmud Fahmi, former vice-president of the *Majlis al-Dawla*, Cairo, May 1992.

[25] For the efforts to create the *Majlis al-Dawla*, see note 23 above. On the boldness of the National Courts, see Salim, *Al-nizam al-qada'i*, vol. II, pp. 278–80.

of the government of Isma'il Sidqi with several recent rulings by the National Courts).[26]

The establishment of the *Majlis al-Dawla* proved to be a new (if eventually abortive) beginning rather than the culmination of the effort to institute more fully a liberal conception of the rule of law in Egypt. The *Majlis al-Dawla* fought several battles with various Egyptian governments over the first decade of its existence; while it proved victorious over the short term in most conflicts, a decisive (and even violent) confrontation with the Revolutionary Command Council (RCC), the group of officers who effectively ruled the country in the aftermath of the 1952 coup, resulted in catastrophic defeat for the proponents of liberal legality.

The legislation creating the *Majlis al-Dawla* placed limitations on its jurisdiction (especially on who had standing to bring a case), but it also established a general assembly for the new judicial body that gave the administrative judiciary a corporate voice. This institution, similar to those established earlier for other Egyptian judicial organs, consisted of judges and other senior personnel from the *Majlis al-Dawla*. The general assembly lent its weight in support of successful proposals to widen the circle of parties who could bring cases and to increase the jurisdiction of the *Majlis al-Dawla*.[27] In 1948 the Administrative Court of the *Majlis al-Dawla* decided in favor of the principle of judicial review of the constitutionality of legislation.[28] This decision resolved decisively a debate among Egyptian courts that had begun when a lower court asserted the principle in 1941 only to have its reasoning rejected by an appeals court.[29]

Over the next few years, as governments, invoking the state of martial law declared in 1948, turned to extraordinary measures against domestic opponents (including the Muslim Brotherhood, radical nationalists, and leftist groups), the *Majlis al-Dawla*'s Administrative Court increasingly stood in their way, ordering reversal of (or compensation for) government decisions to close down newspapers.[30] A 1951 ruling called into question the legal status of the government's dissolution of the Muslim

---

[26] See 'Abd al-Hamid Yunis, "Why is the State Distinct in Litigation?" *al-Ahram*, February 20, 1966. Hill, "Al-Sanhuri," pp. 92–95, discusses the alternative idea that it was a parliamentary initiative. Mahmud Fahmi ascribed the parliament's creation of the *Majlis al-Dawla* to the personal prestige not only of al-Sanhuri but also Muhammad Kamil Mursi, another highly respected jurist, who preceded al-Sanhuri as president of the *Majlis al-Dawla* (personal interview, Cairo, May 1992).

[27] Salim, *Al-nizam al-qada'i*, vol. II, pp. 282–83.

[28] Hill, "Al-Sanhuri," pp. 95–96.

[29] Abdel Rahman Nosseir, "The Supreme Constitutional Court of Egypt and the Protection of Human Rights," unpublished paper, Chicago, 1992, p. 1.

[30] Salim, *Al-nizam al-qada'i*, vol. II, pp. 285–86.

Brotherhood in a case involving a dispute over Brotherhood property.[31] The next year, in the wake of the January riots in Cairo, the Administrative Court ordered the cancellation of an arrest order for two radical critics of the regime, Fathi Radwan and Yusuf Hilmi. The government issued a new arrest order, hoping to meet the Court's objections, but again the order was overturned in the Court.[32]

Increasing jurisdiction, prestige, and boldness brought new enemies. In 1950 the newly elected Wafdist government launched an attempt to rein in the *Majlis al-Dawla*. It was not at first solely (or even primarily) particular decisions that motivated the Wafd, but suspicion of al-Sanhuri, who had become president of the *Majlis al-Dawla*. Al-Sanhuri's affiliation with the Sa'dist party (which had been formed after a bitter rift in the Wafd), personal animosity between al-Sanhuri and several Wafdist ministers (including the justice minister), and a desire for retribution against the Sa'dist party which had dismissed senior Wafdist officials while in power, combined to drive the Wafd to move against him. When al-Sanhuri rebuffed an attempt to provoke his resignation, the cabinet advanced a change in the legislation creating the *Majlis al-Dawla* to prevent former ministers from serving in the body. Since al-Sanhuri had served in a previous Sa'dist cabinet, this would have resulted in his disqualification, a fact that was not lost on anyone. The threat of massive resignations from the *Majlis al-Dawla*, the outcry in the press, and the apparent intervention of the palace forced the Wafdist government to back down. While this attempt to force al-Sanhuri's retirement failed, it foreshadowed a similar but successful measure taken three years later.[33]

The boldness of the *Majlis al-Dawla* under al-Sanhuri's continued leadership insured renewed disputes with the government. On March 22, 1951, for instance, the Administrative Court of the *Majlis al-Dawla* trod on very sensitive ground by deciding that it had jurisdiction to examine a military decision to dismiss an officer.[34] At the end of 1951, therefore, the Wafdist government launched a more modest move to revise the basic law of the *Majlis al-Dawla*. Specifically annoyed by several stays of execution granted by al-Sanhuri (subsequently affirmed by the whole Court), the proposed legislation transferred the authority to grant such stays from the president of the Court to a panel of judges.

[31] Caffery to Department of State, December 8, 1951, USNA 774.21/12–851.
[32] See Lutfi al-Khawli, "Know Your Rights," *Ruz al-yusuf*, August 11, 1952.
[33] For a contemporary account of the confrontation, see the several articles in *Ruz al-yusuf* on February 7, 14, and 21, 1950. For the claim of palace intervention, see 'Abd al-Hamid Yunis, "Why is the State Distinct in Litigation?"
[34] "Work of the Egyptian Council of State," Caffery to Department of State, May 14, 1951, USNA 774.3/5–1451.

It also attached the *Majlis al-Dawla* to the Ministry of Justice. The legal impact of this latter move was unclear but it conveyed a symbolic message offensive to many proponents of the *Majlis al-Dawla*. The general assembly of the *Majlis al-Dawla* condemned the move, especially because the draft legislation had not been submitted to the Majlis for review as required prior to presentation to parliament. The Bar Association joined the condemnation, but the Wafd, with its parliamentary majority, pushed the measure through in January 1952. Jasper Y. Brinton, then serving as legal attaché to the American embassy, wrote: "It is perhaps unfortunate that Sanhouri Pasha was at one time a member of an Egyptian Ministry other than that of the party now in power, but the present opposition is certainly not based so much on political opposition, as on the frequency with which the action of the Government's agents have been set aside by the Court."[35] The measure was partly reversed when Muhammad Kamil Mursi, who had preceded al-Sanhuri as president of the *Majlis al-Dawla*, became justice minister in a non-Wafdist government two months later.[36]

When the Free Officers took power in July 1952, the *Majlis al-Dawla* initially assisted them. Whether it was intimidated by the Officers or simply saw an ally against the Wafd, its new timidity in challenging executive action was striking. The move suspending the activity of political parties received a cautious endorsement from the *Majlis al-Dawla*. When the Officers formed a Regency Council to take the place of the ousted King Faruq, the *Majlis al-Dawla* provided a legal formula that obviated the need to present the measure to the disbanded parliament (as was constitutionally required).[37] The *Majlis al-Dawla* thus worked out a relationship with the ruling Officers, based on the assumption that the authoritarian measures taken by the new regime were emergency measures and that full constitutional and parliamentary life would soon be restored.

This relationship collapsed in March 1954 when a major split occurred within the regime between those who favored the return to parliamentary life and those who supported the continuation of the RCC. While the *Majlis al-Dawla* was not an active participant in the conflict, it was clear where its sympathies lay. Indeed, major rulings against the new regime were rumored to be in the offing, although little subsequent evidence has been adduced to support the idea that the

---

[35] Jasper Y. Brinton, "Modification of the Law on the Council of State," contained in Caffery to Department of State, January 15, 1952, USNA 774.21/1–1552, p. 3. See also Caffery to Department of State, December 8, 1951, USNA 774.21/12–851.

[36] Salim, *Al-nizam al-qada'i*, vol. II pp. 283–84.

[37] Hill, "Al-Sanhuri," pp. 102–104, discusses the relations of the *Majlis al-Dawla* with the RCC.

*Majlis al-Dawla* was contemplating any bold action. At the end of the month, a demonstration by the regime's supporters turned violent when al-Sanhuri's office was stormed and al-Sanhuri himself was assaulted. The general assembly protested strongly to the RCC, which replied with a condemnation of the attack. Al-Sanhuri and most observers, however, believed the attack to have been inspired by some within the RCC itself.[38] Two and a half weeks later, the RCC moved against al-Sanhuri by enacting the measure the Wafd had earlier drawn back from, dismissing all those who had held high partisan positions before July 1952. At least one member of the RCC later described this move as aimed specifically against al-Sanhuri.[39] The loss of al-Sanhuri left the remaining members of the *Majlis al-Dawla* cowed, but they still posed a potential threat to the regime. Whereas the Wafd's earlier attempt had been greeted by the threat of mass resignations from the *Majlis al-Dawla*, this time it was the government which took the initiative. In a measure that marked the complete defeat of the attempt to establish liberal legality through the *Majlis al-Dawla*, a law was enacted one year after the forced resignation of al-Sanhuri that dismissed all its members. While most were immediately reappointed, about twenty of its members were retired or assigned to non-judicial positions (in a foreshadowing of much broader measures taken in 1969).[40] The body's ability to cancel administrative acts and review those sanctioned by the RCC was restricted by law. Robbed of its independence (and of some of its authority), the *Majlis al-Dawla* was no longer able to act to rein in executive authority.

During 1953 and early 1954 the second attempt to increase the institutionalization of liberal legality took place in the drafting of a new, republican constitution. After the RCC decided to move beyond forcing the abdication of King Faruq to abolishing the monarchy altogether, it appointed a body of legal and political experts to draft a new constitution. Al-Sanhuri proved to be among the most influential members of the committee which nearly completed a very liberal and democratic document. The draft would have granted women the right to vote and established a supreme constitutional court to protect the constitution (over the objections of Makram 'Ubayd, another committee member, who argued that this would infringe the prerogatives of the legislature). A Senate was to be established with al-Sanhuri arguing for a strong

---

[38] See the several (sometimes oblique) references in *Al-Sanhuri*. Muhammad 'Ubayd, *Istiqlal al-qada'* (Cairo: Maktabat Rijal al-Qada', 1991), pp. 231–33, includes the text of the correspondence between the RCC and the *Majlis al-Dawla*.

[39] See the portion of 'Abd al-Latif al-Baghdadi's memoirs printed in *Uktubir*, September 5, 1993, p. 46.

[40] 'Ubayd, *Istiqlal al-qada'*, pp. 234–35.

measure of popular participation in electing its members. Work proceeded fairly quickly at first, and by August of 1953 al-Sanhuri promised that the draft would be complete within months, making an extension of RCC rule unnecessary.[41] Yet the work stalled, and when the proponents of the return to constitutional life were defeated in the March 1954 crisis, the fate of the new constitution was sealed. An American account of a meeting on January 15, 1955 between 'Abd al-Nasir and Roger Baldwin, Chairman of the International League for the Rights of Man, described 'Abd al-Nasir as stating "that a constitution had been drafted by a special commission but he did not like this draft since the gains of the Revolution could not be preserved under it. He said he intended to have the RCC go over the present draft and to rewrite it."[42] The abandonment of the liberal draft constitution, along with the taming of the *Majlis al-Dawla*, insured that Egypt's judicial institutions would now operate within an authoritarian context.

## Exceptional courts and the triumph of executive power

The political system developed in some dramatically new ways after 1952. The subordination of all organs of the state to the executive authority (represented first in the RCC and later in the presidency, held by 'Abd al-Nasir) entailed writing a series of new constitutions and basic laws (in 1956, 1958, 1962, 1964, and 1971), the granting of extensive authority to the executive to rule by decree, the creation of a weak parliament, and the foundation of a series of mass political organizations to replace the old, multiparty system. While governments prior to 1952 had used some heavy-handed measures against opponents (especially, but not exclusively, in times when the constitution was suspended), the post-1952 regime proved remarkably intolerant of dissent. Large-scale nationalizations, culminating in the socialist legislation in the early 1960s, led to the state's nearly total domination of the economy. The regime's commitment to equality, demonstrated in 1952 with land reform, climaxed in the adoption of socialist ideology and legislation in the 1960s (and into the 1970s).

Yet through most of the period the regime left the judicial structure alone. States of emergency and the new constitutions granted the regime a fairly free hand in drafting legislation as it wished; the courts (with a fairly positivist orientation often manifested in civil law systems) found it

---

[41] For some contemporary coverage of debates over the constitution including some details on the committee's discussions, see *Ruz al-yusuf*, December 27, 1952; June 1, August 3 and October 19, 1953; and January 11 and February 1, 1954.

[42] Jones to Department of State, January 17, 1955, USNA 774.00/1–1755.

their task to apply the law. Any attempts by the courts to curb executive authority were effectively forestalled by the subjugation of the *Majlis al-Dawla* and the abandonment of the liberal draft of the constitution in the first few years after 1952. For the decade following these moves, the regime showed no interest in introducing fundamental changes in the judicial structure. Yet while the judiciary hardly stood as a major obstacle, neither could it be depended on for favorable rulings in sensitive political cases. The defeat of liberal legality diminished the possibility of direct judicial challenge, but it did not force the judiciary to convict opponents of the regime of political offenses. Therefore, from the first days of the new regime, tools were developed to circumvent the regular courts. None of these tools was unprecedented – indeed, the history of exceptional courts in Egypt was, by 1952, already a long one. The courts to try those involved in the 'Urabi Revolt, the Commissions of Brigandage, the administrative committees empowered to order internal exile, the special courts to try offenses against the British army, and the martial law courts established during the First World War had all had exceptional jurisdiction, composition, and procedures. The three decades after the 1922 declaration of independence offered only a temporary respite from exceptional courts, but they had also witnessed an increased willingness to rely on martial law.

Thus, the first few years of the new regime marked only a renewal of the use of exceptional courts. Only the extent rather than the nature of the courts was new. The use of exceptional courts helps explain why much of the judiciary was accorded some degree of autonomy for so long – the regime had other ways of insuring favorable results. The surface of pre-1952 legality was thus maintained, but methods of moving outside the regular courts were increasingly developed. In Nasserist Egypt, as in many other authoritarian systems, the regime chose to construct special courts for sensitive political cases rather than induce the regular court system to do its bidding. In his conversation with the Chairman of the International League for the Rights of Man in 1955, 'Abd al-Nasir was forthright on the motives behind the use of "People's Courts" and military courts, claiming according to an American embassy account that "it had been demonstrated that the Civil Courts could not be trusted to deal adequately with the Muslim Brotherhood and hence the People's Courts had to be set up" and that the use of military courts would be necessary for another year in order to "secure the Revolution first."[43] A decade and a half later, 'Abd al-Nasir phrased the argument differently when he explained in a dialogue with

---

[43] *Ibid.*

judges that he recognized that the special courts set up after the revolution had a political task. Willing to honor the judiciary's desire to avoid political activity, the RCC had established courts that drew on military officers to avoid implicating the judiciary in the new regime's political activities.[44]

The first exceptional court established was the *Mahkamat al-Ghadr* (Court of Treason), established only five months after the Free Officers came to power in 1952. The *Mahkamat al-Ghadr* established important precedents for the post-1952 exceptional courts: it was bound only by the loosest procedural guidelines; the majority of its members were political appointments with no judicial background; its mandate was extremely broad; and it seemed aimed not simply at punishing but also at embarrassing and discrediting its targets. The decree establishing the court gave it the authority to investigate former political officials suspected of engaging in personal corruption, exploiting their influence, or corrupting the political order. With probably unintended irony, the regime specifically enjoined the court to try those accused of interfering with the judiciary. The court was composed of three senior judges appointed by the minister of justice and four military officers appointed by the commander-in-chief of the armed forces.[45]

In July 1953 the regime established a special military court for Egyptian communists. Both the prosecution and the defendants used the opportunity to try communism as an ideology. The defense made the argument that pamphlets presented by the prosecution as seditious were similar to those that had been circulated by the Free Officers themselves prior to 1952. Defense lawyers argued further that the specific measures communists had called for were similar to those actually enacted by the new regime. In order to support this claim, the defense unsuccessfully asked the court to summon both Muhammad Najib and 'Abd al-Nasir. When the prosecution produced the mufti of Egypt to denounce communism, the defense asked for two former Egyptian ambassadors to Moscow to testify whether communist reality accorded with the mufti's description. While the trial did result in some embarrassment for the regime (the mufti's testimony went beyond a denunciation of communism to a call for an Islamic state), the necessary convictions were obtained for most of those tried.[46]

In September 1953 the *Mahkamat al-Thawra* (Court of the Revolu-

---

[44] The dialogue came in the aftermath of the massacre of the judiciary and is reported in 'Abd Allah Imam, *Madhbahat al-qada*' (Cairo: Maktabat Madbuli, 1976), pp 71–77.

[45] 'Ubayd, *Istiqlal al-qada*', pp. 579–80

[46] For the establishment of this court, see Caffery to Secretary of State, July 9, 1953, USNA 774.001.7/953. For the operation of the court, see the files in USNA 774.001 for 1953 and 1954.

tion) was established. In justifying this new exceptional court, Free Officer Salah Salim frankly stated that although the RCC had confidence in the judiciary for normal cases, the times were not normal and a court not bound by regular judicial procedures was needed. The *Mahkamat al-Thawra* was exclusively military in composition. No appeal was permitted, although the RCC had the right to approve or commute sentences. The court was granted a broad mandate to try crimes against the political order or the revolution, or of supporting imperialism.[47] These offenses could be interpreted very broadly and actions taken before the decree establishing these as crimes could be, and were in fact, prosecuted.[48] For instance, in the trial of Fu'ad Siraj al-Din, former minister of interior and prominent member of the Wafd, the decision by the Wafdist government in October 1951 to abrogate the Anglo-Egyptian treaty of 1936 was treated as tantamount to treason – not because the treaty was sacrosanct but because the government had not taken the necessary steps to manage the resulting confrontation with Great Britain.[49] (When he claimed in his defense that he had actually assisted the Free Officers in actions against the British in the Canal Zone in 1951, 'Abd al-Latif al-Baghdadi, the Free Officer appointed to head the court, rejected the claim based on his personal knowledge of events.[50]) The decree establishing the court gave absolute authority (and little guidance) over both procedures and sentences. Thus the accused was not guaranteed the right of counsel (although the court routinely granted it for its public sessions). In the trial of former Prime Minister Ibrahim 'Abd al-Hadi', who was condemned to death by the court, one charge was heard in camera. When the defendant's lawyer was not allowed to see the documentation related to the charge he resigned in protest and 'Abd al-Hadi' was tried without counsel.[51] The Mahkamat al-Thawra had the (probably intended) effect of airing all charges of corruption and embarrassing behavior on the part of the pre-1952 political leadership (or at least all charges that the new regime wished to have aired). Old regime politicians often raced to testify against each other, supporting not only the idea that they were corrupt as a group but also that they were incapable of concerted action in the nation's interest.[52] The task of the Mahkamat al-Thawra can therefore be viewed as producing show trials in all senses of the term.

[47] 'Ubayd, *Istiqlal al-qada'*, pp. 580–82.
[48] Hankey to Foreign Office, September 15, 1953, FO 371/JE10118, File 1.
[49] See *Egyptian Gazette*, "Serag El Din guilt 'amounts to treason,'" January 18, 1954.
[50] Hankey to Foreign Office, December 14, 1953, FO 371/J10118, File 44.
[51] See *Egyptian Gazette*, September 30, 1953.
[52] See, for example, Caffery to Department of State, November 18, 1953, USNA 774.13/ 11–1853.

In May 1954, just as the *Mahkamat al-Thawra* was preparing to conclude its work, the regime decreed the establishment of a second chamber of the court to deal with "all acts of sedition which took place on April 28," the date of an abortive military rising against the new regime. The new chamber served to embarrass Muhammad Najib (still president but isolated from the rest of the RCC) because of the rebels' support for him. Finally, at the end of June 1954 al-Baghdadi announced the completion of the work of the Mahkamat al-Thawra.[53]

The following November, *Mahakim al-Sha'b* (People's Courts) were established to suppress the Muslim Brotherhood in the wake of an unsuccessful assassination attempt on 'Abd al-Nasir. Once again, the courts were given a broad mandate to deal with "actions considered as treason against the Motherland or against its safety internally and externally as well as acts considered as directed against the present regime or against the bases of the Revolution." As with its predecessors, the *Mahakim al-Sha'b* were given wide latitude with regard to both procedures and punishments. They were required only to give the accused notice of charges twenty-four hours before the hearing. Once begun, cases could not be adjourned more than once or for more than forty-eight hours. No appeal from their verdicts was permissible, although once again the RCC had the authority to approve or commute any sentence. The first court was established with three members of the RCC: Gamal Salim (described by the American ambassador as the "wild man" of the regime whose appointment was designed to frighten Brotherhood members), Anwar al-Sadat, and Husayn al-Shafi'i.[54] Defendants had difficulty in obtaining the counsel they wished: the would-be assassin of 'Abd al-Nasir unsuccessfully appealed to several leading politicians to defend him; and Hasan al-Hudaybi, the general guide of the Brotherhood and a former judge on the *Mahkamat al-Naqd*, was turned down when he appealed to the Bar Association for aid. The proceedings of the court (in which several Brotherhood leaders either distanced themselves from the organization or blamed each other for its perceived excesses) were broadcast on radio until some of those on trial began to denounce the regime too stridently. After the first trial, seven members of the organization (including al-Hudaybi himself) were sentenced to death. Apparently not wishing to create a martyr, the RCC commuted al-Hudaybi's sentence citing his advanced age and ill-health. Yet after the conclusion of the first trial, the RCC announced that the

---

[53] See Stevenson to Foreign Office, May 24, 1954, FO 371/JE10118, File 5; Caffery to Department of State, May 24, June 7, and June 30, USNA 774.00/5–2454; 6–754; and 6–3054.

[54] Caffery to Department of State, November 2, 1954, USNA 774.00/11–254.

work was so great that it would form three new all-military People's Courts so that matters could be resolved quickly. When the new trials began, the American embassy observed that the Brotherhood itself was being tried; any association with it could be considered criminal:

The charge against the six stated that as members of the Guidance Council they participated in directing the policy of the Brotherhood towards violence and terrorism and approved of an armed secret system for overthrowing the present regime. With respect to this charge the only pertinent contention of the prosecution was that they took no action to dissolve it. The prosecution made no attempt to establish the fact that any of the accused were members of the secret organization or that they committed any overt act against the regime.

With the trial of these secondary leaders of the Ikhwan, the Tribunal has moved away from the original purpose of attempting to prove that the accused participated, through the secret organization; [sic] in a plot to assassinate NASIR and overthrow the regime. The objective of the court now appears to be that of showing that membership in the Brotherhood itself is a crime against the nation. This shift of orientation probably results from the fact that the trials are more an implement of internal propaganda than a legal proceeding and their object is that of devising a means for dispersing and destroying the leadership of the Ikhwan rather than punishing those involved in the plot.[55]

Eventually hundreds of Brotherhood members were tried.[56]

The termination of the *Mahakim al-Shaʿb* in 1955 constituted the end of the regime's routine construction of exceptional courts (although the *Mahkamat al-Thawra* was revived in the wake of the 1967 war and again in 1971 to try ʿAli Sabri and other rivals of Sadat). In subsequent years, rather than constructing new courts, the regime simply transferred sensitive political cases to the military courts. Once a case entered a military court no appeal to the civilian judiciary was possible. As part of the armed forces, military judges could be counted on to render the desired verdicts on most occasions. The law of procedure for military courts was amended to allow for necessary measures such as trials *in absentia*. There were numerous indications that the military courts convicted on the basis of evidence obtained in dubious circumstances. In a 1957 trial of a group accused of plotting against the regime, one defendant suddenly uncovered his feet to show wounds he claimed had been inflicted during torture.[57] The same year several alleged plotters (including two former ministers) were convicted almost entirely on the basis of signed confessions. In camera trials were also common.[58]

---

[55] Caffery to Department of State, December 3, 1954, USNA 774.00/12–354.
[56] For reporting on the work of the *Mahakim al-Shaʿb*, see the various files in USNA 774.00 for late 1954 and early 1955.
[57] Hare to Secretary of State, August 15, 1957, USNA 774.00/8–1557.
[58] See USNA 774.00 for 1957 and 1958 for various reports on political trials in military courts.

The use of military courts and exceptional measures to confront, harass, punish, and embarrass political opponents were certainly contrary to any conception of liberal legality but they had a strong legal basis. That basis originated not in the coup of 1952 but can be traced directly back to the British declaration of martial law in 1914. That declaration included the appointment of a British military governor with emergency powers and the removal of the actions of the military authority from the jurisdiction of the courts. Early on, the actions of the military authority were limited, but as the war moved closer to Egypt, more extensive actions were taken. The British used martial law as a justification for several measures that were not allowed under prevailing interpretations of the capitulations, such as imposing taxes on foreigners.

The usefulness of martial law during the war led the British and Egyptian leaderships to provide a regular legal basis for its possible return. In the 1923 constitution, provision was made for the declaration of emergency. The 1936 Anglo-Egyptian treaty allowed the British the right to call for a state of emergency in Egypt. This step was actually taken in 1939.[59] The declaration that year named the prime minister rather than the army commander as the military governor of the country, which seemed to allow for greater use of martial law against political opponents. More importantly, the prime minister's dual position prevented any political oversight of martial law actions (by merging political and military authority in a single person). One American legal expert argued that this step, and the wide scope of actions taken under martial law, exceeded the bounds of the 1923 constitution. Martial law was reinstated during the Palestine war of 1948. On this occasion, a lower level military court went so far as to question the constitutional grounds of some of the measures taken under the state of emergency, but it also argued that only the legislative authorities could nullify such actions.[60] Martial law was lifted in 1950 but reimposed following the rioting of January 1952; it was in force when the coup took place the following July.

Thus, the emergency law the regime inherited in 1952 had two chief features: it gave the government very strong powers (for instance, verdicts of military courts could not be appealed but were submitted to the military governor for approval), and it could be portrayed as a

---

[59] The declaration of a state of emergency in 1939 was a disappointment to the British who wished Egypt to declare war on Germany and "prepare" to declare a state of emergency. The Egyptian government was deeply split on the matter and stopped short of declaring war. The declaration of a state of emergency was an attempt to placate the British in the spirit of the 1936 treaty. See FO 371/J3369.

[60] The information in this paragraph was taken largely from "Martial Law in Egypt 1914–1949," prepared by Judge Jasper Y. Brinton, May 27, 1949, USNA 883.00/5–2749.

creation of the British. By 1952 critics of the old regime and liberal jurists were denouncing Egypt's emergency law. The *Majlis al-Dawla* was becoming bolder in scrutinizing actions taken under martial law, leading the government to attempt to remove its power to review such measures.[61] When the Free Officers came to power, therefore, many critics hoped that the new regime would not simply cancel the existing state of emergency but rewrite the law which allowed for such extensive emergency powers. In 1953, Ihsan 'Abd al-Qudus called boldly and publicly for such a step, arguing that 'Urabi, Mustafa Kamil, and Sa'd Zaghlul all led without the benefit of martial law because they had broad popular support. Since Najib had a similar level of support, martial law was not necessary.[62]

The new regime rejected these calls. Not only was the state of emergency continued, but in October 1954 a new law on the subject was enacted that actually strengthened the hand of the military governor by transferring to him some authority that had earlier been given to individual ministers or the cabinet as a whole.[63] In 1958 a more comprehensive law was issued, which in many ways was more appropriate for a country in which a state of emergency had become the rule rather than the exception. (It was at that time that the term "martial law" [*hukm 'urfi*] was largely replaced by "state of emergency" [*halat al-tawari'*] out of recognition that exceptional measures had far exceeded the military sphere of affairs; see chapter 4.) By this time, even the legalities required by the broadened law could be ignored – the state of emergency declared at the beginning of the Suez Crisis in 1956 was not submitted to the parliament until June 1964 (in spite of the legal requirement that any declaration be submitted to the next parliamentary session).[64]

The initial wave of trials had required special courts because of the volume of cases and the ambiguous nature of the offenses and because there was more desire for publicity than for harshness. Once that wave was over, the regime, armed with a strong emergency law and a near-continuous state of emergency, was able to transfer to pliable military courts routine political cases.

---

[61] See, for instance, Lutfi al-Khawli, "Know Your Rights. Martial Law," *Ruz al-yusuf*, July 7, 1952, August 11, 1952 and May 25, 1953; see also the story on martial law, *Ruz al-yusuf*, October 27, 1952, p. 20. For the stand of the Bar Association, see Ziadeh, *Lawyers*, pp. 84–86.

[62] "When Will It Be Decided for Egypt to Rule without Martial Law?" *Ruz al-yusuf*, August 3, 1953.

[63] Caffery to Department of State, October 19, 1954, USNA 774.00/10–1954.

[64] See "Light on the Emergency Law," *al-Wafd*, June 8, 1994.

## The clash between the judiciary and the regime and the emergence of socialist legality

The judicial structure in Egypt by the end of the 1950s differed only slightly from what had existed ten years earlier. Those changes that had been effected – the unification of the judiciary and the subjugation of the *Majlis al-Dawla* – were based on proposals that predated 1952. Yet the political system had changed greatly. The monarchy had been abolished, political parties (other than the sole organization sponsored by the regime) dissolved, and authority was increasingly concentrated in the presidency. Far from treating the judiciary as an obstacle to the operation of executive power, the regime simply made use of the military courts for sensitive political cases and relied on executive domination of the parliament (and extensive presidential authority to issue decrees) to enact legislation the courts were bound to carry out. This situation continued even as the regime turned in the 1960s to the construction of a socialist order. In the early 1960s extensive nationalizations and the cultivation of a socialist ideology laid the groundwork for the construction of Arab socialism in Egypt. As this effort progressed, however, a confrontation between the judiciary and the regime began to build. The confrontation, culminating in a 1969 event now referred to as the "massacre of the judiciary," resulted from a perception among some leading members of the regime that the judiciary was insufficiently enthusiastic in supporting the socialist transformation and indeed was coalescing into a powerful interest group critical of many features of Egypt's new political order.[65]

### The new socialist legality

Beginning in the mid-1960s a group of leading political and legal figures began to call for a transformation in Egypt's legal culture, arguing that fundamental changes were needed as part of the effort to build a socialist society. From the point of view of the judiciary, a portion of the public discussion on the topic was fairly innocuous, because it dealt with introducing new legislation supportive of socialist

---

[65] The use of the term "interest group" may seem odd, because judges are state officials. Yet their corporate identity has at times allowed them to act coherently in defense of their material interests as well as their political vision. Additionally, the prestige of the judiciary is sufficient to garner them some support from the legal community (although lawyers and judges often operate as rivals as well). The emergence of a judicial "interest group" will become more clear in the following chapter.

transformation.[66] Yet many writers went much further, arguing for fundamental changes in both the ideological orientation of the judiciary and its structure.

On an ideological level, the new socialist legality involved a repudiation of the idea of the separation of powers and a reliance on socialist principles in jurisprudence (even at times at the expense of the letter of the law). The doctrine of separation of powers was denounced as naive and capitalist in origin; it resulted in distancing the judiciary from its proper political role. Socialist jurisprudence depended on a recognition on the part of the judiciary that Egypt's social and political system had undergone fundamental changes. In cases in which the law was ambiguous or uncertain, judges should consider the values of the new order in making their decisions. Indeed, the government went to the extent of preparing draft amendments to the civil code that would require judges to apply the bases of the socialist order when the law was unclear (the existing civil code enjoined judges to consider Islamic law, other legal systems, and general principles of law).[67] In 1966 Jamal al-'Utayfi, a prominent legal scholar, extended this view by arguing that legislation that predated the 1952 revolution deserved special scrutiny by the judiciary. He specifically cited the 1948 law regulating relations between landlord and tenant. Arguing that the law was the product of the capitalist era and gave the landlord too strong a position, al-'Utayfi observed that this kind of law subverted socialist transformation. Changing all such legislation in parliament would simply take too long. Thus the judiciary faced a dilemma between applying the letter of the law or the spirit of the age. Al-'Utayfi argued that following modern socialist principles was preferable to a punctilious literalism. He therefore lauded the recent decision by a Cairo ibtida'i (primary) court on a case involving subletting. While the 1948 law made it nearly impossible for a landlord to evict a tenant, it did allow the landlord to retake possession of an apartment if the original tenant sublet the property. The court found the law a product of a time when imperialism, feudalism, and capitalism prevailed in Egypt and therefore reflected only the interests of the landlord. While the law was still in effect, it was deemed outdated, and the court refused the landlord's suit to evict the tenant.[68]

[66] See, for instance, "Changing of the Laws," al-Akhbar, August 28, 1966, p. 4; the editorial, "The Legal Revolution," al-Jumhuriyya, August 28, 1966; and Jamal al-'Utayfi, "On the Road to Socialist Legality," al-Ahram, October 20, 1967.

[67] "The Law Applies the Bases of the Socialist Order in Case of the Absence of Legislative Texts that Can be Applied," al-Akhbar, December 7, 1967.

[68] Jamal al-'Utayfi, "The Revolutionary Face of the Judiciary," al-Ahram, February 14, 1966.

The argument that a new socialist jurisprudence was needed in Egypt was given a strong impetus by a series of front-page editorials that appeared in the daily *al-Jumhuriyya* in March 1967. The editorials, signed by 'Ali Sabri, the secretary-general of the Arab Socialist Union (ASU), attracted great attention because they appeared to augur a major new initiative of the regime. While the tone was outwardly respectful towards Egypt's judiciary, the editorials argued for a reconceptualization of the role of the judicial branch in socialist Egypt. In an initial editorial, 'Ali Sabri observed that only the judiciary had been excluded from any role or participation in the ASU. The doctrine of separation of powers had been used to justify exclusion. The practical effect was to separate the judiciary from the popular base of the society. The judiciary alone, of all the working forces of the nation, was not performing its proper political work. Yet the doctrine of separation of powers, which Egypt had imported, was not even applied in capitalist countries, because in those countries judges always originated in the ruling class and applied the law of the ruling class.[69] Two days later, 'Ali Sabri criticized conflicting judgments that often came from different courts in similar cases; he extended the argument further by claiming that the separation of the judiciary led to judges sometimes applying the people's laws contrary to popular desires.[70] In a further editorial, he claimed that while individual judges before 1952 issued judgments that favored the people rather than the ruling class, "the popular bases cannot find an explanation for some judgments issued after the revolution, for instance, which clearly oppose the people's concepts and the movement of their struggle."[71] While the independence of the judiciary was a laudable goal, so too was its participation in political work – participation which should go beyond mere formalities.[72] The alternative was the creation of a distinct judicial class, separated from the interests and struggle of the people. 'Ali Sabri summarized the task of the judiciary in socialist society: applying the law and explaining it according to the goals that motivated the legislation; suggesting and participating in drafting new legislation appropriate for socialist transformation; and developing the existing laws in accordance with the current circumstances and needs of

---

[69] "The Judicial Sector and the Theory of Separation of Powers in the Society," *al-Jumhuriyya*, March 18, 1967.

[70] "The Political Separation between the Men of Justice and the National Position of the Masses," *al-Jumhuriyya*, March 20, 1967.

[71] "Those Who Dealt with the Masses of the People before the Revolution and those who Supported the Power of the Ruling Class," *al-Jumhuriyya*, March 22, 1967.

[72] "The Opinions of the Men of the Judiciary Have Importance in Defining the Method of Representing them in Popular Organizations," *al-Jumhuriyya*, March 26, 1967.

the society, preventing gaps which might allow exploitative elements to operate.[73]

The institutionalization of the new socialist legality entailed a series of structural changes, according to 'Ali Sabri and others. 'Ali Sabri himself focused on the inclusion of the judiciary in the ASU, and this topic drew the most attention in public discussions (and probably in private deliberations of the political leadership of the country). Yet while attention was devoted to the idea, proposals remained fairly vague. 'Ali Sabri, while he insisted that judicial participation in the ASU be truly effective, recognized that judges, like those in the armed forces, could not be treated like other constituent groups in the ASU. He insisted that they should be represented at the level of the central committee, and reassured the judiciary that it would have a role to play in determining the precise institutional arrangements.[74] More well-defined proposals were suggested by those in less authoritative positions. One year before the series of al-Jumhuriyya editorials, Jamal al-'Utayfi suggested in al-Ahram that an organization be constructed for all those working in legal fields, including judges, members of the niyaba, law professors, and lawyers. The purpose of the organization would be to insure that all involved were working together in the interests of the new society. Al-'Utayfi claimed he had no wish to violate the independence of the judiciary or force judges to rule according to public opinion, but that judges must be connected with the values of the revolution, limiting exploitative property and protecting socialist property.[75] Some members of the judiciary publicly endorsed proposals for their inclusion in the ASU, though – as became clear – they were probably a minority.[76]

Another idea attracting great attention was popular participation in the judiciary. Various proposals were put forward, most centering on some use of the jury system or introducing popular representatives without judicial background to the bench. This was deemed consistent with the new socialist ideology. Since professional judges would still be in the majority, the proposals were presented as no threat to the judiciary itself.[77]

---

[73] "Concerning the Issue of the Participation of the Men of Justice in Political Work," al-Jumhuriyya, March 25, 1967.

[74] 'Ali Sabri, "Opinions of the Men of the Judiciary."

[75] Jamal al-'Utayfi, "Towards a Unification of the Laws Realizing the Representation of the Judiciary in the Socialist Union," al-Ahram, May 22, 1966.

[76] See Mustashar Rashad al-Khallaf, "When is the Law in the Service of the People?" al-Masa', 23 February 1966; and the "Popular Base" page, al-Masa', February 24, 1966, in which several members of the niyaba and judiciary write in support of an earlier proposal.

[77] These proposals were discussed extensively in the journal of the Bar Association, al-Muhama, in the late 1960s and early 1970s. Most issues contained discussion of various forms of popular participation in the courts.

In order to further the goal of developing a centralized and coherent judicial system, other proposals were put forward. One suggestion was to remove the judicial function from the *Majlis al-Dawla*, returning administrative cases to the *Mahkamat al-Naqd*. The *Majlis al-Dawla* was criticized as a creation of Isma'il Sidqi, an authoritarian prime minister under the old regime; as discriminatory, allowing some parties the right to resort to a special judiciary; and as a departure from the idea of a single, unified judicial structure.[78] Reforms in the *niyaba* that would have placed it under greater executive control were also discussed. Jamal al-'Utayfi called for the transformation of the *Mahkamat al-Naqd* into a supreme court, empowered not simply to rule when cases were brought to it, but to issue reinterpretations of existing law on its own. This would greatly speed the task of socialist transformation and insure a unified interpretation of the law.[79]

### The massacre of the judiciary

The series of editorials by 'Ali Sabri in March 1967 augured a new initiative by the regime. Yet no real initiative was taken, perhaps because the 1967 war and the resulting political crisis led to the placing of priorities elsewhere. The regime initially adopted none of the proposals put forward to establish the new socialist legality. The various proposals had attracted the attention of the judiciary, and probably the quiet opposition of most of them. In 1968 and 1969 judges made use of their existing autonomy as private misgivings gave way to public confrontation. For many judges, it was clear that it was only a matter of time before their institutional autonomy, respected by the regime since 1952, would be seriously eroded. There was little public debate on the ideological level (perhaps because once 'Ali Sabri had endorsed the new socialist legality, any but the most oblique challenge would have been risky). Some judges enthusiastically and publicly supported the various proposals (and some apparently even joined the ASU's semi-clandestine vanguard organization), but the proposed structural changes in the judiciary, especially the inclusion of the judges in the ASU, were viewed by most as tantamount to making them an organ of executive power. The respectful tone of 'Ali Sabri and others did not obscure their denunciation of judicial autonomy. That autonomy – represented in a large measure of judicial self-governance in selection, assignment, and promotion and in the Judges Club – made it possible (though still highly risky) for the judges to resist the proposals as a body.

[78] 'Abd al-Hamid Yunis, "Why is the State Distinct in Litigation?"
[79] Jamal al-'Utayfi, "Revolutionary Face."

The regime had its own grievances against the judiciary. One possible complaint was a series of decisions taken that could only displease the political leadership of the country. In a case beginning in 1967 related to the Kamshish incident (in which a former large landowning family was accused of murdering a village ASU activist for challenging their position in the village), a civilian court issued an acquittal verdict in a case the regime had cited as justification for far-reaching measures against the old landowning elite. The following year a state security court acquitted someone accused of conspiring against the regime, and a second state security court acquitted a former ambassador accused of espionage for a foreign country. The connection between these cases and the radical steps eventually taken remains unclear, although the president of each of the two state security courts was dismissed in the massacre of the judiciary.[80]

Yet it was probably not the independence of individual judges that bothered the regime (which always had ways of avoiding regular courts), but the independence of the judiciary as a corporate body. Egyptian judges are educated in a small number of law schools; it is not uncommon for judges to have several relatives who preceded them in entering the judiciary. Largely self-governing in matters of appointment and promotion, proud of an institutional history going back to the late nineteenth century, and very conscious of their prestigious position, Egyptian judges form a community (at times it seems almost a caste) possessing a strong identity and sense of mission. By the late 1960s, the regime had come to dominate most of the country's interest groups and most of the society's institutions were either directly under government oversight or effectively dominated by a part of the state apparatus or the ASU. Judges remained almost alone in their strong sense of independence and distance from the regime (though not from the state as a whole). Past groups that had played powerful and autonomous roles in Egyptian politics – such as the Bar Association, labor unions, or university students – found their autonomy seriously eroded in Egypt in the 1950s and 1960s.[81] To make matters more critical, the political crisis that gripped Egypt after the 1967 war was accompanied by a new bid for independence by several groups (particularly students and unions). As the regime struggled to retain its strong control over the Egyptian polity, the judiciary stood out as a corporate group resistant to the regime's domination.

It was not simply a desire by the regime to dominate the judiciary for its own sake that led to the strong mutual suspicions and eventually to

[80]  See 'Ubayd, *Istiqlal al-qada'*, p. 241, note 2.
[81]  Robert Bianchi, *Unruly Corporatism* (New York: Oxford, 1989).

confrontation. After all, the regime had lived with the autonomy of the judiciary for a decade and a half. The regime increasingly showed signs of frustration with the judiciary because of an ideological gap that seemed only to grow. For the regime, the judiciary remained wedded to prerevolutionary ideas and unwilling (or at least reluctant) to share in the officially sanctioned Arab socialist ideology. The judiciary, for its part, still largely inclined to liberal ideas of legality and fiercely jealous of its autonomy, reacted to signs of regime frustration with alarm. The editorials by 'Ali Sabri set many judges on edge, and in 1968 and 1969 a series of events led the judges to defend their interests increasingly boldly and publicly.

The first step came in March 1968 when the general assembly of the Judges Club used signs of growing unrest and hints of a move towards political liberalization as an opportunity to issue a statement responding to calls to change judicial organization. The statement, publicly distributed and published in *al-Quda*, the journal of the Judges Club, expressed opposition to including judges in any political organization as well as other proposals that had been suggested in the press (such as the participation of non-judicial personnel in trials or reorganization of the *niyaba*). Explicit denunciation of these proposals was coupled with oblique calls for liberalization, the end of the use of special courts, and greater respect for the constitution and the rule of law.[82] The timing of the statement could not have been worse for the regime. Not only did it occur in the midst of popular unrest, it also came two days before a major address by 'Abd al-Nasir. After learning of the intention of the Judges Club to issue the statement, the minister of interior requested that it be delayed until after the president's speech, arguing that the judges would soon discover their own statement superfluous. The officers of the Club refused, contributing to the impression that 'Abd al-Nasir's March 30 call for limited liberalization (including defending the revolution "under the protection of the sovereignty of law") came under heavy domestic pressure.[83] Ambiguously, 'Abd al-Nasir also called for a new supreme court, though it was not clear whether he intended this as a revival of the old liberal proposal of a constitutional court or an endorsement of the calls for an avowedly political court to bring the judiciary in line with socialist transformation.

The initial government response to the statement was guarded. On April 18, 'Abd al-Nasir stated "I am not inclined at the present time to

---

[82] Portions of the statement can be found in English translation in Delwin Roy and William Irelan, "Law and Economics in the Evolution of Contemporary Egypt," *Middle Eastern Studies*, 25(2), 1989, pp. 167–68.

[83] See Imam, *Madhbahat al-qada'*, pp. 53–54.

include the judiciary or the armed forces or the police in the political organization [the ASU]. I say at the present time. It is first necessary to complete the political organization and confirm its effectiveness and to confirm the veracity of its expression of the working forces of the people." Only after that was done could the inclusion of the judiciary and other sectors in the ASU be discussed.[84]

The statement of the Judges Club left the judiciary divided. While some saw the statement as a courageous call for the regime to honor the rule of law and the independence of the judiciary, others viewed it as hypocritical – it constituted a political statement by a judiciary claiming it wanted to distance itself from politics.[85] The Judges Club divided into pro- and anti-statement groups. As elections for Club offices approached in March 1969, two slates emerged, one identified with the regime (and, according to its critics, actually formulated by the minister of justice) and one identified with the March 1968 statement. The pro-statement slate won a resounding victory.

In August 1969 the regime finally responded with a series of presidential decree-laws aimed directly at all aspects of judicial autonomy. The effect was the subordination of the judiciary to executive power. The first established a new Supreme Court, superior to the *Mahkamat al-Naqd*, whose members served short (three-year) terms by direct presidential appointment. The motivation for the creation of a new court with sharply curtailed autonomy was clearly spelled out in an explanatory note which echoed many of the arguments for further centralization and socialist legality made earlier by Jamal al-'Utayfi and 'Ali Sabri:

It has become clear in many cases that the judgments of the judiciary are not able to join the march of development which has occurred in social and economic relations. This is a result of the inadequacy of legislation or a result of interpretations unsuitable for the new relations.

While the state has dealt with many of the most apparent inadequacies of legislation, it is the task of the judiciary in interpreting and applying that activates stagnant texts. The legislator depends on, or is hindered by, his task according to what is handed down in the way of interpretation of texts, especially because legislation is not always able to follow the changes which occur in a society with the necessary speed. This makes the task of the judge in the stage of transition to socialism of the utmost importance and assures his vanguard role and his responsibility to preserve the values of the society and its principles as an element completing his independence. The independence of the judge is not a characteristic the society bestows on him; rather it is established in the interests of justice and the people.

---

[84] Imam, *Madhbahat al-qada'*, p. 45, note 1.
[85] Much of the discussion can be found in the course of Imam's frank defense of the regime's actions in *Madhbahat al-qada'*.

Among the aspects of the shortcoming in our inherited judicial system is the multiplicity of judicial agencies. A fundamental reform of the judiciary was realized when the *Shari'a* and *Milli* Courts were abolished by Law 462 of 1955, and the personal status sections became a part of the regular judiciary. But the multiplicity in judicial agencies continues to exist.[86]

Thus, the task of the new court was to develop the new socialist jurisprudence and to insure a single, authoritative interpretation of legal texts.

A second presidential decree-law formed a new body, the Supreme Council of Judicial Organizations (to replace the exclusively judicial Supreme Judicial Council and other similar bodies). The Council, with control over judicial appointments and promotions, was largely composed of judges, but it was headed by the president (with the minister of justice as vice-chairman), giving far greater executive control of the judiciary than had existed previously. A third decree-law went further, using the reorganization as justification for requiring that all judicial personnel be subject to immediate reappointment. Those not reappointed would be retired or reassigned to non-judicial work. This measure came to be called the "massacre of the judiciary" because more than 200 judicial personnel lost their positions as a result. The victims included the entire board of the Judges Club, the president (and many other members) of the *Mahkamat al-Naqd*, and numerous lower court judges and members of the *niyaba* and other judicial organizations. A final presidential decree-law dissolved the board of the Judges Club and substituted appointment for election of its officers. These measures were similarly justified by the need to prevent contradictory rulings, insure the unity of the judiciary and of the interpretation of laws, and aid socialist transformation.[87]

Yet just as the subjugation of judicial to executive power was complete and the stage was set for the implementation of the new socialist legality, the regime changed course once again, allowing for the unmistakable (if gradual and incomplete) return of liberal legality to Egypt.

[86] The text is printed in Imam, *Madhbahat al-qada'*, pp. 136–37.
[87] The explanatory notes for all these decree-laws are included in the appendices to Imam, *Madhbahat al-qada'*.

# 4　Egyptian courts, 1971–1996: the reemergence of liberal legality

In 1969, Egypt's political leaders made the decision to bring the judiciary under executive domination. More than any specific rulings made by the courts, the move seemed to stem from the corporate independence of the judges coupled with the ideological clash between the liberal legality of the judiciary and the aspirations of the regime for socialist transformation. Yet the commitment of the regime to socialist ideology was never unqualified, and it began to diminish rapidly in the 1970s. Indeed, official ideology gradually placed greater emphasis on the rule of law, democracy, and the independence of the judiciary. From 1971 on, the several measures taken during the massacre of the judiciary were either undone or transformed beyond recognition. By the mid-1980s, Egypt's judges had gained more ground than they had lost in 1969 in their efforts to assert their independence and corporate interests. While the impact of the measures taken in 1969 were potentially far-reaching, the actual institutional changes were fairly modest; they were therefore not difficult to reverse. Yet the reemergence of liberal legality on an institutional level was still a very gradual process and it remains incomplete.

In this chapter, the historical record of the reassertion of liberal legality will be followed by an analysis of the limitations of the current institutional structure of Egypt's judiciary from a liberal standpoint. The chapter will conclude with a consideration of the nature of liberal legality in Egypt on an ideological level, its meaning, and the reasons for its reemergence.

## Reversing the impact of the massacre of the judiciary: the emergence of the judicial lobby

In 1971, Egypt received a new constitution, the fourth such document to govern the country since the 1952 coup. The constitution came in the wake of the "Corrective Revolution" of May 15 – in which Anwar al-Sadat decisively defeated his rivals (led by ʿAli Sabri) in a battle for succession following 'Abd al-Nasir's death the previous September. Besides 'Ali Sabri, who headed the Arab Socialist Union, several of those defeated had commanded the security and intelligence service. Sadat accordingly portrayed himself as the lawful leader of a state of institutions, victimized by a conspiracy of extralegal "centers of power." While the reinstitution of the "Court of the Revolution" to try his opponents may have left some to doubt Sadat's sincerity, the new president gave concrete meaning to his claim by apologizing – in a speech to the Bar Association – for the massacre of the judiciary, offering to reinstate the dismissed judges.[1] The 1971 constitution contained a similar ambivalence: it primarily reflected existing institutional arrangements but gave vague (though increasingly important) nods in the direction of liberal legality.

A reading of the constitution at the time would probably have led to a description of the document as containing only vague assurances of the rule of law while it embedded still further the decisions of August 1969. On the one hand, the constitution proclaimed that "the rule of law [*siyadat al-qanun*] is the basis of rule in the state" and promised the independence of the judiciary, the right to legal counsel, and the presumption of innocence. It assured that there would be no punishment not based on law, no *ex post facto* laws, and no arrests without charges. No administrative act would be removed from the purview of the courts. Government employees resisting a court order would be criminally liable.

At the same time, three more specific measures seemed to undermine guarantees of the rule of law. First, the Supreme Council of Judicial Organizations (with the president of the republic at its head) was transformed from a body created by presidential decree-law in 1969 to a constitutionally mandated instrument of judicial appointment and promotion. Since the legal status of 1969 decree-law was being challenged in the courts (eventually successfully, on the fairly cogent grounds that the president's decree power did not allow him to amend the existing law of judicial organization), this step assured continuing executive oversight of the judiciary. Second, the constitution made explicit provisions for courts that had been designed to control or bypass the regular judiciary. The Supreme Court created in 1969 was renamed the Supreme Constitutional Court. Its duties and organization were either identical to the earlier body or were left to legislation. State

[1] Enid Hill, *Mahkama! Studies in the Egyptian Legal System* (London: Ithaca Press, 1979), p. 36.

Security Courts were also given a constitutional basis, although their specific organization and competence were left to legislation. Finally, the 1971 constitution created an entirely new office, the Socialist Public Prosecutor, responsible for "taking procedures to secure the rights of the people, the safety of the society and its political system, and commitment to socialist behavior."[2]

During the 1970s the proponents of liberal legality lost considerable ground in the area of special courts and quasi-judicial organs with exceptional jurisdiction. The Socialist Public Prosecutor, the Court of Ethics, and the Parties Court (which will be examined below) were inventions of the Sadat presidency. These bodies, unlike the exceptional courts of the mid-1950s, were constructed with the participation of the regular judiciary. For many judges, this only made them more noxious, because they compelled the judiciary to associate itself with structures and procedures in which it had little confidence. But it also made them less likely to ignore all conceptions of due process or operate outside of the law. Egyptian law still gave the president the authority to transfer cases to military courts. The Egyptian government continued to move outside of the regular judiciary on occasion and, indeed, multiplied the number of tools that allowed it to do so.

Yet despite the proliferation of exceptional courts, the thirteen years after 1971 witnessed an almost complete reversal of the decisions taken in August 1969. In general, the proponents of liberal legality in Egypt fought for a series of measures that would have had the effects of turning the vague assurances of the 1971 constitution into concrete realities and reversing the executive domination of the judiciary. These proponents were a mixed group, consisting of the judiciary itself, the leadership of the Bar Association, several leading lawyers and intellectuals, and (after 1977) opposition political parties.[3] They lobbied a regime that was sympathetic to some of the demands, though very slow in responding to them.

---

[2] The 1971 constitution is still in force so copies are widely available; this analysis is based on the Arabic text published in *al-Muhamah*, 51 (10), 1971, and an English version, published by the Ministry of Information in September 1971. I have provided my own translation, guided by the official version in meaning but avoiding its infelicities. Part four, articles 64–72, concern the rule of law. Article 179 covers the Socialist Public Prosecutor. Actually, the Socialist Public Prosecutor had been mentioned in legislation a few months before the 1971 constitution was issued, although it was just being established. The committee that drafted the 1971 constitution apparently had other ideas in mind and actually decided against proposals for similar positions but was overruled. See Muhammad 'Ubayd, *Istiqlal al-qada'* (Cairo: Maktabat rijal al-qada'), p. 708, note 2.

[3] In the 1984 parliament, the leader of the opposition Wafd party was Mumtaz Nassar, the president of the Judges Club, who had been forced into retirement in the massacre of the judiciary in 1969.

As a result of the changes introduced between 1971 and 1984, Egypt's current judicial system probably approaches liberal conceptions of legality more closely now than at any time in the country's history.[4] Its various components have asserted, sometimes quite vigorously, a new vision of the rule of law in Egypt. There are important limitations on the operation of the new liberal legality, however, and the political leadership of the country shows little willingness to move further than it has already.

### Regaining Judicial Autonomy

For members of the judiciary, the most important battle concerned judicial appointments and promotion. The new body created in 1969, the Supreme Council of Judicial Organizations, chaired by the president of the republic, when coupled with the simultaneous dismissal of a large number of sitting judges for political reasons, communicated the message very effectively that judicial independence had been largely abandoned. Judges demanded the return of the previous body, the exclusively judicial Supreme Judicial Council. In this they worked directly against article 173 of the 1971 constitution which provided that the Supreme Council of Judicial Organizations, "presided over by the president of the republic, shall supervise the affairs of the judiciary organizations." A 1972 law of judicial organization had given this body primary authority in matters of appointment and promotion. In 1984 the judiciary finally prevailed by securing a change in the 1972 law. The Supreme Council of Judicial Organizations could not be dissolved because it was specifically mandated in the constitution, but most of its duties were given to a reconstituted Supreme Judicial Council, with a completely judicial composition.[5] The 1984 changes marked a real

---

[4] Admirers of the Mixed Courts saw them as guaranteeing the rule of law, but if anything they did so too much: while liberal legality involves limiting the state in the domestic arena, the Mixed Courts enforced strong limits on the country's sovereignty.

[5] The provisions of the 1984 law and an analysis are provided in 'Ubayd, *Istiqlal al-qada'*, pp. 290–305. The reinstitution of the Supreme Judicial Council insulated the judiciary not only from the executive branch but also from the parliament. In March, 1994, some members of the People's Assembly complained that some of the new members of the judicial corps were less qualified than others who had been rejected. The clear implication was that there had been favoritism, presumably towards relatives of other judges. The speaker of the Assembly refused to discuss the matter, claiming that the Supreme Judicial Council alone was responsible. See "No Supervision from the People's Assembly on the Judicial Authority," *al-Ahram*, March 18, 1994. (Earlier, a leading judge had denied that there was any favoritism. See the letter by Counsellor Ibrahim al-Tawila, vice-president of the *Mahkamat al-Naqd*, *al-Ahram*, February 10, 1994).

landmark in Egyptian judicial history, and they came amidst a general
liberalizing climate. Once the regime made the concessions they were
difficult to retract. No new massacre could be taken in the name of a
socialist legality the regime had abandoned. (Instead of reversing the
1984 decisions, the regime has had to resort to the old tactic of avoiding
the regular judiciary, as will be seen.)

The judges' victory was just short of complete. There was no attempt
made to amend the 1971 constitution, making the recreation of the
Supreme Judicial Council reversible. Inspection and disciplining of
judges still operates from the Ministry of Justice, which has led one critic
to describe judicial independence as "imaginary."[6] Yet this seems at
best hyperbolic, because all of those involved in the inspection process
are judges, approved by the Supreme Judicial Council (after nomination
by the minister of justice) and their decisions are all subject to the
approval of the Supreme Judicial Council.[7] Potentially more serious was
the continued subordination of the *niyaba*, responsible for investigating
and prosecuting crimes, to the Ministry of Justice and the Supreme
Council for Judicial Organizations. The 1984 law did extend the
principle of irremovability to members of the *niyaba* for the first time,
meaning that, like judges, they may serve until they reach the mandatory
age of retirement. But appointment of the official heading the *niyaba*, *al-
na'ib al-'amm*, remains an executive branch prerogative. While all
members of the *niyaba* are considered part of the judiciary, there is at
least circumstantial evidence of reluctance of the *niyaba* to bring
politically inconvenient cases (especially, as will be seen, those involving
charges of torture by the security services) to court.

The hard-won autonomy of the judiciary allowed courts to take fairly
bold stands restricting executive authority or reversing executive actions.
The majority of Egypt's legal opposition political parties owe their
official status to court decisions after their applications were rejected. In
the 1980s the administrative court structure ancillary to the *Majlis al-
Dawla* regained the boldness it lost when al-Sanhuri and others were
dismissed three decades previously.[8] Some lower-court judges even
experimented with decisions based not on legislated law, but on the
*shari'a*, claiming that article 2 of the Egyptian constitution, which states
that "the principles of the Islamic *shari'a* are the chief source of

---

[6] 'Ismat al-Hawari, "The Imaginary Independence of the Judicial Authority," *al-Wafd*,
January 8, 1994. For a similar charge, see Muhammad al-Hayawan's column, "A Word
of Love," *al-Wafd*, April 29, 1995.

[7] Dr. 'Isam Muhammad, personal interview, Washington, D.C., March 1994.

[8] See James Rosberg, *Roads to the Rule of Law: The Emergence of an Independent Judiciary in
Contemporary Egypt*, Ph.D. dissertation, Department of Political Science, Massachusetts
Institute of Technology, 1995.

legislation," mandated such an orientation. A new, shari'a-based jurisprudence failed to emerge, however. The culprit is not the executive but the newly autonomous judiciary itself. The reinstitution of the Supreme Judicial Council sufficiently enhanced the judiciary's corporate identity to allow it to rein in those whose decisions do not accord with the prevailing positivist judicial culture.[9]

The most strikingly bold decisions – or at least the ones attracting the most attention within the country – related to those accused in cases of political violence, particularly those in which Islamicist groups were implicated. Most cases have gone to the State Security Courts and particularly to its Emergency Section, which was constructed to expedite trials and limit appeals. The judges of the State Security Courts have come from the regular judicial corps, and they have used their independence since the mid-1980s to issue acquittals in cases in which defendants claim to have been tortured. In the first such instance, the "al-Jihad Organization" case, the State Security Court ruled in 1984 that the confessions of many of those accused in political violence surrounding the Sadat assassination in 1981 were obtained through torture. The decision acquitted many of those accused, especially of the more serious charges. The court, describing the use of torture during interrogation as medieval, inappropriate for the modern age, and a violation of human rights and the constitution, urged the niyaba to investigate the security services.[10] Forty-four members of the security services were eventually charged, but they were all acquitted – a verdict the Supreme State Security Court explained was based on the superficial niyaba investigation of the torture allegations (a rare public instance of judicial criticism of the niyaba).[11] In 1990, the trial of those accused of involvement in a violent Nasserist organization resulted in a set of acquittals when the State Security Court refused to consider confessions because of evidence that defendants were tortured. This time the judges involved were particularly bold: not only did they overturn an earlier

<hr/>

[9] One of the most senior judges in the country claimed in a personal interview in 1991 that judges who insist on the superiority of the Islamic shari'a to positive legislation will find their careers stalled.

[10] For a detailed summary of the ruling, see 'Ali 'Abd al-'Al al-'Isawi, Ashhar al-muhakimat fi al-ta'rikh (The Most Famous Trials in History), (Beirut: Dar al-Jil, 1991), pp. 190–203.

[11] Husayn 'Abd al-Raziq, "Al-ta'zib bayna al-niyaba wa-l-sahafa wa majlis al-sha'b" (Torture among the Niyaba, the Press and the Parliament), al-Yasar, 52, November 1994, pp. 4–6. Judicial calls for investigations by the niyaba were not received well by all members of the niyaba–a leading member declared that judges had no authority to order the niyaba to conduct specific investigations. See Ahmad 'Abd al-Zahir al-Tayyib, "The Relationship of the Niyaba 'Amma with the Judiciary of Judgment," al-Quda, (5/6), May/June 1986.

ruling by a different panel, but they also announced the verdict before the defense had presented the case and engaged in a bitter public argument with the *niyaba*, all but accusing it of concealing evidence of torture.[12] When Islamicist political violence reemerged in the early 1990s, the State Security Courts reacted similarly, refusing to accept as evidence confessions that had apparently been obtained under torture. In 1993, all twenty-seven accused in the 1990 assassination of Rif'at al-Mahjub, the speaker of the People's Assembly, were acquitted of murder. Only ten were convicted on lesser charges of carrying unlicensed weapons and forged identifications. The court argued that evidence that had been obtained through illegal means could not be considered. Later that year, eight of the thirteen Islamicists accused in the murder of secularist author Faraj Fawda were acquitted; among those found not guilty was Safwat 'Abd al-Ghani, the reputed military leader of the radical *al-Jama'a al-Islamiyya* organization. These verdicts provoked great controversy: in the al-Mahjub case, the court's ruling was publicly denounced by the editor of one of Egypt's government-owned dailies.[13] At the same time, Islamicists who denounced Egypt's political system for its rejection of *shari'a* for civil law were moved to praise the civil law judiciary. Ma'mun al-Hudaybi, a Muslim Brother-hood leader, praised Egyptian courts for according defendants all of their rights.[14] After his acquittal, 'Abd al-Ghani himself expressed his trust in the integrity of the Egyptian judiciary, and his lawyer, Muntasir al-Zayyat (himself later detained for his involvement with Islamicist groups), termed the verdict "just, making clear that in Egypt the judiciary has integrity."[15]

[12] An earlier trial resulted in acquittals for some of those charged because of lack of evidence. When the case was sent to the president for approval (as provided in the emergency law), the *niyaba* announced it had accumulated additional evidence against those acquitted. The president therefore ordered the case to be retried, and the later court acquitted all those involved. The first court had rejected defense charges that the *niyaba* had concealed torture; the second court not only gave credence to the charges but also called for judicial supervision over investigation of political cases. While there were some in the *niyaba* who resented the 1984 call by judges in the al-Jihad case for an investigation of torture, this time the argument broke out into the open, partly because of the decision's clear implication that the *niyaba* had concealed evidence. See 'Atif Faraj, "The *Niyaba* in the Prisoner's Dock," *al-Musawwar*, March 16, 1990.

[13] See the editorial by Mahfuz al-Ansari, *al-Jumhuriyya*, August 19, 1993. Al-Ansari argued that while torture is criminal, evidence obtained under torture is still valid evidence; the crime of torture should not be allowed to erase evidence of another crime. This argument is expressly rejected by the Egyptian constitution which states that a confession obtained under torture is invalid.

[14] "Judicial and Party Personalities Praise the Egyptian Judiciary after the Ruling in the al-Mahjub Case," *al-Hayah*, August 16, 1994.

[15] "Acquittal of 8 from the Jama'a in the Faraj Fawda Case," *al-Hayah*, December 31, 1993.

Assisting the judiciary in its bid for corporate autonomy has been the revitalization of the Judges Club. The decision in 1969 to reorganize the Judges Club (and depoliticize it) was soon reversed, and judges again were allowed to elect their own officers. The Judges Club slowly returned to the position it had gained in the late 1960s, the time when it was transformed from a social organization concerned at most with the material needs of judges into a forum for debating those political issues relevant to the judiciary (and, by 1968, an agent representing their political perspective). The Judges Club continues to reject any image of itself as a political organization, but it has been active in the effort to further liberal legality in Egypt. Most notable in this regard was the 1986 National Conference on Justice, sponsored by the Judges Club, which issued far-reaching recommendations (examined below) on Egypt's legal system.[16] In the 1980s, the journal of the Judges Club became a forum for public issues concerning the judiciary; its pages, for example, included calls for the abolition of all exceptional courts.[17]

Indeed, for many (including some judges) the revitalization of the Judges Club has been excessive in that it has involved judges in some very political (and very divisive) issues. By the 1980s, elections to the Judges Club had become heated contests, often pitting those who wish to eschew confrontation with the government against those less shy. In March, 1987 – less than a year after the National Conference on Justice – the Supreme Judicial Council felt compelled to issue a public statement calling for members of the judiciary (including the *niyaba*) to cease granting interviews to the press about political topics or discussions in the Judges Club.[18] In 1989, however, several matters pushed divisions out into the open. During that year the parliament chose to ignore a report from the *Mahkamat al-Naqd*, confirming irregularities in the election of eighty-seven members of parliament. The speaker of the parliament refused to act on the report, arguing that while the *Mahkamat al-Naqd* was legally responsible to investigate electoral complaints, the parliament had the final voice on its own membership. (A similar dispute took place in 1991 and 1992 over a much smaller number of deputies; once again the parliament refused to act on the judicial report.[19]) In

---

[16] It should also be noted that one of the most thorough works on judicial organization in Egypt is 'Ubayd, *Istiqlal al-Qada'*, published by the Judges Club and containing forthright calls for liberal legality.

[17] Mustashar Wajdi 'Abd al-Sammad, "Studies in the Exceptional Laws," *al-Quda*, (5/6), May/June 1986, pp. 20–24.

[18] "Statement from the Supreme Judicial Council: Men of the Judiciary and the *Niyaba* Must Refrain from Giving Political Speeches," *al-Ahram*, March 6, 1987.

[19] The dispute led one prominent judge to suggest that the constitution be amended to forgive the *Mahkamat al-Naqd* all responsibility of the matter, which only seemed to put them in the middle of a political dispute. See Mustashar 'Adli Husayn, "The Task of

October, 1989, security forces arrested a student suspected of involvement in Islamicist groups, held him for several days, and apparently tortured him. The arrest took place at 2:00 a.m. at the house of the student's father.[20] The only element rendering the event unusual was that the student's father was a prominent judge on Cairo's Court of Appeals and vigorously took up the case (even challenging the legality of the emergency law and the current parliament).[21] Other judges supported him, partly because the security forces had violated judicial prerogatives by entering a judge's house without permission from the Supreme Judicial Council. The son was released after several days of intense pressure from the judiciary.

As a result of resentment over these matters, when elections took place in December 1989 for offices in the Judges Club, divisions between those perceived as pro- and anti-government were as strong as they had been for twenty years. In a stormy session, the outgoing board, perceived as too willing to accommodate itself to the government by some judges, was replaced by a more aggressive leadership.[22] Despite the divisive session, advocates of a less confrontational line could continue to adduce many favorable measures taken by the government in support of their positions and their candidate, Muqbil Shakir, was later elected to the presidency of the Judges Club.[23]

Judges had many issues that they wished the government to act on, and in the late 1980s and early 1990s most of their material requests – for higher salaries, computerization, better courtroom facilities – were being met (though sometimes in a dilatory manner). Indeed, the Judges

the Naqd Court," al-Ahram, December 14, 1991. One of those who was thus barred from taking a seat sued the parliament in the administrative court. While the court did not have the authority to overturn the parliamentary action, it did order compensation.

[20] The torture allegations are contained in references to the case in the Middle East Watch report, Behind Closed Doors: Torture and Detention in Egypt (New York: Human Rights Watch, 1992). As in most torture cases in Egypt, the sole person willing to provide an account is the victim himself. The Middle East Watch report does omit some information – as an explanation for the arrest it gives only the son's conjecture that it may have been related to a decision given by his father (p. 144). There is no mention of the son's alleged political activities. Yet his account of torture is sufficiently consistent with other descriptions to render it credible.

[21] The father argued that the 1958 emergency law used to justify the arrest of his son was void because it had been issued by decree and not submitted to the parliament and that the parliament's extension of the state of emergency in 1988 was invalid because irregularities in the election of seventy-eight deputies rendered the parliament itself invalid. See Ahmad al-Lutfi, "Judicial Proceedings Assure the Invalidation of the Emergency Law," al-Wafd, December 10, 1989.

[22] For one account of the session, see "Two General Assemblies for the Judges in One Day!" al-Sha'b, December 19, 1989.

[23] As a victim of the massacre of the judiciary, Muqbil Shakir could hardly be described as too willing to curry favor with those in power, but he quickly took a conciliatory line.

Club became in one sense an effective lobby for judicial interests, expressing itself on numerous questions from the retirement age for judges to budget allocations for the judiciary.[24] High government officials, including President Husni Mubarak himself, have periodically met with leading judges and the board of the Judges Club, listening to their requests with a sympathetic ear.[25] Judges, for instance, have successfully turned government attention away from proposals to increase the number of judges as a way of solving the problem of slow litigation, arguing that would only result in diluting the quality of the judges and producing conflicting judgments.[26] Instead they have called for increasing technical and administrative support and procedural reforms to break the logjam. Indeed, some lawyers complain privately that the judges have become sufficiently powerful to block those reform efforts which violate their interests. The more confrontational tone of the late 1980s has softened, but judges won real concessions in the process.

### The transformation of the Supreme Constitutional Court

The development of the Supreme Constitutional Court from a check on the judiciary into the boldest judicial actor in the country demonstrates how institutional continuity does not preclude dramatic changes in the role of the judiciary. The Supreme Court was created in 1969 not only to make jurisprudence more uniform but also to make it more consistent with socialism (and executive branch policy). Following the promulgation of the 1971 constitution, the renamed Supreme Constitutional Court was to be organized by legislation. Yet implementing legislation did not become effective for eight years, primarily because of strong judicial suspicions of the Court. Accordingly, the Supreme Court established in 1969 continued operating until 1979 when it was finally replaced by the Supreme Constitutional Court. The idea of a separate constitutional court was not new; indeed, the draft constitution written after 1952 had provided for such a court.[27] (That provision was a victim of the many revisions made by the regime before the constitution was promulgated.) Yet in the 1970s the idea of such a court was

---

[24] For some idea of the positions advanced by the Judges Club, see the interview with Muqbil Shakir in *Uktubir*, December 1, 1991.

[25] See, for instance, the several stories in *al-Ahram*, October 5, 1988, and the front-page article in *al-Ahram*, June 22, 1988 for accounts of meetings between Mubarak and leading judges.

[26] See, for instance, the interview with Ahmad Shawqi al-Maliji, who had just assumed the dual position of president of the *Mahkamat al-Naqd* and chairman of the Supreme Judicial Council, *al-Ahram*, July 5, 1988, p. 6.

[27] See *Ruz al-yusuf*, February 1, 1954, p. 10.

controversial indeed. Judges worried that the constitutional stipulation requiring the Court to be an independent judicial body would only be honored halfway – the Court would be independent from the rest of the judiciary but far from independent from the executive branch. These suspicions had a firm foundation because of the strong presidential role in appointments to the Supreme Court and the short (three-year) tenure of judges in that body.

In the end, the judges lost on the issue of the relationship of the Court to the rest of the judiciary but won on its independence from the president. The Court was to be entirely separate from the rest of the judicial structure. The budget, legislative basis, and administrative support of the Court are entirely separate from those of the regular judiciary. On the other hand, the method of appointment provided for in the legislation establishing the Court effectively removed it from presidential control. While the presidency and membership in the Court are still formally made by presidential appointment, the legislation established a general assembly for the Court (consisting of the member judges) who forward nominations (through the Supreme Council for Judicial Organizations) for membership to the president of the republic. In practice, the president of the Court has been its senior member, and all the appointments recommended by the general assembly have been approved automatically by both Sadat and Mubarak. Many judges regarded this as an unhappy compromise, because the Court still stands apart from the rest of the judiciary, and because presidential prerogatives regarding appointments, though not exercised, are still theoretically extensive. As recently as 1986 the National Conference sponsored by the judiciary called for abolition of the Supreme Constitutional Court.[28] However, the judiciary gained more than it realized in this compromise, because, as will be seen, the Court has been a strong and effective supporter of liberal legality in Egypt.

The Supreme Constitutional Court was given three tasks, the most prominent of which is to decide on constitutional issues raised by cases in other courts.[29] If one of the parties to a dispute argues that a

---

[28] Opposition to the Supreme Constitutional Court among the judiciary has declined (though not disappeared). Counsellor Muqbil Shakir, the current president of the Judges Club, endorsed the Court and its work in a personal interview, Cairo, May 1992.

[29] This description of the Supreme Constitutional Court is based on conversations with several of its members, particularly Dr. Muhammad Abu al-'Aynayn and 'Abd al-Rahman Nusayr (both vice-presidents of the Court), and with members of the Commissioners Body, particularly Dr. 'Adil 'Umar Sharif and Najib 'Ulama. The Commissioners Body consists of generally younger judges (though they carry the rank of *mustashar*, the higher of the two judicial titles) and prepares advisory opinions for the Court.

constitutional issue is involved, an Egyptian court may refer the issue (or allow the party to refer it) to the Supreme Constitutional Court. Only the Court may rule on the constitutionality of legislation, although other bodies are not barred from examining the constitutionality of lesser matters (such as individual administrative decisions and private contracts) on their own. A ruling by the Court that a legislative provision is unconstitutional renders it void. The other two tasks assigned to the Court are vestiges of its initial role as providing not simply constitutional oversight but also a measure of centralization. The Court may be asked by high officials (through the minister of justice) to render a definitive interpretation of a legislative text. The final task is to decide cases of conflicting judgments or jurisdiction among other Egyptian courts.

In the 1980s the Court issued a series of judgments that established it as the boldest judicial actor in restricting executive action even in cases with significant political aspects. Perhaps the two cases which involved the greatest public notice involved challenges to Egypt's electoral laws. In 1987, the Court ruled that the 1983 law governing the 1984 parliamentary elections unconstitutionally restricted the right of citizens to elect their representatives. The law, which provided for proportional representation, prevented independents from running for parliament. The Court's ruling was bold not only because of the political implications, but also because it was based not on a strict application of a clear text but on a plausible but hardly inevitable reading of the 1971 constitution.[30] The parliament passed a new electoral law for parliamentary elections in 1987 which again divided the country into multimember districts but allowed for one seat in each district to be open to independents. (Remaining seats would be divided according to proportional representation, as in 1984.) A preliminary ruling found this law unconstitutional, criticizing both the unequal size of the districts and the restricted opportunities for independents. In both cases, legislation passed by the parliament prior to the decision was allowed to stand. The practice of publishing advisory judgments by the Court's Commissioners Body (*hay'at al-mufawwadin*) (which has responsibility for preparing the case for the entire Court) gave the government and the parliament sufficient warning of the Court's possible intentions to allow new legislation to be passed before the final decision was announced. The two rulings (and a similar judgment in 1989 regarding elections to the

---

[30] Article 62 of the 1971 constitution provides that "citizens shall have the right to vote, to nominate and express their opinions in referenda, according to the provisions of law. Their participation in public life is a national duty." The court ruled that the 1983 law unconstitutionally restricted candidates to members of existing parties.

consultative *Majlis al-Shura*) has thrust the Supreme Constitutional Court to the center of the political stage. Not only has the Court twice forced the dissolution of parliament, but it has also left important ambiguities in its electoral law rulings that all but guarantee future disputes. The opportunities for independents and the one-person one-vote principle read into the 1971 constitution have not been fully defined by the Court.[31]

The boldness of the Court was also illustrated in a 1985 decision regarding Egypt's law of personal status. In 1979, President Sadat had decreed changes in the law, strengthening the position of women in divorce and custody cases. The Court ruled that the president had exceeded his authority by doing so. The government argued that the dire need for updating the personal status law and the paralysis of the legislature in considering changes constituted by themselves an emergency situation allowing the president, under article 147 of the 1971 constitution, to issue a decree-law. The Court rejected this reasoning, and ruled that the desire to amend existing legislation was not sufficient to invoke article 147.[32] It was primarily the implications for personal status law that drew most public attention (the ruling came at a time of debate over the implementation of Islamic law; the 1979 amendment had been criticized by Islamicists for its departure from the *shari'a*). Yet the enduring importance of the decision was related not to the substance (the parliament quickly passed a modified version of Sadat's 1979 decree-law) but instead to the Court's daring to restrict executive authority to define emergency situations.

A series of rulings has established the Court's willingness to rely on very general constitutional provisions in striking down restrictions on both political rights and private property. For instance, a law barring the establishment of political parties opposed to the 1979 Egyptian–Israeli peace treaty was struck down as inconsistent with freedom of expression and the multiparty system promised in the 1971 constitution.[33] (At the same time, the Court refused to strike down that part of

---

[31] Indeed, the 1990 electoral law was itself challenged on new constitutional grounds. Kamal Khalid, who was elected to parliament after successfully challenging the previous electoral law, claimed that judicial supervision of elections, mandated under Article 88 of the 1971 constitution, was implemented inadequately. The Commissioners Body advised rejecting the suit, arguing that since Khalid had been elected in 1990 he was not harmed and had no standing to raise the suit. See "Today the Claim of the Unconstitutionality of the Majlis al-Sha'b is Examined," *al-Wafd*, October 1, 1994.

[32] 'Awad el-Morr, "The Supreme Constitutional Court of Egypt and the Protection of Human and Political Rights," in Chibly Mallat (ed.), *Islam and Public Law: Classical and Contemporary Studies* (London: Graham and Troutman, 1993). Dr. el-Morr is the current president of the Supreme Constitutional Court.

[33] El-Morr, "Supreme Constitutional Court," pp. 237–39.

the law that banned parties that were not distinguished from existing parties.[34]) A 1981 law that dismissed the leadership of the Bar Association (then involved in a dispute with President Sadat) was overturned by the Court as an infringement on the right of association.[35] The Court has also ruled that legislation passed by popular referendum (a device used by the government on several occasions, especially under Sadat) is still subject to constitutional review.[36] A series of rulings established that the Court takes constitutional guarantees of property very seriously, and several decisions taken in the 1960s to nationalize land and capital with little or no compensation have been reversed.[37]

The Court's boldness has not been unlimited, as will be seen. And it is forced to rely on the cooperation of other judges to refer cases. Such cooperation has not always been forthcoming (as the example of the military courts will demonstrate).[38] The 1995 press law is an example of how such jurisdictional issues can hamper the liberalizing efforts of the courts. In May, 1995, with little warning, the government introduced a new press law in the parliament.[39] The law caught almost all parliamentary and opposition actors completely by surprise (it was not on the parliamentary agenda and the government had failed even to refer it to the *Majlis al-Dawla* for comment). The government's majority was sufficiently loyal to pass it immediately and without serious examination. When journalists and opposition leaders had time to read the new law they expressed outrage, claiming that it was vague, tendentious, and threatening in content. Indeed, it arguably violated constitutional guarantees of freedom of the press. The law removed the ban of preventive custody for journalists and criminalized writings that damaged national security and even the national economy. Yet for the Constitutional Court to rule on the law, it would be necessary for the

---

[34] Salah al-Din Hafiz, "The Judiciary is the Protector of Democracy . . . So Why the Argument and Embarrassment?" *al-Ahram*, May 18, 1988.

[35] Abdel Rahman Nosseir, "The Supreme Constitutional Court of Egypt and the Protection of Human Rights," unpublished manuscript, Chicago 1992.

[36] Nosseir, "Supreme Constitutional Court," pp. 9–10.

[37] El-Morr, "Supreme Constitutional Court," pp. 246–59. For a recent ruling along these lines, see 'Ali 'Afifi, "Return of Vacant Land to its Owners Whatever Its Value," *al-Akhbar*, May 17, 1992.

[38] The Egyptian Supreme Constitutional Court is not unique in this regard. The problems in raising constitutional challenges to the Kuwaiti Constitutional Court are discussed in chapter 6. In Italy as well, judges were reluctant to refer constitutional cases to the Constitutional Court established after the Second World War. See Mary L. Volcansek, "Judicial Review in Italy: A Reflection of the United States?", *Policy Studies Journal* 19 (1), Fall 1990, p. 135.

[39] This discussion is based on contemporaneous press accounts. The controversy surrounding the law was extensive. See, for example, *al-Wafd*, May 30, 1995.

government to use the law to prosecute a journalist and then have the matter referred to the Court. Until that time the law would hang as a threat which the government could invoke at any time: journalists could be detained and investigated and, as long as formal charges were not brought, it would be difficult to challenge the constitutionality of the law. The government finally agreed to refer the law to the Constitutional Court based on political rather than legal reasons: the outcry was sufficient to lead to the search for methods of defusing or delaying the issue. Yet the government's referral of the law was necessarily rejected: the Court can only rule on constitutional issues that arise in the course of a concrete dispute. By requesting an abstract ruling (not connected to any case) the government effectively moved the issue out of public debate for several months while the Court prepared its ruling that it had no jurisdiction.

When it does receive cases, the Supreme Constitutional Court has a stronger record in pursuing liberal legality than even the *Majlis al-Dawla* under al-Sanhuri. What is especially remarkable is the Court's ability to go beyond the positivism characteristic of the Egyptian judiciary to develop an innovative jurisprudence supporting liberal legality in Egypt. This jurisprudence (which will be analyzed more fully below) is especially ironic given the Court's origins in the subjugation of the judiciary in 1969.

Why has liberal legality reemerged in Egypt over the past two and a half decades? Why have judges managed (albeit slowly) to reassert their vision of the rule of law without a direct confrontation with the executive authorities? Why have executive authorities not only tolerated the reemergence of liberal legality but at times even encouraged it? While in some ways quite remarkable, the version of liberal legality that has emerged in Egypt is less restrictive of executive authority than initially appears. To understand how, one must first examine the institutional limitations that allow executive authorities to continue avoiding the judiciary. More subtly, one must then explore the ideological limitations of the liberal legality of the Egyptian judiciary.

## Institutional limitations on liberal legality in Egypt

Executive authorities in Egypt complain about the construction of a "government of judges" because of the numerous political cases that are decided by the courts rather than the cabinet and administrative agencies. By 1996, such complaints had reached the point that the government began to consider changes in the legislation governing the

Supreme Constitutional Court.[40] These concerns cannot obscure the numerous institutional mechanisms that allow the executive to stave off judicial action and even avoid it altogether. The Egyptian government is no different from other litigants in its ability to exploit the sluggish pace of litigation to its advantage (see chapter 7). Unfavorable rulings can be appealed; final verdicts can be hamstrung by difficulties in implementation; and actions that the courts have overturned can be repeated in the secure knowledge that the resulting litigation – even if the final judgment is not in doubt – will delay matters several years.

Less savory than employment of the sort of dilatory tactics common to many legal systems (though perhaps more finely developed in Egypt) is the use of remaining executive influence to rein in judicial organs. Critics of the government levy numerous charges here, referring to the remaining government control over the budget of the courts, the practice of delegating judges to non-judicial work (especially the boards of public-sector companies), and other bureaucratic provisions that tie the judiciary to the Ministry of Justice.[41] While such criticisms are often echoed by judges themselves, no evidence has been presented that these minor considerations impinge on judicial autonomy.[42] On one major issue, however, circumstantial evidence suggests that executive influence over the *niyaba* – perhaps through presidential appointment of its head – lingers. Despite numerous and consistent reports of the use of torture by the security services, documented by human rights organizations and on occasion given credence by trial judges, the *niyaba* has displayed great reluctance (indeed all but refused) to investigate individual cases.[43] In 1994, 'Abd al-Harith al-Madani, an Islamicist lawyer, died while being held by security forces. Government claims that he died of asthma could explain neither his sudden affliction with a condition he had never

---

[40] See the interview with Fathi Surur, the speaker of the Egyptian parliament in *al-Musawwar*, March 15, 1996.

[41] These kinds of criticisms are a staple for the opposition *al-Wafd* newspaper, partly because of the large number of lawyers (and former judges) who contribute articles. Mustafa Kamil Murad occasionally writes in *al-Ahrar* on similar themes – see for instance his columns on January 29, 1990 and January 31, 1994.

[42] One leading judge did mention to me one budgetary practice that would seem to rein in judicial autonomy. In a personal conversation in Cairo in May, 1995, the judge alleged that the perceived budgetary independence of the Supreme Judicial Council is illusory. He claimed that the judicial structure as a whole is underfunded, with the result that courts routinely run out of funds before the end of the fiscal year. This forces them to resort to the Ministry of Justice for supplementary funding on a regular basis.

[43] See Middle East Watch, *Behind Closed Doors*, and 'Abd al-Raziq, "Al-ta'zib." In 1993 matters had reached the point that even the Cairo high military court felt compelled to order the *niyaba* to investigate torture complaints by Islamicists. See the Agence France Press report, in FBIS Daily Report, Near East and South Asia, September 30, 1993, FBIS-NES-93-188, p. 11.

previously suffered nor the multiple wounds on his body. The Bar Association (with strong Islamicist representation in its leadership) claimed that the *niyaba* obstructed any investigation and issued a strike call in protest.[44]

While the issue of torture gained salience as Islamicist violence began to rise in the early 1990s, institutional constraints on liberal legality touched matters much wider than the *niyaba*'s apparent reluctance to challenge the security forces on their routine use of torture. Egypt's judicial structures grew (especially since 1969) largely by accretion; each new addition worked alongside (rather than replaced) older structures. Thus, in contrast to the trend up to the 1950s of unification of the judiciary, recent years has seen the dispersal of jurisdiction among various judicial and quasi-judicial bodies. Unlike the temporary bodies established immediately after 1952, the new bodies are generally permanent rather than temporary creations. The construction of the Supreme Constitutional Court fits such a pattern. Other bodies are not regarded by proponents of the rule of law as so benign, however. Frequent discussion of "exceptional courts" in Egypt generally refers to three bodies: the Socialist Public Prosecutor (founded in 1971 and later associated with a new "Court of Ethics"), the State Security Court system (especially the Emergency Section), and the military courts (and their jurisdiction over civilians).[45] Each of these judicial structures was founded in a different era and justified at that time in terms of ideas or institutional arrangements (socialism, authoritarianism, and the British occupation) that have since been repudiated or disappeared. Yet the usefulness of these exceptional courts is demonstrated by their survival under a regime that otherwise has shown a genuine (if sporadic and uneven) commitment to the rule of law.

Perhaps the most threatening institution on paper is the Socialist Public Prosecutor, given a vague mandate under the 1971 constitution to protect the society, the political system, and socialism.[46] The post was to be filled by presidential appointment and was to assume responsibility – working with a new Court of Sequestration (*Mahkamat al-Hirasa*) for impounding the assets of political and economic adversaries of the

---

[44] See "Lawyers' Strike in Egypt Paralyzes Judicial Activity," *al-Sharq al-awsat*, May 16, 1994. The strike was eventually called off, but not before violent clashes between lawyers and security forces.

[45] The Parties Court is often included in the list of exceptional courts; though in practice its role has been superseded by the administrative courts (and, to a much lesser extent, the Supreme Constitutional Court) because of their willingness to overturn the decisions of the Parties Court (and, on occasion, the legislative basis for such decisions).

[46] One of the most comprehensive treatments of the Socialist Public Prosecutor and the Mahkamat al-Qiyam is 'Ubayd, *Istiqlal al-qada'*, pp. 687–752.

prevailing order. Coming as it did shortly after the "Corrective Revolution" but before the full ideological reorientation of the regime, the new structure seemed designed to give legal legitimacy to the sequestrations of the 'Abd al-Nasir period. Yet neither the Socialist Public Prosecutor nor the Court of Sequestration was strictly judicial in nature, because both were given vague mandates that went beyond enforcing clear legal texts to defending the social, political, and economic order.

The Socialist Public Prosecutor was thus established just as the regime began to turn towards limited economic and political liberalization. Even as its socialist ideological basis eroded, the institution continued unchanged. In the late 1970s the regime began to retreat from political liberalization and the Socialist Public Prosecutor was given renewed attention. Two laws – the 1978 Law of Protection of the Internal Front and Social Peace (*himayat al-jabha al-dakhiliyya wa-l-salam al-ijitam'i*) and the 1980 Law of Protection of Values from Dishonor (*himayat al-qiyam min al-'ayb*) – broadened the political jurisdiction of the Socialist Public Prosecutor, based on the argument that democratization thus far had failed to balance the rights of the individual and the rights of the society.[47] The second law introduced a new structure, the *Mahkamat al-Qiyam* (generally translated as the Court of Ethics), which took the place of the Court of Sequestration and furthered the transformation of the Socialist Public Prosecutor into a largely investigative body charged with bringing cases of offenses against the political and economic order. The *Mahkamat al-Qiyam* was to consist of two levels and mix a judicial and a non-judicial element. (Since the 1960s there had been discussion of introducing a "popular" element into the judiciary; the Court of Sequestration and the *Mahkamat al-Qiyam* drew on vestiges of this discussion by introducing respected public personalities into a quasi-judicial position.[48])

The laws in question would seem to give sweeping authority to the Socialist Public Prosecutor to pursue virtually anyone who had accumulated wealth or criticized any public policy. The Socialist Public Prosecutor and *Mahkamat al-Qiyam*, acting together, were authorized to sequester funds and to prevent individuals from traveling outside the country and practicing political rights. Yet three factors have led the Socialist Public Prosecutor and the *Mahkamat al-Qiyam* to define their

---

[47] See the explanatory note for the Law of Protecting Values from Dishonor, quoted in 'Ubayd, *Istiqlal al-qada'*, p. 701.

[48] The procedure for appointing non-judicial personnel to the Court is described in "Recomposition of the Two Courts of Ethics for the New Judicial Year Next October," *al-Ahram*, September 6, 1987.

functions fairly conservatively (and confine their activities largely to the economic rather than political realm). First, both structures, though they lie completely outside the normal judicial framework, contain a strong judicial element. Senior positions in the Socialist Public Prosecutor's office have been delegated from the regular judiciary, and senior judges have dominated the *Mahkamat al-Qiyam*. More important, the regular judiciary has achieved considerable authority over those in the two organs. Since 1984, the Supreme Judicial Council (and not any executive branch-dominated organ) has assigned members of the judicial corps to both bodies. Second, the politically restrictive laws of the late 1970s have been challenged in the courts, often on constitutional grounds, with some success. An ambitious and highly political Socialist Public Prosecutor would probably be reined in by the administrative courts and especially the Supreme Constitutional Court. Most important, however, has been the attitude of the regime. The renewed pursuit of political liberalization during the 1980s made the political duties of the Socialist Public Prosecutor seem as anachronistic as its title. Broad political repression of potential dissidents has been replaced by petty harassment and highly targeted repression (which involve the use of tools other than the Socialist Public Prosecutor). Indeed, by 1994 the actions of the courts and especially the development of other mechanisms had sufficiently gutted the political responsibilities of the Socialist Public Prosecutor that the government removed it from political work as a limited gesture to the opposition.

The Socialist Public Prosecutor has hardly been inert, however. In the economic sphere, its actions have been prominent on at least two occasions. In 1985 it moved against black market currency dealers, leading to a highly public battle with the minister of economy over economic policy. In the late 1980s it moved against unregulated investment companies (most of which claimed to have been acting in accordance with Islamic principles), alleging that some represented nothing more than pyramid schemes, offering large returns only by paying out of current deposits. The ensuing collapse of most of the investment companies left the Socialist Public Prosecutor in charge of obtaining and overseeing distribution of their assets. As a result of such activities, criticisms of the system grew not only from a legal but also a financial perspective.[49] In 1994, under parliamentary criticism that his office had grown both excessively powerful and inefficient, Socialist

---

[49] See, for example, Sana' Mustafa, "Funds Threatened by Storms," *al-Wafd*, June 18, 1990. See also "The Socialist Public Prosecutor Responds to *Ruz al-yusuf*," *Ruz al-yusuf*, April 3, 1995.

Public Prosecutor Jamal Shuman revealed that he was responsible for assets valued at 1.8 billion Egyptian pounds.[50]

The State Security Court system – and the Law of Emergency establishing it – have roots in very different conditions than the Socialist Public Prosecutor.[51] The Law of Emergency is a direct descendant of measures taken by the British during the occupation (see chapter 3). One of the major innovations of the post-1952 regime in emergency rule in Egypt was to introduce a new special set of courts to deal with security issues. The State Security Courts were established in 1958 to establish a more suitable structure for long-term emergency rule than the military courts (although the use of military courts was hardly terminated, as will be seen). The new courts became such a part of the judicial landscape of Egypt that the 1964 and 1971 constitutions contained an article providing for them.[52] And the measures taken in the name of national security since the Second World War are sufficiently broad that the State Security Courts have been given surprisingly wide competence. Cases involving key money and violations of price controls on basic commodities generally go to the State Security Courts on the argument that they involve economic and public security.

With the diverse nature of cases before the State Security Courts, the structure had split into two distinct systems by the 1970s. The first system forms part of the regular judicial structure, in that it is formed by members of the regular judiciary and largely follows its procedures and structures. Its jurisdiction reflects the idiosyncracies of past definitions of national security more than current political realities. The legal basis of what might be called the "regular" State Security Courts rests on a 1980 law that contains only vestigial elements of the origins of the system (for example, rights of appeal are slightly limited, and the president of the republic does have the option, not currently exercised, of appointing some military officers to judicial panels). In many ways, the regular State Security Courts are better seen as special sections of the regular judiciary with jurisdiction over specific cases than as an exceptional court system.

The second structure that bears the name State Security Court (often called the "Emergency Section" of that Court) deviates much more

[50] "The Socialist Public Prosecutor and the Clear Facts!" *al-Ahram*, May 6, 1994.

[51] 'Ubayd, *Istiqlal al-qada'*, provides a comprehensive analysis of the legal basis, structure, and procedure of the State Security Courts; see pp. 617–77. This section is largely based on 'Ubayd's work. Hill, *Mahkama!*, contains an abbreviated (and now dated) but excellent summary; see pp. 35–36.

[52] Article 171 states vaguely that "the law shall regulate the organization of the State Security Courts and prescribe their jurisdiction and the conditions to be fulfilled by those who occupy the office of judge in them."

from the composition and procedures of the regular court system. The president of the republic is given wide discretion in determining the competence, procedure, and composition of the Emergency Section. While in practice the president has used few of the powers available to him in determining the nature of the Emergency Section, the legislative basis exists for far more intrusive executive actions. In general, the Emergency Section has been composed of judges from the regular judiciary and has been very respectful of procedural guarantees for defendants. The jurisdiction of the Emergency Section – determined by the president during a state of emergency (which has been in effect with a few exceptions since the Second World War) – has been largely confined to cases of organized political violence. In only one respect has the president availed himself of the almost boundless authority available to him, but that exception is an important one. While no judicial appeal is possible from the verdict of the Emergency Section, the law gives the president the authority to approve verdicts of the courts. This is not simply a formality, because the president can lighten sentences, cancel judgments, and, if a cause is adduced, order a retrial. Thus an individual acquitted in one trial might simply find the verdict rejected by the president, with the result that an entirely new trial is ordered. (If an acquittal is issued in a retrial, the president is required to approve the judgment.) On two prominent occasions, the president has used his authority to overturn acquittals. One occasion, referred to above, involved those tried in political violence attributed to a Nasserist organization in the 1980s. The second occasion involved the trial of ʿUmar ʿAbd al-Rahman and a large number of his followers, accused of participating in political violence in a 1989 riot in al-Fayyum. When the Emergency Section acquitted all those involved in 1990, the president withheld any action. In 1993, in the midst of a wrangle with the United States over ʿAbd al-Rahman's alleged involvement in the World Trade Center bombing and his possible extradition to Egypt, President Mubarak ordered that he be tried again.[53]

In confronting political opposition, the Emergency Section in the 1980s and 1990s acted at times less like a terrifying weapon of the regime and more like a nuisance to executive authorities. Not simply did it issue acquittals in prominent cases, but it often took years to do so. Further, on several occasions the acquittals were coupled with accusations of torture by the security forces, as described above. Finally, trials in the Emergency Section sometimes involved inviting expert witnesses whose testimony was incendiary or embarrassing. For example, in the

---

[53] "Military Governor Orders Retrial of ʿAbd-al-Rahman," *al-Ahrar*, March 1, 1993.

trial of those accused of assassinating Faraj Fawda, Shaykh Muhammad al-Ghazali, a widely respected though controversial religious scholar, denounced those who opposed imposition of Islamic law. While he stopped just short of condoning Fawda's assassination, his testimony also implied that the government was operating outside the bounds of Islam (a claim that echoed the argument of radical Islamicist groups without endorsing their call for rebellion against such a government).[54]

It was perhaps displeasure with the delays, verdicts, and embarrassments associated with the Emergency Section of the State Security Court that led the government in the 1990s to turn to the most reliable exceptional court system – the military courts. Indeed, for a regime seeking to avoid the regular judiciary, the military courts represent an ideal structure in many ways. The 1966 law governing the military courts allows trials of civilians in military courts in one of two conditions: either they commit a crime on a military base or related to the armed forces, or the president of the republic decides to transfer jurisdiction over a crime to the military courts.[55] The first condition has been used to intimidate journalists and others associated with the opposition. In several incidents writers (including several prominent journalists) have been summoned for interrogation after writing articles that touch on military subjects; in general charges have been dropped or (more often) the investigation suspended after the point is made that journalists should exercise discretion.[56]

In 1992, however, after an upsurge in Islamicist violence, use of the military courts went beyond harassment. President Mubarak began using his authority to transfer cases involving Islamicists to the military courts. The appeal of these courts was clear: they could be extremely quick and they issued verdicts (usually convictions) which could not be appealed. After a conviction is issued, a defendant has only fifteen days to file a petition (and may only do so on the grounds that there was a violation or misapplication of the law or a crucial error in procedure) before the case is referred to the president for final consideration.[57] While military judges claim that they undergo specialized training and observe all the procedural safeguards necessary to guarantee the rights of

---

[54] See "al-Ghazali: No punishment in Islam for Anyone who Kills an Apostate," *al-Hayah*, June 23, 1993.

[55] See 'Ubayd, *Istiqlal al-qada'*, pp. 597 and 607 and the interview with the president of the High Military Court, "The President of the Military Judges, General 'Abd al-Ghaffar Hilal: The Military Courts are not Exceptional Courts." *al-Musawwar*, January 8, 1993.

[56] See Muna al-Taji, "Journalists, but They are Tried before the Supreme Military Court," *al-Sahafiyyun*, 13, May, 1991, pp. 212–17.

[57] See "Cairo: Approval of the Judgments in the Sidqi Assassination Attempt Case," *al-Hayah*, April 4, 1994.

the accused, critics claim that lack of appeal and short periods of appointment (two years, though renewable) insure that military judges will feel more responsible to the military hierarchy than to any judicial ethic.[58] In practice, the critics have much evidence in their favor: verdicts are quick, harsh, and frequently issued *in absentia* (meaning that no effective defense can be offered). Military courts are also less patient with appeals for additional time or complaints of torture.

The use of military courts to try civilians initially did not go unchallenged. When President Mubarak began to refer individual cases to the military courts, an administrative court ruled that the 1966 law had been interpreted too broadly. The law mentioned the president's authority to refer "crimes" to the military courts; critics argued that only whole classes of crimes could be transferred and therefore the president's decision to transfer individual cases (after the crime had been committed) was invalid. The government directed the Supreme Constitutional Court to issue an authoritative interpretation of the text; in January, 1993 it ruled in favor of the broadest interpretation of the president's authority.[59]

A second legal attack on the transfer of cases is theoretically much stronger but practically much more difficult to argue. The Egyptian constitution proclaims in article 68 that "every citizen has the right to refer to his natural judge." The precise meaning of "natural judge" is ambiguous at best, but leading legal authorities have argued that the trials of civilians before military courts, the absence of appeals, and the lack of independence of the military judiciary render the president's authority to transfer cases unconstitutional.[60] Yet while the Supreme Constitutional Court might be sympathetic with such an approach, the military courts claim, based on the 1966 law, that they alone have the right to determine their jurisdiction, making it unlikely that they would refer the constitutional issue to the Supreme Constitutional Court. (The 1992 ruling by the Court, while only an authoritative interpretation of statute, has also been misconstrued as an approval of the constitutionality of the military courts' jurisdiction over civilians.[61]) In a sense, the

[58] See 'Ubayd, *Istiqlal al-qada*' and "The President of the Military Judges," *al-Musawwar*, January 8, 1993, for a strong attack on, and a strong defense of, the military courts.

[59] "The High Constitutional Court Affirms the Right of the President of the Republic to Transfer any Crime to the Military Judiciary under a State of Emergency," *al-Ahram*, January 31, 1993.

[60] See 'Ubayd, *Istiqlal al-qada*' and al-Taji, "Journalists" for versions of this argument. One member of the Supreme Constitutional Court gave me a sympathetic version of the argument during a private meeting in June, 1991.

[61] In 1995, President Mubarak transferred the trial of scores of Muslim Brotherhood leaders to the military courts. The decision marked a departure not only in the number of civilians but also in the nature of the charges. The Muslim Brotherhood leaders were

military courts (and President Mubarak) are exploiting a gap in the competence of the Supreme Constitutional Court – it can only decide on cases that have been referred to it. Thus the use of military courts to avoid the regular judiciary seems both secure and effective.

Having successfully maintained channels of moving outside the normal judiciary, the regime has insured that the reemergence of liberal legality need not affect the most sensitive political cases (especially those which are regarded as posing an existential challenge to the regime). The harshness of the military courts, in this sense, has made possible the independence of the rest of the judiciary. Yet this explanation of the reemergence of liberal legality remains incomplete, because it risks overstating the opposition between the regime and the judiciary. The liberal legality of the judiciary is more harmonious with official ideology and practice than might initially appear.

## The uses and meaning of liberal legality in Egypt

The "rule of law" is a broad term but not an empty one; it has many possible shadings and connotations. What does it mean to Egypt's judiciary and to its executive authorities? Both Egypt's judges and its highest executive officials invoke the phrase in support of their visions of the proper role of courts and law in the country.

### *Judicial visions of the rule of law*

The best way to discover the meaning of the phrase to the country's judiciary is to examine the most developed, well-articulated, and unconstrained judicial visions of the rule of law. The first such public vision involves the National Conference on Justice, held in 1986 under

not charged with specific acts of political violence and terrorism but of undermining the political order and subverting the constitution. A number of prominent lawyers (some, like Ahmad al-Khawaja, normally hostile to Islamicists of any sort) volunteered to serve in their defense. Some filed a suit against President Mubarak in administrative court, claiming that the 1966 law's provision for trying civilians in military courts was unconstitutional. The administrative court referred the constitutional issue to the Supreme Constitutional Court, a move that the military courts had refused to take. As of this writing, the Court has issued no ruling. The case presents a difficult legal (and not simply political) dilemma to the Court. On the one hand, some members are clearly scandalized by the use of the military courts to suppress political dissent. On the other hand, the Supreme Court (the pliant predecessor of the Supreme Constitutional Court) issued a ruling in a similar case. Since Court rulings are final and authoritative, the Court must either honor the precedent or find a way around it. The legal conundrum combined with the political sensitivity of the case seems to account for the uncharacteristic procrastination of the Court.

the sponsorship of the Judges Club. The second involves the jurisprudence of the Supreme Constitutional Court. Far more than any other
judicial body, the Supreme Constitutional Court, by reason of its
structure, jurisdiction, and composition, has been able to develop and
pursue a consistent approach to the fundamental legal issues confronting
the country.

In April, 1986, the Egyptian judiciary achieved its greatest success in
directing the country's attention to legal matters. The Judges Club
invited leading lawyers, professors, intellectuals, and political leaders to
join with judges in discussing the Egyptian legal system. President
Mubarak spoke near the beginning of the conference, citing his respect
for the law, the judiciary, and legal institutions. With that background,
five committees were established, devoted to legislation, civil procedures, criminal procedures, judicial affairs, and administrative support
for the judiciary. The conference concluded by approving a bold
statement on the rule of law and a disparate collection of recommendations, some quite far-reaching. The general statement contained a clear
directive to the executive authorities to respect liberal legality, arguing
that it was the primary basis of political legitimacy:

The establishment of justice among the people is a mission of the ruler and a
trust imposed upon him. There is no path to the realization of justice without the
sovereignty of law. The sovereignty of law is not realized merely by the
submission of individuals to its texts or their being forcibly bound to its
judgments . . . but it means in the first place that law springs from the conscience
of the nation and expresses its desire truly and accurately and the authority
submits to its judgments and is the only basis of its legitimacy and legality in its
works.[62]

Without elaboration, the statement claimed that the judiciary "is prior to
the creation of the state itself," and that without the judiciary the law
degenerates into slogans and democratic life loses its basis.

In its specific recommendations, the conference concentrated on the
reunification of the Egyptian judiciary. The multiplication of exceptional
courts offends the professional sensibilities and the corporate interests of
the Egyptian judiciary; it is also portrayed as a violation of legal equality
when separate judicial structures have jurisdiction according to the
nature of the individuals involved and of the case itself. Accordingly, the
conference statement claimed in general that "the resort to exceptional

---

[62] The complete text of the statement was published in *al-Jumhuriyya*, April 26, 1986,
p. 1. While there was extensive press coverage of the conference, no other national
newspapers published the complete text of the final statement, though it is not clear
whether this was simply because of its length or due to political sensitivities regarding
some of the recommendations. All other quotations from the final statement are from
the version published in *al-Jumhuriyya*.

legislation, if it is prolonged, corrupts the nature of the people and shakes trust in the law and the system." Specifically, the conference demanded abolishing the Socialist Public Prosecutor, the *Mahkamat al-Qiyam*, the State Security Courts, and even the Supreme Constitutional Court (with its jurisdiction transferred to the *Mahkamat al-Naqd*). The law organizing the military courts was criticized for its provision for trying civilians. This set of recommendations demonstrates again how similar institutional changes can serve very different ends. Between 1883, when the National Courts were established, and 1949, when the Mixed Courts were abolished, the call for judicial unification was motivated by nationalist concerns. During the attempt to establish socialist legality in the 1960s, judicial unification was seen as an authoritarian measure. Over the past two decades it has become a liberal rallying cry.

Another series of recommendations concerned procedural and administrative improvement to facilitate the efficiency of litigation. The committee on legislation found itself the locus of a heated debate on the application of *shari'a* law; the proponents of the *shari'a* managed to achieve a vague statement in the final document calling for the application of *shari'a* law in accordance with article 2 of the Egyptian constitution.[63]

The legality endorsed by Egyptian judges (and their guests) in the conference thus is based explicitly on the rule of law. This means not only that the executive authorities themselves are bound by legal procedure, but also that all judicial authority is exercised by a single judicial structure. Deviations from these principles throw the legitimacy of the political order in doubt, and thus it is in the interest as well as the responsibility of the executive authorities to construct the necessary institutional arrangements and abolish those which detract from an independent, unified judiciary. Defense of political and property rights, while very much the business of the courts, do not merit detailed consideration in the conference recommendations. More concerned with procedural and structural issues, the Egyptian judiciary seems content to leave the content of legislation to the legislature (except when it is connected with either procedural or constitutional issues). The rule of law as envisioned by judges focuses on achieving fairness and equity in application of the law much more than it focuses on making good law.

---

[63] The statement was strong enough to satisfy *shari'a* proponents, but it was sufficiently general (and couched in constitutional language) to serve as a compromise measure. For some details on the debate in the legislative committee, see Ahmad 'Abd Allah, "Justice in the Prisoner's Dock!" *Al-Ahali*, May 12, 1986.

As will be seen, this is a vision of the rule of law that is largely palatable to executive authorities.

The Supreme Constitutional Court, however, has departed from this traditional judicial focus to advance a substantive, and not simply procedural, view of the rule of law. When its decisions over its first decade and a half are taken together, a vision emerges of an admittedly political jurisprudence limiting executive (and legislative) authority and guaranteeing political rights and private property.[64] Two features of the Court have allowed it to venture beyond the traditional positivism of the Egyptian judiciary in a coherent way. First, the mandate of the Court to render authoritative rulings on constitutional issues compels a more adventurous interpretive role than is usual for Egyptian courts, because of the vagueness (which often seems intentional) and contradictions contained in the 1971 constitution. (As mentioned above, one of the chief characteristics of the constitution is to combine vague liberal language on rights and freedoms with specific, often authoritarian, language empowering the executive.) Working with such a text it becomes virtually impossible to claim that the Court is simply mechanically applying a self-evident text. Second, the small size of the Court and its authority to select its own members allows it to pursue its mandate in a fairly coherent manner.

The current president of the Court, 'Awad al-Murr, is frank on his conception of the Court's mission with regard to human rights:

The struggle for human rights will therefore never come to an end, as long as encroachments persist through systematic state actions which relinquish or impair prescribed constitutional guarantees. Both for the protection of political and civil rights, and for the protection of the right of property, the Egyptian Supreme Constitutional Court has covered some ground in the pursuit of human rights and dignity in the past decade. It shall, God willing, continue to perform in the future the role prescribed to it by the Constitution.[65]

With some exceptions, the Court has exercised its discretion in a manner favorable to civil and political rights: provisions related to executive authority have been interpreted fairly narrowly and guarantees of equal opportunity and individual rights have been interpreted fairly liberally. Al-Murr describes the Court's general principle: "restrictions on political rights which are neither mandated by the nature of a given right nor by the requirement of its exercises shall not stand."[66] An

---

[64] One member of the Court admitted to me in a personal conversation that "every constitutional case is political." This contrasts strongly with the consistent public stand of the regular judiciary that Egyptian judges operate outside of politics.

[65] El-Morr, "The Supreme Constitutional Court," p. 260.

[66] El-Morr, "The Supreme Constitutional Court," p. 232.

example of the Court's ambitious jurisprudence is its approach to international treaties and declarations related to human rights. The Supreme Court, the predecessor to the Supreme Constitutional Court, ruled in 1975 that the United Nations Declaration on Human Rights is not a treaty (but merely a non-binding recommendation) and, even if it were, treaties have the force only of legislative texts and can therefore be limited by subsequent or more specific legislation. The Supreme Constitutional Court has not challenged this argument directly, but it has insinuated the text of international human rights documents into Egyptian constitutional law by using them as aids in interpreting vague constitutional guarantees. In striking down an article in the Customs Law that punished as smugglers those who simply could not produce appropriate documentation that duties were paid, the Court ruled that this violated the presumption of innocence, guaranteed in the constitution and explicated in international documents.[67]

The Court has been similarly expansive in its interpretations of individual property rights. Al-Murr has written of the Court's aim to transform "abstract constitutional commands into concrete restrictions which would make real the conceived or anticipated protection of human rights, particularly in the field of economic rights which had long been ignored or avoided."[68] With a few exceptions (such as the right to form and join trade unions) most of the economic rights the Court has dealt with involve private property. Despite some recent modifications, much of the Nasserist legislation regarding urban and rural real estate remains in force, allowing the executive strong rights to confiscate property and giving renters very strong positions. The Court has acted to restrict the prerogatives of both the executive and (to a lesser extent) renters, adducing a general right to private property not simply in the 1971 constitution, but in Egyptian constitutional tradition. While admitting a legislative right to regulate property, al-Murr writes:

All Egyptian Constitutions were anxious to establish the principle of the preservation of property except for limitations specifically provided for constitutionally. Safeguards are established to maintain the performance of the social function of property in service of the national economy. This qualified protection was established with a view to the fact that the ingredients of private property are rooted in an individual's activities, which constitute the machinery for progress and the source of public wealth.[69]

[67] This passage is based on Nosseir, "The Supreme Constitutional Court," pp. 45–50.

[68] 'Awad al-Murr, "Human Rights in the Constitutional Systems of Islamic Countries," *Cairo University Law Review*, 1, 1988, p. 7; quoted in Adel Omar Sherif, "The Supreme Constitutional Court in the Egyptian Judicial System," unpublished paper, Chicago, 1992, p. 12.

[69] El-Morr, "The Supreme Constitutional Court," p. 256.

Government confiscations without compensation or without allowing resort to the courts has been struck down, as has a law allowing landlords only one-half of the proceeds when a renter of commercial property sells his rights to a new renter.[70]

In one important respect, however, the Supreme Constitutional Court has been deferential to the executive. The idea of "acts of sovereignty" has inhibited the Court – though not at all predictably – in restricting some actions of the executive. ʿAbd al-Rahman Nusayr, a vice-president of the Court, explains:

The general guidance given by the court in this concern is that such political questions (or acts of sovereignty) are closely interrelated with the sovereignty of the State internally and externally, and encompass, by their nature, profound political considerations which justify giving the legislative or executive branches full discretionary power in order to realize the security and well-being of the country. As a result, this category of political questions (or acts of sovereignty) may not be subjected to judicial control, neither on its constitutionality nor its legality. In addition, the judiciary does not have available to it the necessary information to control such questions or acts. Furthermore, it is not appropriate to discuss these political questions or acts of sovereignty publicly in court sessions.[71]

The Court has accepted the principle sparingly. Nusayr admits "neither in its earlier or in its recent decisions has the court given precise criteria for both acts of sovereignty and/or political questions, preferring to give itself, case-by-case, the power to determine whether or not the challenged law is considered an act of sovereignty or a political question."[72] While rejecting several claims that certain state actions were acts of sovereignty, the Court has accepted the idea on at least two occasions.[73]

Thus, the concentration of the regular judiciary on procedural rather than substantive issues of law, and the Supreme Constitutional Court's acceptance of the principle of acts of sovereignty have helped to make judicial conceptions on the rule of law more palatable to the regime. But the extent of congruence between executive and judicial conceptions of the rule of law is still more extensive and profound than this suggests.

---

[70] On property rights generally, see el-Morr, "The Supreme Constitutional Court," pp. 246–59. On the case of renters, see Nosseir, "The Supreme Constitutional Court," pp. 37–38.

[71] Nosseir, "The Supreme Constitutional Court," p. 13.

[72] Nosseir, "The Supreme Constitutional Court," p. 12.

[73] Nosseir, "The Supreme Constitutional Court," p. 13, mentions two instances in which the Court accepted the idea of "acts of sovereignty." The first involved a treaty among Arab states on the establishment of Arab armies; the second involved the presidential decision to hold a referendum on dissolving the parliament (after the Court had overturned the electoral law in 1990).

*Executive conceptions of the rule of law*

Centralizing and even authoritarian regimes have little objection to (and much use for) strong courts and legal structures in most circumstances. The Egyptian system, with its hierarchical courts, positivist orientation, and reliance on state-codified law has enforced executive will fairly faithfully for over a century. With the legislative authority clearly (if at times unofficially) under executive domination, it would be surprising if matters were otherwise. It is only in exceptional (generally political) cases that the verdicts of an independent judiciary might regularly clash with executive desires, and Egypt's executive authorities have dealt with such cases by constructing exceptional courts on several occasions.

Given this general compatibility between the executive and judicial branches, how can the clash of 1969 be explained? Part of the explanation lies within the executive branch itself, where legal desires may not be so clearly expressed, especially in a sprawling bureaucracy containing competing interests and pursuing different (sometimes contradictory) policies. It was partly the incoherence of the executive branch that led advocates of socialist transformation in Egypt to begin to look to the judiciary as a potential ally, though only if it was itself transformed and inculcated with a political (and socialist) conscious-ness. Yet such advocates had achieved nothing until 1968 when judges began to confront them openly. At that point judicial autonomy began to be perceived as a threat not because of specific decisions but because of a general political and ideological orientation deemed excessively independent of the regime.

This does not imply that judicial notions of the rule of law have no content, only that they are more easily accommodated than may initially appear. With some important exceptions – regarding important political cases and restrictions on executive action – Egyptian regimes have gone far in realizing judicial conceptions of liberal legality. What is remarkable in recent years is how far the regime has limited these exceptions. Important political cases are generally (though not exclusively) tried in the regular courts, and the courts (particularly the Supreme Constitu-tional Court) have been allowed to impose restrictions on executive action.

This can partly be explained by an official ideology which increasingly (since 1971) cites liberal conceptions of the rule of law in support for its legitimacy. During the early 1970s, as some of the authoritarian measures taken under 'Abd al-Nasir were reversed, Egyptian leaders (especially President Sadat) spoke of the rule of law and of a state of institutions (as opposed to arbitrary rule). While the last few years (and especially the last month) of Sadat's presidency saw a renewed imposition of heavy-handed measures to suppress dissent, rhetorical commitment to the rule of law did not disappear. In the 1980s, a limited but genuine emergence of democratic practices became a theme in many of the major statements and speeches in which the basic contours of the regime and its policies were defended and elaborated. Since that time, judicial themes have become a staple of presidential (and prime ministerial) speech-making. Respect and praise for the judiciary are combined with vaunting of the material and institutional measures taken to meet judges' independence and requirements. After returning from Ethiopia after an attempt on his life in 1995, the president's praise of the judiciary became almost hyperbolic. The judicial leadership, one of the first groups to meet with Mubarak after his return, was told "Before the members of the judiciary I get tongue-tied out of respect for the pillars of justice, the bedrock of democracy. Members of the judiciary: I thank you with all my heart. I know of your feelings for me. I share the same feelings and appreciation."[74] In a more detailed exposition in 1986, during a speech at the National Conference on Justice, Mubarak stated:

If democracy is the first pillar of government then there is no democracy without justice and no justice without a law giving everybody his right and defining for every one of us duties and obligations on the basis of equality among citizens and non-discrimination between one group and another, no matter how strong.

I share with my countrymen in their esteem for the Egyptian judiciary and its men and I consider them among the vanguards of the working forces to secure the society and provide stability to its movement and make possible realizing progress in its march of reform . . .

For that reason I cannot imagine the existence of enmity between the judicial authority and the other institutions of government because we all strive to realize the same goals. We govern according to the texts of the constitution and the dictates of the law which is applied on the ruler and the ruled equally, and the strong submit to it before the weak and the rich and the poor without difference or discrimination.

It is not permitted for any authority to intervene in cases or in the affairs of justice . . .

I committed since the beginning of my assumption of responsibility to wait for the judgment of the judiciary in all matters which by their nature are appropriate for it.

I guarantee the respect of all institutions of state to the judgments of the court in letter and spirit. I tell you frankly that there were some important questions in which it was possible for the president of the state to decide according to his constitutional prerogatives, but I preferred not to issue a decision because [the

---

[74] The remarks were reported in FBIS Daily Report, Near East and South Asia, FBIS-NES-95-126, June 30, 1995, p. 9.

matter] was in front of the judiciary. It is necessary for the president of the state to wait for the rule of the judiciary and the word of justice and right.[75]

On some occasions members of the judiciary have returned the favor: in 1988 the president of the *Mahkamat al-Naqd* claimed that under Mubarak the rule of law and the independence of the judiciary had changed from slogans into a basis for action.[76]

It remains to be seen whether rulers' continued citation of the rule of law enhances the legitimacy of the regime, but there can be no doubt that leading political figures do rely on their respect for the judiciary in their public efforts to justify the political system. Yet the congruence between the judiciary and the executive leadership, though incomplete, rests not only on public efforts at legitimation but also on complementary visions on the proper role of legal institutions and the judiciary.

The battles over exceptional courts and institutional guarantees of independence, though quite real and important, obscure the degree to which the Egyptian judges perceive themselves and act as agents of the state. As suspicious as they may sometimes be of executive influence, Egyptian judges tend not to behave as freestanding actors mediating between that state and the society or between different social actors, but as enforcers of state policy, no matter how impartially and principled. Indeed, in one sense judges are responsible not only to the law and their own consciences but also to each other. The battles over the independence of the judiciary have largely concerned institutional autonomy of the judiciary as a corporate entity – with the result that it makes much more sense in Egypt to speak of the independence of the judiciary rather than the independence of individual judges. While judges may have full authority to reach their own decisions, the frequency of multiple-judge panels, extensive rights of appeal, and judicial control over matters of appointments and promotion combine to give the judiciary a very strong sense of corporate identity. And the judiciary as a body shows every willingness to distance itself from the executive but little interest or willingness to distance itself from the state. The acceptance, however limited, of the concept of "acts of sovereignty" is itself evidence of this sense of state. Another indication is the language generally used to justify judicial independence and liberal jurisprudence. Individual rights are not only (or even primarily) cited as ends in themselves or self-evident truths, nor is the rule of law always its own justification. Instead, Egyptian judges will often argue in terms of the social and political

---

[75] The text of the speech is printed in *al-Ahram*, April 21, 1986.
[76] *Al-Ahram*, July 5, 1988, p. 6. For another example, see Dr. Muhammad Majdi Marajan (president of the Cairo Court of Appeals), "Mubarak . . . and the Judiciary," *al-Ahram*, February 1, 1994.

benefits accruing from judicial independence and observance of individual social and political rights. The National Conference on Justice, for instance, described emergency measures as corrupting because they ultimately undermine popular support for the political order.[77] 'Awad al-Murr, in a presentation of the achievements of the Supreme Constitutional Court in the field of human rights, wrote "Human rights exercise a direct impact on the legality and stability of governments."[78]

Indeed, Egyptian judges can quickly cast aside their liberal principles when their corporate honor or professional interests are at stake. For them law is a matter to be left to professionals; ordinary citizens should not only be barred from deciding cases but also prohibited from discussing them (even after a verdict).[79] Legal matters should be restricted to those with the proper training and state-granted authority.

Perhaps the most subtle expression of this sense of state relates to the application of *shari'a* law. While many judges are devout Muslims, and while the National Conference on Justice called for the application of the *shari'a* in accordance with the constitution, the judiciary as a corporate body has upheld the role of state-legislated positive law at almost every opportunity. The most serious challenge to positive law has been based on the second article of the Egyptian constitution, which reads (as amended in 1980) that "the principles of the Islamic *shari'a* are the principal source of legislation." While far from converting the Egyptian legal system to one largely based on *shari'a*, the amendment would seem to narrow the realm for positive legislation by barring any law clearly incongruent with the *shari'a*. (The most prominent areas thus thrown into doubt included criminal penalties, personal status, and commercial interest.) A few lower-court judges used this text to justify rulings that contradicted existing legislation.[80] Yet the Supreme Constitutional Court, while stopping short of robbing the amendment of all its meaning, has endorsed interpretations that not only rescue positive legislation but specifically endorse the idea that the legislative authority requires broad discretion. In a key ruling in 1985, the Court held that the amendment would only apply to laws enacted by the parliament subsequent to the 1980 amendment; all pre-1980 legislation could be

---

[77] See the final statement as printed in *al-Jumhuriyya*, April 26, 1986, p. 1.

[78] El-Morr, "Supreme Constitutional Court," p. 260.

[79] See the series of comments by judges in Mahanna Anwar, "When is it Permissible to Comment on Judicial Rulings?" *Uktubir*, January 31, 1993. While there is disagreement about whether public discussion of a verdict by non-experts is illegal, there is no quarrel with the idea that it is unethical and undesirable. Similarly, discussions with judges on the American legal system often lead to comments on the inappropriateness of the jury system, in which non-professionals are given the power to render verdicts.

[80] See Faraj Fawda, "It is Truly a Strange Resignation," *al-Ahram*, October 3, 1985.

aligned with *shari'a* only by fresh parliamentary action.[81] More recently, in 1993, wide discretion was granted to the legislature even after the 1980 amendment. The Court argued that the *shari'a* can be divided between fixed principles (which must be observed) and rules subject to contestable and changeable rules (in which the legislature may exercise its discretion according to changing needs and conditions).[82] By subscribing to an unabashedly modernist view of the *shari'a*, the Court has not simply upheld existing legislation. Also preserved was a vision of what constitutes law: the Court has clearly supported the general view within the Egyptian judiciary that the source of law is the state. Few judges would question the viability or legitimacy of the *shari'a*, but most would view it as a body of law that informs (and places general restrictions on) positive law, as expressed in clear legislative texts. The second article of the Egyptian constitution, then, has not occasioned the imposition of a sharply narrowed field for positive legislation in Egypt. Rather than restricting the state to enforcing conceptions of justice whose origins precede the state, law in Egypt continues to enable the state to shape and guide the society. Executive authorities, while often annoyed by the exercise of judicial power, have no quarrel with such a vision of law.

## Rule of law, liberalism, and authoritarianism

We may now return directly to the first of the three questions posed by this study: why have Egypt's political leaders constructed and sustained an independent and European-style judicial system over the last century? The examination of Egyptian judicial history in the past three chapters affirms a central assumption that underlies the question: the judicial system was a conscious creation of the political leadership in the late nineteenth century; it has been both sustained and modified by successive generations of political leaders. The degree of judicial independence has varied (and in 1969 briefly but systematically challenged), but on no occasion has it been negligible. During two periods – the years prior to the construction of an authoritarian political order in the mid-1950s and the years since the mid-1980s – judicial independence has been sufficient to enable the courts to construct real restrictions on executive authority. Thus the central puzzle of Egyptian

---

[81] See Enid Hill, "Al-Sanhuri and Islamic Law," *Cairo Papers in Social Science*, 10 (1), 1987, pp. 126–27.

[82] See Hatem Aly Labib Gabr, "The Interpretation of Article Two of the Egyptian Constitution as Envisaged by the Supreme Constitutional Court," unpublished manuscript, April 1994.

judicial development is why Egypt's rulers would seem to have tied their own hands. The three approaches adduced in chapter 1 – imposed law, liberal legality, and law as domination – vary greatly in their helpfulness in solving this puzzle.

Imposed law is of limited use in answering the question. The Egyptian judicial system came under strong European influence at the beginning, but its formation and especially its continued existence were in no way imposed. Legal reform was initiated before European penetration was acutely felt, and, as shown in chapter 2, the key periods in legal reform hardly coincided with the height of imperial penetration. The construction of the Mixed Courts and the decision to construct the National Courts both predated the British occupation of 1882. Both survived the occupation despite, and not because of, the British presence. The Mixed Courts were seen as a bastion of non-British foreign influence; British officials denounced the National Courts as culturally inappropriate and often excessively nationalistic. The National Courts were also held to foster litigiousness in civil cases while they simultaneously protected criminal elements with their legalistic judicial scruples. The judicial system of the late nineteenth century certainly betrays European influence, but it was constructed as much to contain imperialism as to enforce it; in some ways its existence was even entirely independent of imperialism. And once created, the system was sustained (and in many ways strengthened) by governments which proclaimed resistance to imperialism as a primary mission. The Wafd tolerated the Mixed Courts as a temporary curb on British influence; the Nasserist regime reined in judicial independence but acted to further the authority and centralization of the system in other ways.

If the system was not imposed, neither was it solely a domestic attempt to foster liberal legality in Egypt. To be sure, liberal ideas about judicial independence, individual rights, and private property have been influential at times. Unsurprisingly, such liberal ideas have been given freest rein at times of official tolerance for other liberal tendencies, such as pluralism and free expression. The National Courts were founded partly on liberal principles, and the 1940s saw further institutionalization, especially of judicial independence and individual rights. Since the early 1980s ideologies predicated on the rule of law have played a far greater role both within the judiciary and among the senior political leadership. Especially recently, the autonomy allowed the courts has generally followed closely the autonomy granted non-official actors. Yet at no time has any conception of the rule of law been used in an attempt to transform the basic nature of the regime. Liberal legality as understood and pursued in Egypt has generally been consistent with the fundamental interests of the executive authorities. Even authoritarian regimes have managed to work with (or around) the judiciary on most occasions.

Those who view law as predominantly a form of domination offer the most help in understanding Egyptian judicial development. Yet one of the strongest themes that emerges in writings from this perspective – the role that law plays in legitimating a prevailing order – does not seem as helpful in the Egyptian context. This is partly because, as will be seen, there is little evidence that the Egyptian legal system has ever played any legitimating role in the eyes of most Egyptians (whose view of legal institutions has been extremely instrumentalist). If the Egyptian legal system legitimates the prevailing order, it probably does so chiefly in the eyes of the political elite. That is, the legal order may provide a sense of self-justification to Egypt's political leadership even if it does not justify the leadership in the eyes of the remainder of the population. Even here, however, Egyptians who argue that the prevailing order is legitimate because the law operates in a fair and just manner have been far from dominant. Since the presidency of Anwar al-Sadat such claims have increased in frequency and forcefulness, but they have been used just as much to call the regime to account (for failing to live up to its proclaimed principles) as to justify it.

The relationship of law to domination and authority is generally more political than ideological in nature. The legal order constructed in the late nineteenth century augmented the authority of the central state even as it placed (sometimes feeble) limitations on specific individuals and office holders. Legislation became the exclusive domain of the state. The French system, with its centralized and hierarchical courts and its positivist orientation, insured that Egyptian courts would enforce state-mandated law as faithfully as possible. Egyptian rulers, just as much as Egyptian citizens, can take a very instrumentalist view of the courts and of law in general. Even when it has been fairly independent, the Egyptian judiciary has never been worse than annoying to the country's political leadership; far more often (even at the present) it serves their ends.

Egypt's legal system has been used as a conscious model throughout the Arab world. Some of the most faithful adoptions of Egyptian practices and institutions have occurred in the Arab states of the Gulf. Direct British intrusions, fears of Egyptian political domination, and fealty to Islamic authenticity make the extent of Egyptian influence surprising. Why did the Gulf states build the legal systems that they did? In the next two chapters we will consider if the explanation developed here for the evolution of the Egyptian system obtains for these states as well.

# 5    Legal reform in the Arab states of the Gulf

In the Arab states of the Gulf, legal reform took place in a very different international and domestic setting from that prevailing in Egypt over the past century.[1] The imperial influence was greater (thus the likelihood of imposed law should have increased). Additionally, the forces for liberal legality were weaker. Yet if the historical experience of Egypt over the past century is any guide, the adoption of European-style legal systems – and legal reform more generally – cannot be explained primarily in terms of imperial imposition or liberal legality. While imperialism was hardly irrelevant to the Egyptian experience, the European presence at most set the context for a series of far-reaching reforms that was pursued for independent reasons by an ambitious, centralizing Egyptian political elite. And while the system adopted had several characteristics of liberal legality, it could also be accommodated to a variety of political systems. To be sure, the lawyers and judges of Egypt's National Courts were always one of the strongest forces advocating liberal legality, but they also posed few obstacles to (and occasionally have facilitated) unchecked executive authority.

One would expect that the Arab states of the Gulf would have been both more susceptible to imperial pressure and more suspicious of institutions associated with liberal legality. The British presence excited less nationalist opposition (with the possible exception of Bahrain) and came at a time when the administrative structure was far more rudimentary than in Egypt. And the regimes of the Gulf have been unabashedly autocratic; with the exception of short periods in Bahrain and much longer periods in Kuwait, liberal democratic institutions and practices have generally not even existed on a nominal level. Thus the field was much more open to imperial influence, though much less open to institutions associated with liberal legality. Had imperialism or liberalism been the paramount forces for legal reform in the Arab world,

[1] The countries covered in this and the following chapter are Bahrain, the United Arab Emirates (formerly the Trucial States), Kuwait, and Qatar.

129

Gulf systems should have been more British and less liberal in inspiration.

In fact the historical experience of the Arab states of the Gulf demonstrates that the lessons of the Egyptian experience are of more general applicability. Legal reform first and foremost served state-building purposes; imperialism and liberalism were at best of secondary importance. Even with more favorable terrain for imposed law, the British failed in their attempt to construct Gulf legal systems on an Anglo-Saxon rather than an Egyptian (and French) model, largely because of decisions made within the local political systems. As in Egypt, autocratic regimes have increasingly operated in a legalistic manner, able to bend the institutions of liberal legality to serve non-liberal ends. Efforts have occurred (in Bahrain in the 1950s and in Kuwait over the past decade) to use the legal system to liberal ends; such efforts have not succeeded.

Prior to the establishment of the permanent British presence in the nineteenth century, the Arab societies of the Gulf had only rudimentary administrative structures. The paucity of written records makes it difficult to describe the judicial and legal structure in all but the vaguest terms. While the view is widespread in the region that *Shari'a* Courts existed and exercised general jurisdiction, the reality was probably more complicated.[2] Four sets of courts operated. First, the courts of general jurisdiction were most likely the rulers' courts; important disputes would be submitted to the ruler, who issued judgments according to custom (*'urf*, perhaps informed by or consistent with – but formulated largely outside of – the *shari'a*). Second, tribal populations would have submitted disputes to tribal leaders. Third, merchants and artisans had courts and arbitration committees to resolve disputes according to their own customs. Finally, *Shari'a* Courts operated, especially in matters of personal status. Only the *Shari'a* Courts had a well-defined and written body of law and a semblance of fixed procedure. Their importance probably increased in some areas (especially Qatar) under the influence

---

[2] This view of the historical role of *shari'a* courts is often – though not exclusively – adduced by those who see the *shari'a* as the only legitimate basis for the legal system of an Islamic society. It is particularly widespread in Qatar, a country where documentation on the political legal system prior to the twentieth century (and even for the first half of the century) is extremely sparse. 'Abd al-'Aziz al-Khulayfi, the current vice-president of the *Shari'a* Courts in Qatar (and a former judge on the civil courts) claims that the *Shari'a* Courts were the primary (if not the sole) courts in Qatar from the earliest days of Islam until 1971 (personal interview, Doha, December 1994; the claim was also made in a 1994 meeting with Qatari law students). In Qatar the claim is rarely contested. See, for instance, Yusuf Muhammad 'Ubaydan, *Ma'alim al-nizam al-siyasi al-mu'asir fi qatar* (The features of the contemporary political system in Qatar) (n.p., 1984), p. 256.

of the Wahhabi movement and with the growth in the size and political complexity of the societies (and the consequent demand for specialized courts as opposed to the informality of rulers' tribunals).[3]

In the twentieth century, two important changes were introduced in the Gulf states. First, Great Britain successfully asserted jurisdiction over non-Muslim foreigners and authority to legislate for them. Second, a large degree of formality, hierarchy, and codification was brought to the preexisting legal systems. As part of this process, tribal and customary procedures either disappeared or lost authority. *Shari'a* Courts were not totally immune from this process; indeed, in some places (including Kuwait) they eventually fell victim to it. The result was that shortly before (or sometimes shortly after) independence, the states of the Gulf had written codes, fixed legislative processes, and formalized courts, largely with written procedures and well-defined jurisdiction.

To what extent were the legal systems that resulted a product of British imposition or influence? And why was the dominant source for both legislation and court structure neither Britain nor the *shari'a* but Egypt? The history of judicial and legal development in the Arab states of the Gulf in the period before independence consists largely of a British attempt to develop local legal systems with mixed results, and a separate (though not always unrelated) indigenous movement to build a centralized and hierarchical court system based on codified law.

### The assertion of British jurisdiction and the attempt to develop and anglicize Gulf law

In the nineteenth and early twentieth centuries, the Arab states of the Gulf all reached arrangements with Great Britain that ceded control over foreign affairs and defense in return for British protection. Nothing in the various agreements indicated that they affected jurisdiction. Still, British mistrust of local legal systems led them to induce local rulers to make a series of pledges granting authority over most foreigners to

---

[3] The investigation of pre-imperial law and courts is most developed for Kuwait. See 'Adil al-Tabataba'i, *Al-nizam al-dusturi fi al-kuwayt* (The Constitutional System in Kuwait) (Kuwait: n.p., 1994), pp. 243–62; 'Uthman 'Abd al-Malik al-Salih, *Al-nizam al-dusturi wa-l-mu'assasat al-siyasiyya fi al-kuwayt* (The Constitutional System and Political Institutions in Kuwait) (Kuwait: Kuwait Times Press, 1989), pp. 40–89; and "Lamha hawla tatawwur al-qada' fi al-kuwayt" (A Glimpse at the Development of the Judiciary in Kuwait), *al-Ra'y al-'Amm*, February 7, 1994. A. Nizar Hamzeh contends that in Qatar most disputes were settled according to tribal law until the Wahhabi movement made the *shari'a* supreme. While plausible, there is no documentation for the claim. See A. Nizar Hamzeh, "Qatar: The Duality of the Legal System," *Middle Eastern Studies*, 30 (1), January 1994, p. 79.

British-administered courts. The origins of British jurisdiction differed in each state, but in no case was the matter seen as critical for either side.

Bahrain preceded other Gulf states in assenting to British jurisdiction; a treaty signed in 1861 stipulated that "all offenses which (British subjects of every denomination) may commit, or which may be committed against them, shall be reserved for the decision of the British Resident, provided that the British Agent located at Bahrain shall fail to adjust them satisfactorily."[4] (At the time the British resident, the top political official in the Gulf, was based in Bushire in Iran; the British were represented locally by a political agent. In 1946 the residency was transferred from Bushire to Bahrain.) In 1909 the ruler of Bahrain asked the British to assume jurisdiction in cases involving foreigners and that joint courts, consisting of British and local judges, be established for mixed cases (those involving subjects of both systems). While there was some subsequent disagreement about defining both foreigners and mixed cases, these were resolved amicably.[5] Indeed, Bahrain's rulers were consistently the most open to British legal influence.

In Kuwait, the agreement establishing British dominance in defense and foreign affairs (but omitting any mention of internal politics) was signed in 1899. The status of Kuwait was still contested, however, especially because the Ottoman Empire considered Kuwait part of its territory. After the First World War and consequent Ottoman collapse, the fate of former Ottoman territories was the subject of extended international negotiations. Thus, while the British considered an attempt to assert jurisdiction over its citizens (and perhaps others) as early as 1911, uncertainty over Kuwait's status discouraged them from pursuing the matter for ten years. When the matter was finally officially raised in 1921, the amir of Kuwait indicated that he had no objection to the British government assuming jurisdiction over its own citizens and other Europeans (though ceding jurisdiction over citizens of non-Christian states was less palatable to the amir). It was not until 1925 that the British presented a draft Order in Council establishing British jurisdiction to the amir, Ahmad al-Jabir Al Sabah, which he ambivalently accepted. The Order in Council allowed British jurisdiction only over citizens of governments that had accepted it, but the British government did not approach any other government to attain its assent to British jurisdiction over its citizens in Kuwait. In 1934 the British addressed this lacuna by obtaining the amir's agreement to transfer jurisdiction over

---

[4] See Annex IV in "Report on a visit by the Legal Advisor to the Foreign Office to the Persian Gulf States," June 6, 1952, FO 371/EA 14./6.

[5] *Ibid.*

citizens of non-Muslim states to the British without obtaining the permission of those states.[6]

In Qatar the British assertion of jurisdiction came as part of bargaining over the oil concession in 1935. Short of funds and concerned about the continuation of his family's rule, Shaykh 'Abd Allah ibn Qasim Al Thani made an explicit bargain with the British.[7] He agreed that "disputes between British subjects, British protected subjects, and the subjects of non-Muslim foreign powers should be settled by the nearest office of the High British Government i.e., the Political Agent, Bahrain, or his representative," and that a joint court would be established to adjudicate disputes between Qatari and British citizens. The agreement came "on the condition that the Government undertake to give their full support to me and to my heir apparent, my son Hamad, when he succeeds me and that they do acknowledge him as my heir apparent and support him when he succeeds me."[8] The joint court never came into operation, however, and it was not until the 1950s that any cases were brought to the British court under the agreement.[9] By that time a political agency had been opened in Qatar so that cases were tried in Doha rather than referred to Bahrain as anticipated in the original agreement.

While the relationship between the British government and the rulers of the Trucial States (currently the United Arab Emirates) was of longer standing than its relationship with the Al Sabah family of Kuwait or the Al Thani family of Qatar, it was not until 1945 that the British established jurisdiction over British citizens and other foreigners there. While the treaty between the British and the local rulers came into force in 1853, the British interest in the area was purely strategic and unconcerned with internal matters until the prospect of oil concessions arose in the twentieth century.[10]

Despite the different dates and circumstances of the British assumption of jurisdiction, the agreements shared two features. First, there was a subtle difference between the perceptions held by local rulers and the British concerning the rationale for ceding jurisdiction. For local rulers, the *shari'a*, even when not fully implemented, retained its full legitimacy

---

[6] See "H.M.G.'s Jurisdiction in Kuwait," enclosure no. 1 in Pelly to Burrows, January 9, 1954, FO 371/EA 1643/1.

[7] The political background to the agreement is explained in Hassan Mohammad Abdulla Saleh, *Labor, Nationalism and Imperialism in Eastern Arabia: Britain, the Shaikhs and the Gulf Oil Workers in Bahrain, Kuwait and Qatar, 1932–1956*, Ph.D. dissertation, University of Michigan, 1991, p. 56.

[8] "Translation of letter No. 7/54 dated the 14th Muharram 1354," included in Burrows to Eden, April 3, 1954, FO 371/EA 15413.

[9] Haines to Home, April 14, 1961, FO 371/B 14./4.

[10] H. Y. Mudawi, "Recommendations on the Legal System in the State of Dubai Trucial States," January 8, 1961, FO 371/B 1644/3.

for Muslims; non-Muslims were always to be governed at least in part according to their own law. Thus the view that the law applied depended on an individual's religion was fully acceptable (even where the arrangements agreed to differed from those supported by Islamic jurisprudence). The rulers had no serious objections to allowing a Christian power (which already exercised control over defense and foreign affairs) assume jurisdiction over Christians, yet they generally insisted on retaining jurisdiction over Muslims. For the British, their assumption of jurisdiction was predicated not on any religious basis but on the inadequacy of local courts. Local legal systems inspired little confidence because they were increasingly based on the *shari'a* (which most British officials denigrated as fossilized and unsuitable for modern conditions), had little or no mechanism for legislation, and had neither written procedures (and often no written records or registers) nor many procedural guarantees.

The difference in perspectives explains some of the conflicts that developed between local rulers and the British. One ambiguity was whether British jurisdiction covered all foreigners or simply Christians or non-Muslims. In most cases, local rulers accepted British jurisdiction over Indian Muslims but opposed it over Arab Muslims. Beyond such an obvious source of conflict, local rulers were reluctant to accept the establishment of joint courts for mixed cases, because they might involve forcing *shari'a* judges to share the bench with British judges. Also, they expanded the number of cases involving Muslims in which a British official would sit in judgment. British officials in general felt little sympathy with local reluctance to establish joint courts, often ascribing it to the obscurantism and obtuseness of the rulers. For instance, during a 1954 effort to persuade the amir of Qatar to establish joint courts as agreed upon in 1935, Judge C. H. Haines visited Doha on behalf of the Foreign Office. He wrote that the amir

explained that the only Court he can recognize officially is the Sharia Court. We tried to explain to him how in modern systems, Civil and Criminal law is separated from personal status law and that in our own Courts we apply to Moslems Sharia law only in matters of marriage, divorce, and inheritance, but I do not think he really understood . . .

I am afraid that there is at present no hope of establishing a Joint Court on the lines we had in mind although we could have one with the [British] Adviser sitting. Such a court would in the Ruler's eyes and indeed in the eyes of all Qataris be a British Court.[11]

---

[11] Notes by C. H. Haines on visit to Doha, March 24, 1954, included in FO 371/EA 16413.

In fact, the amir probably did understand what Haines wanted; it was Haines who failed to understand the strong ideological attraction to the *shari'a* and the strong political influence of the *shari'a* judge.

The second feature these agreements shared is a failure to specify the law that would be applied in the British courts. Since British officials unanimously regarded local law as undeveloped and indeterminate at best, there was no possibility of their acceptance of that law in British courts. On the other hand, there was an increasing desire, as will be seen, to establish the British courts as models which local rulers would feel compelled to emulate in their own systems. This made British officials anxious that the law they applied be seen as appropriate to local conditions. Until Indian independence, the British courts simply applied the nineteenth-century Indian code. In the 1950s this code came to be seen as both inadequate and complex, and new legislation was issued.[12] At all times the British treated the matter of law to be applied as their own prerogative; local rulers would be consulted but had, in British eyes, ceded not only jurisdiction but also all legislative authority over non-Muslim foreigners. With few exceptions, local rulers did not challenge the British claim, partly because there was little local positive legislation to apply and little desire to apply the *shari'a* to non-Muslims. (On only one occasion did the amir of Qatar make an ineffectual effort to have the *shari'a* applied to foreigners.)

Especially in the 1950s and 1960s the British increasingly felt the need to promulgate new laws for their Gulf courts. These laws were generally presented to local rulers in order to encourage them to issue parallel legislation for their own citizens. When local legislation was enacted in a matter in which the law of the British courts was silent, British officials would attempt to issue parallel legislation for their courts. For instance, laws governing renting of residential properties and prohibitions on the importation of artificial pearls (which threatened the local pearling industry) were generally issued by the rulers of the region and then copied by British officials for their courts. (The British were slightly less forthcoming on alcohol but did closely regulate its importation to satisfy local rulers.)[13]

While there were occasional conflicts between the British and local rulers, the system was far less controversial than the Mixed Courts and the capitulations in Egypt. There were some acrimonious debates over

[12] After Indian independence and the Foreign Office's assumption of responsibility for the Gulf, new legislation was issued upon the order of the foreign secretary on the recommendation of the British political resident in Bahrain. For a description of the process, see the Foreign Office minute by Eric Beckett, April 20, 1951, FO 371/EA 14./2.

[13] On the matter of pearls and alcohol, see FO 371/EA 16410, file, 1952.

the British role (especially in Bahrain where British legal influence was particularly strong), but these were remarkably few given the struggles over restrictions on sovereignty elsewhere in the Arab world. At first British courts excited little controversy because they were relatively inactive. This was especially true before 1947 when British interests in the Gulf fell under the responsibility of the British government in India, as a Foreign Office official explained in 1959:

For many years the Government of India was responsible for manning the Persian Gulf posts, and that Government seems to have concerned itself with only two things: (1) that no threat to communications with India should ever develop from the Persian Gulf; and (2) administering justice to the limited classes – the classes at that time not being very numerous – of persons in Her Majesty's jurisdiction. The Government of India would have looked with horror at any suggestion that it was responsible for creating a respectable indigenous judicial system.[14]

This attitude became less tenable when the British Foreign Office assumed responsibility from the India Office for the Gulf with Indian independence in 1947. The number of Gulf residents falling under the jurisdiction of the British courts steadily increased, and the prospect of large-scale oil production motivated the British government to widen its concern with the Gulf beyond matters of security and transportation. British officials increasingly felt a need not only to protect the Gulf states from external threats but also to develop their administrative and economic capacity. Further, the rise of Arab nationalism and the global decline of British imperialism made many officials feel that their position was not permanent. A different basis for protecting British interests would eventually have to be secured. While this feeling was particularly widespread and acute after the Suez Crisis of 1956, the earliest discussions in the Foreign Office concerning judicial and legal affairs in the Gulf were predicated on the eventual end of British jurisdiction. For instance, in reporting on a 1952 tour of the Gulf states, Eric Beckett, the legal adviser for the Foreign Office, stated "I am convinced that for political reasons we shall have to be ready to agree at some future time that the present dual judicial system shall be replaced by a single judicial system, which will all be under the Ruler, and that therefore, in all that we do now, we should have this probably ultimate development in mind."[15]

Accordingly great attention was given, beginning in the early 1950s, to developing the Gulf legal systems, and, where possible, building them

[14] Foreign Office minute by J. L. Simpson, April 24, 1959, FO 371/BA 1644/6.
[15] "Report on a Visit by the Legal Advisor to the Foreign Office to the Persian Gulf States," June 6, 1952, FO 371/EA 1642/6.

on British lines. Several instruments were advocated by various British officials to bring this about. Officials in the region and in London often differed in their estimation of the advisability and especially the practicality of the various instruments and on which combination of them to use. The least controversial elements of British policy involved encouraging local rulers to send members of their families to Great Britain to study law and suggesting the appointment of Sudanese, Palestinian, and Jordanian judges or legal advisors, all of whom came from countries where British legal influence was high. The first of these strategies showed few obvious results; the second was frustrated by a desire by most (though not all) rulers for Egyptian judges and advisers, as will be seen.

Most British officials also believed that their courts could serve as models, attracting the admiration of local populations and rulers. For this reason, there was an effort to diminish the judicial functions of the political resident and the political agents and designate specific officials whose duties would be restricted to the legal realm. The hope was to impress on local rulers the need to separate the judiciary from administration. Pessimists argued that the British courts were neither imposing nor impressive. Local (and indeed all Arab) residents were always likely to prefer local courts and unlikely to pressure rulers to emulate British courts.[16] In 1953, the British political agent in Bahrain wrote: "Unfortunately, although Her Britannic Majesty's Court for Bahrain is, of course, open to the public, the Bahrain public does not display the slightest interest."[17] Whatever the merits of the British courts, these pessimists proved accurate in their prediction that even advocates of far-reaching legal reform would rarely cite the British courts as models.

Other tools of British influence would have probably been more effective had they proved more viable. British legal advisers could have overseen local legal development had local rulers been induced to appoint them. Bahrain's longstanding British adviser, Charles Belgrave, though not designated as a legal adviser, did much legal work and even sat as a Bahraini judge. (In 1954 he was joined by a judicial adviser.) Yet outside of Bahrain, Gulf rulers displayed no interest in British advice on matters inside their own courts (in the late 1930s the ruler of Kuwait had requested a general adviser during a time of political instability; the minimalist approach prevailing at the time prevented a positive British

---

[16] See, for instance, the 1950 proposals of the British political agent in Kuwait, H. G. Jankins, in his letter to the political resident in Bahrain, Sir Rupert Hay, December 12, 1950, attached to Hay to Fry, January 29, 1951, FO 371/EA 1644/4.

[17] J. W. Wall to B. A. B. Burrows, September 2, 1953, FO 1016/164115/9.

reply).[18] Joint courts were seen as an instrument of securing British influence and judicial development simultaneously. Local judges would have sat with British judges (ruling, it was hoped, on the basis of the British-authored codes); these judges would gain experience and familiarity with the law and gradually replace the British element. Yet while joint courts did operate in Bahrain, rulers in other countries viewed them with suspicion, as did *shari'a*-minded elements in the population. Even in Qatar, where a joint court had been agreed upon in 1935, rulers dragged their heels and prevented its establishment. More ambitious plans for joint courts – that they would assume jurisdiction for all (not simply mixed) cases, and that they would eventually be turned over to local governments – were occasionally mooted but never instituted.

Another possible instrument of British influence – and at times the centerpiece of the British effort – was a British-authored law code, designed to suit local conditions. When the Foreign Office assumed responsibility for the Gulf, an early determination was made that the Indian code, though the product of British influence, was outdated and too complex to be adopted immediately for the British courts of the Gulf. A direct application of English law was also unsuitable (presumably because it was less likely to be accepted in the Gulf). Work began immediately in the Foreign Office on developing a new code, based on a simplified version of the Indian code, elements of British law (generally English but occasionally Scottish), and, in some areas (such as procedure), Egyptian law.[19] The clear goal was to promulgate the code for the British courts and to induce local rulers to promulgate it for their own citizens. With British and local courts operating on the basis of the same law code, it would then be possible to contemplate unification of the two systems – under the auspices of local rulers but under strong British influence. The code, however, was long in preparation, and, as will be seen, led to political disaster when finally introduced.

A final strategy was to hold out retrocession of jurisdiction as a carrot to local rulers in order to persuade them to construct legal systems that the British would recognize as just and adequate. In other words, as soon as rulers promulgated suitable laws or built suitable courts, the British would cede them areas of jurisdiction. As local reform progressed, British jurisdiction would gradually be reduced and finally renounced. One of the major flaws with this strategy is that outside of

---

[18] Glen Balfour-Paul, *The End of Empire in the Middle East: Britain's Relinquishment of Power in her Last Three Arab Dependencies* (Cambridge: Cambridge University Press, 1991), p. 109.

[19] "Draft Record of Meeting Held at the Foreign Office on 6th January, 1950," FO 371/ EA 1643/4.

Kuwait the British were more enthusiastic about the idea of retrocession than local rulers. Rulers rarely displayed any interest in assuming the jurisdiction they had earlier handed to the British.

The flaws in these various strategies were not unknown in the early 1950s when they were first debated, but they were probably underestimated. In any case, the need to develop a policy led to a careful examination of the various strategies and, indeed, a reasonably consistent policy was in fact pursued. Its ultimately lackluster record should not lead to the conclusion that other strategies would have achieved greater success; as has been observed, equally formidable (if initially unimposing) obstacles stood in front of all the possibilities considered. Perhaps if local officials had taken a less contemptuous and disparaging view of the *shari'a* and not worked with the declared objective of subverting its influence in all but personal status they would have been able to work more closely with local rulers on codification or unification of jurisdiction. But on the rare occasion when an official did express a more positive attitude towards the *shari'a* – as did a British adviser to the amir of Qatar in 1954 – his view was dismissed and termed "disturbing."[20]

The first attempt to draw a comprehensive policy for the Gulf states came in 1950, when the general principle was established that unification of British and local courts under local rulers was a long-term goal. To reach that goal, and to insure just and efficient courts in the interim, local British officials were instructed to concentrate on joint courts, advice, and drafting and implementing appropriate legislation. The British political agent in Kuwait, H. G. Jankins, objected that such a policy was too perfectionist and ignored political realities, at least in Kuwait, where demands for retrocession of jurisdiction and objections to joint courts were likely to be particularly strong. Jankins argued that the focus should be shifted instead to encouraging the establishing of adequate local courts as soon as possible; the more successful this project, the more retrocession of jurisdiction could be used as an incentive.[21] (While this position met disapproval by higher officials, by the end of the decade there were few alternatives.)

The pursuit of joint courts and the appointment of judicial advisors showed no signs of success. In 1952, Eric Beckett, the legal advisor to the Foreign Office, made a tour of the Gulf and wrote a comprehensive report on regional policy on legal and judicial matters. He advocated continued efforts to persuade local rulers to employ British legal officials. His report did include a slight retreat on the matter of joint

[20] See the correspondence on the matter in 1954 in FO 371/EA 16413, file.
[21] See the correspondence in FO 371/EA 1644, file, for 1951.

courts, noting that efforts on the matter would likely be counter-productive in Kuwait (though Beckett did call for renewed efforts in Qatar and the Trucial States). Indeed, since the Kuwaiti government soon attempted to persuade the British government to allow mixed cases to be tried in Kuwaiti courts, Beckett's retreat was a bow to political necessity.[22] Most notable, however, was the increasing prominence given to codification. Beckett recommended that the codes be produced and enacted for the British courts as soon as possible.[23] The intent, of course, was to have them copied for the local courts.

With the lack of success on judicial advisers and joint courts, the new code soon became the focal point of British efforts in the region. By 1954 the first result of the codification effort, a draft penal code, was finally ready. The strategy of the British Foreign Office had been to present it to local rulers only when it was ready to promulgate for British courts. Fear about its reception and contempt for local rulers had led British officials to consult in advance only with the amir of Bahrain. A Foreign Office official wrote in 1954 that consulting each of the rulers in advance would be a lengthy process and that

the Rulers are so ignorant that it would be a complete waste of time and would only invite them to suggest all sorts of impossible amendments to which we could not agree. We therefore decided to consult only the Ruler of Bahrain on the draft of the Code and we feel reasonably satisfied that if the rulers want to do so, they will be able to adopt it satisfactorily in its present form without undue difficulty from the points of view of religion and local custom.[24]

A month earlier a Foreign Office official had recommended more explicitly to the political resident in Bahrain to "rely upon the example of the more advanced state of Bahrain to bring [the Ruler of Qatar] gradually round to the idea of adopting secular penal and civil codes and transferring a large measure of jurisdiction from the Sharia to the secular Courts."[25]

The British had reason to be optimistic that this course of action would produce favorable results. When presented with the code, the amir of Bahrain indicated a willingness to consider adoption for Bahraini courts. The British therefore decided to delay introducing the code for their courts until he had studied it more closely, hoping for simultaneous promulgation.[26] And in 1955, while the draft penal code was under

[22] See the 1954 correspondence contained in FO 371/EA 1643, file.
[23] W. E. Beckett, "Report on a Visit by the Legal Advisor to the Foreign Office to the Persian Gulf States," June 6, 1952, FO 371/EA 1642/6.
[24] Foreign Office minute by W. V. J. Evans, June 18, 1954, FO 371/EA 1645/7.
[25] Fay to Burrows, May 12, 1954, FO 371/ EA 16413.
[26] See the 1954 correspondence in FO 371/1645, file.

review in Bahrain, Sa'd al-'Abd Allah Al Sabah, the son of the Kuwaiti amir and commander of the police (and much later the crown prince and prime minister), and other Kuwaiti officials pressed the British for copies of the draft code so that they could study it for local adoption.[27] In Bahrain itself, the amir came under increasing pressure from an opposition which made codification of law one of its central demands.[28] In 1955 the British reached agreement with the amir of Bahrain for simultaneous promulgation after the amir's advisers had produced some minor modifications in the version to be applied in local courts.

Yet when the code was finally published it provoked a storm of criticism and aggravated a political crisis in Bahrain.[29] The Bahraini opposition, led by a self-proclaimed High Executive Committee, charged that the code was a foreign imposition rather than one derived locally. The code was also denounced for being too harsh and too permissive of authoritarian steps. Especially noxious was a host of provisions on associations, assembly, and sedition which the High Executive Committee felt could be used against the opposition. While British officials thought these criticisms unfair or "political" rather than legal, some had to admit that, at the least, sheer clumsiness had aggravated the matter. The code criminalized offenses against the Queen and the British government; on this score the British residency in Bahrain confessed that parts of the code were "inappropriate, and some even ridiculous." Especially embarrassing was the code's confusing language on incest and bigamy; provisions here seemed to be in conflict with the shari'a. The amir, in his discussions with the British, had insisted that these matters therefore be left to separate shari'a courts. After negotiation the articles in question remained in the code, and a separate statement was issued that the Shari'a Courts would be consulted. This hardly satisfied the opposition. And the opposition was able to lampoon the code for its criminalization of harsh treatment of fish in the "cruelty to animals" section.[30]

The controversy forced the amir to agree to postpone adoption of the code while a Muslim legal expert was consulted to suggest revisions. 'Abd al-Razzaq al-Sanhuri, the Egyptian jurist, was approached. Forced to hesitate because of his uncertain political status in Egypt (see chapter 3) and inability to obtain a passport, he finally accepted the assignment. While the matter was suspended in Bahrain, the British decided to delay

---

[27] Pelly to Burrows, February 28, 1955, FO 371/EA 1642/5.
[28] See Balfour-Paul, *End of Empire*, p. 112, and Saleh, *Labor, Nationalism and Imperialism*.
[29] The correspondence on the episode is contained in FO 371/EA 1642.
[30] The local criticisms are summarized in Residency to Eastern Department, September 20, 1955, FO 371/EA 1642/27.

adoption of the penal code for their courts in the Gulf. Yet al-Sanhuri worked too slowly for the British, and in September 1956 the Foreign Office allowed the code to come into force for all British courts outside of Bahrain.[31] The Suez Crisis at the end of October resulted in serious political disturbances in Bahrain, and the British and the amir both felt they could wait no longer. The authoritarian provisions that the opposition had decried were needed by the government to suppress local dissent. On November 7, 1956, the amir put the code into effect. Although some controversial and ridiculed clauses (such as offenses related to marriage and cruelty to animals) were suspended, provisions on sedition, association, and assembly were retained – and immediately acted upon.[32] A Foreign Office official noted the link between the hasty promulgation and the political disturbances: "The recent unrest in Bahrain caused by the local reaction to British intervention in Egypt made it advisable to increase the powers of the local courts and of the police force."[33] The British shortly followed suit, putting the penal code into force in their courts in Bahrain. (In 1957 al-Sanhuri finally submitted his suggestions. Rather than revise the British-authored code, his proposal was based on the Egyptian and the French codes and was ignored in Bahrain.[34])

The episode in Bahrain left British policy in a shambles. While the new penal code had been introduced in all the British courts, only Bahrain had adopted it domestically, and the process there was unlikely to convince other rulers of the desirability of following suit. In May 1956, even before the extent of the débâcle in Bahrain was apparent, the Foreign Office ordered its officials in the region to strike a more compromising pose:

we should strongly encourage the codification of the Ruler's law. Where an English model does not prove acceptable, we should not oppose an Egyptian one which would often mean a European code somewhat adapted. However inferior such a code might be to the best English law, it would be greatly preferable to the type of law that the Sheikhs would apply if they had failed to accept our advice and had followed their own inclinations.[35]

Other indications of the retreat were the suggestions made by British officials during 1956: to concentrate on encouraging the training and selecting of appropriate Arab personnel for the courts; consult more closely with local officials on legislation; and exhibit greater willingness

[31] See the correspondence in FO 371/EA 1642/21.
[32] See the records in FO 371/EA 1644/5 (1957).
[33] Foreign Office minute by F. A. Vallat, December 5, 1956, FO 371/EA 1642/24.
[34] See the handwritten minute by Judge Haines, June 26, 1957, FO 371/EA 1644/5.
[35] The draft of the letter (Riches to Burrows) is contained in FO 371/EA 1642/10.

to cede jurisdiction over some nationalities.[36] In July 1956 the British discovered that Kuwaiti officials had considered and rejected the draft penal code. While some ascribed the rejection to a generational conflict between younger reform-minded shaykhs and the obscurantist senior figures, the flaws in the code and the controversy then brewing in Bahrain undoubtedly were factors as well.[37] The Kuwaiti rejection of the British-authored penal code was accompanied by an effort to rely increasingly on Egyptian expertise; by the time Kuwait gained independence in 1961 there were only a few traces of British legal influence.

Thus, by 1957, just as the Suez Crisis began to make many feel a greater need to anticipate the eventual end of British jurisdiction, three of the most ambitious tools the British had hoped to use – joint courts, judicial advisers and codification of law – had failed to produce any concrete results (except for a Pyrrhic victory in Bahrain). While there was no declaration of defeat, British goals became more modest. In general, however, simply less ambitious versions of the same policies were pursued. In 1959, for instance, George Middleton, the British political resident, wrote to the Foreign Office on possible policies to be pursued to foster judicial development in the Gulf. Gone was any hope of a comprehensive regional policy; indeed, Middleton admitted to difficulty in advancing any positive suggestions. He concluded that "the only practical way of effecting any reform in the legal position in the Gulf is by gradual evolution and not by abrupt revolution" and abandoned any idea of a uniform regional policy.[38]

The idea of joint courts, the focus of much effort in the early and mid-1950s, was not dropped.[39] Yet while the idea was still taken quite seriously by British officials (generally those more removed from the realities on the ground), few concrete actions were taken to follow a course of action that most officials on the scene regarded as holding little promise.[40] In Bahrain, where joint courts existed for mixed cases only, there was little local interest in building them into a system that would have jurisdiction in all cases. In Kuwait, the approach of independence made the idea, always regarded as unpalatable by the country's rulers, unthinkable. In Qatar, the agreement on paper to establish joint courts

[36] See FO 371/EA 1642, especially piece 23, Burrows to Lloyd, September 17, 1956.
[37] Residency to Foreign Office, July 21, 1956, FO 371/EA 1642/18.
[38] Middleton to Beaumont, June 1, 1959, FO 371/BA 1644/9.
[39] A prominent British lawyer in the Gulf, William Ballantyne, was a particularly strong supporter of the idea. See W. M. Ballantyne, *Legal Development in Arabia* (London: Graham and Troutman, 1980). This book reprints a series of articles on the subject of law in the Arabian peninsula; on joint courts, see p. 5 and p. 15. I am indebted to 'Abd Allah al-Muslimani for bringing this book to my attention.
[40] See the 1958 correspondence in FO 371/BA 16415/3158.

for mixed cases was finally abandoned in 1960, and the British resident signed an agreement to try cases in the court of the defendant.[41] Only in the Trucial States did the effort to establish joint courts bear any fruit, and there rulers agreed only to have mixed cases heard by the new structures. (Ironically, an agreement to establish a joint court in Abu Dhabi in 1960 occasioned a bitter dispute in 1963 when a British judge, unaware of the agreement, refused to allow a local judge to sit in a mixed murder trial.[42]) The more ambitious hope of establishing joint courts with general jurisdiction, organized after British courts and enforcing British-authored codes (eventually transforming into British-style but wholly local courts) was abandoned.

On the matter of the codes themselves, the débâcle with the British-authored criminal code in Bahrain left the British no choice but to hope to legislate by example. In 1957 the Foreign Office advised the British resident in Bahrain to concentrate on developing law that could be seen as a model by local rulers; no longer was the prospect of local promulgation of British-authored codes regarded as realistic.[43] By 1961, the highest British judicial official in the country, Judge Haines, gave faint hope that local rulers would enact new laws promulgated for the British courts: "We cannot expect the Rulers to pay much attention to these and our best course will probably be to advise them to engage competent lawyers to draft suitable laws in much the same way as Kuwait has done."[44]

Even on the matter of judicial advisers, the British showed signs of retreat. In the years after Suez, there was little thought of British judicial advisers. There was a great British preference, however, for an adviser trained in Britain or in a country under strong British legal influence. Thus Jordanian, Palestinian, and Sudanese advisers were viewed more favorably than Egyptians. Even here, however, British officials were far from insistent. While they generally seized any opportunity to put forward a British-trained adviser (and British-trained judges as well), by the late 1950s it was clear that Egyptian influence was going to be strong in the Gulf (with the possible exception of Bahrain). When the amir of Qatar appointed an Egyptian lawyer and diplomat, Hasan Kamil, to the post of legal adviser, most British officials realized that there was little hope in expanding their regional legal influence. (Indeed, Kamil soon became involved in a heated exchange with British officials over whether

---

[41] See the minute by C. H. Haines, April 7, 1960, FO 371/BA 1649/3.
[42] During the dispute, British officials accused the shaykh of Abu Dhabi of interfering with the course of justice; he in turn began to refuse to refer cases to the British courts. See the 1963 correspondence on the Das Island case, FO 371/B 1641.
[43] Riches to Burrows, October 31, 1957, FO 371/EA 16410/10.
[44] Haines to Home, April 14, 1961, FO 371/B 1642/4.

or not Qatar could expel those under British jurisdiction; his argument seemed to be based on the claim that Qatar had ceded jurisdiction, but not all legislative authority over foreigners.[45])

The final tool the British could use in molding Gulf legal development was the use of retrocession of jurisdiction as an incentive. During the decade between Kuwait's independence and the independence of the other Gulf states, this was virtually the only realistic policy the British could pursue. It was hampered by the lack of interest Gulf rulers showed in retrocession. Further, retrocession was generally linked in practice to political circumstances rather than judicial development. In Kuwait, where the political agent wrote three years before independence that "it is probably hopeless to expect [the Kuwaiti judicial system] to reach what we should regard as an adequate standard," retrocession proceeded quickly and smoothly once the decision had been made that Kuwait would become independent. In Bahrain, on the other hand, with its British legal advisers, joint courts, and British-authored law codes, retrocession proceeded very slowly until the decision was made to withdraw from the Gulf by 1971.

Yet this does not mean that British influence in the legal development of the Gulf was negligible. When explaining the establishment of the civil courts in Qatar, most officials inside and outside the system today claim that some civil court system was a British condition for independence. This view is certainly exaggerated – it is unimaginable that the British would have remained in Qatar solely because of the continuation of *shari'a* courts as courts of general jurisdiction. More-over, the civil courts were actually created prior to independence in 1971 though they were sharply limited in jurisdiction. Yet the oft-cited claim does point to the influence the British did have. By continually advancing the subject of legal and judicial development in dealings with local rulers, it is probable that the British did contribute greatly to the acceptance of a professionalized judiciary and the adoption of written law codes. The role of the *shari'a* judiciary has been minimized even in states where its political support remains strong (especially Qatar); in Kuwait it was abolished altogether (with civil courts ruling on the basis of codified *shari'a* law). In short, the British succeeded in determining that there would be a new legal and judicial order in the Gulf that would not be solely *shari'a*-based, but they failed in most locations in shaping that order to any great extent.

If this is the case, then how can we understand what legal systems did

[45] See "Minutes of a Meeting in Dr. Kamel's Office on Wednesday, February 13, 1963," FO 371/B 1642/14, and "Record of discussion with Dr. Hassan Kamel on July 31, 1963," FO 371/B 1641/35.

emerge in the Gulf? Why did the Egyptian model prove so attractive? And why were local regimes willing to pursue judicial reform, sometimes in the face of opposition from *shari'a* judges and their supporters?

### The domestic roots of legal reform in the Arab states of the Gulf prior to independence

While the Arab states of the Gulf pursued legal reform in different ways and at different paces, the results did not display tremendous variation. In general, the construction of judicial systems and the enactment of codified law, although related, proceeded separately.

Bahrain was the first country to embark on the creation of a centralized, civil judiciary. The influence of the *Shari'a* Courts was weaker in Bahrain than in almost all the other states of the Gulf, and, as is already clear, the openness to British advice was much greater. Like other Gulf states, there were three sets of domestic courts operating: *Shari'a* Courts, commercial courts, and the courts of the ruler. Because of the relative weakness of the first, they were confined largely to matters of personal status by the early 1950s. By that time, the commercial courts had also become marginalized and under the domination of the ruling family. On the other hand, the ruler's courts, with virtually all of their judges from the ruling family (the major exception was Belgrave, the British adviser), had developed a hierarchical (three-tiered) structure and had become the courts of general jurisdiction.[46] Thus, at a time when most of the other Gulf states were not yet contemplating wide-ranging judicial reform, Bahrain had already constructed a framework for a centralized and hierarchical judiciary. The staffing of the courts proved controversial, however, as judicial positions continued to be nearly monopolized by the ruling family throughout the 1950s. The reform movement that crested in Bahrain in the mid-1950s demanded greater independence for the judiciary. In October 1955 the opposition extracted a pledge from the ruler to appoint a professionally trained judge (rather than a member of the ruling family; this would have necessitated hiring a foreigner). When the opposition was suppressed the following year the pledge was forgotten (even though British inclinations favored the hiring of foreign judges).[47] British officials believed that the amir simply viewed judicial functions as an integral part of the ruling family's prerogatives.[48] (This belief was firmly based; to this

[46] Haines, "Bahrain Government Courts," December 1951, FO 371/EA 1644/26.
[47] Gault to Riches, January 12, 1959, FO 371/BA 1544/2.
[48] See Burrows to Lloyd, September 17, 1956, FO 371/EA 1642/23.

day the State Security Courts in the country are headed by a member of the ruling family.) A secondary factor may have been fiscal: all new legal personnel would have initially come from outside the country, and remarks by the president of the courts in 1961 indicated that this was regarded as too expensive.[49]

Yet the growing complexity of legal disputes in Bahrain and the increased economic activity in the country, put severe pressure on the ruler-dominated courts. Called upon to solve increasingly complex disputes, the courts did increase in specialization (with separate civil and criminal divisions), but the chief judge was still a member of the ruling family the British believed to be illiterate. When a Bahraini student specializing in Gulf law received a Ph.D. from Cambridge, he failed to find a position with the Bahraini government.[50] Finally, in 1963, the amir allowed the Chief Judge of the British courts in the Gulf to travel to Amman and Jerusalem to hire three judges for the Bahraini courts. Yet the new judges were allowed only to sit with judges from the ruling family.[51] Thus, while the Al Khalifa did promote a hierarchical and professional judiciary, they resisted both domestic and foreign pressure, allowing judicial positions to open to those outside of the family only with extreme caution.

The work on codification of law proceeded similarly. Demands for law codes and legislation governing matters such as labor and housing were the staple of both the nationalist opposition and the labor movement. The ruling family responded slowly.[52] Law remained a mixture of custom and *shari'a*, though by the 1950s (perhaps under Belgrave's influence), the ruler's courts were beginning to apply the Sudanese penal code (itself modeled on the Indian code).[53] As pressure increased, the amir responded by agreeing to enact the British-authored penal code (itself based on the Sudanese penal code already informally in force). As described above, the opposition reacted angrily (denouncing both the substance of the code and the process by which it was adopted). The code, put into force in 1956 with some controversial elements suspended, represented the last serious effort at codification in over a decade (though some less comprehensive legislation was

[49] See the note on the visit by the Lord Privy Seal to Shaikh Daij, January 19, 1961, FO 371/B 1642/7.
[50] Whyatt to Home, March 27, 1962, FO 371/B 1642/4. The student's failure to find employment was not permanent; decades later he served as minister of state for legal affairs.
[51] See the correspondence in the file FO 371/B 1641 and B 1642.
[52] See the sections on Bahrain in Saleh, *Labor, Nationalism and Imperialism*.
[53] Haines, "Bahrain Government Courts," December 1951, FO 371/EA 1644/26. See also the sections on Bahrain in W. E. Beckett, "Report on a Visit by the Legal Advisor to the Foreign Office to the Persian Gulf States," June 6, 1952, FO 371/EA 1642.

enacted). When the Jordanian judges arrived they found very little legislation in place. Thus, by the end of the 1960s, with independence approaching, the legal framework was still quite limited. A committee working hastily followed the general practice in the Gulf, long resisted in Bahrain, of adopting Egyptian codes.[54]

In Kuwait, judicial development generally preceded codification.[55] As in Bahrain, the courts of the ruler had general jurisdiction, and they ruled according to custom (informed, on some issues, by the shari'a). The ruler did refer cases involving personal status or religious questions to an appointed shari'a judge, but no separate shari'a judiciary ever crystallized. Merchants and craftsmen had arbitration bodies to rule in specialized disputes. Various official institutions, such as the Kuwait municipality, also set up dispute resolution boards. Rarely a truly absolute ruler, the amir of Kuwait operated under the watchful eyes of prominent merchants as well as other members of the Al Sabah family. In 1938 some merchants, supported by dissident members of the Al Sabah, compelled the amir to convene an assembly and then to assent to its basic law.[56] Extremely brief, the law charged the assembly with writing many laws, including one to organize the judiciary. The short life of the assembly prevented it from carrying out its mandated program, but a significant restructuring did provide the basis for the future development of a professionalized judiciary. Judicial salaries were raised, and the courts were included in the state budget and given a fixed location and hours of operation. A greater and a lesser court were created and the assembly determined to build an appeals court and engage a legal expert to lay down a more complete judicial structure.[57] While the appeals court did not materialize, an Egyptian judge was hired in the 1940s (although he was not given the full responsibilities envisioned by the short-lived assembly).[58] In 1948 the amir ordered a further reorganization of the courts, establishing a separate section for personal status and vesting authority for approving or overturning verdicts in a court president. While there was thus no formally established appeals court, the court president would consult

---

[54] Ballantyne, *Legal Development in Arabia*, p. 23.

[55] Despite the paucity of documentation, there is general consensus on most of the features of judicial development in Kuwait. See al-Salih, *Al-nizam al-dusturi*, al-Tabataba'i, *Al-nizam al-dusturi*, "Lamha hawla tatawwur al-qada' fi al-kuwayt," and 'Abd al-Rida 'Ali Asiri, *Al-nizam al-siyasi fi al-kuwayt* (The Political System in Kuwait) (Kuwait: Matba'at al-watan, 1994).

[56] The text of the law, arguably Kuwait's first written constitution, can be found in al-Salih, *Al-nizam al-dusturi*, pp. 107–108.

[57] Al-Salih, *Al-nizam al-dusturi*, p. 111.

[58] On the Egyptian judge, see "Lamha hawla tatawwur al-qada' fi al-kuwayt."

with a *shari'a* expert and a panel of judges when reviewing difficult cases.[59]

Despite these efforts at judicial development, in 1954 the British political resident in Kuwait described only a rough division of labor among judges.[60] The following year a Palestinian judicial official employed by the British reported that the courts followed extremely informal procedures and that Egyptian judges were restricted to personal status matters. Members of the Al Sabah held other judicial positions.[61] This situation continued up until 1959 when Kuwait's first law of judicial organization was enacted by an amiri decree.[62] The law completed the unification of the judiciary (thus ending the judicial functions of the specialized arbitration boards, though some arbitration mechanisms continued). Judicial specialization increased and a separate appeals court was finally established. Clearly following an Egyptian model, a judicial council was established (headed by the minister of justice) for appointments and promotions, and a *niyaba* system was adopted. The preference for Egyptian judges manifested itself by larger-scale hiring of Egyptian judges. The Kuwaiti constitution of 1962 enshrined Egyptian practice even further, borrowing language on the independence of the judiciary, allowing (but not requiring) the establishment of a *majlis al-dawla* system, and mandating the establishment of the supreme judicial council, administrative court, and *niyaba*.

By contrast, codification proceeded very slowly until the late 1950s. While rulers pledged observance of the *shari'a*, local custom seems to have been more influential in determining criminal and civil matters.[63] No amir claimed legislative authority until 1932 when the law creating the Kuwait municipality was issued by decree.[64] The reformist 1938 assembly did turn its attention to codification only briefly, but specifically enjoined judges to rule on the basis of the Ottoman-authored *majalla*, the nineteenth-century effort to codify the *shari'a* following the framework of the French code. From that date, the *majalla* was regarded as in force in all Kuwaiti courts; legislation by amiri decree continued and gradually broadened in scope but covered only a few areas. British observers still felt that Kuwaiti courts were operating without anything

---

[59] See al-Salih, *Al-Nizam al-dusturi*, pp. 126–30, and Tabataba'i, *Al-Nizam al-dusturi*, pp. 308–311.
[60] Pelly to Burrows, January 9, 1954, FO 371/EA 1643/1.
[61] See the report by Ahmad Hijazi, June 23, 1955, and the attached minute by C. H. Haines, June 27, 1955, FO 371/EA 1641/7.
[62] See al-Salih, *Al-nizam al-dusturi*, pp. 130–134.
[63] Al-Salih, *Al-nizam al-dusturi*, pp. 41–42.
[64] Al-Salih, *Al-nizam al-dusturi*, p. 84.

except vague guidance by the *shari'a*.[65] This feeling, even though it may have been exaggerated, seems to have been shared by some judges from the Al Sabah. In the mid to late 1950s, British officials reported contradictory statements from leading members of the ruling family, some calling for greater efforts at codification (and even consideration of the British-authored penal code) with others (including the amir) claiming that the *majalla* was sufficient.[66] After the adoption of a more complex judicial structure in 1959, the reformers finally won out, and legal attention turned away from judicial matters to codification. This shift was undoubtedly assisted by the determination of the Kuwait government to assume jurisdiction over foreigners (a rare attitude among Gulf rulers); since the British had always been critical of deficiencies of Kuwaiti law some steps towards codification seemed to be a necessary price of retrocession.

At this time, Egyptian codes were the obvious choice for several reasons. First, they were the only comprehensive codes available in Arabic (this was partly due to the resistance of Kuwait and other Gulf states to the British codification effort). Second, Egyptian legal personnel had been employed in the Kuwaiti legal system for some time. Third, the Egyptian codes, based as they were on the French codes, closely resembled the *majalla* in structure (even if they differed in content), making their adoption a less radical step. Finally, the British, even though they at times resented the increasing reliance on Egyptian models, viewed the Egyptian codes as adequate (though overly complex) and modern. Accordingly, the Kuwaiti government requested al-Sanhuri to take charge of drafting codes, based on his previous work in Egypt. Thus a combination of internal pressure and external circumstances brought about an Egyptian-style legal system in Kuwait.

In Qatar, the *Shari'a* Courts proved to be much more powerful, and they deeply affected – and continue to affect – the course of judicial and legal development. It is probably the case that arbitration boards operated in disputes in the pearl industry and tribal leaders resolved disputes arising among the rest of the population. Unlike most of the other states of the Gulf, however, no real courts seem to have operated under the amir, who, though he may have heard some simple cases, referred most disputes and criminal matters to the *shari'a* judge, at least

---

[65] This attitude surfaced regularly in British reports on the Kuwait courts. See, for instance, W. E. Beckett, "Report on a Visit by the Legal Advisor to the Foreign Office to the Persian Gulf States," June 6, 1952, FO 371/EA 1642/6.

[66] See, for instance, Burrows to Lloyd, September 17, 1956, FO 371/EA 1642/23, and the minute by G. W. Bell, August 16, 1957, FO 371/EA 16411/4.

since the mid-nineteenth century.[67] Heavily influenced by the Wahhabi movement, Qatar proved highly resistant to any official deviation from Islamic jurisprudence. 'Abd Allah bin Zayd Al Mahmud, the *shari'a* judge, whom the British regarded as obscurantist and an obstacle to proper legal development, proved a major influence not only on the ruling family but on the population as a whole. He is credited with transforming the *Shari'a* Court from an informal to a regularized structure after his appointment in 1938. After establishing a court register, he founded the Presidency of the *Shari'a* Court (the administrative office for the courts) in 1957.[68] The amir did establish a separate court in 1950, with his sons as the judges.[69] Yet the new court's relationship with the *Shari'a* Court was the opposite of that prevailing in most other Gulf states. Instead of the ruler or members of the ruling family serving as judges with general jurisdiction, referring only personal status cases or technical legal issues to the *Shari'a* Court, the amir's sons served to prepare cases before referring most of them to the *Shari'a* Court. Judge Haines describes what he found in a 1954 visit:

On the morning of the 20th of March I sat in the Qatar Government Court with Shaikh Ahmed, Shaikh Khalifa [sons of amir] and Mr. Hancock [a British adviser to the amir]. At the beginning Shaikh Ahmed stated that the Court was subordinate to the Sharia Court. There were 25 cases for hearing all of which were civil cases, except one. No evidence at all was taken by the Court. The defendant in each case was asked if he acknowledged the debt. If he did he either paid the money to the plaintiff in Court and a note of this was made on the record or if he did not pay at once a decree was issued usually giving him time to pay. If the defendant denied the debt, the case was forthwith referred to the Sharia Court. When the [*Shari'a* Court] Qadhi's judgment is received the Court Clerk records it as a judgment. The same procedure is followed in Criminal Cases but in at least one case the Qadhi's finding was made a judgment of the Court in the presence of the accused. Thus in effect the Qatar Government Court applies Sharia Criminal Law.[70]

While the amir's sons wished to play a more active role, they both said that 'Abd Allah Al Mahmud would object and would be able to prevent any encroachment on the jurisdiction of the *Shari'a* Court. In the early 1960s, with labor unrest in the oil industry, the amir agreed to a suggestion by his newly appointed Egyptian adviser, Hasan Kamil, to hire an Egyptian judge to write a labor law which would establish a

[67] Interview, Judge Yusuf al-Zaman, Vice-President of the Appeals Court of Qatar, November 1994, Doha.
[68] 'Ubaydan, *Ma'alim al-nizam*, pp. 58–59.
[69] W. E. Beckett, "Report on a visit by the Legal Advisor to the Foreign Office to the Persian Gulf States," June 6, 1952, FO 371/EA 1642/6.
[70] C. H. Haines, report on visit to Doha, March 24, 1954, FO 371/EA 16413/2.

separate labor tribunal (on which the Egyptian judge would sit). When
the judge arrived, however, Kamil found him excessively obsequious
and had him dismissed.[71] Qatar then requested a second judge to be
sent, though the ruler insisted that he should have the right to dismiss
the judge on one month's notice.[72] In the late 1960s two other
specialized tribunals were established: a traffic court (headed by a later
amir), and a court in the municipality. With the coming of independence, Qatar came under tremendous pressure from the British to
develop its non-*shari'a* based courts. In 1970 a criminal court was
established, taking the place of the municipal court, which ruled in some
criminal matters.[73] The following year, independence resulted in a hasty
attempt to establish courts (and codes), but no effort was made to define
the relationship between the *Shari'a* Courts and the new "National
Courts" (*al-Mahakim al-Wataniyya*; they later came to be called the
"Justice Courts," *al-Mahakim al-'Adliyya*, presumably based on nineteenth-century Ottoman terminology). While containing general references to judicial independence, the Qatari constitution made no
mention of the organization of the courts. Much of this indeterminacy
can be ascribed to the opposition of the *Shari'a* Courts; 'Abd Allah Al
Mahmud, the *shari'a* judge, referred to the new courts as the "courts of
Satan."[74] Since the police had been under British command, they had
taken upon themselves a prosecutorial function (on the Anglo-Saxon
model). Qatar has not followed most other Arab states in establishing a
*niyaba* system in which prosecution is a judicial rather than police
function. Thus litigants in civil cases and the public prosecutor (in the
Interior Ministry) in criminal cases effectively had to choose whether to
file a case in the *Shari'a* or *'Adliyya* Courts. The *'Adliyya* Court system
was clearly modeled after the Kuwaiti (in turn modeled on the
Egyptian), with separate civil and criminal sections and a unified appeals
court. It took on the functions of the specialized tribunals (the traffic,
labor, and criminal courts).

[71] Kamil was offended by what he considered sycophantic behavior and specifically by the
judge's attendance at a mosque, which Kamil thought beneath the dignity of an
Egyptian professional. See "Minutes of a Meeting in Dr. Kamel's Office on Wednesday,
February 13, 1963," FO 371/B 1642/14.

[72] *Ibid.*

[73] The information on the various specialized tribunals comes from my personal interview
with Judge al-Zaman, November 1994. Regarding the British role in forcing the
establishment of the *'Adliyya* Courts, there is no documentation yet publicly available.
Nevertheless, judges in both the *'Adliyya* and *Shari'a* Courts make the claim freely, as
do other high officials in Qatar, that the establishment of the system was a condition of
independence. By 1970 it was probably the case that the British were in no position to
determine the nature of the new system, beyond insisting on its establishment, however.

[74] Interview with a legal official in Qatar, November 1994.

Unlike Kuwait and Bahrain, the major effort at legislation was directly connected with the construction of a complex non-*shari'a* court structure. In the 1950s, the amir issued some specialized legislation by decree, but he remained resistant to any comprehensive efforts, as the British resident in the Gulf noted in 1956:

The Ruler of Qatar has agreed to a number of specialised Regulations for Traffic, Customs, Dangerous Drugs, etc. and in that respect has shown himself more amenable to legislative progress than his colleague in Kuwait, but he is perhaps even further from accepting the idea that there is a need for codified laws on subjects which, to his way of thinking, are covered by the Sharia and he would almost certainly think the acceptance of such an idea to be unorthodox and impious. It must probably therefore be concluded that at least during the life of the present Ruler there is no prospect of securing the introduction of a general penal code, even one adopted from a Moslem country or prepared by a Moslem jurist. There is, however, a tendency to develop case law. The local Court before passing a sentence considers what sentences have been given in comparable cases in the past . . .[75]

Having enacted some specialized legislation, the amir seemed reluctant to go further until labor disturbances occurred in 1963. At that time Hasan Kamil drafted a statement which the amir issued pledging:

Amongst the most important problems to the study of which and the means of implementation of which we are now giving attention is the problem of issuing a body of laws necessary for the regulation of our society, and the relations between the people who live in its compass. The most important of these laws are the Civil Law, the Commercial Law, the Law of Civil Appeal and the Law of Criminal Procedure. When the preparation of these basic laws is completed (and their preparation will require much time and effort), we shall hasten to establish the Courts of Law which the application of these Laws will require.[76]

Yet the return of labor peace led to longer delays than the announcement implied. Only a labor law was issued in the short term; five years later a law governing the municipality was issued but no effort at codification was in evidence.

Thus, by 1971 Qatar only had a few specialized laws. A few days before independence, a series of codes – a law of punishments, a law of criminal procedure, a civil law, and a commercial law – were suddenly issued. Although an Egyptian element predominated, those responsible for these codes came from different countries and tended to draw on

---

[75] Burrows to Lloyd, September 17, 1956, FO 371/EA 1642/23.
[76] The document, "Explanatory Announcement Concerning the Comprehensive Program of Work for the Progress of the Country," was shown to British officials by Hasan Kamil. See "Record of discussion with Dr. Hassan Kamel on July 31, 1963," FO 371/B 1641/35.

their native codes heavily. The work was hasty and gaps remained.[77] Yet Qatar, when independence became effective several days after the new codes were promulgated, had a set of codes and the framework of a centralized, hierarchical judiciary.

In the Trucial States, much less documentary information exists, even for the larger amirates of Dubai and Abu Dhabi. This is partly because of the low British interest in the area. But it is also true that the small populations and low level of economic activity made judicial and legal issues much less salient. The same combination of rulers' courts, merchants' tribunals, tribal law, and *shari'a* courts (generally staffed by appointment by the ruler) probably prevailed. What is notable is the degree to which the issues debated elsewhere in the Gulf – the role of *Shari'a* Courts, the desirability of codification, the staffing of the courts – drew much less attention. This seems to have been particularly the case in Dubai, where the *shari'a* judge expressed no objection to codification (at one point even expressing interest in the British-authored criminal code) but did scrutinize proposed legislation for its compatibility with the *shari'a*.[78] Yet while the amir of Dubai did accept a British offer to recruit a legal adviser from Jordan, there was little movement toward legislation or codification.[79] Thus, of all the states of the Gulf, the Trucial States had made the smallest efforts at legal reform by the time of independence (at which point they became the United Arab Emirates). Upon independence, the UAE followed the course of other Gulf states by constructing a legal system generally along Egyptian lines (both with regard to judicial structure and codes), though as in Qatar the *Shari'a* Courts retained some vitality.

This survey of legal reform in the Gulf states reveals that the systems cannot be seen as externally imposed – either by Britain, the colonial power or by Egypt, the most significant source of codes and judicial models. British influence did prod some societies and rulers to move in the direction of the construction of new legal systems, but except for Bahrain the British did not substantially affect the course of that effort. Instead Egyptian influence was predominant. Yet in spite of the strong political role played by Egypt in the Arab world during the period of legal reform in the Gulf, there is little evidence that the systems were an

---

[77] One leading Qatari official mentioned that there was no law of bankruptcy – a gap that has not yet been rectified – because influential Qataris objected to the draft, forcing its removal from the codes issued.

[78] See C. H. Haines, "Workings of Dubai Qadi Court," February 11, 1959, FO 371/BA 16410/7, and the note by John Whyatt, July 7, 1961, FO 371/B 1644/3.

[79] The correspondence related to the recruitment of the legal adviser is included in the 1963 records of the recruitment of judges in Bahrain, FO 371/B 1642.

Egyptian imposition. Some Gulf leaders may have looked to Egypt as a counterbalance to the British, but at the time Egypt's ambitious and self-proclaimed revolutionary foreign policy could hardly have made it attractive to Gulf rulers. In fact, in the case of Bahrain, there seems to have been a conscious effort to avoid Egyptian influence. It is notable that perhaps the two most important Egyptian legal experts active in the Gulf were far from Nasserists. 'Abd al-Razzaq al-Sanhuri had been purged from the Egyptian judiciary by the Nasserist regime and, as British documents make clear, was hampered in his efforts to work on Gulf legal issues by the actions of the Egyptian regime.[80] Indeed, he traveled to Kuwait to work on the Kuwaiti codes only after the amir of Kuwait personally appealed to 'Abd al-Nasir to grant al-Sanhuri the right to travel outside of Egypt.[81] And Hasan Kamil had served as Egyptian ambassador in Hungary but resigned as a result of differences with the government.[82] His political inclinations may be surmised from a 1963 conversation in which he agreed with a British official who expressed reservations about bringing East Bank Jordanian lawyers to the Gulf because of their "Nasserite tendencies."[83]

The attraction of the Egyptian model did not therefore lie in a political preference for Egyptian over British influence. In most Gulf states different, generally internal, concerns were far more relevant. In all states rulers were anxious to retain their prerogatives – this was one of the major reasons for the long delay in accepting outside judges and in giving them real responsibilities once they were hired. And in some states shari'a judges watched the effort to build a new system with new codes with great suspicion. The Egyptian system, with its hierarchical and centralized structure, and with comprehensive codes that could be issued by amiri decree, undoubtedly held greater attraction for rulers than a British-style system based partly on precedents and on significant judicial discretion. And while the Egyptian system was in turn based on the French, some efforts had been made (especially by al-Sanhuri) to use Islamic jurisprudence to inspire amendments in the civil code. The resemblance between the shari'a-based majalla and the Egyptian codes in form undoubtedly assisted as well. Thus the Egyptian system seemed

---

[80] For instance, when he wished to work on the Bahrain penal code, British officials believed that 'Abd al-Nasir personally ordered that al-Sanhuri not be granted a passport. See the relevant correspondence in 1956 in FO 371/EA 1642.

[81] See 'Abd al-Razzaq al-Sanhuri min khilal awraqihi al-shakhsiyya ('Abd al-Razzaq al-Sanhuri through his Personal Papers) (Cairo: al-Zahra' li-l-a'lam al-'arabi, 1988), p. 309, note 2.

[82] Whyatt to Home, March 27, 1962, FO 371/B 1642/4.

[83] "Minutes of a Meeting in Dr. Kamel's Office on Wednesday, February 13, 1963," FO 371/B 1642/14.

more consistent with a *shari'a*-based system, no matter how far it was removed from Islamic roots. In the effort to retain the control of the rulers and to avoid unnecessary offense to *Shari'a* Courts, the Egyptian system had much more to offer than the alternatives. (And, by the time that the later Gulf states finally exhibited an interest in legal reform, there were no real alternatives available, the British having abandoned the effort.) Thus, while imperialism was not irrelevant to legal reform in the Gulf, the systems in place by (or shortly after) independence cannot be seen as imposed; in most cases they had real domestic roots. In no case was legal reform seen as a limit on the rulers' authority; indeed, the rulers of the Gulf states were generally most resistant to legal reform when it seemed connected to a diminution in the prerogatives of the ruling family. (This explains the delays in accepting foreign judges as well as the reluctance to accede to popular demands for reform or to follow through on public pledges on the issue.)

These systems were thus created partly because they were not seen as threatening ruling families; there was a feeling that autocratic rule could operate within a legalistic framework. Indeed, Egypt has shown that is the case. But Egypt has also shown that an independent judiciary can, if given the right legal tools, strain at the limits imposed by an autocratic or authoritarian system. How have Gulf judiciaries coexisted with autocratic executive authorities?

# 6 The legal system and the rule of law in Kuwait and Qatar

The Egyptian experience indicates that the sort of legal and judicial systems erected by the Gulf states should have been able to accommodate themselves to the autocratic political systems generally prevailing in the area. The judicial vision of legality in Egypt has only rarely been inconsistent with the desires of the country's rulers. This has made possible a fair degree of judicial independence as well as official observance of legality in the bulk of governmental affairs. On matters deemed too critical to leave to a strict legal framework, rulers have generally escaped constitutional and legal restrictions less by attacking than by avoiding the judicial structure. At certain periods when political pluralism, if not full-fledged democracy, has operated, the judiciary has worked for a more ambitious conception of liberal legality and enforced some significant constraints on executive action.

The experience of the Gulf does not contradict the lessons of the Egyptian experience, but it does suggest some refinements. In an effort to understand the political role played by Gulf legal and judicial systems, special attention will be given to Kuwait and Qatar. Kuwait, with its history of an assertive (and sometimes adversarial) parliament, viable associational life, and constitutional development, probably provides the most fertile ground in the Gulf for the emergence of liberal legality. Qatar, with a far less politicized society, organized only informally by family, and with constitutionally unrestricted executive authority, would seem to provide the least fertile ground.[1] Thus, the comparative study of Kuwait and Qatar will reveal the extent of the pliability of the legal and judicial systems in the area and the likelihood of their serving as a base for the emergence of liberal legality.

---

[1] See Jill Crystal, *Oil and Politics in the Gulf: Rulers and Merchants in Kuwait and Qatar* (Cambridge: Cambridge University Press, 1990).

## Liberal and illiberal legality in Kuwait

In Kuwait, many of the same issues debated in Egypt in the past century have arisen, though often in different forms. In particular, controversy about the independence of the judiciary and the resort to exceptional courts in Kuwait have been intimately connected with debates over the extent of the rule of law. However, perhaps the most notable feature of the Kuwaiti scene has been the weak role played by the judiciary in the fundamental legal and constitutional issues that have arisen in the country. This is not to say that advocates of liberal legality are weak in Kuwait. Indeed, they are stronger at the current time than almost anywhere else in the Arab world. Their strength lies outside the judiciary, however, for reasons related to the political and legal structure as well as the unassertive judicial outlook. If the Egyptian experience is any indication, tolerance of political pluralism in Kuwait (currently at historically high levels) may eventually lead to the limited institutionalization of liberal legality.

### Judicial independence in Kuwait

The independence of the judiciary from the executive emerged as a key issue in political debates inside Kuwait in the 1980s, although few claim the judiciary's political meekness is wholly due to executive domination. As in Egypt, appointments, transfers, and promotions are the responsibility of a Supreme Judicial Council, mandated in article 168 of the Kuwaiti constitution of 1962. Besides stipulating the existence of the Council, however, the Kuwaiti constitution leaves its composition and organization entirely to the field of legislation. And Kuwaiti legislation has given great authority to the executive branch in this regard. The minister of justice is involved in the appointment of almost all senior judicial officials. Lower appointments fall to the Supreme Judicial Council but it, in turn, is composed primarily of those senior judicial figures under the influence of the minister of justice. Further, the Supreme Judicial Council is devoid of budgetary independence, and all the administrative support for the courts is part of the Ministry of Justice rather than being attached to the courts or to the Council. In the mid-1980s, a group of parliamentarians, led by Mishari al-'Anjari, attempted to legislate far greater independence for the judiciary, giving it the fiscal and institutional autonomy from the Ministry of Justice comparable to its Egyptian counterpart (after 1984). With the 1986 suspension of parliamentary life that effort was aborted; indeed a leading parliamentary advocate of the reform believes the proposed law was one of the causes of the government's decision to dissolve the parliament indefinitely.[2] In 1990 the amir issued by decree a new law of judicial organization that actually strengthened executive control over the judiciary.[3] Mishari al-'Anjari won a seat in the elections occasioned by the 1992 restoration of parliamentary life. The prime minister-designate, Sa'd al-'Abd Allah Al Sabah (also the crown prince) was compelled to invite al-'Anjari into the government. Colleagues report that he was offered several ministries but insisted on assuming the position of minister of justice and exacted a pledge from the prime minister that the cabinet would support a new law of judicial organization.[4] Indeed, a new law was introduced by several members of parliament and the government prepared its own draft.[5] When a complex dispute between the parliament and the government erupted over the legal status of legislation enacted in the absence of parliament (to be examined more fully below), however, the proposed law became a victim of an agreement between parliamentary leaders and the government to suspend action on affected legislation until the courts had ruled in relevant cases.[6] The agreement involved a suspension of parliamentary action on decree-laws enacted in the absence of parliamentary life and therefore barred only discussion of the 1990 decree-law, not action on a new law of judicial organization. Yet the distinction was initially lost and only in early 1995 did the legislative committee of the parliament resume examination of the new proposals. There is clear momentum for increasing judicial independence, but work so far has moved at a glacial pace.

The authority and composition of the Supreme Judicial Council is not the only issue critics cite blocking the independence of the Kuwaiti judiciary. Unlike many other constitutions in the Arab world, the Kuwaiti constitution does not provide for the irremovability of judges, stating in article 163 only that "Law shall guarantee the independence of the judiciary and shall state the guarantees and provisions relating to judges and the conditions of their irremovability." While judges have

---

[2] Mishari al-'Usaymi, personal interview, Kuwait, April 1994.

[3] For details on the 1990 decree-law see Lawyers' Committee for Human Rights, "Kuwait: Building the Rule of Law: Human Rights in Kuwait After Occupation," report dated April 1992, p. 22.

[4] Mishari al-'Usaymi, personal interview, Kuwait, April 1994; see also Lawyers' Committee for Human Rights, "Laying the Foundations: Human Rights in Kuwait Obstacles and Opportunities," report dated April 1993, p. 21.

[5] For the text of the law proposed by parliamentary deputies, see al-Tali'a, April 13, 1994.

[6] 'Abd al-Rusul 'Abd al-Rida, personal interview, Kuwait, January 1995; see also Muhammad al-Salman, "Parliament Suspends Examination of all Decrees Issued in its Absence, and the Legal Affairs [Committee] Changes its Direction and Stops Examining the Law of the Judiciary," al-Watan, July 22, 1994. Al-'Anjari's defeat in the 1996 parliamentary elections dealt a blow to efforts to revise the law.

not been dismissed in Kuwait for political reasons, critics consider this constitutional text excessively weak (especially since implementing legislation only guarantees the irremovability of senior judges) and in need of amendment.[7] A further concern sometimes voiced in Kuwait involves the employment of foreign judges by short-term contracts. With the heavy reliance on judges from countries where salaries are far lower (especially Egypt), some critics charge that such judges will be unlikely to offend executive authorities, fearful that their contracts will not be renewed. In most of the small Gulf states foreign judges are in the majority. Even in Kuwait, with its longer judicial history and well-established law school, only slightly more than half of judicial personnel are Kuwaiti.[8] The criticism of reliance on foreign judges may not be without foundation, but it is certainly exaggerated: the Egyptian Supreme Judicial Council limits Egyptian judges to four years of service overseas (if they wish to remain longer they lose their judicial rank in Egypt); this certainly must diminish the concern about contract renewal.

In spite of numerous criticisms concerning the independence of the Kuwaiti judiciary, there are few indications – or few charges – of direct political interference in judicial decisions. Indeed, Kuwaiti judges are more likely to avoid politically sensitive issues than to impose government will. Yet the strong executive role in judicial affairs has certainly decreased the corporate independence of the Kuwaiti judiciary. In short, what is at issue is less the independence of the individual judge than the independence of the judiciary (as in Egypt). Without a judges club, without control over senior positions, and without budgetary and administrative independence, the Kuwaiti judiciary has not been able to be a corporate actor for its own interests (much less on behalf of a specific legal vision) as has the Egyptian judiciary in recent years.[9]

### Exceptional courts in Kuwait

While the Kuwaiti judiciary has had far less success securing corporate independence, the government has only rarely resorted to exceptional courts. Military courts, which have been used extensively against members of Islamicist groups in Egypt since 1992, have played no role

[7] 'Uthman 'Abd al-Malik al-Salih, *Al-nizam al-dusturi wa-l-mu'assasat al-siyasiyya fi al-kuwayt* (The Constitutional System and Political Institutions in Kuwait) (Kuwait: Kuwait Times Press, 1989), p. 610.

[8] Figures for 1995 provided me by the Ministry of Justice in Kuwait indicate that out of 374 judicial personnel (including both judges and members of the *niyaba*), 204 are Kuwaitis, 164 are Egyptians, and 6 are Syrian.

[9] While no judges club exists at present, there has been a recent attempt to begin one. Judge Riyad al-Hajiri, personal interview, Kuwait, April 1994.

in Kuwaiti society. Article 164 of the constitution restricts military trials of civilians (perhaps because of the role of military judges in post-1952 Egypt): "except when martial law is in force military courts shall have jurisdiction only over military offenses committed by members of the armed and security forces within the limits specified by law." Indeed, the legal basis for military courts remains incomplete. In 1992, before the reestablishment of parliament, the amir issued a decree-law establishing such bodies; the law was attacked by liberal critics and the newly elected parliament rejected it.[10]

A second exceptional court, for trying government ministers accused of crimes, is suggested in the constitution. Article 132 reads: "A special law shall define the offenses which may be committed by ministers in the performance of their duties, and shall specify the procedure for their indictment and trial and the competent authority for the said trial, without affecting the application of other laws to their ordinary acts or offenses and to the civil liability arising therefrom." The provision was probably included to insure that ministers could be brought before courts of some kind. Political courts for such purposes, often operating out of parliamentary bodies, were common features of nineteenth- and early twentieth-century constitutions. In Kuwait it took twenty-eight years before the constitutionally mandated law was promulgated as the parliament and the cabinet clashed over the issue without clear result. In 1990, in the absence of parliament, the amir issued a decree-law which outraged much of the opposition, since it stipulated that unless four judges in a special five-judge panel voted for conviction the minister would be acquitted. The opposition argued that the constitutional text was designed to insure that ministers were accountable for their actions as much as, if not more than, ordinary citizens. The decree-law had the opposite effect by requiring the special judicial majority. In 1994 the parliament rejected the law, setting off the most complex constitutional battle in Kuwaiti history (as will become clear below). In 1995 the government and parliament finally compromised on a new law.

The only truly active exceptional courts have been the State Security Courts and the Martial Law Courts (al-Mahakim al-'Urfiyya). The first were, until quite recently, a permanent part of the Kuwaiti judiciary. In 1969 the parliament passed legislation allowing for the establishment of

[10] See 'Abd al-Rida 'Ali Asiri, Al-nizam al-siyasi fi al-kuwayt (The Political System in Kuwait) (Kuwait: Matba'at al-watan, 1994), p. 245. For the criticisms of the law, see 'Uthman 'Abd al-Malik al-Salih, "The Draft Law of Military Law and Punishments," Majallat al-huquq, March–June 1993, p. 11. See also the remarks of Mishari al-'Usaymi in the parliament, January 19, 1993. The parliamentary action places the law in the same category of other decree-laws rejected by parliament (including the law to try ministers); their status is still unclear.

State Security Courts, although the implementing regulations were not issued until 1975. While composed of regular judges, the Courts' members were appointed by the justice minister. Further, until 1991 a judgment from the Court was final unless issued *in absentia*. In 1976 the constitutionality of the Courts was challenged on the grounds that they subjected ordinary citizens to an exceptional court even when martial law was not in force, and that the lack of a right of appeal violated a constitutionally guaranteed right to resort to the courts. The Constitutional Court upheld the law, however, stating that the constitution allowed the organization of courts to be determined by law, and that the right to resort to the courts did not imply a right to appeal.[11] Defendants were not without rights in the State Security Courts: sessions were often public and the Courts referred those who claimed to have been tortured to medical examiners (though critics charged that the Courts still admitted evidence gained under torture).[12]

State Security Courts played a very prominent role in the aftermath of the Iraqi invasion. Initially, as will be discussed below, Martial Law Courts were established. When these came to an end in June 1991, State Security Courts took on the work of crimes related to the invasion and occupation. Before the State Security Courts assumed jurisdiction, however, the Kuwaiti government yielded to international pressure and issued a decree-law amending their procedures. First, judges were to be appointed only after the Supreme Judicial Council was consulted, although ultimate authority remained with the minister of justice. Second, a limited right of appeal was granted: in cases in which defendants argued that the law had been misapplied they were allowed to appeal to the *Mahkamat al-Tamyiz* (the highest court in Kuwait, equivalent to Egypt's *Mahkamat al-Naqd*).[13] While this procedure was still criticized as granting insufficient rights of appeal, an international human rights group noted in a 1993 report that half of those brought before State Security Courts had been acquitted.[14] In 1995 the law establishing the State Security Courts was repealed, in an effort led by human-rights parliamentarians and with government assent, on the grounds that such special courts were no longer required.[15]

Martial Law Courts had a far more terrifying record. Their basis lies

[11] 'Adil al-Tabataba'i, *Al-nizam al-dusturi fi al kuwayt* (The Constitutional System in Kuwait), Kuwait, n.p., 1994, pp. 878–83. See also Asiri, *Al-nizam al-siyasi*, p. 247.
[12] Middle East Watch report, "A Victory Turned Sour: Human Rights in Kuwait Since Liberation," September 1991, p. 42.
[13] Lawyers' Committee, "Kuwait: Building the Rule of Law," p. 16.
[14] Lawyers' Committee "Laying the Foundations," chapter 2.
[15] See Ghunaym Muhammad al-Mutayri, "Kuwait Abolishes State Security Court," *al-Sharq al-awsat*, July 10, 1995.

in article 69 of the Kuwaiti constitution, which allows the amir to proclaim martial law (though it requires him to refer the matter to the parliament). In 1967 the implementing legislation was passed, modeled partly on the Egyptian law. It involves appointing a military governor (who in practice has been the prime minister, as in Egypt) with extensive, even extra-constitutional, emergency powers. The 1967 law also provided for Martial Law Courts composed of officers (appointed by the military governor) and professional judges (appointed by the minister of justice). Judgments of the courts cannot be appealed, but they are submitted to the military governor for approval. Martial law was declared in July 1967 (several weeks after the June Arab–Israeli war) and stayed in effect until January 1968, but the Martial Law Courts did not play a prominent role. The government did attempt to broaden its constitutional powers to declare martial law in 1980 but failed.[16]

Immediately after the eviction of the Iraqi army from Kuwait, martial law was declared for the second time in Kuwaiti history. This time Martial Law Courts played an extensive role, and continued operating until June 1991 when martial law was ended and pending cases were transferred to the State Security Courts. Martial Law Courts thus actually operated for only slightly over a month, but during this period they convicted 118 of 164 individuals brought before them. The trials came under heavy criticism for their use of confessions obtained under torture, harsh sentences, and failure to grant defendants and their lawyers the time or opportunity to present a defense.[17]

Despite the record of the Martial Law Courts, most of the harsh measures taken during the period immediately following the Iraqi occupation occurred completely outside of the framework of the courts. Armed gangs, some apparently composed of members of security services, engaged in arrest, torture, and murder of suspected collaborators. In most cases, those involved escaped punishment, though in one particularly prominent case (the Nur Farhat case) some members of the security services were eventually convicted.[18] Most notable, perhaps,

[16] The proposal was made in the "Committee to Improve the Constitution" established before the resumption of parliamentary life. The details on the legal basis of martial law and martial-law courts are based on Tabataba'i, *Al-nizam al-dusturi*, pp. 621–33 and al-Salih, *Al-nizam al-dusturi*, pp. 451–63.

[17] Middle East Watch, "A Victory Turned Sour," pp.35–36.

[18] Details on the Nur Farhat case can be found in the various human rights reports that were issued in the aftermath of the occupation. "Laying the Foundations" includes a letter from the head of the *niyaba* to Ghanim al-Najjar, head of a Kuwaiti human rights group, reporting investigation of fifty-seven cases of alleged crimes committed by members of the security forces. The letter also reported the status of the cases: 13 referred to the courts; 20 investigation closed; 10 misdemeanors referred to investigation department; 14 cases under investigation.

was the deportation of (and refusal to allow reentry to) Kuwaiti residents of those nationalities accused of excessive sympathy with Iraq. Unlike the extralegal and illegal actions of the security forces, deportation was often carried out in accordance with the legal prerogatives granted to the minister of interior. In other words, while none of these actions was reviewed by the courts, Kuwaiti law allowed the deportations to take place. The minister of interior is legally authorized to deport any non-Kuwaiti in the interest of public welfare, security, or morals.[19] Yet while extrajudicial measures – both legal and illegal – were used extensively in 1991, they have diminished remarkably since then. Stung by criticisms from international human rights organizations and under pressure from a parliament increasingly interested in human rights (a pressure that may have been welcomed by the new reform-minded minister of justice), Kuwait's various government agencies have exhibited greater respect for judicial procedures. On several occasions, members of the police have been tried for beating suspects; on one occasion, the Ministry of Interior was ordered to pay compensation to the victim.[20] As will be seen in the following chapter, the legal guarantees for some (especially foreign workers) are quite weak, but there is evidence of a willingness, at least in parts of the Kuwaiti government, to see these guarantees enforced.[21]

Thus, unlike Egypt, exceptional courts have not played a major role in Kuwait. The structure of such courts is much less developed and they have been used far more rarely. Even on the one occasion that they were used extensively, what was more notable was the extent of actions that took place completely outside of the judiciary. Kuwait's executive authorities have found far less need to construct quasi-judicial alternatives to the regular courts. In fact, even the court with the greatest ability to pose

[19] See Middle East Watch, "A Victory Turned Sour," p. 47; see also the Middle East Watch report, "Nowhere to Go: The Tragedy of the Remaining Palestinian Families in Kuwait," October 23, 1991. This authority is still exercised. In a controversial case in early 1995 a Palestinian resident in Kuwait sent a caustic but unthreatening poem by fax to a Kuwaiti journalist known for his sarcastic attacks on Palestinians. The journalist complained to the interior minister who ordered that the Palestinian be deported immediately. No recourse to the courts was possible under Kuwaiti law and the deportation was effected.

[20] In February 1994, a court ruled that the Interior Ministry should pay compensation of 18,000 KD to a citizen who was beaten. The text of the ruling is printed in al-Tali'a, February 16, 1994, p. 6. Al-Watan, January 17, 1995, p. 9 reports on the trial of police for beating somebody into signing a confession.

[21] The Ministry of Justice has recently established an Office of Human Rights, within its International Relations Department. The current Assistant Undersecretary of Justice, Jamal Ahmad al-Shihab, was active in the 1989–90 movement that called for the restoration of the parliament; he served as the attorney for a leading member of the movement, Ahmad al-Rub'i (later minister of education), when the latter was arrested for his activities.

a real challenge to executive authority – the Constitutional Court – has been far more timid than its Egyptian counterpart. An examination of the Court shows this stark contrast, which is especially surprising in view of the constitutional text the Court is designed to protect.

### Kuwaiti constitutionalism and the Constitutional Court

The Kuwaiti constitution of 1962 is one of the few constitutions in the Arab world that can be described as having constituted the political order as much as it was constituted by it. With independence in 1961, the ruling family of Kuwait (most notably the amir, 'Abd Allah al-Salim Al Sabah) conceded the need to have a constituent assembly responsible for writing the constitution. The motives were partly international and partly domestic. Internationally, Kuwait's sovereignty was not yet secure. Iraq's claims on Kuwait led to an international crisis which was only temporarily resolved in 1963. The heavy British influence on the state both before and after independence made it a target of Arab nationalist criticism. The Kuwaiti leadership seemed determined to demonstrate that it had all the accoutrements of a sovereign state and full popular support. A constituent assembly seemed an obvious answer to such concerns. Domestically, disputes within the ruling Al Sabah family had led to some severe crises in the past (including, in one instance at the end of the nineteenth century, fratricide); the amir was apparently concerned that succession procedures be clearly delineated in a constitutional document to prevent future struggles within the Al Sabah.[22] Additionally, Kuwait had several important political actors besides the Al Sabah. These included an Arab nationalist movement (strongest among students and recent graduates) and historically powerful merchant families. The amir, who had himself headed the abortive 1938 national assembly, apparently viewed a constituent assembly as a means of reaching an accommodation with such autonomous forces.

Accordingly, elections for twenty positions in the Constituent Assembly (al-Majlis al-Ta'sisi) were held at the end of 1961. The twenty elected delegates were joined by all the ministers who had not won election in their own right; the result was a body of thirty-one members, eleven of whom were from the Al Sabah.[23] Elected members included

---

[22] According to the president of the al-Majlis al-Ta'sisi, succession was one of the key concerns on which the amir focused during the writing of the constitution. See al-Salih, Al-nizam al-dusturi, pp. 206–207.

[23] See Salah al-Ghazzali, Al-hayah al-dimuqratiyya fi al-kuwayt (Democratic Life in Kuwait) (Kuwait: National Union of Kuwaiti Students, 1985), pp. 9–13.

representatives of Kuwait's merchant families, leaders of bedouin groups, and Ahmad al-Khatib, an Arab nationalist leader. At the same time, foreign experts in constitutional law were engaged to assist with the drafting work. The chief drafter was 'Uthman Khalil 'Uthman, an Egyptian colleague of 'Abd al-Razzaq al-Sanhuri, who had himself just completed work on drafting Kuwait's law codes. 'Uthman produced a draft for the assembly. A constitutional committee then reviewed the draft, making some changes. The constitution was then referred to the entire assembly. While members of the assembly did raise many issues, the transcripts of the sessions reveals them to have been largely satisfied with the explanations of 'Uthman (who was present to address the members' questions). The matters which excited the most concern included whether to amend the draft to mandate the *shari'a* as "the main," rather than "a," source of legislation. The assembly maintained the original wording, though the controversy has continued intermittently to the present day. A second controversy was over the provision prohibiting ministers carrying on outside business while holding office. Finally, some wished to extend the constitutional requirement that ministers hold native Kuwait citizenship to deputy ministers. On all three matters a majority of the assembly was convinced by 'Uthman's defense of the original draft.[24] After minor modifications, the draft was approved.

The outcome of Egyptian drafting, Al Sabah concerns, and popular participation was a curious and often ambiguous document. The cabinet seemed torn between responsibility to the amir and to the parliament; the relationship has remained contested during much of the time that parliaments have been in session. The constitution was also accompanied by an explanatory memorandum (which had become standard practice for Egyptian legislation), the legal status of which has been the subject of sometimes acrimonious debate. In several key areas, the constitution clearly reflects concerns that arose in Egyptian constitutional debates. 'Uthman, a member of the committee that authored the fairly liberal 1954 draft constitution in Egypt, probably sought to remedy in Kuwait many of the flaws that liberal constitutionalists found in Egyptian constitutional life.[25] He therefore not only borrowed Egyptian

---

[24] See Richmond to Home, "Constitutional Advance in Kuwait," November 19, 1962, FO 371/BK 1015/50.

[25] Kamal Abu al-Majd, an Egyptian constitutional expert who was a student of 'Uthman and has served as adviser to the amir of Kuwait and dean of the law school at Kuwait University, maintains that 'Uthman saw Kuwait as an undeveloped, tribal society. 'Uthman's goal was therefore to draft a constitution that would assist Kuwait's political development along modern lines and therefore included elements that he considered highly advanced. Personal interview, Cairo, November 1994.

language on judicial independence and the right of recourse to the courts, but also included provisions barring some of the limits on liberal legality that had arisen in Egypt. For instance, in article 169, the administrative court was specifically authorized to nullify as well as order compensation for illegal administrative acts. This was an authority the administrative courts of the *Majlis al-Dawla* had claimed, only to find the Nasserist regime remove it by law. A similar attempt in Kuwait would have been a clear violation of the Kuwaiti constitution of 1962 (the Egyptian constitution of 1971 finally adopted similar wording). As mentioned above, article 164 prohibited military courts from trying civilians except during times of martial law, a probable reaction to the heavy use of military courts in Egypt after 1952. And the constitution, while granting the amir extensive emergency powers, also contained strong provisions for parliamentary supervision of such powers. As will be seen, the provisions have proven too strong for the government on two occasions.

Also demonstrating Egyptian influence, article 173 mandated the construction of a judicial body for constitutional disputes. The right of judicial review of the constitutionality of legislation had been difficult to establish in Egypt, and provision for a specialized constitutional court was included in the constitution drafted by al-Sanhuri, 'Uthman, and others after 1952 only to be rejected by the regime. 'Uthman seemed to wish to grant the Kuwaiti judiciary what the Egyptian judiciary exercised uncertainly and only after protracted battles. The explanatory memorandum justified the existence of the court in terms of centralization, a major concern of Egyptian judicial development, arguing that if judicial review were dispersed among the various courts it may lead to conflicting judgments. During the deliberations, the Al Sabah-dominated cabinet of the time attempted to remove both this article and article 169, which dealt with an administrative court, maintaining that the Kuwaiti judiciary was not yet sufficiently developed for the task.[26] Yet the result of the drafting process not only maintained the provision for a constitutional court but strengthened it by adding the sentence: "In the event that this body determines that a law or regulation is unconstitutional it will be considered retroactively void [*ka'an lam yakun*]."

It took twelve years before the Constitutional Court actually began operating. Not until 1971 did the parliament take up the matter when some members proposed legislation to establish a court. Their plan provided for an eight-member court composed of senior judges and law professors chosen by the government, the parliament, and the judiciary.

[26] Richmond to Walmsley, August 15, 1962, FO 371/BK 1015/37.

The chair of the Department of Public Law at Kuwait University would also have served as a member. The government at the time responded to the parliamentary initiative with its own plan for a five-member court consisting only of senior Kuwaiti judges selected by the Supreme Judicial Council. The government argued that the dearth of constitutional cases would make it preferable that the judges selected continue with their duties on other courts and meet as the Constitutional Court only when needed. Further, the government plan restricted to itself and the parliament the right to resort directly to the Court. Other constitutional issues would have to be referred to the Constitutional Court by other courts. If a court decided, despite the arguments of a party to a dispute, that no constitutional issue was involved, that party could resort to a "Committee to Examine Challenges" (lajnat fahs al-tu'un) consisting of three judges from the Constitutional Court. If the Committee decided that the challenge was serious, it was to refer the case to the full Court; otherwise the constitutional challenge would be dismissed. In 1973 the government plan was passed by the parliament, and the Court was established in October of that year.[27]

The law came under criticism from legal scholars and opposition parliamentarians on the grounds that the Court would be weak and even unconstitutional. The explanatory memorandum to the constitution mentioned that the government and the parliament would participate in forming the Court. Thus, the plan advanced by members of parliament would come far closer to the Court as originally intended and would be a more appropriate forum for deciding political struggles over the meaning of the constitution. Proponents of the government plan argued that the explanatory memorandum was not binding.[28] In 1983 the parliament passed legislation amending the composition of the Court, but the amir withheld his consent arguing that the legislation was based only on the explanatory memorandum which he could not accept as binding. The parliament was deterred from an attempt to pass the legislation over the amir's veto by a government threat to go directly to the Court to obtain a binding interpretation of the constitutional provision. Feeling that the Constitutional Court was unlikely to declare itself unconstitutional, parliamentary leaders abandoned the effort.[29]

Criticism also centered on the procedure for individuals to bring constitutional challenges, especially because article 173 read that "the law shall guarantee the right of the government and concerned parties to

[27] Al-Salih, Al-nizam al-dusturi, pp. 665–67.
[28] See al-Salih, Al-nizam al-dusturi, pp. 645–49, and Tabataba'i, Al-nizam al-dusturi, p. 894.
[29] Al-Salih, Constitutional Review, pp. 62–64.

challenge the constitutionality of laws and regulations before the body."
Since individuals faced two possible hurdles – the original court hearing
the case and the Committee to Examine Challenges – critics argued that
the law obstructed rather than guaranteed their right to challenge a law
or regulation constitutionally. One leading Kuwait constitutional scholar
also argued that allowing the original court to decide the seriousness of a
constitutional challenge violates the clear intention to establish a single
court empowered to decide constitutional issues.[30] It is theoretically true
that by allowing appeal to the Committee, the Kuwaiti law does give
individuals a stronger right to resort to the Constitutional Court than
they have in Egypt where a decision by the original court not to refer a
challenge is final.[31] Yet in practice, it has been virtually impossible for
any individual to convince the Committee to refer a case to the full court;
indeed, it has still yet to do so on any occasion.[32] And the Committee
itself has been allowed to determine its own constitutionality. In 1992,
during a period of press censorship, a writer protested a decision by the
minister of information to prevent publication of his column in the daily
al-Watan on the grounds that it violated constitutional guarantees of
freedom of expression. When the original court refused to refer the issue
to the Constitutional Court, the writer appealed to the Committee; he
also argued to the Committee that the constitution guaranteed him the
right to resort directly to the Court and not to the Committee. The
Committee rejected both claims thereby ruling that its own existence
could not be legitimately challenged on constitutional grounds.[33]
Indeed, the Committee has played such an important role that the Court
and litigants have begun to behave as if the Committee's decisions are
precedents almost comparable to decisions by the entire Court.[34]

[30] Al-Salih, *Al-nizam al-dusturi*, pp. 611–12, 656–61, and 684–93.
[31] Tabataba'i, *Al-nizam al-dusturi*, p. 894.
[32] Al-Salih, *Al-nizam al-dusturi*, p. 692. 'Adil al-Tabataba'i, personal communication,
February 1995.
[33] See constitutional case 1 of 1992; the judgment is published in *Majallat al-qada' wa-l-
qanun*, 14, December 2, 1993, p. 13. The claim that prior press censorship violated
constitutional guarantees was rejected because such censorship had been lifted by the
time the case reached the Court. According to the law establishing the Court,
individuals who bring cases must have a direct personal interest; the Court ruled that
the end of censorship meant that the author no longer had an interest in overturning
censorship. It is difficult to escape the impression that the Court followed the reasoning
only to avoid a politically sensitive case. While censorship had been lifted the
government did not abandon its claimed authority to reimpose it. Further, the end of
press censorship did not erase the harm caused by the original act of censorship.
[34] Most constitutional authorities in Kuwait would argue that the decisions of the
Constitutional Court are binding on other courts while the decisions of the Committee
are binding only with regard to the specific case at hand. Yet the Court has never acted
to reverse any precedent created by the Committee, giving the Committee's decisions
greater authority than they would otherwise have.

Have the criticisms of the Court's structure and procedure proved valid in practice? And if they have, has the Kuwaiti constitution remained unenforceable? An answer to these questions can begin by an examination of the Kuwaiti Oil Tankers Corporation case, which is still before the Kuwaiti courts. This case involves almost all of the most sensitive constitutional issues in Kuwait: the emergency powers of the amir, the authority of the Constitutional Court, the relationship between the parliament and the government, the authority of the parliament itself, and the accountability of the Al Sabah family. Moreover, the ultimate result of the dispute will not be of mere symbolic value but will go far in determining the meaning of many contested articles of the Kuwaiti constitution.

On January 18, 1994 'Ali al-Khalifa, a former minister of oil and a member of the Al Sabah family, was charged with embezzlement along with Hasan Qabazard, a leader of a prominent merchant family, and several top officials of the Kuwaiti Oil Tankers Corporation.[35] They were accused of arranging the sale of oil tankers to the Corporation for several times their market value and pocketing the difference (amounting to tens of millions of dollars). Two years later, however, the legal dimensions of the case had proved so complex that the court had only begun to look into the merits of the accusation.

'Ali al-Khalifa's lawyers immediately claimed that the court where the charges were first heard – a regular Kuwaiti criminal court – was not competent to hear the case. The claim was based partly on article 132 of the constitution which mandated a special law and court for offenses committed by ministers in performance of their public duties. In fact, parliament had never passed such a law, although, as discussed above, the amir had issued a decree-law in 1990 to fulfill article 132. Just days before 'Ali al-Khalifa was charged in court, however, the parliament had rejected the decree-law, claiming the right to review (and cancel) all decree-laws issued in its absence. 'Ali al-Khalifa's lawyers argued that the parliamentary action was invalid and that the justice minister, Mishari al-'Anjari, had played an improper role and encouraged the parliament to take the step, knowing that 'Ali al-Khalifa was about to be charged. In effect, the parliament and a member of the government stood accused of interfering in judicial matters, a violation of the constitution. Even if the parliamentary action was valid, however, it was still unclear whether an ordinary criminal court could have jurisdiction over a minister, especially because the parliament had not yet passed any legislation to replace the repealed decree-law for trying ministers.

[35] This account of the case is based on newspaper accounts in *al-Hayah*, *al-Qabas*, and *al-Watan* (which is owned by 'Ali al-Khalifa).

Yet the core of the defense claim was that parliament could cancel a decree-law promulgated during the suspension of parliamentary life only by issuing legislation (subject to government veto); a simple resolution citing article 71 and indicating rejection of a decree-law (not subject to government veto) was insufficient. Indeed, the government and the amir had not invoked article 71 when issuing this and other decree-laws. The defense claimed that the amir was not exercising his emergency powers and thus was not subject to constitutional oversight. Instead, the cabinet and the amir constituted the *de facto* authority in the country and legislation issued by them, even if it did not satisfy the terms of the Kuwait constitution, was valid. It was for this reason that it would take separate legislation and not a mere parliamentary resolution to render the law ineffective.

The criminal court, faced with this complex web of constitutional issues, referred the matter to the Constitutional Court. When faced with some of these issues after a past suspension of parliament, the Constitutional Court had generally avoided the most difficult matters. When parliamentary life was resumed in 1981 after a suspension lasting four and one-half years, the constitutional status of decree-laws and parliamentary authority had arisen in two important cases.[36] In the first, the Court avoided addressing directly whether the amir had exceeded his authority by suspending parliament and whether the parliament had the power to review decree-laws. In the second case, the Committee to Examine Challenges refused to refer an objection to a decree-law to the entire Court. The Committee did so by seeming to endorse the government argument that a decree-law passed during the suspension of parliamentary life did have validity stemming from its promulgation by the *de facto* authority in the country.[37] At the same time, the Court noted (without mentioning article 71) that the parliament had affirmed the decree-law.

Having failed to resolve the issues earlier, the Constitutional Court was faced with them again in 1994, though in much more complex form. Yet the trial court posed the question only in the simplest way: was the act of parliament cancelling the decree-law constitutional? While mentioning the 1982 Committee ruling (thus hinting decree-laws issued in the absence of parliamentary life had a different status than those issued on the basis of article 71 of the constitution) the Court seized on

[36] Muhammad al-Muqatti', chair, Department of Public Law, Kuwait University, personal interview, Kuwait, April 1994.
[37] Ibrahim Muhammad al-Humud, "The Effects Resulting from the Parliament's Refusal of Law Number 35/1990, Issued in the Period of the Suspension of Parliamentary Life," *Majallat al-huquq*, 18 (3), September 1994, p. 560.

the narrowness of the question posed to rule that it had no jurisdiction. The parliamentary action rejecting the decree-law to try ministers was not itself a law, and the Court argued that it did not have the authority to rule on non-legislative parliamentary actions. Thus it referred the matter back to the original court to decide whether or not it had jurisdiction over 'Ali al-Khalifa.[38] (In 1995, the parliament finally passed new legislation for trying ministers and the case was taken up by a newly constituted special court.)

By sidestepping the most difficult issues, the Court seemed to be vindicating its critics. It is true that the Court has issued some bolder rulings – such as its 1992 judgment overturning the election of two members of parliament.[39] But during the spring and summer of 1994 the Court issued two other judgments that seemed to lack political courage. When some journalists argued that their inability to obtain a permit to establish a newspaper was an infringement of their constitutional rights, the Court avoided addressing the matter of press freedom by arguing simply that the case had been brought to the Court improperly.[40] And in a case stemming from the parliament's rejection of a decree-law which granted pension benefits for members of the *al-Majlis al-Watani* (a quasi-parliamentary body established in the absence of the regular parliament in 1990), the Court also ruled that this was a parliamentary action not falling within its jurisdiction.[41] And critics point not only to the indeterminate nature of the Court's rulings but also to their number. Partly because of the refusal of the Committee to refer cases to the Court, the Court has not issued more than three dozen rulings over its two decades of existence.

Some argue that the problem is the unassertiveness of the Kuwaiti judiciary as a whole. The reluctance of the judiciary to confront constitutional issues is of long standing. In the eleven years between the promulgation of the constitution and the establishment of the Constitutional Court, ordinary Kuwaiti courts were several times asked to rule

---

[38] The ruling, constitutional case 3 of 1994, is printed in *al-Kuwayt al-yawm*, year 40, no. 162.

[39] The Constitutional Court has been designated by law as the body ruling in disputes relating to parliamentary elections. In 1992 two deputies were elected in districts where some members of the military were allowed to vote (which they are prohibited from doing). Since the number of military members voting was greater than the margin of victory, the Court invalidated their election and the parliament ordered by-elections. See Hamad al-Jasir, "Kuwait: Revoking the Membership of Two Deputies," *al-Hayah*, December 30, 1992.

[40] The text of the ruling, constitutional case 1 of 1993, is printed in *al-Kuwayt al-yawm*, year 40, no. 149, April 3, 1994.

[41] The text of this ruling, constitutional case 1 of 1994, is included in *al-Kuwait al-yawm*, year 40, no. 156, May 22, 1994.

on constitutional issues. Since the constitution clearly endorsed judicial review the courts could have plausibly claimed jurisdiction over constitutional disputes before the establishment of the Constitutional Court; since the constitution designated a special court the courts could have also plausibly denied it. In 1969 the Court of Appeals chose the latter path, to the disappointment of several leading legal scholars.[42] The administrative court has also come under attack for accepting the doctrine of "acts of sovereignty," and for applying it unnecessarily broadly. The law organizing the judiciary forbids it from examining acts of sovereignty but does not define the term. The law has been challenged on the grounds that it unconstitutionally restricts the right to resort to the courts, but the Kuwaiti administrative court has ruled that the issue is not sufficiently strong to merit the attention of the Constitutional Court. Moreover, the court has been far less restrictive in its application of the doctrine than have Egyptian courts in recent years.[43]

While charges of direct executive interference in the courts are rare in Kuwait, it is judicial timidity in political matters that has led liberal critics to revive older proposals to broaden the Constitutional Court beyond senior judges to include former parliamentarians and law professors and to weaken or abolish the Committee to Examine Challenges. While such proposals clearly have the support of some leading deputies, the parliament has yet to consider the matter in a sustained manner.[44] Ironically, the proposals of the advocates of liberal legality in Kuwait contradict those of their counterparts in Egypt, illustrating again that political context can often be more important than precise institutional arrangements. In Kuwait, the inclusion of non-judicial (though expert) personnel is seen as a step towards greater boldness and independence. In Egypt, the participation of non-judicial personnel is viewed as anathema to the rule of law.

More generally, the situation in Kuwait differs from Egypt where the major issue attracting the attention of advocates of liberal legality has been the executive's ability to avoid the regular judicial system. In Kuwait, with the exception of the period immediately after the Iraqi withdrawal, that has not been as great a concern.[45] Instead, attention

---

[42] Al-Salih, *Al-nizam al-dusturi*, p. 664; Tabataba'i, *Al-nizam al-dusturi*, pp. 885–93.

[43] See Dawud Sulayman al-'Isa, "Commentary on the Judgment of the High Appeals Court, Tamyiz Section–Commercial, Issued in its Session Held November 25, 1987" *Majallat al-huquq*, 18 3, September 1994, p. 865.

[44] 'Abd Allah al-Rumi and Mishari al-'Usaymi, personal interviews, Kuwait, April 1994. In a personal interview with Mishari al-'Usaymi, Kuwait, January 1995, he speculated that such legislation would likely meet a government veto.

[45] There are sometimes thinly veiled accusations that members of the Al Sabah family do not fully come under the scrutiny of legal authorities, however.

has focused on the authority to issue legislation itself, and especially the constitutionality of decree-laws issued in the two periods when parliamentary life was suspended. This dispute is worth examining in some detail, particularly since the restoration of parliament in 1992 has made the issue more, rather than less, acute.

In 1976, the amir of Kuwait, Sabah al-Salim Al Sabah, dissolved the parliament and issued a decree suspending several constitutional provisions: the portion of article 56 specifying the size of the cabinet relative to the parliament; article 107 requiring that new elections be held within two months of the dissolution of parliament (and requiring the immediate reconvening of the old parliament if elections are not held); and article 174, governing the amendment process. Leaving no stone unturned, the amir also suspended article 181, which specifically prohibited him from taking the actions he was in fact taking: "No provision of this constitution may be suspended except during martial law within the limits defined by law. In no circumstances may the sessions of the parliament be suspended during this period, nor shall the immunities of its members be infringed." The decree granted the cabinet all the powers exercised by the parliament and announced that legislation would henceforth be issued by decree. Further, a committee to improve the constitution would be established. The decree adduced no basis for its authority, nor did it explain the reasons for the actions beyond vague charges that democracy was being exploited.[46] Members of the disbanded parliament were unable to claim that article 107 was still in force (which would have recalled the dissolved parliament in the absence of new elections), nor was there any serious challenge in court to the amir's decree.

A committee to improve the constitution was indeed appointed, but only in 1980 after the death of the amir and the succession of the former prime minister, Jabir al-Ahmad al-Jabir Al Sabah. Rather than implement the threat implied in the decree of 1976 of amending the constitution by decree, the government agreed to submit amendments proposed by the committee to a restored parliament in accordance with constitutional procedures. In 1981 parliamentary life (and the suspended articles of the constitution) were therefore restored. The government passed on some of the proposed amendments to the new parliament, but eventually withdrew them because of lack of support.[47] The government also informed the parliament of decree-laws issued in

---

[46] The text of the decree is included in al-Ghazzali, *Al-hayah al-dimuqratiyya*, pp. 118–19. The exploitation of democracy presumably referred to a series of policy differences between the parliament and the cabinet which had led to several confrontations.

[47] Al-Ghazzali, *Al-hayah al-dimuqratiyya*, pp. 137–44 and 173–74.

its absence, without explicitly stating that they would be subject to article 71 of the constitution. Article 71 required the submission of emergency legislation to parliament. Those decree-laws not approved would be retroactively invalid. The government in effect claimed, as ʿAli al-Khalifa's layers claimed thirteen years later, that the decree-laws were as valid as other legislation and needed no parliamentary agreement to be effective. To repeal them, the parliament would have to pass new legislation, which would have to be submitted to the amir who could withhold approval. (Article 66 does provide mechanisms for promulgating legislation that has not gained the amir's approval; however, they are difficult to exercise and in fact have never been used.) Without clear guidance from the Constitutional Court (as discussed above), the matter was resolved by a parliamentary decision to approve most of the 500 decree-laws submitted to it, although a restrictive press law was specifically rejected.[48] Some laws never received parliamentary approval, leaving their status unclear.

In 1986, the amir again dissolved parliament and suspended the constitutional clauses preventing him from doing so. The parliament again took no immediate action, but three years later a group of former parliamentarians led a campaign to restore parliamentary life. By early 1990 the campaign had gathered sufficient force that the government responded – first by trying forcefully to suppress the movement, then by offering a limited pledge (including elections for a consultative body, the *al-Majlis al-Watani*) which the opposition rejected. During the Iraqi occupation, a popular congress was held in the Saudi city of Jidda; the opposition exacted a concession from the ruling family to restore parliamentary life after liberation. After elections in 1992, parliament reconvened and once again was faced with over 500 decree-laws promulgated in its absence. After rejecting some decree-laws, including that related to trying ministers, parliamentary leaders reached an agreement with the government to suspend the issue of the decree-laws until the outcome of the ʿAli al-Khalifa case (and another case related to the prerogatives of members of the short-lived 1990 consultative body) was clear. Because all motions and appeals in the ʿAli al-Khalifa case could easily take years to resolve, and because of the indeterminate role played by the Constitutional Court, the effect of the agreement was to postpone the issue of decree-laws beyond the life of the current parliament. While some parliamentarians were clearly frustrated by the agreement, the parliamentary leadership was apparently cowed by a threat by the government to go to the Constitutional Court for a binding ruling – and

---

[48] Al-Ghazzali, *Al-hayah al-dimuqratiyya*, p. 171; Mishari al-ʿUsaymi, personal interview, Kuwait, January 1995.

given past decisions by the Court there was a strong fear that it would uphold the view that article 71 did not apply and that the parliament could only cancel decree-laws by issuing subsequent legislation.[49]

Liberal parliamentarians and most (though not all) Kuwaiti constitutional scholars agree that the parliament has the right to reject the decree-laws retroactively simply by parliamentary resolution rather than by legislation, which would likely be blocked by the government.[50] The argument of the government and its supporters would seem at first glance to be tenuous. The actions of the amir in suspending parliament and granting its authority to the cabinet were clearly unconstitutional. And the claim that emergency circumstances necessitated such action is also unconvincing – not only on the political grounds that policy differences hardly constitute national emergency, but also on the constitutional grounds that emergency situations were anticipated by – and provided for – in the 1962 constitution. Not only did the government not avail itself of the constitutional remedies; the amir in his decrees had directly and consciously violated the few constitutional limitations placed on emergency powers. The amir and the government were clearly operating outside the constitution and the law. The response of the government and its supporters would initially appear to be sophistry: it is precisely because the actions were unconstitutional that they cannot be judged by constitutional mechanisms. Their legitimacy cannot be questioned because they occurred in a different constitutional framework, one in which the executive had seized legislative powers. Decree-laws issued under such circumstances have the same validity as laws passed in accordance with the constitution.[51] Thus, the government was effectively asking not only the parliament but also the court specifically entrusted to guard the constitution to sanction

---

[49] The government threat was widely rumored; it was made public by a leading member of the cabinet when some parliamentarians threatened to break the agreement by raising some decree-laws for discussion in January 1995. See the statements of 'Abd al-'Aziz al-Dukhayl in *al-Qabas*, January 30, 1995, p. 1.

[50] A strong and comprehensive presentation of the case for the parliament's authority to review decree-laws enacted in its absence is 'Adil al-Tabataba'i's article *"Mada ikhtisas majlis al-umma bi-nazar al-marasim bi-qawanin al-sadira fi halat al-hall"* (The Extent of the Jurisdiction of the National Assembly in Examining Decree-Laws Issued in the Case of Dissolution), unpublished copy, 1994. I am grateful to Mishari al-'Usaymi for providing me with a copy of the article; a version was published in *Majallat al-muhama* in 1994.

[51] For a forceful defense of this position, see al-Humud, "The Effects Resulting from the Parliament's Rejection of Law Number 35/1990." The author is able to adduce several Egyptian court decisions concerning similar circumstances both under the 1923 constitution (which was also suspended twice) and after 1952. He apparently confuses the Egyptian *Majlis al-Dawla* and the Supreme Court with the Supreme Constitutional Court, however.

actions whose only justification was that they were so clearly unconstitutional that they in themselves formed a new constitutional order.

The arguments of the government and the reaction of its parliamentary and scholarly opposition seem puzzling at first and can be understood better if they are moved outside the narrow framework of the dispute over decree-laws to a far more fundamental clash regarding the meaning of constitutional life in Kuwait. In that context, what is at issue is not simply the validity of the government actions but the basis of its authority and legitimacy. Those who support the full legal status of decree-laws generally see the executive – and perhaps the ruling family – as prior to the constitution both politically and historically. Since the constitution was brought into being by amiri decree, it can be abrogated or suspended, even in part, by amiri decree. The amir, as head of state, and the executive, as the effective power exercising sovereignty in the country, possess ultimate authority. Not only does this allow them to act as necessity requires, but they are the ultimate judges of that necessity. This view is internally consistent and historically based, but it is profoundly anti-constitutional in inspiration. Scholars of constitutionalism have often admitted the need to exceed constitutional constraints on extraordinary occasions, but neither time did the amir announce any clear reasons for his suspension of parts of the constitution.[52] Further, the Kuwaiti constitution, like most others, does provide for emergency situations, but the amir made no attempt to use constitutional remedies for the unnamed problems before taking drastic action.[53]

Opposed to this is a constitutional vision of liberal parliamentarians and most constitutional scholars. Their historical image of Kuwait is quite different: it was a society which invited the Al Sabah to rule but only in a spirit of collegiality and consultation. Elected assemblies in 1921 and 1938 and the basic law issued by the 1938 assembly were merely formalizations of the social and political contract between Kuwaitis and their rulers. The 1962 constitution was similarly a contract between the amir from the Al Sabah and the members of Kuwaiti society, and that contract cannot be unilaterally abrogated by the amir.[54]

In 1995 the government moved to resolve the dispute by asking the Constitutional Court to rule on the applicability of article 71 to decree-

---

[52] As an indication of the failure of the amir to express clear reasons, Kuwaitis continue to adduce a wide variety of foreign and domestic reasons for both actions.

[53] For a comprehensive treatment of the subject of constitutionalism and emergency powers, see John E. Finn, *Constitutions in Crisis: Political Violence and the Rule of Law* (New York: Oxford University Press, 1991).

[54] This view is best articulated by Kuwait's leading constitutional scholars, ʿUthman ʿAbd al-Malik al-Salih and ʿAdil al-Tabatabaʾi whose works have served as a basic reference for this section. See especially al-Salih *Al-nizam al-dusturi*, pp. 202–208.

laws issued in the absence of parliament. The timing and method employed showed elements of both clumsiness and heavy-handedness. Earlier, the government had suspended *al-Anba'*, a normally tame newspaper, for a short period. While the reasons were not specified, the newspaper had just published an interview with a leading Islamicist who seemed to criticize the influence of the Al Sabah in the country. The interview was published shortly after the amir had criticized press excesses in a holiday address. The government adduced a decree-law issued during the suspension of parliament as the authority for the suspension, even though the parliament had voted to reject the law in question. The government erroneously argued that the parliamentary action rejecting the decree-law had not been published in *al-Kuwayt al-yawm*, the official gazette, and therefore had no legal standing. Since the parliamentary action had in fact been published the government found itself in a legally weak and politically embarrassing position. Rumored to be on the brink of collapse, the cabinet instead struck a very aggressive pose: it abandoned its earlier agreement to postpone the issue until the 'Ali al-Khalifa case was resolved and asked the Constitutional Court to rule on the constitutional status of the decree-law. This angered almost all parliamentarians, who regarded the Constitutional Court as weak and unlikely to disappoint the government. Ahmad al-Khatib, one of only two members of the 1992 parliament who had been elected to the Constituent Assembly, went so far as to call for a *niyaba* investigation of the entire cabinet for violating the constitution and high treason.

The question the government submitted to the Court was cast narrowly as the applicability of article 71 to decree-laws issued in the absence of parliament, not the larger issue of the constitutionality of the specific decree-laws enacted. Since article 71 covers the authority of parliament between sessions, the government has argued that it does not apply to prolonged periods of suspension. Thus the Constitutional Court, with its predilection for narrow rulings, could simply find that article 71 does not apply to the decree-laws – dealing the parliament and the constitution a severe defeat – without passing judgment on the blatant unconstitutionality of the decree-laws themselves. Since the entire dispute erupted during a period in which the parliament appeared divided (chiefly between Islamicists and liberals) and unable to confront the government in a unified and sustained manner, government motives in suddenly provoking a constitutional crisis and confrontation with the parliament were unclear. The most likely objective was simply to recover from the legal and political blunder caused by the suspension of *al-Anba'*. Thus few Kuwaitis were surprised when the government bowed to parliamentary pressure and agreed to withdraw the request for a

Constitutional Court ruling and leave the entire matter unresolved. In a sense the parliament won a victory because none of the decree-laws it rejected has been enforced. Yet the al-Anba⁻ controversy showed the government's ability to reopen the matter at any time and to use the Constitutional Court to intimidate parliamentary opposition.

That such a struggle is not resolved after over three decades is not unexceptional, but that the strongest defenders of constitutionalism lie in the parliament and the academy and not on the court specifically charged with interpreting the constitution must be regarded as anomalous. In one important sense, the anomaly underscores an important lesson of the Egyptian experience: judicial institutions matter, but not outside of the political environment that surrounds them. In Egypt, the judiciary has emerged as an effective advocate of liberal legality only at times when a pluralistic political order has been tolerated. Outside of those periods, the same judicial institutions operate as only a very weak check (and sometimes as a great facilitator) of executive authority. Similarly, the Kuwaiti courts have at all times served the general purpose of governing and administering Kuwaiti society. They have not served the additional purpose of enforcing constitutional limits on the executive, largely because the political environment has not allowed them to do so. The intention of some parliamentarians to amend the structure of the courts is an effort to insure that the Constitutional Court will play such a role; that effort will succeed only so long as there is a parliament (or other political force) able to secure the political environment for such a constitutionalist judiciary. As with the Egyptian judiciary, the Kuwaiti judiciary has proved itself quite capable of serving both authoritarian regimes and those allowing for significant (though limited) political pluralism.

### The role of courts and the prospects for liberal legality in Qatar

In Kuwait, the courts have shown that in the absence of favorable political circumstances they cannot be a force for liberal legality; even in favorable circumstances they have yet to play such a role. The Kuwaiti judiciary lacks the corporate independence to articulate such a vision. While not wholly devoid of institutional tools and constitutional authority to pursue such a mission, they have as yet shown little inclination to do so. Without either the structural bases for independent action or an activist outlook, the Kuwait judiciary has never pursued a liberal legal vision of any sort.

The situation in Qatar would seem to be even less promising. In the absence of parliamentary life or political pluralism, it would seem that liberal legality would be irrelevant. This might suggest that the courts are non-participants in Qatari political (as opposed to legal) life and are powerless to regularize, much less rein in, executive action. While such a conclusion seems plausible, the empirical evidence suggests that it is exaggerated: the courts are involved (and are in fact actors) in an admittedly muted struggle over the political identity of the country. What the Qatari case affirms above all, however, is that a civil judiciary exercising some independence is not incompatible with a non-liberal and non-democratic political system.

Qatar has two completely independent court structures and, as a result of matters left unresolved since independence, the relationship between them is still not completely defined. On the one hand, the *Shari'a* Courts (formerly free-standing, now administratively attached to the Ministry of *Awqaf*) have jurisdiction in personal status cases, murder, and crimes related to morals (such as adultery and possession of alcohol). The *'Adliyya* Courts legally have jurisdiction over all civil matters and those criminal matters not falling to the *Shari'a* Courts. In addition, all criminal cases in which Muslims are neither accused nor victims fall under the jurisdiction of the *'Adliyya* Courts.

Yet from independence in 1971 until the end of the 1980s, the legal definition of the jurisdiction of each system was not always observed. The *Shari'a* Courts accepted the existence of the *'Adliyya* Courts grudgingly and slowly. The president of the *Shari'a* Courts referred to the *'Adliyya* Courts as "courts of Satan" in the 1970s. The current vice-president of the *Shari'a* Courts refers to them as the *"qanuniyya* courts," indicating that they are based on positive law without endorsing the idea that they are based on justice as the term *"'adliyya"* implies.[55]

As a result of the rivalry between the two court systems, individuals could choose the system they wished.[56] *Shari'a* Courts would only refuse jurisdiction in a civil suit if the matter clearly involved commercial interest in a way prohibited in Islamic law; rather than penalize those involved they would simply reject the case.[57] Moreover, the public prosecutor, attached to the police in the Ministry of Interior (Qatar did not adopt the *niyaba* system in which prosecution is the task of judicial personnel attached to the courts) would often bring criminal cases (especially theft) to the *Shari'a* Courts.[58] To prevent conflicting

[55] 'Abd al-'Aziz al-Khulayfi, personal interview, Doha, December 1994.

[56] Al-Khulayfi, personal interview, Doha, December 1994; Ahmad Fakhru, judge in the *'Adliyya* courts, personal interview, Doha, November 1994.

[57] 'Abd al-'Aziz Hanafi al' Usayli, legal adviser to the crown prince, personal interview, Doha, November 1994.

[58] Al-Khulayfi, personal interview, Doha, December 1994.

judgments, both systems had a "gentlemen's agreement" (the English term is used widely among judges in both systems to describe the arrangement) to refuse to consider a case once it had been filed in the other court system.

The struggle for jurisdiction between the two courts was not bitter. Judges in the *Shari'a* Courts resented the diminution of their jurisdiction but accepted their establishment as within the authority of the amir.[59] Judges in the *'Adliyya* Courts viewed the *Shari'a* Courts as operating without fixed codes or procedures, but recognized that their claims to legitimacy in a Muslim society were strong. Even if the struggle was not bitter, however, it involved fundamental issues about the nature of the Qatari polity. For the *'Adliyya* judges and their supporters, modern states have certain requirements, and these include courts of law with fixed codes, written procedures, and guarantees of due process. For the *Shari'a* Court judges and their supporters, the *shari'a* is an essential and basic component of any Islamic society. While they do not reject codification and fixed procedures that are based on the *shari'a*, they have moved only slowly and uncertainly in that direction.[60]

Thus both a legal and an ideological and religious contest are involved. The Qatari government has taken actions to defuse the conflict, though it has shied away from a definitive pronouncement on the subject. The appointment of 'Abd al-'Aziz al-Khulayfi, a judge from the *'Adliyya* Courts trained partly in positive law, to the vice-presidency of the *Shari'a* Courts has worked to keep friction to a minimum. With the incapacitation of 'Abd Allah bin Zayd Al Mahmud, the president of the *Shari'a* Courts since 1938, al-Khulayfi effectively operates as president. Judges from the *'Adliyya* Courts admit that al-Khulayfi is more accommodating than his predecessor, although al-Khulayfi himself makes no secret of his preference for his new work and his wish that the *Shari'a* Courts be recognized as the courts of general jurisdiction for Qatar. Beyond al-Khulayfi's appointment, the Qatari government directed the *Shari'a* Courts several years ago to stop accepting cases that were designated as falling within the jurisdiction of the *'Adliyya* Courts.[61] While that order has largely been observed, the fact that it was

[59] 'Abd al-Rahman Al Mahmud, personal interview, Doha, November 1994. Al Mahmud currently chairs the board of directors for the Qatar Islamic Bank; he previously worked as a top administrative official in the presidency of the *Shari'a* Courts. His father has been the president of the *Shari'a* Courts since 1938.

[60] Both al-Khulayfi and Al Mahmud stated in personal interviews that codification and written procedures were not inconsistent with a *shari'a*-based system, though both seemed to regard such formalization as needed to respond to criticisms of the courts rather than as an end in itself.

[61] Al-Khulayfi, personal interview, Doha, December 1994.

issued at all only highlights the low regard of the *Shari'a* Courts for positive legislation, at least in the past. The 1971 decree-law establishing the *'Adliyya* Courts and designating its areas of jurisdiction was largely ignored by the *Shari'a* Courts; it took direct instructions for them to begin to observe it.

Both sets of courts have themselves taken the initiative to resolve the conflict by pursuing legislation. The *Shari'a* Courts and the *Awqaf* Ministry have proposed a law defining the relationship between the *Shari'a* and *'Adliyya* Courts, which would return to the *Shari'a* Courts what they felt they had lost. The *'Adliyya* Courts and the Justice Ministry responded with their own draft law which tilted the relationship in their direction. The matter has gone to the cabinet on two separate occasions without a decision having been taken; clearly the government regards the matter as highly sensitive politically.[62]

Thus the two court systems are not only involved in a low-intensity but fundamental struggle over Qatar's political identity; they have become active participants in that struggle. In fact, as the British discovered several decades earlier, the political influence of the *Shari'a* Courts is extensive; in one sense they represent the only political force in the country to operate autonomously of the executive authority in a formal and open manner.

Yet even if the *'Adliyya* Courts are a political actor in this limited sense, do they themselves have the independence that is a necessary element for the establishment of liberal legality? Qatar's judges do have constitutional guarantees of independence and irremovability.[63] In one sense their comparative lack of institutional development probably enhances their independence: there is no system of judicial inspection (as operates in Kuwait and Egypt) with the result that promotion operates almost exclusively on the basis of seniority. There is similarly no judicial council as in Kuwait and Egypt, with most of the functions of such a body being assumed by the president of the *'Adliyya* Courts.[64] Thus there are none of the institutional mechanisms that exist in Egypt for the judiciary as a whole to exercise a kind of corporate independence, but the tools available to executive authorities to punish judges who issue inconvenient rulings are probably slightly less than in Kuwait and in Egypt between 1969 and 1984.

[62] 'Abd Allah al-Muslimani, director of the technical section of the secretariat to the cabinet, personal interview, Doha, November 1994.

[63] Yusuf Muhammad 'Ubaydan, *Ma'alim al-nizam al-siyasi al-mu'asir fi qatar* (The Features of the Contemporary Political System in Qatar), n.p., 1984, p. 257.

[64] This information is based on interviews in November 1994 in Doha with Ahmad Fakhru, as well as with Yusuf al-Zaman, vice-president of the Court of Appeals, and Bihzad Yusuf Bihzad, a prominent Qatari lawyer.

In fact, even in private conversations, lawyers and litigants claim that there is no executive interference in the work of the courts. While some claim that there is discrimination against non-Qataris, especially in criminal cases, they admit that the courts do not hesitate to issue judgments against the government and members of the Al Thani family in civil disputes. In criminal cases the situation differs, but not because of the judiciary. Since investigation and prosecution of crimes falls to the Interior Ministry, rather than to a more independent *niyaba*, some privately claim that influential figures in the country can obstruct the course of criminal cases and have charges dropped.[65] If Qatari judges (if not the judiciary as a corporate body) do show signs of independence, how can this be explained in a political order that shows no other features of liberal or democratic practices? In fact, the *'Adliyya* Courts are hardly in any position to restrict executive action, even if they can rule against the government in specific disputes. First, the Qatari system lacks the administrative courts established elsewhere in the Arab world on the Egyptian model. While administrative acts can be – and in fact are – reversed by the courts designated for civil disputes, the absence of a specialized body for this purpose probably makes judges less sure of their ground. Second, and more important, the Qatari constitution gives almost no basis for the courts to restrict executive authority. The constitution itself, written within the royal palace (rather than a constituent assembly) and issued by decree, is modestly termed the "Temporary Amended Basic System." Since all legislative and executive authority is vested in the amir, and even the constitution itself can be amended by amiri decree, the constitution in effect places no checks on his authority. A consultative body is mandated by the constitution (though provisions to have its members elected have never been implemented). Thus, the political atmosphere does not exist for the emergence of liberal legality, and the constitution provides little basis for it.[66] The absence of liberal legality does not imply the absence of legality altogether, however. The amir governs by way of law that is enforced by the courts; it is the constitution and the legal order itself that place no restrictions on executive authority. Thus, unlike Egypt since 1952 there has been no temptation to resort to exceptional courts; Qatar's rulers have full legal authority to do as they wish.

[65] This is based on private conversations with Qatari lawyers. The most bitter complaint I heard expressed against the courts was from a Qatari citizen who filed suit against a member of the ruling Al Thani family in a commercial dispute. His anger stemmed not from the decision, which was favorable to him, but from the delays in executing the court order which would have been likely to occur no matter who the litigants were.

[66] In fact, not a single Qatari judge or lawyer could name one case in the history of the courts that had a constitutional dimension.

Indeed, if any limitation to executive action can be found it lies not in the *'Adliyya* but in the *Shari'a* Courts. Since the law they enforce is based on independent scholarship (and in fact since the courts themselves until now have been given no basis in positive legislation) the *Shari'a* Courts are potentially far more independent not only in their enforcing of law but also in the law that they enforce. And while the Courts generally subscribe to the Hanbali school of Islamic jurisprudence, they do on occasion resort to other schools, giving them even wider latitude.[67] At present, they show no inclination of attempting to develop the potential to issue judgments restricting the executive authorities. Nevertheless, the institutional basis for them to do so still exists. The *Shari'a* Courts have not been immune from the general development of hierarchical and formalized courts throughout the Arab world – they have instituted registries, appeals procedures, and built formal courtrooms. Yet they retain greater independence than many other judiciaries in the region. If the Qatari judiciary ever works to regularize or limit executive authority (which seems unlikely), it will be *Shari'a* judges and not *'Adliyya* judges who play that role.

The historical development of the legal systems in the Arab states of the Gulf affirm most of the lessons of the Egyptian experience. Gulf societies, with less nationalist resistance to British domination and with legal systems that were institutionally less developed, still moved in a direction different from that favored by the British. Just as in Egypt, imperialism hastened the development of non-*shari'a* based systems but it hardly imposed a new legal order. The operation of the systems in the Gulf has also shown that the feature of such systems that is most attractive to executive authority is their centralized nature that makes it possible to enact and enforce positive legislation. Legalism in the Gulf is fairly well developed, as it is in Egypt. Finally, as in Egypt, legalism need not imply liberal legality, constitutionalism, and the regularization or limitation of executive authority. When institutional and political conditions are favorable the judiciary has worked to pursue a limited but real vision of liberal legality in Egypt. Judges have not done so in the Gulf, even in Kuwait, despite the effort of liberal parliamentarians and legal scholars to develop a constitutionalist vision and a supportive institutional framework. The judicial institutions of the Gulf are sophisticated, their codes well-developed, and their judges independent (as individuals). Resort to exceptional courts is rare. Yet this system serves executive authorities and does not challenge them, even when

[67] 'Ubaydan, *Ma'alim al-nizam* , p. 263; 'Abd al-'Aziz al-Khulayfi, meeting with students from the Qatar University Department of Law, 1994.

others within the political community (especially in Kuwait) have done so. Executive and judicial visions of legality remain very much in harmony throughout the Gulf.

### Gulf judiciaries and the Egyptian experience

We may now turn to the second of the three questions that have informed this study of courts in the Arab world. Why have the major features of the Egyptian system been recreated throughout the Arab world? The motivations guiding legal and judicial development in the Gulf do not differ substantially from those in Egypt.

As in Egypt, the usefulness of viewing non-indigenous legal systems as externally imposed is limited. The circumstances for imposed law were far more favorable in the Gulf than they were in Egypt, because the British presence was less controversial and the local administrative structure was far more rudimentary when the British arrived. Nevertheless, while the degree of British influence was greater in the Gulf than it was in Egypt, British officials were more often than not frustrated in their attempts to guide legal development. Only in Bahrain did the British achieve any permanent success. In the other states the British presence (and the withdrawal) did sometimes provide an impetus for legal reform, but the content of that reform was locally determined. Egyptian influence proved to be far greater than British influence, largely because of decisions made by local rulers.

If imposed law provides little guidance, liberal legality provides even less. While there has been some evidence of an ideological attraction to the rule of law in Kuwait, even there liberal visions of legality have been weak. In much of the rest of the region such visions have been non-existent. Even in Kuwait, the center of a liberal constitutionalist vision has been in the parliament and the academy; little support has been found in the courts. In other Gulf states, rulers have generally respected the courts, but the legal basis for any liberal vision is extremely weak.

Gulf rulers have been drawn to legal reform, then, for much the same reason as their counterparts in Egypt. Centralized law codes and codified law increase the authority and effectiveness of the central state. Also as in Egypt, they do not necessarily increase regime legitimacy. In Kuwait, there has been a vague connection between respect for the rule of law and regime legitimacy, but in Qatar the relationship is probably negative. The contest between the *Shari'a* Courts and the *'Adliyya* Courts, while it hardly threatens the regime, leaves it open to the criticism that it is abandoning the legitimate Islamic model in favor of a system imported from France by way of Egypt. In Egypt, the debate over the abandonment of the *shari'a* occurred many decades after the event; in Qatar it is occurring (albeit in a muted fashion) concurrently with the emergence of civil courts. The attraction of such courts, then, lies not in how they legitimate but in how they operate in a daily fashion to enforce the laws and the policies dictated by the political authorities.

Up to now, we have focused primarily on political elites, probing their actions and intentions in the construction of legal systems. We now turn our focus from elite intentions to social consequences, as we study how Egyptians have taken the legal system built over the past century and made it their own.

# 7　Popular uses of the courts

The little plaintiff or defendant, who was promised a new rocking-horse when Jarndyce and Jarndyce should be settled, has grown up, possessed himself of a real horse, and trotted away into the other world. Fair wards of court have faded into mothers and grandmothers; a long procession of Chancellors has come in and gone out; the legion of bills in the suit have been transformed into mere bills of mortality; there are not three Jarndyces left upon the earth perhaps, since old Tom Jarndyce in despair blew his brains out at a coffee-house in Chancery Lane; but Jarndyce and Jarndyce still drags its dreary length before the Court, perennially hopeless.[1]

Charles Dickens, *Bleak House*

In 1987, Musa Sabri, a prominent Egyptian journalist was angered by an article mentioning him in the opposition newspaper *al-Wafd*. He filed a libel suit against the paper's editor, Mustafa Shardi, and the leader of the Wafd party, Fu'ad Siraj al-Din, the two officials held responsible under the press law for the contents of the paper. It took seven years before Sabri's suit was rejected by the *Mahkamat al-Naqd* which ruled that the responsibility mentioned in the press law was undefined.[2] Long before this the plaintiff and one of the two defendants had died, yet the case continued on, possessed of its own life, until the highest court in the country had ruled.

In 1961, a resident of Cairo learned from his father that the family was a beneficiary of a *waqf* (endowment) consisting of some urban real estate valued at eight million dollars and decided to go to the Ministry of

---

[1]　Charles Dickens, *Bleak House* (New York: Dell, 1965), p. 38

[2]　See "Egypt: Demand for Execution of Two People Accused of Killing Two Christians," *al-Hayah*, December 2, 1994. The case was not unique. In December 1989 *al-Ahali*, the weekly newspaper published by the Tajammu' party, published an article on Tharwat Abaza that led to a defamation suit. In March 1995 a court finally ruled that the editor of *al-Ahali* and Khalid Muhi al-Din, the party leader, should pay LE 5,000 in compensation. See Husayn al-Marsafawi, "Requirement that Khalid Muhi al-Din and the Former Editor of *al-Ahali* Pay LE 5,000 as Compensation to Tharwat Abaza," *al-Akhbar*, March 3, 1995. However, a few months later the Supreme Constitutional Court ruled that the responsibility mentioned in the press law could not be extended to editors in such cases.

*Awqaf* to have it divided among the many heirs. That required getting a court's approval, which in turn required that all of the heirs – who at that point numbered between eight and nine hundred – be notified. When the case actually went to court, however, a judgment was delayed because some of the heirs listed by the Ministry of *Awqaf* had died. The court postponed the case, insisting that the heirs of those recently deceased be contacted. Yet when the beneficiaries returned to court the case was delayed again for the same reason: some beneficiaries had died in between the two sessions, and the court ruled that their heirs had to be notified. This repeated itself for fifteen years, with the large number of heirs and the considerable delays between court sessions rendering a resolution of the case virtually an actuarial impossibility. About a tenth of the heirs were lawyers, and some very prominent attorneys were among the group. When one of the heirs was appointed minister of justice, the court finally agreed to end the delay (the minister of justice at that time generally chaired the Supreme Council of Judicial Organizations, representing the president), and in the mid-1970s a ruling was issued to the Ministry of *Awqaf* to divide the *waqf*. Yet at that point the matter ground to a halt again, this time because the *waqf* administrators insisted that they were entitled to one-tenth of the share of each beneficiary for their work in dividing the *waqf*. They also insisted that they be paid in advance rather than from the proceeds of the division, fearful that they would otherwise not receive their money. Yet many of the beneficiaries could not afford to pay before receiving their share. As of this writing, the court's judgment has yet to be implemented.[3]

Stories such as these are very familiar to most Egyptians. If they do not know somebody involved in seemingly endless litigation personally, they can read one of the numerous newspaper accounts: a divorce case pending for twenty-five years; a dispute within a family over ownership of a factory that is older than a quarter of a century but unresolved; a court that took ten years to rule that it did not have jurisdiction only to have this ruling reversed on appeal.[4] Egyptians would be fully justified in

---

[3] This information is based on an interview with one of the beneficiaries. In June 1991 I supervised thirty-one interviews (participating in some of them) with Cairenes who had been involved in civil and criminal cases. The interviews involved working-class, middle-class, and professional Cairenes, both male and female, and were loosely structured, focusing on the details of the case: the nature of the dispute; the decision to go to court; the course of the litigation; the attempt (if any) to negotiate outside of court; and the lawyer–client relationship. They focused on divorce, housing, employment, inheritance, supply, and forgery. As will become clear, even seemingly purely civil cases often involve the criminal law as well.

[4] On the divorce case, see Muhammad al-Sadafi, "In a Seminar at the Judges Club: A Respectable Wife has Looked for Divorce in the Courts for 25 Years," *al-Ahali*, January 19, 1994. On the factory case, see Badr al-Din Adham, "So that Justice is not Lost

feeling that in their country lawsuits are far more certain than taxes and on occasion survive death itself. Nor are Egyptians alone in these complaints. In other countries which have borrowed large parts of the Egyptian system similar stories are now being heard. Why would Egyptians bring their problems to courts which are almost universally described as slow, riddled with corruption (though not necessarily at the judicial level), inefficient and complex? And how do their experiences – and the system of courts more generally – affect the legitimacy of the political system as a whole?

## Working the system

The Egyptian system as it has emerged over the past century has generated consistent complaints that it encourages litigiousness. The history of such criticisms dates back to the late nineteenth century, as discussed in chapter 2. And half a century ago a new minister of justice described his ideas to an American diplomat for improving the physical facilities, personnel and procedures of existing courts – goals that still occupy the attention of the Egyptian government today.[5] Most previous writings on the imposition or importation of European-style systems focuses on its cultural inappropriateness. Yet the experience of Egypt indicates that – at least for the urban population that now comprises half the society – the legal system is far more often perceived as far too integral a part of Egyptian culture. The problem is not that Egyptians do not know how to work the system but that they work it too well.

Claims of Egyptian litigiousness would seem to receive strong support from statistical evidence on the use of the courts. Contradictory estimates on the case load of the courts suggest that there are so many lawsuits that the authorities literally cannot count them fast enough. In 1991, the deputy minister of justice for judicial inspection estimated that there were twelve million new cases brought before the various Egyptian courts each year.[6] The actual figure is probably lower, although in 1988, Salah Muntasir claimed that the most recent published figures at that time (from 1978) indicated 6.6 million cases and that the total number

Because of the Slowness of Litigation," *al-Akhbar*, December 17, 1985. On the reversed ruling of lack of jurisdiction, see Yusuf Jawhar, "Sound and Echo in the Court," *al-Ahram*, June 11, 1988.

[5] See S. Pinkney Tuck to Secretary of State, December 6, 1947, USNA 883.041/12–647. Indeed, for a description of legal delays earlier in this century with a very contemporary ring, see Latifa Muhammad Salim, *Al-nizam al-qada'i al-misri al-hadith* (Cairo: Markaz al-dirasat al-siyasiyya wa-l-istratijiyya bi-l-ahram, 1984), vol. II (1914–1952), pp. 384–87.

[6] 'Atif Faraj, "The Judges Retire . . . and 12 Million Cases are in the Courts," *al-Musawwar*, October 11, 1991.

had probably doubled in the interim.[7] To claim that the number of lawsuits doubled in a decade is not implausible; between 1952 and 1982 the number of cases quadrupled.[8] More recently, the minister of justice reported that in 1991 Egyptian courts produced judgments in seven million cases.[9] While no precise statement is possible, it seems safe to say that the number of new court cases a year approaches one per household. While cross-national comparisons are difficult, especially with a decentralized system like the United States', it is probable that Egyptians are as litigious, if not more so, than Americans.

Without a precise breakdown on the nature of cases, it is difficult to ascertain which sectors of society generate the most lawsuits, but indications are strong that, at least in urban areas, it is middle-class and working-class households that generate most cases. As will be indicated below, such families are more likely to resort to the courts for divorce and personal status cases than the more affluent. One judge in the *Mahkamat al-Naqd* estimated that even at the level of his court, the highest in the country, more than half of the cases heard were related to labor law and housing.[10]

Court cases can consume enormous amounts of time, but they do not necessarily cost enormous amounts of money. Court fees are low; to raise an appeal to the highest level, the *Mahkamat al-Naqd*, requires posting a bond of 25 Egyptian pounds, an amount that was fixed in the 1930s (and is now equivalent to approximately 8 US dollars). Yet the number of cases is still such that the Ministry of Justice actually generates revenue for the state, taking in over twice as much as it costs to administer.[11]

Expensive lawyers are most certainly available for those who can afford them, but others come with far lower fees. There is approximately one lawyer for every 400 Egyptians – a ratio similar to that in the United States. While not all those with law degrees practice law, the population of lawyers is still increasing faster than the general population.[12]

---

[7] Salah Muntasir, "On Litigation," *al-Ahram*, May 30, 1988.

[8] Badawi Mahmud, "Between You and Me is the Court," *al-Jumhuriyya*, April 24, 1986. Based on Ministry of Justice figures, the author claims that the number of civil, commercial, administrative, criminal, and personal status cases before the courts stood at 1,681,064 in 1952; by 1963 the figure reached 3,595,740. In 1973 the number was 5,477,489; in 1982 it was 6,100,924 (slightly lower than Salah Muntasir's claim for 1978).

[9] *Al-Ahram*, January 22, 1992.

[10] See the statement by Ahmad Makki, quoted in Mahmud, "Between You and Me is the Court."

[11] Ibid.

[12] There are approximately 130,000 lawyers in Egypt and 7,000 new law school graduates each year. This makes the annual growth of rate of lawyers higher than the crude birth

Attempts to legislate legal fees and to monitor lawyer–client relations have produced few effects.[13] Lawyers' fees vary considerably and are often negotiable. For most criminal cases, lawyers most often charge for the case, though they will sometimes ask for additional amounts if the case drags on. For civil cases, they will often ask for an amount based on the value of what is at issue, but whether this is paid partly in advance or is dependent on the outcome of the case varies. Because of the large number of people with law degrees able to prepare simple cases (even if they are not practicing law full time), most working-class Egyptians can find a lawyer, though not necessarily a good one.

Yet it is not simply the accessibility of the courts that accounts for the delays in reaching and implementing verdicts. In Qatar, judges in both the *Shari'a* and *'Adliyya* Courts acknowledge that the strongest attraction of the former for those who seek swift justice is their lack of complex procedure and ability to reach quick decisions. In the *'Adliyya* Courts in Qatar, and in the Kuwaiti courts, the problem of delayed justice is a frequent topic of discussion. The procedures of Egyptian courts, and of Egyptian-style courts in the Gulf, seem to guarantee overburdened courts along with numerous opportunities for litigants who seek, for whatever reason, to delay a final judgment. A consideration of these procedures reveals much about the multiplicity of tools available to customers of the courts.

The chief legitimate tool in the hands of those who wish to delay or reverse a judgment is the right of appeal. As in most civil law systems, an appeal generally consists of a higher court retrying the case rather than reviewing the conduct of the lower court. In almost all cases at least one appeal is possible; it is often the case that two levels of appeal after the initial judgment are available. In an ordinary civil case it would be unusual to complete the three levels in less than three years should one or both of the litigants choose to exercise their appeal rights.

There are further mechanisms for those who wish to delay the course of litigation. One of the most frequently discussed is an appeal for a judge to be recused in a case (*radd al-qadi*). While such a motion is seldom successful, it is referred to another panel of judges who rule on it. The sole cost of such a failed motion is a lost deposit. There is no limit to the number of such motions that can be filed in a case, offering a litigant the opportunity for almost endless delays. In 1986, *al-Ahram* reported a case that at that point had been before the courts for thirteen years, solely because one of the parties filed repeated *radd al-qadi*

rate for the country. See Ahdaf al-Bandari, "The 'Whirlpool' of Litigation . . . the Game of Courts," *al-Ahram*, 6 August 1992.

[13] 'Abd al-'Azim al-Basil, "Judgment after Negotiation," *al-Ahram*, June 6, 1990.

motions.[14] The Conference on Justice held that year recommended limitations on the use of *radd al-qadi*. In 1992 the parliament finally passed some amendments to the law of civil procedure which raised the deposit required and levied a fine for frivolous motions.[15] The effect may have been to put use of *radd al-qadi* as a delaying tactic beyond the reach of all but the affluent.[16]

A second (and probably far more common) source of delay is the courts' heavy reliance on expert opinions. For advice and examination on a whole series of issues – forgery, business practices, architectural soundness of buildings – courts will generally refer a case to specialized court employees. Egyptian judges themselves rarely develop their own specialization, increasing their reliance on such experts in any case with a technical dimension. As with most court employees, experts complain that they receive more cases than they can possibly investigate; they also complain not only of low salaries but that their expenses in connection with their work are not met.[17] While rumors of corruption among experts are not uncommon, their reputation is better than that of other employees, as will be seen. But when confronted with the charge that court decisions are frequently delayed for unreasonable periods, many judges respond (often with the concurrence of lawyers) that the primary source of delay lies not with them but with the experts.[18] Mindful that involving an expert entails considerable delays, some litigants will use this to their advantage. A claim that a key document or signature has been forged, for instance, will require consultation with an expert that could set back a case by an entire year. Since a false claim results in no penalties, an unscrupulous litigant can charge forgery seeking only a delay.

Administrative employees of the court are the object of the most complaints. The positions of *amin al-sirr* (a clerical employee responsible for maintaining and recording documents) and *muhdir* (bailiff and process-server) are generally singled out as among the most corruptible

[14] 'Abd al-Nasir Salama, "*Radd al-Qadi* . . . and the Slowness of Litigation!" *al-Ahram*, January 22, 1986.

[15] Interview with Rajab al-Banna (then assistant editor and legal correspondent for *al-Ahram*), May 1992.

[16] Kuwait imported *radd al-qadi* when it adopted large parts of the Egyptian codes. This allowed 'Ali al-Khalifa (in the case described in chapter 6) to file for *radd al-qadi* after the Constitutional Court had returned the case to the original trial court. When that motion was turned down it was appealed. The case was thus delayed for half a year.

[17] See Jihan Sha'ib, "The Expert Decides about Millions – and Gets 6 Pounds for Transportation Costs – 1000 Experts – One Investigates 400 Cases," *al-Akhbar*, December 18, 1985.

[18] Personal interview, Fathi Jawda, judge in the *Mahkamat al-Naqd*, May 1991; see also al-Bandari, "The 'Whirlpool' of Litigation." Similar complaints are heard in Kuwait.

in the system. Once again, low salaries and educational levels of these employees are held responsible. Often referred to in public as "the mafia of the courts," these employees are often charged with losing key documents, delivering papers to the wrong address, forging signatures to indicate that papers were served that actually were not, and failing to find a valid address – often in return for a bribe from one of the litigants. The amendments to the law of civil procedure raised fines for those accused of such bribery and liberalized the rules for notifying parties of a suit by newspaper announcement. But tales of renters facing eviction after losing an unknown lawsuit, or of cases dismissed when key documents disappeared, are still common in the press.[19] Even if the claims of corruption are exaggerated, judges and judicial personnel believe them to be true.[20] The result is that judges are far more willing to delay cases if a party does not appear, and, even if a judgment is issued *in absentia*, a litigant who appeals, claiming that he received no notice, will receive a sympathetic hearing.

Even a litigant who has received a favorable ruling in the courts will face a new set of delays in implementing the judgment. Parties who win a civil suit over money or property will often face adversaries who simply refuse to accept the judgment; they must then return to the courts and ask an implementation judge (*qadi al-tanfiz*) to have officials implement the ruling. If the dispute involves a sum of money there might be longer delays as the property and bank accounts of the loser of the suit are investigated. Indeed, Egyptian law is currently fairly lenient on those who drag their heels in obeying court rulings in civil cases.[21]

All of these problems and sources of delays are well known to those involved in the Egyptian courts (and indeed to the general public). They are discussed privately, in the press, and in legal circles. The 1986 Conference on Justice issued a series of recommendations for speeding the work of the courts. While only some of the suggestions have been implemented, the Conference succeeded in attracting national attention to the issue, and further suggestions are routinely mentioned in the press. Procedural reform receives much attention, with proposals focusing on limiting rights of appeal, restricting *radd al-qadi* motions, and constructing a mechanism to prevent frivolous or inappropriate cases from reaching the courts (some of these suggestions were included

[19] See Adham, "So that Justice is not Lost"; Alfat Ibrahim, "Enemies of Justice!" *al-Ahram*; March 20, 1993; and 'Atif Faraj, "The Mafia of Stealing Cases and Forging Rulings Shakes the Throne of Justice," *al-Musawwar*, October 25, 1991.

[20] Personal interviews with Khalid 'Abd al-Ghaffar, member of the *niyaba*, June 1991, and Bakri 'Abd Allah, Socialist Public Prosecutor office, May 1992.

[21] Haniya Fahmi, "So that the Judgments of the Judiciary are not Transformed into Judgments [only] on Paper!" *al-Ahram*, May 24, 1986.

in the 1992 amendments to the law of civil procedure). Others focus more on institutional changes, such as establishing small-claims courts or arbitration boards not bound by the complex procedures of the regular court system. Currently a *niyaba* exists only for the criminal and administrative courts; the 1986 Conference on Justice endorsed the idea of a *niyaba* for the civil courts responsible for preparing cases and ensuring that they were ready for trial. The United States Agency for International Development has expressed interest in supporting technological reforms, including a computerized case-tracking system. Finally, some have focused on the staffing of the system, arguing for more stringent standards (and higher salaries) for administrative personnel and extending the retirement age for judges.[22] In 1987 the minister of justice even ordered that a special section be established in the *ibtida'iyya* (primary) courts to decide cases over three years old.[23]

While some of the proposals made over the past decade have been (or will be) adopted, others encounter difficulty for institutional or fiscal reasons. Judges remain wary of (though not uniformly opposed to) measures that reduce the procedural safeguards offered litigants. Reducing the number of cases before the courts by arbitration or screening also draws judicial suspicions that the justice system is being closed to many people. More important, perhaps, are the costs involved in many of the proposals. While judicial salaries and physical facilities have been improved over the past decade, the construction of a civil *niyaba* or a comprehensive effort to raise the level of administrative personnel have so far been deemed too costly by the executive authorities.

Even if the institutional and fiscal obstacles to reform were all removed, however, complaints about litigiousness and overburdened courts would continue. The legal project begun over a century ago with the construction of the National Courts has succeeded too well, and Egyptian courts have insinuated themselves – or been brought – into the

[22] For some of the press discussions of reform of the legal system, see Ahmad Husayn, "A New System for Examining Appeals in the *[Mahkamat] al-Naqd*," *al-Ahram*, October 7, 1985; Iman Mustafa, "Application of the System of Conciliation Councils [*majalis al-sulh*]," *al-Ahram*, November 2, 1985; Hasan 'Abd al-Mawjud, "On the Bench they Rule on the People's Cases," *al-Ahram*, October 17, 1985; Mustafa Kira, "Justice and the Simplification of Litigation Procedures," *al-Ahram*, November 1, 1987; Mahanna Anwar, "The Judge. Will We Keep Him . . . Or Retire Him?" *Uktubir*, March 6, 1988; Dina Rayyan, "A Court for the Family–Its Implementation is Lost," *Akhbar al-Yawm*, January 7, 1990; "How do we Speed Justice?" *al-Ahram al-Iqtisadi*, September 9, 1991, pp. 30–33; 'Atif Faraj "The Judges Retire . . . and 12 Million Cases are in the Courts" and Rajab al-Banna, "How Will '*Radd al-Qadi*' be a Right that is Not Misused?," *al-Ahram*, October 11, 1991. For the recommendations of the Conference on Justice, see *al-Jumhuriyya*, April 26, 1986, p. 1.

[23] Ahmad Husayn, "A Section in Every Court to Decide in Old Cases Starts Today," *al-Ahram*, October 1, 1987.

most intimate of relationships. The legal system has been used for over a century by the country's political leadership to realize different goals. In the late nineteenth century, centralization was a prominent concern connected with the construction of the courts. In the Nasserist period, there was a concerted effort to meet the demands of rural Egyptians for land and urban Egyptians for housing and jobs – demands that political leaders attempted to meet partly through legal changes. More recently, the rights of women have drawn some attention and legislative action. It should be no surprise, then, that when Egyptians have troubles with housing, land, employment, and divorce they look to the courts for the remedies that have been promised them.

Accessible courts, affordable lawyers, and laws that offer wives, renters, and workers substantial rights and prerogatives have resulted in the entry of the Egyptian courts into many of the spheres of daily life in Egypt. Two areas of legal and court activity in Egypt – divorce and housing – will draw special attention in this chapter in an effort to ascertain how, when, and why Egyptians use the courts. These areas have been chosen because they comprise a good deal of the burden courts shoulder in civil litigation. When working- and middle-class Egyptians go to court, it is likely to be over one of these two issues.

The Egyptian courts respond to wives and renters partly because they have been designed and instructed to do so, and partly because potential litigants are familiar with their legal status. In a third example we will discover how an Egyptian-style legal system presents itself to domestic workers in Kuwait, a group that lacks these advantages. While their legal position will be shown to be unfavorable, there are surprising similarities with other groups in the ability to bargain and combine different fora for resolution of disputes.

### Divorce

Egyptian marriages are of course very often based primarily on love, but they can never escape economics. If they become troubled they often do not escape the courts. A web of personal status law, customs (some based on the law, others designed to minimize its effects), and intensive pre-marital bargaining forms the backdrop to all marriages. Divorces occur within the same framework, but it is not at all unusual for informal family intervention and the criminal law to play roles as well. (The law and practice for Egyptian Christians are very different, and divorce is extremely difficult. This section concerns only Egyptian Muslims.)

Egyptian personal status law is based on *shari‘a* sources and an Islamic conception of marriage as a contractual agreement between a husband who pledges support and a wife who pledges obedience. As such it shares essential features with personal status law in other predominantly Muslim countries. But the law has been codified since 1929 and has undergone some substantial changes since then.[24] Even in its first incarnation, the law gave substantial rights to a wife to divorce from her husband if he failed to provide support or caused her harm.[25] The husband's right to divorce his wife is virtually without legal restriction, although Egyptian personal-status law does include procedural requirements designed to insure that he will not do so recklessly. (Technically, a husband can directly divorce his wife; a wife does not directly divorce her husband but asks a court to order divorce.) In 1979, President Anwar al-Sadat issued a decree-law giving the wife stronger guarantees; when the Supreme Constitutional Court ruled in 1985 that al-Sadat had exceeded his constitutional powers by failing to submit the decree to parliament a new, slightly diluted, law was duly passed. Two of the principal changes adopted in 1979 and 1985 were to make it easier for a wife to claim harm (and thus demand a court-ordered divorce) if her husband married a second wife, and to require that the husband provide housing for his divorced wife and children still under her care. A further change implemented gradually in the 1960s and 1970s related to *bayt al-ta'a* (literally, "house of obedience"). A husband whose wife has left his house (as will be seen, joint property is virtually unknown and housing is usually provided by and belongs to the husband) can ask a court to order her return. Formerly, such an order could be forcibly implemented by the police. Over the past three decades that practice has virtually disappeared, but a wife who ignores a *bayt al-ta'a* order will forfeit many of her legal rights.

The impact of the law can only be understood in the context of Egyptian customs and bargaining related to marriage. Since husband and wife retain separate ownership, much of the pre-marital bargaining concerns what each side will bring to the marriage or pledge to the other. In general, a husband is expected to provide an apartment and major appliances. A wife may provide some of the furnishings for the apartment. A husband also is required to pay a *mahr* (bride-price) to his wife (or to her family to hold in trust for her), often consisting of two

[24] See John L. Esposito, *Women in Muslim Family Law* (Syracuse: Syracuse University Press, 1982), chapter 3; Carolyn Fleuhr-Lobban and Lois Bardsley-Sirois, "Obedience (Ta'a) in Muslim Marriage: Religious Interpretation and Applied Law in Egypt," *Journal of Comparative Family Studies*, 21 (1), Spring 1990, p. 39; and Enid Hill, *Mahkama! Studies in the Egyptian Legal System* (London: Ithaca Press, 1979), chapter 3.

[25] For a thorough study of the issue in the *Shari'a* Courts, see Ron Shaham, "Judicial Divorce at the Wife's Initiative: The *Shari'a* Courts of Egypt, 1920–1955," *Islamic Law and Society*, 1 (2), 1994, p. 217.

separate amounts. The *mahr muqaddim* (advance bride-price) is paid at the time of the wedding. A *mahr mu'akhkhar* (delayed bride-price) is also sometimes pledged to be paid in the event of divorce (or death). A husband is also expected (and required by law) to provide financial support for the family; so long as the husband provides the proper home and support, a wife is expected (and required by law) to live with her husband.

These arrangements leave tremendous room for bargaining and protracted financial negotiations to precede (and often prevent) a wedding. With housing scarce and expensive and financial resources tight for all but the very affluent, the families of the bride and groom are generally very anxious to insure that the needs and interests of their side are guaranteed; they are also careful to safeguard the interests and property of their side should the marriage end in divorce. The social standing of the two sides, the earning power of the groom, and quality of housing he can provide all affect the outcome. As a result, although the law would seem to give a husband far greater divorce rights than a wife, the situation in practice often depends on the arrangements made in advance of the marriage and the nature of the marital difficulties.[26] If a wife can show harm – perhaps because of physical or verbal abuse (or, since 1979, because the husband marries a second wife) – she will not only be able to divorce her husband, but may also be able to demand the *mahr mu'akhkhar*, child support, and housing. If, however, she leaves her husband and is unable to satisfy a court that she is justified, she may face a *bayt al-ta'a* order giving her the choice of returning to the home she fled or forfeiting most of her financial rights.

The result is that a troubled marriage often erupts in a tangled web of lawsuits and even criminal charges, which in turn provoke formal and informal attempts at mediation. For instance, in order to substantiate charges of harm, a wife will sometimes go to the police to swear a statement that she was subject to physical or verbal abuse. A husband will seek to gain legal advantage by filing a *bayt al-ta'a* suit to make clear to the wife that she will face potentially disastrous legal and financial consequences unless she returns. A creative spouse can find a variety of ways to invoke personal status, civil, and criminal law on his or her

---

[26] Egyptians here are not unique. In an extensive study of divorce in Iran and Morocco, Ziba Mir-Hosseini found courts used, especially by women, to negotiate marriage relationships. She also found several similar social practices that had the effect of strengthening the bargaining position of women (though precise customs varied as did court attitudes towards such practices). She even found that legal and social practices often had the effect of undermining the *shari'a* conception of marriage. Ziba Mir-Hosseini, *Marriage on Trial: A Study of Islamic Family Law, Iran and Morocco Compared* (London: I. B. Tauris, 1993).

behalf; such attempts generally provoke a similar set of moves by the other spouse. What is especially noteworthy is the wide variety of fora that are employed, often simultaneously. Husbands and wives will deal directly with each other, use the mediation of relatives and friends, and use the criminal, civil, and personal status courts in complex strategies to obtain (or prevent) a divorce on the most favorable terms.

The following case illustrates how litigants can use the courts and informal mediation (and even physical violence) in a protracted and bitter breakup of a marriage.

### Case 1 (Informant: friend of husband; relative of wife[27])

A friend of mine married my relative; she was studying to be a teacher. He was from a poor family, from a *sha'bi* [popular] neighborhood. After the engagement they quarreled over money and over her friends. He lived with her for about two months after the wedding. He lived in the same apartment building as his father. Whenever somebody would visit her, his relatives would look on. That annoyed her. She liked to go out with her friends and he forbade that. She wanted to help out her family because her father was old. He refused to help. They had a bad quarrel, and her family intervened. Then things really got bad – he was barred from her family's house. Not even the police could help. After the end of the school year he was beating her every day. She wanted to go out; he did not want her to go out. She left him. She demanded a divorce from him but he refused. He filed a *ta'a* suit against her and charged her with *khiyana* [betrayal, in this case infidelity]. She filed a suit demanding divorce and possession of the furnishings [that she had provided], claiming that he had taken them. He denied that he had them. We tried two or three times [to settle], but she wanted her furnishings. One of her relatives, a good, older man, was helping. They [the husband's family] attacked him [verbally] in the street. He raised a slander suit. Once the husband saw his wife in the street and quarreled with her. He grabbed her. He had to pay a fine.

The suits went on for four or five years or more. A session, another session, the lawyer did not show up, then the lawyer would come but the witnesses did not show up, then they came but the judges delayed the case. It was delayed once or twice a month. At the end he won the *ta'a* suit [requiring her to return], but she refused [to return] unless they would find a new house far away from his family. He refused. They [the wife's family] appealed to the High Court for divorce. She did not abandon the suit for the furnishings, but he won it because she did not return to his house. They kept on going for more than seven years. She would file a case, he would file a case; from one case to another all the way to the High Court. After seven years, the court ruled for divorce.

While it is impossible to ascertain the extent of physical violence in

[27] These interviews were supervised, translated and transcribed by the author. The interviewers are personal acquaintances of the informants. The words are the informants', but I have edited them for clarity and succinctness.

family relationships, the courts tend to take the matter extremely seriously. Battery is not simply grounds for divorce but also a criminal offense; if a wife charges battery she exposes her husband to criminal charges even while strengthening her rights to a divorce. A husband might also charge that a wife's family has beaten him. Thus, criminal and civil cases often are intertwined, as the following case demonstrates.

### Case 2 (Informant: husband's uncle)

A young man, a house painter, fell madly in love. He was a youth, with all those feelings. They got married. He got a simple apartment with simple furnishings. There were problems, but there was love. Her mother would come to stay for a week or a month. Naturally, a man wants to stay in a house by himself. Then her sister came. That is where the problem began. So she went to her mother and siblings for a month. He said he would not give her money for household expenses. She left him [for good]. He filed a [bayt al-taʿa] suit against her. She swore a mahdar [statement] that he had beaten her and had not been paying household expenses. They went to the police station. He denied beating her and withholding the money, but he hit her in front of the police officer. They made out a mahdar there. Later he saw her walking in the street with a man. He then agreed with a friend to go to the police station and complain that the friend had been having an affair with his wife. The officer did not believe the story; the husband went crazy and hit the officer. He was summoned to the police station [for having hit the officer]. He went to another officer, whose house he had painted, to intervene. They dropped the complaint after he apologized.

I went with him to his apartment. There was nothing there – even the pictures on the wall were gone. He asked his friend who had a shop in the building about it, and he told him that his wife had come and taken everything. He asked his friend how he could sit back and watch that happen. Then he insulted and hit his friend. He went on to his wife's relatives. They were butchers. There was a fight. When he got home he found threats written in blood on the walls. He did not complain to the police because he wanted to get even.

He divorced her and paid support [nafaqa] of LE 60. They had a son. When he turned twelve, the husband filed suit to obtain guardianship, as was his right. He wanted to get the boy so that he would no longer have to pay support to his wife. But the boy did not want to go, so the judge ruled that the boy would stay with his mother. The husband still pays the support. He has brought suit to reduce it. The ex-wife wants to get remarried but does not want to lose the support payments. That case is still going on. She brought proof of poverty, and he brought proof that she is living well.

The husband filed a suit to gain the furnishings [from the apartment the couple had lived in]. They inspected the apartment to make sure it was empty. His friend the police officer advised him to get witnesses that she had taken what was there. But he could not get evidence. Everyone was scared of her family. The case is still going on. It has lasted five years. The case about the beating is still going on as well. The ex-wife has also sworn a mahdar that he brought women to the apartment. She has said she would drop her cases if he drops his regarding the furnishings and guardianship of the son. He wants to get rid of the case. He wanted to get married again, but the ex-wife's family went to his prospective bride's family, and the marriage fell through.

Working-class and middle-class Cairenes tend to be very aware of the provisions of the personal status (and other relevant) law, and this affects their actions both before a marriage and in the course of a marital conflict. Thus some of their strategies are essentially preemptive – to gain a stronger bargaining position in case marital difficulties occur. This takes the fairly obvious form of carefully recording the material obligations of both sides in a written marriage contract, but it can also take more subtle forms. In one instance, a fiancée's engagement seemed about to collapse in an argument over finances and her prospective groom's wish to travel to Saudi Arabia to work. She therefore insisted that he write her a check for the value of the household furnishings he had pledged to provide. (In Egypt checks are often used not to exchange money but as guarantees of good faith, or they are postdated and used as promissory notes.) He agreed, but when the engagement finally collapsed he withdrew the money from the bank account. She then took the matter to the police, because writing a check without sufficient funds is a criminal offense punishable by a jail sentence. Her family then used the criminal case to increase their bargaining power.

The extensive use of the courts by working- and middle-class Cairenes in marital disputes suggests that the formal legal system is hardly seen as the forum of last resort. With the prolonged nature of litigation surrounding divorce (according to one estimate, the average life of a divorce case in the courts is seven years[28]) early resort to the courts is almost necessary. Yet the courts are hardly seen as a forum of first resort either. The various methods for settling marital problems – formal and informal, direct and manipulative, obvious and inventive – are all used, very often simultaneously. The courts and the legal system have become part of the social landscape, not simply accepted but actively sought out by those with severe marital difficulties. Indeed, it is probably the affluent who can afford to take a more reticent attitude towards the courts. When difficulties in a marriage occur, the material conflicts of wealthy Cairenes (over apartments, furniture, and child support) can be less pressing and more easily resolved informally outside of a legal framework.[29]

Once the courts have been introduced into a dispute, their role tends to escalate because of the actions of the parties themselves. Suits

[28] Al-Sadafi, "In a Seminar at the Judges Club."
[29] See especially Hill, *Mahkama!*, chapter 3.

provoke countersuits; criminal charges are filed to buttress a civil claim; and appeals and delaying tactics insure that the matter can be postponed for a momentarily disadvantaged party.

While debates over the current and desired relationship between *shari'a* law and the personal-status code have at times sharply divided the Egyptian polity, these concerns are rarely cited by those actually before the courts. Litigants seek concrete goals rather than abstract justice. Egyptians seem to be quite aware not only of the provisions of the personal-status law available to them but also other legal provisions (such as criminal prohibitions of slander and assault) whose relevance to marital dispute is not obvious until invoked by litigants. Even those with a relatively weak legal position devise tactics to make their claims on property, spouses, or custody of children.

In one sense, Cairenes seem exceptional in the Arab world only in the full range of legal tools available to them and their need and inventiveness in using them. In Qatar, where all divorces are handled by *Shari'a* Courts unbound by complex procedural guidelines, the number of divorces in one year is generally one-third or one-quarter the number of marriages.[30] In Kuwait, the number of divorces is generally one-fifth or one-quarter of the number of marriages.[31] These figures are comparable to those of Egypt. There is nothing about Egyptian marriages that is more tenuous. But the economic pressures are less intense in Kuwait and Qatar (where family and government assistance are more available for women who leave their husbands, particularly with regard to housing), and it is more difficult for a woman in the Gulf to obtain a court-ordered divorce. As a result, divorces in Kuwait and Qatar tend to be far less complicated affairs and are processed far more quickly by the courts. In Jordan, on the other hand, where divorce is also handled by *Shari'a* Courts but resources are more limited, Richard Antoun noted generally regarding personal status cases:

The pursuit of a court claim is frequently only one in a set of in-court and out-of-court tactics pursued by family members, mainly husbands, wives, and their fathers, toward certain ends. From the litigant's point of view it is not an attempt to obtain Islamic justice in some abstract sense. Rather, each litigant, explicitly or implicitly pursues a strategy that may involve certain moves in the Islamic court, certain moves in the civil court, certain developments in the framework of village custom, recourse to government officials (to a land registry officer, subdistrict officer, or police chief) or to tribal arbitrators (the Pasha). When the particular end has been achieved in any of the above arenas, the litigant drops his

[30] Ministry of *Awqaf*, State of Qatar, *al-Taqrir al-ihsa'i 1411–1412 h* (Statistical Report, 1411–1412 A. H.). The cited figure is based on marriages among Qatari citizens.

[31] State of Kuwait, Ministry of Justice, *al-Kitab al-ihsa'i al-sanawi* (Annual Statistical Book), various years. Again, the cited figure is for Kuwaitis married to Kuwaitis.

court case regardless of the satisfaction or nonsatisfaction of the narrower court claim.[32]

For Cairenes involved in marital problems, the legal system is not an alien, inappropriate, or terrifying presence but a potential ally or a set of tools. Some of these tools are generally helpful to one side and some to the other, but all are used, sometimes early and sometimes often.

### Housing and real estate

If Egyptians are ingenious and litigious when it comes to marital disputes that involve property indirectly, they can be equally so when property is directly at stake. Once again, the law itself provides many openings to several different sorts of parties. Landlords and tenants in urban and rural Egypt have a variety of tools at their disposal, sometimes by the design of political authorities and sometimes not. Legislation dating back to the period of Arab socialism (and sometimes before) has offered opportunities to those who are far from affluent to seek legal solutions to their problems. Recent attempts to modify property relations by law are hardly likely to remove the courts from being called upon in disputes.

Agricultural land was governed for forty years by a series of land reform measures undertaken within months after the new regime came to power in 1952. A significant amount of land was redistributed from large landowners to small owners. Perhaps more significant was rent control, which not only fixed the amount of rent that a landlord could charge (seven times the land tax) but also made it virtually impossible to evict a renter from the land. In 1992 a new law governing landlord–tenant relations in agricultural land loosened some of these requirements. While the full impact of the law is not yet clear, it seems extremely unlikely that attempts to evict tenants under its provisions will result in fewer lawsuits.

In urban areas, rent controls were introduced by the martial law authority during the Second World War and legislated into permanent existence after the war by the parliament.[33] Legislation also made it virtually impossible for a landlord to evict a tenant (subletting is the only common ground for eviction). Children could generally inherit rental

---

[32] Richard Antoun, "Litigant Strategies in an Islamic Court in Jordan," in Daisy Hilse Dwyer (ed.), *Law and Islam in the Middle East* (New York: Bergin and Garvey Publishers, 1990), pp. 39–40.

[33] A good summary of policy and legislation concerning urban real estate is Milad M. Hanna, "Real Estate Rights in Urban Egypt: The Changing Sociopolitical Winds," in Anne Elizabeth Mayer (ed.), *Property, Social Structure and Law in the Modern Middle East* (Albany: State University of New York Press, 1985).

rights from their parents. The 1952 regime actually rolled back rent on several occasions. In the 1960s and 1970s rents on new construction were fixed by neighborhood committees. By the 1980s landlords had come to feel that renting an apartment was essentially selling it, so difficult had it become to change rents or evict tenants. As a result, new construction since that time has generally been sold directly to occupants, generally even before it has been completed. Reforming landlord–tenant relations for urban residential property has drawn much discussion, but so far no legislation has been issued. Once again, it is unlikely that granting landlords greater authority to evict their tenants will reduce lawsuits related to housing. Rental of commercial property is also governed by strict legislation, and amounts are also fixed by neighborhood committees.

In both urban and rural areas, the legislation of the past half-century has given sufficiently strong guarantees to tenants that eviction, even for reasons sanctioned by law, has become very difficult. If a farmer claims ownership of land and refuses to pay rent, then those who claim to be his landlord will be able to retake the property only after prolonged litigation. If a tenant of an apartment sublets, the landlord will be able to obtain actual eviction only after launching a lawsuit that, after appeals are exhausted and an implementation order is obtained, could take years. Complicating matters still further are the illegal practices that have developed, especially with regard to urban real estate, to circumvent the law. Chief among these are key money for residential apartments and excess rents (often not recorded in the contract) for commercial property. This in effect ties the civil and criminal law systems together; indeed, since rent control originated in a martial law measure, the State Security Courts are at times involved.

Thus as much as the law represents an effort to define the relationship between renter and landlord, its actual effect is to provide a collection of tools and opportunities that can be used in inventive ways.

### Case 3: (Informant: landlord of an apartment and a commercial property)

I had an apartment I rented to a group of Algerian students. [The student I had signed the contract with] finished his studies and left, and he gave his key to one of his colleagues. This went on for a while – as soon as one would finish his studies he would leave and turn the key over to somebody else. I went to the apartment and tried to reach an agreement. I explained that this [subletting] was illegal in Egypt. The occupant has to leave the key with the owner when he leaves. The student there became angry and refused. I made him understand that if he did not change his mind I would go to court, but he said that he would not give me the key or give up the contract. I talked to him for several months but it was no use.

So I went to my lawyer and we filed an eviction case. This was at the end of 1984. The case continued in court for more than three years. If a paper is missing then the judge can delay for a month. Also, the opposing lawyer would delay things. He would use gaps in the law. He was frank – he told me that I would win the case but instead of a month it would take a year.

The Algerian returned to Algeria but he gave the lawyer power of attorney [tawkil]. The lawyer would always try to convince the judge [to delay the case because] the Algerian was about to come back. The lawyer offered me a settlement in which I would get back the key and end the contract for LE 500. At first I refused. But all the delays caused problems. I wanted to get the apartment ready for my fiancée [so that he could get married]. It was causing problems between me and her family. Finally I agreed.

The lawyer himself wanted to take over the apartment – he was young and wanted to open an office there. Once I went to the apartment and found the lawyer there. He had some files, dossiers, and books. He was using the apartment [as an office], so I went to the police to get an order that ownership was in dispute and that nobody could occupy it.

Finally I gave him the money. He had no case, but the time involved was more important. But the settlement was delayed – he had photocopied the contract but the judge needs to see an original. In the end, we settled the case ourselves and the case will eventually expire in the courts.

I had another problem with real estate. I owned a store used by somebody who sold car paints. He was always late with the rent. He got way behind, paying only one or two months worth every six months. I got fed up. I tried to solve the problem and I used all sorts of intermediaries. He listened to nobody. I went to court in 1988. I went to the lawyer who had worked against me in the first case. I thought I could exploit his nature in my favor this time instead of having him work against me. He told me my case was won; it was easy. He said it would be a quick eviction case. I knew he had no integrity, but I was happy when he said this. I agreed, and he filed the case. It was supposed to take a month. I asked him when the final judgment would be, and he said "Leave that to me. That is what you pay me for. I will call you." But he was really trying to get money from both of us.

The final judgment was for forced eviction. The lawyer went and offered him a deal – the tenant paid him LE 200. Then the lawyer came to me and told me to leave the case alone, it had been settled. He said the tenant would now pay his rent on time. But the tenant called me to tell me what happened. Finally another person selling car paints paid the old tenant a sum and me a sum to take over the shop.

As in divorce cases, the landlord here hardly regarded the courts as a final alternative. Although he did not resort to legal action immediately, he did not demonstrate any reluctance to do so. And once legal proceedings had started, negotiations continued. As the lawsuits proceeded, bargaining positions shifted according to the strength of the parties; in both cases the courts played an important role but did not determine the outcome. Indeed, in both cases the course and nature of legal proceedings proved as important (if not more so) than any final decision the court might render. In neither case was the landlord naive – he was aware of his legal rights and knowledgeable about how to assert them. However, his resort to the legal system to achieve goals was frustrated on both occasions by a lawyer even more expert in using the legal tools available and quite able to subvert the landlord's legal position, as strong as it was in theory.

The most obvious legal tool available to at least one party to a dispute is delay. If a document is missing or a party fails to appear in court, judges generally delay a case. While they will not delay indefinitely, this does usually make it possible to postpone examination of a case for up to a year (especially because civil courts are closed for all but emergency matters for three months during the summer). In cases in which more than two parties are involved, delays can be much more prolonged. This is especially true in *waqf* cases where all beneficiaries must be present or sign over power of attorney to a lawyer who will be present. The case cited at the beginning of this chapter had almost farcical aspects but is not unusual for a *waqf* case. One case involving a smaller number of beneficiaries went through the courts for twenty years when the judge who had been handling it (on appeal) died, leading to further delays. In addition, property cases often involve, or can be made to involve, expert reports (on matters like the authenticity of documents, the soundness of buildings, or the nature of changes made in a building).

Since so many property transactions involve aspects that are not simply illegal but criminal (such as key money or excess rents) an enterprising litigant can at times strengthen his or her position by revealing to legal authorities complete details of a transaction.

### Case 4: (Informant: son of the renter of an apartment)

About three or four years ago, we took an apartment. The owner of the building took about LE 500 from each resident in illegal key money. After about six months, the landlord came back and wanted two or three hundred additional pounds from each resident for repairs in the building. There were about thirty-six apartments in the building. Some residents talked to a brigadier in the army about it, then to somebody in the 'Abdin police station, then to a big judge. They all said, this man [the landlord] is a thief. We called the landlord to the police station. The chief of the station asked him about the [key] money. He said that he had taken nothing and demanded proof that he had. He was about seventy years old. One resident said he had not paid key money; he was a coward. The second said his brother had paid it, but his brother was in Saudi Arabia [and thus could not come to join the suit]. My father said he knew people in the *niyaba* and he would raise it with them. The *niyaba* took up the case and decided to call in all the people in the building and the owner. They brought over a couple of residents at a time.

The next day five of the residents filed suit against the owner. He had also taken money from people in the building to pay electricity bills, but he did not put this in the contract. But they found out that he had been bribing employees at the electric company rather than paying the bills. The employees lived in another building the landlord owned, and he had taken key money from them too. When they found out they were in trouble [for accepting bribes from him] they told about the key money, and they had all the receipts.

The judge said there are three cases – key money, [unpaid] electricity, and bribery. He told the landlord: "You are in trouble. You are a forger, a thief, and a liar – and you are seventy years old. If you give all the money back, you can escape the five-year jail sentence." But the man was a miser. You could take away his life, but you could not take a piaster from him. The judge told him he could pay half the money now and the other half within a year. If he did not pay there would be a second case. The man agreed. He paid the first half, but he did not pay the second. So the residents filed another suit, but the owner had a heart attack. My father said he would not keep quiet. He found out that the landlord owned some land in 'Abdin. He asked the court to force him to sell that land to pay the second half. When the landlord got notice of that case he fainted and went to the hospital. As soon as he got out of the hospital he said he would pay and he did. The landlord tried to make problems for us. We were on the top floor. He started keeping animals – including water buffalo – on the top floor. We got an order from the court to have them removed, and the place cleaned up – and a fine paid. The owner came to kiss my father's hand. He offered to clean things up but wanted the fine taken away. My father refused.

In this case criminal law was used as a bargaining chip not directly by the parties but by the court itself. It is more common for litigants to make allegations of criminal violations and to offer to drop them in return for a favorable settlement of the civil suit.

### Case 5: (Informant: renter of commercial property)

I had a store in Faysal Street in Giza. I rented it from somebody, he took from me LE 6,000 in advance rent. He wrote me receipts for it. I would only pay half the rent each month; the other half would be deducted from the advance rent I paid. The law says that somebody may take two years' advance rent up to LE 2,000.

Once I asked him to date the contract, so that I could give it to the local government. The contract had fixed the rent at LE 60 until the neighborhood rent control commission had been appointed and defined rents. He was angry and refused [apparently fearing that dating the contract would oblige him to return any back rent that exceeded the amount the commission might set]. I did not say a thing, but about two weeks later a *muhdir* from the court brought me an announcement [of an eviction notice] for bringing plumbing into the store, adding a *sandara* [small storage area], and removing a wall. So I showed a copy of the contract and the announcement to a lawyer. He told me these things were permitted as long as they were not structural changes. If the owner did not like the changes he could ask me to return things to the way they were when I left the property.

The truth of the matter was that rents had gone up and he could get LE 9,000 or LE 10,000 instead of the LE 6,000 I paid. I had been there for about two or three years. This was in the summer of 1985. I needed to rescue my good name. I also needed to assure myself that he would not take the store while I was gone, even though he was in Kuwait. I was traveling to the Arabs [Arabian peninsula] on a regular basis. He was a civil engineer working in the port. His wife was a doctor for women. These were educated people, not doormen.

I had earlier rented an apartment and paid LE 5,000 in advance. The man [constructing the building] had collected LE 35,000 for apartments and then went abroad, leaving the building incomplete and empty. I went to the State Security *niyaba* about that. While there I told them the story [about the advance rent for the commercial property]. He asked me if I knew that was against the law. I said yes. He asked me if I had the contract and the receipts. I gave him photocopies. He took over the matter. The case went along for a little less than two years. They ordered him to return LE 4,650 to me. There was also a judgment for the government. He had to pay double this amount to the Ministry of Housing for violating the housing law. He had to pay the same fine to the court for violating the law of the state.

We were both outside the country. He was in Kuwait, but he did nothing. According to my information after three years the judgment would no longer be valid [and the case would have to be renewed]. The last day the judgment was valid would be December 31, 1990. Then the events in Kuwait happened [the Iraqi invasion of August 1990] and he left [to return to Egypt]. He came to me and pretended to know nothing about the case. He asked for back rent. I told him why not sell me the property? We had talked about this before the case started. I told him I would pay the same amount we had agreed before [five years earlier].

The judgment against him [of the fine and return of back rent] was not implemented. It would have been a month in jail too . . . I don't remember exactly. He kept coming to me, asking me to sign the [sales] contract. I said, "You know what happened in Kuwait. I have the same problems [with available cash] you do." Before the case he was very hard-headed, his behavior was bad. But because of the judgment . . .

The matter ended there. We signed the contract of ownership. The judgment threatened him.

In this case heavy civil and criminal penalties could be documented by the contract and the receipt for the payments. Indeed, even in cases where illegal advance rent or key money is paid, written contracts and receipts are not unusual, giving the renter real bargaining power – it is the landlord, not the tenant, who can be prosecuted over key money. Yet even if the criminal law is not obviously involved, litigants can invoke it in creative ways. In one case, the owner of a building attempted to evict a married couple. The owner claimed that they had not made the required payments; the couple claimed they had and that the owner simply wanted to sell the apartment at a higher price. Since the owner lived in his building, the disputants were neighbors who saw each other frequently. This proximity led to several quarrels. After one quarrel with her landlord, the wife threatened with eviction went home and scratched herself with a razor blade to make it appear as if she had been attacked. She then went to the police, and with witnesses willing to testify that there had been a quarrel, was able to secure a criminal judgment against the landlord. The criminal charges in this case did not serve as a useful bargaining chip, because the two parties failed to reach an agreement.[34]

The law and court procedures affect the bargaining positions of the parties, but they hardly supplant bargaining. Even those in a relatively weak position are able to find tools in the legal system. In one case, a man renting an apartment illegally sublet it to a watchmaker. When the watchmaker was late with the rent, the original leaseholder would have seemed to be without legal recourse, since his sublet to the watchmaker was illegal. After trying various legal stratagems in vain, he was able to reach an agreement with the apartment owner to file an eviction suit against the watchmaker because of the subletting. The dispute lasted eleven years, but ended with a new lease agreement between the landlord and the original renter.

The instances of divorce and housing examined thus far have involved areas in which several legal tools are available to both sides. While most of the conflicts are long and frustrating, neither side is powerless nor are they by any means inert. Yet what if the legal tools available are far fewer? If we turn our attention to domestic laborers in Kuwait, we find a situation where there is no socialist legislation protecting them and indeed where their employment relationships fall largely outside of a legal framework. Yet in areas in which the law does offer them protection (from physical abuse) and in which the courts are willing to play an active role, the same bargaining process occurs. In Egypt, the tools available to litigants matter far more to them than abstract debates about the cultural or religious appropriateness of the law. Extensive legislation and active (if dilatory) courts insure that many such tools are available to be used to complement rather than to replace other problem-solving strategies. If we move outside of Egypt, do we still find the legal system presenting itself

---

[34] The informant in this case was from the side of the tenants.

(from the viewpoint of potential litigants) as a set of tools? And do we find that the legal system is viewed not as a forum of last resort but as part of the bargaining process? We can answer these questions by examining a group which has none of the advantages of the Egyptian litigants discussed above. Foreign laborers in Kuwait do not share the nationality (or generally language) of their employers or the court personnel, and they have far fewer legal protections available to them. They should be among the least able to take an instrumentalist approach to law – yet even they can show surprising legal entrepreneurship.

### Domestic labor in Kuwait: bargaining and the criminal law

In Kuwait, labor legislation currently in effect offers little to the numerous domestic workers in the country. Far from their home countries and with few legal tools available, such workers would seem to be the least likely to resort to the courts. Yet when offered tools some do use them, again not in an attempt to obtain justice in an abstract sense but to compensate for a weak economic and social position. Even those exposed to physical abuse (including rape) have a weaker legal position than wives seeking divorce or tenants seeking to avoid eviction in Egypt. Yet as in Egypt, their legal status is the outcome of the interaction of several different kinds of law. In general, immigration law combined with criminal law define the position of abused domestic labor; that definition leaves them in a weak position but with room for bargaining and maneuver.

Treatment of domestic labor in Kuwaiti homes is governed only loosely by law and custom. The use of domestic labor has been fairly common since the beginning of the oil era. Initially it was most common to hire males from other Arabian peninsula states where there were bonds of language, culture, and religion. Yet with the spread of oil wealth throughout the peninsula, other sources of domestic labor were found. Initially males from the Indian subcontinent were most common, but in recent years (especially with the increasing child care responsibilities given to domestic labor) women, especially from the Philippines, have been brought into Kuwaiti homes.[35] The cultural, linguistic, and

---

[35] Jamal al-Shihab, Assistant Undersecretary for Legal Affairs and International Relations, Ministry of Justice, personal interview, Kuwait, January 1995. Al-Shihab argued to me that many of the problems with domestic servants have arisen because of strong cultural differences which did not present a problem when most of those hired came from other Gulf states.

sometimes religious gaps between employer and employee can be great, and the social effects of reliance on domestic labor is a frequent topic of discussion in the Kuwaiti press.[36] By 1993 the number of domestic workers in Kuwait exceeded 168,000.[37] Incoming domestic workers were split almost evenly between males and females.[38] About 35,000 were from India and 22,000 from the Philippines.[39] Sri Lanka and Bangladesh are other major sources of domestic labor.

Domestic laborers can enter and work in Kuwait in one of two ways. First, they may be recruited directly from their country of origin and granted a visa specifically for the purpose of domestic labor. These workers are far more likely to have written contracts. A model labor contract suggested by the Ministry of Interior Office of Household Labor requires the sponsor to provide housing, clothes, medical care, and a return ticket at the end of the contract period. (The Interior Ministry contract does not require a weekly day off, though it does require an annual paid vacation of one month.) Disputes are to be referred to Kuwaiti courts. A different model contract recommended by the Philippine embassy guarantees at least one day of rest a week, food and housing without charge, fifteen days of vacation per year, and a round trip ticket to the Philippines if the contract is renewed (generally after two years). Laborers are required to attend an orientation session that covers their obligations, rights, and household duties before leaving the Philippines. The contract also mandates mediation by the embassy before the dispute is referred to local authorities. Yet the Philippine government, mindful of complaints from laborers in Kuwait and of reports of unscrupulous employment agencies, took action in September 1988 to ban hiring domestic workers except in restricted circumstances. Philippine and Kuwaiti authorities in Kuwait, however, acknowledge that the ban is easily circumvented.

Second, domestic laborers may come to Kuwait in ways that are, at

---

[36] For a lurid example of such discussion see "Some of the Servants are Students of Satan!" al-Watan, supplement, July 1993. Most discussion centers on the desirability of relying on non-family members (and non-Muslims) in taking such a large role in child care responsibility. Certainly not all press discussion is unfavorable to the domestic servants. A local radio program devoted to legal subjects focused on the legal rights and obligations of Kuwaitis employing domestic servants.

[37] "The Minister of Interior: Servants are 168 Thousand in Kuwait and Assault by Employers on Servants . . . Does Not Represent a [General] Phenomenon," al-Qabas, July 23, 1993.

[38] Jasim al-Shamari, "The Political Crisis of 'Maids' between Kuwait and the Philippines," al-Majalla, September 19, 1993, p. 29.

[39] See "The Ambassador of India: 115 Thousand Indians in Kuwait Working in Various Sectors, Among them 35,000 Working as Servants in Houses," al-Ra'y al-'Amm, January 19, 1993; Philippine figures collected by the Embassy of the Philippines in Kuwait.

best indirect, and are often deceptive of both officials and laborers. Since measures have been taken to limit and regulate hiring of domestic labor directly from the Philippines, they may be brought first to other Gulf countries and then to Kuwait. They may also be brought as nurses, tutors, or non-domestic labor (and even be promised such work) in order to evade visa restrictions on household labor. Employment agencies are even rumored to trade in large numbers of such laborers, so that a woman who has been hired as a nurse in Bahrain may find that her contract has been sold to an agency that intends to have her travel on to Kuwait to work as a domestic worker.[40]

Workers in the second category have very few legal protections. They generally have no written contracts and any arrangements they may have agreed to orally were generally discussed in their country of origin. It should be no surprise that their Kuwaiti employers cannot be held accountable in Kuwaiti courts for oral arrangements the laborers made with distant agencies. Once in Kuwait they are governed by local visa and labor laws and regulations. While the Kuwaiti labor law does provide some protection to workers, domestic labor and low-wage employees are not effectively covered. If they are dissatisfied with their employers or convinced that their contracts are being violated, they thus have little recourse. Nor can they leave their employers easily – they must complete two years of employment with their sponsor before they may be legally hired by another employer. A worker who leaves before this period is considered a runaway and can be arrested.[41]

While other workers will often complain about deceptive practices by employment agencies and ill-treatment by employers, domestic workers, especially females from the Philippines, have attracted particular (even global) attention, largely because of the number of Filipino domestic workers seeking refuge in their embassy. During 1994, 1,488 Philippine citizens went to the embassy: only 53 of these had complaints unrelated to their employers (such as illness, pregnancy, and homesickness); 908 complained of maltreatment or verbal abuse; 23 charged that they had been raped; 81 cited other forms of molestation. The remainder complained of other conditions relating to their work (such as delayed payment or contract substitution).[42]

---

[40] Since such agencies were only loosely regulated in the past, it is difficult to ascertain the prevalence of such practices, but they are believed by members of the Filipino community in Kuwait to be widespread. The Interior Ministry did establish an Office of Household Labor in 1992 to regulate the agencies operating in Kuwait.

[41] For a general analysis of the problem, see Middle East Watch, "Punishing the Victim: Rape and Mistreatment of Asian Maids in Kuwait," Women's Rights Project report, August 1992.

[42] Figures collected by Philippine officials in Kuwait.

Most Kuwaitis feel that their society has been unfairly singled out for criticism. Since Kuwait is generally more open than other Gulf societies, it is probably the case that those interested in the issue can investigate it more fully in Kuwait than elsewhere. The problem has hardly been ignored inside the country. Indeed, extensive press and parliamentary discussions have been joined by a strong official response.[43] In 1992 a law was enacted by amiri decree which required that household labor agencies obtain a permit to continue operating and established an office to regulate their conduct and inspect their operations.[44] A police station (al-Dasma) has been designated to handle most of the cases. Police officials have cooperated with the Philippine embassy (and other relevant embassies), and there is generally an official from the embassy present when a complaint is investigated. The official procedure is very clear: if a criminal offense is alleged, the matter is turned over to the *niyaba* for immediate investigation. (Kuwaiti law, like Egyptian, distinguishes between a *junha*, a crime punishable by less than three years in prison, and a *jinaya*, punishable by more than three years. In Kuwait a crime classified as a *jinaya* – such as rape or a serious assault – is investigated by the *niyaba* whereas a *junha* is handled by the police.) If the complaint does not involve a major crime an attempt is to be made to bring the laborer together with the employer, in the presence of the police and an embassy official. In a *jinaya*, officials are neither to participate in nor obstruct negotiations between the parties. And if an amicable solution is reached, the issue must generally be presented to a court before charges may be dropped.[45] (As will become clear below, police procedures differ from what is officially mandated.) While investigation and negotiations are proceeding, Philippine domestic workers are generally allowed to continue to stay at the embassy. The result is that there are, on average, 200 women using the embassy as a refuge at any given time.

Yet even if they do seek refuge in the embassy the legal position of domestic workers is weak. If their complaints stem from contract violations or work conditions, they can do little to substantiate their claims and cannot leave their employer without permission until they have completed two years of work. If their complaints are related to physical or verbal abuse, they will likely be able to produce no witnesses. And while cases of rape may be treated seriously, there are again rarely

---

[43] For example, see "The Minister of Interior," *al-Qabas.*

[44] Salah Ahmad al-Najim, director of Office of Household Labor, Ministry of Interior, personal interview, Kuwait, February 1995.

[45] The procedures were described in personal interviews in Kuwait, January 1995, with Muhammad al-Ansari, director of the Department of International Relations at the Ministry of Justice, and Fallah al-ʿUtaybi, director of investigations for the Capital Governorate in the Ministry of Interior.

witnesses. In cases where they claim more than one rape, skeptical authorities will probably question them on why they did not escape after the first occurrence. In this way, a victim of multiple rape can often be treated less seriously than the victim of a single rape.[46] Finally, if the authorities are not convinced that an abuse has taken place, workers are required by immigration law to return to their place of employment.[47]

Yet while domestic workers find numerous and serious obstacles when resorting to the legal system, the official actions taken on their behalf have given them some legal tools. There is every evidence that they use them. As in marital and housing disputes in Egypt, however, legal tools are used in the bargaining process, not to supplant it. And police procedure, while it may actually weaken the position of the domestic worker alleging abuse, facilitates bargaining.

A charge of battery, verbal abuse, or rape rarely results in a prosecution in Kuwait (although there have been some highly publicized trials in the past few years). Instead it results in direct and indirect bargaining between accuser and accused. Before proceeding with investigation (or referring a case to the *niyaba*), police at the al-Dasma station ask the domestic laborer for his or her preferences.[48] Options include returning to the home country, finding a new employer, returning to the employment agency, returning to the original employer, and prosecuting the case. These options are not mutually exclusive, but unless laborers clearly and specifically state that they wish the case prosecuted, police will try to arrange informal solutions. Even after charges are filed, the option to bargain for an informal solution still exists. Officials justify this practice with the argument that they cannot prosecute a crime without the cooperation of the victim (though they make no effort to secure such cooperation) and that they wish only to follow the wishes of the victim.[49]

---

[46] Several of those who have dealt with such cases expressed the belief that allegations of multiple rape often indicate consensual sexual relations – or at least will be regarded that way by the courts. And in one case which I became personally familiar with, a maid alleging multiple rapes reported that the police questioned her about her failure to escape after the first rape and expressed doubts about her claims because she was not pregnant.

[47] I was once interviewing a Kuwaiti lawyer when he received a call from a distraught client who had earlier been accused of raping his maid. An investigation led authorities to conclude that there was insufficient evidence to pursue the case. The police then contacted the employer and ordered him to take the maid back to his house, a prospect that horrified both parties. The lawyer described police conduct in such cases as "stupid" but admitted they were operating in accordance with the law.

[48] This information is based on interviews with criminal investigators at al-Dasma in February 1995. In the course of conversation with the investigators, several cases were dealt with in my presence, including one rape case.

[49] It is probably the case that a more aggressive attitude by the police would place the

Kuwaiti families in such situations generally have two concerns. First, and most seriously, is the criminal charge itself. Second, families who employ domestic labor generally pay a substantial fee to the agency which covers the laborer's trip to Kuwait. If a domestic laborer leaves their employment they will have to pay this fee again in order to secure a replacement (unless the departure takes place in the first few months of service, in which case they can usually demand that the agency supply a replacement without payment of the fee). Thus they will typically seek to have the charges dropped and to recover the fee if the domestic worker will not return. Domestic workers will want either to find new employment in Kuwait or to return to their country of origin. (In cases where their complaints relate to working conditions rather than physical abuse, many will also agree to return to the original place of employment as long as their complaints are addressed.)

In Egypt, marital problems, if they result in the wife leaving the house, will often result in the husband filing a *bayt al-ta'a* suit while the wife makes criminal charges of battery or mistreatment. Similarly, in cases involving domestic workers in Kuwait, the worker will make criminal charges while the family complains to the police that the worker has deserted them (in violation of immigration and labor law). Having resorted to their legal tools, the two sides will then bargain.

Once the bargaining begins, it is extremely rare for the legal issues to go to court. If the Kuwaiti family feels the charges are strong, they may offer to pay for the laborer's return to the country of origin or to allow the transfer to a new sponsor. If the charges are weak, they may demand that the initial fee they paid the agency be repaid – if not by the agency then by anybody wishing to hire the worker and assume sponsorship. Of the domestic workers who sought refuge in the Philippine embassy in 1994, roughly one-third were repatriated, a second third returned to the original place of employment, and the remainder found new employment (either with the assistance of the embassy or by returning to the agency). The total number alleging criminal violations to an embassy official was over 1,000; there were only twelve prosecutions. The courts

laborers in a far stronger position. Yet in one way it probably does protect some laborers from prosecution for making false charges. Officials involved in the investigation of crimes against domestic laborers claim that a large number, even the majority, of allegations are false and designed only to obtain release from a labor contract. Even if this claim is exaggerated it probably has a strong basis. False charges undoubtedly are made because they offer one of the few avenues for escape from an undesirable situation. A domestic servant who is verbally maltreated or not paid will probably have to live under such conditions for two years. One who alleges a serious crime will probably be able to settle for a transfer of the contract to a new employer or a plane ticket home. Thus, official diffidence in the pursuit of formal criminal charges makes it less likely that those making false (or merely unproven) charges will be prosecuted.

and the legal system were hardly inert on the issue, but their chief role (sometimes intentionally and sometimes not) was to establish more clearly the bargaining position of the two parties. Indeed, bargaining does not even necessarily stop if a case does go to court. In 1994 a Kuwaiti couple accused in the beating to death of their maid offered to pay *diya* (in Islamic law a payment in the event of death that the family of a victim may accept in return for dropping criminal penalties).[50] Kuwaiti courts are not obliged to accept the payment of *diya* as are some Islamic-based courts, but the payment often results (as it did in this instance) in a reduced sentence.

Unless criminal charges are made the bargaining position of the laborer is quite weak. Kuwaitis involved in the issue often claim that criminal charges are falsely made when a laborer is simply dissatisfied with working conditions or wishes to find more lucrative employment elsewhere in the country.[51] This is very difficult to substantiate, but it must be recognized that immigration and labor law give a laborer few tools to change employment other than criminal charges. It would be no surprise if some use the only tools at their disposal. Kuwaitis often claim that they are the victims of crimes by domestic workers (especially theft). But their bargaining power is so strong – since they are the worker's sponsor and often hold his or her passport as well in defiance of official policy – that there is little need to resort to the police in such cases. In 1994, only thirty-three Kuwaiti families made criminal complaints against Filipino domestic workers.[52]

The low prosecution rate in charges domestic workers make against their employers is thus related not to the attitudes of the *niyaba* or the courts. Instead it is directly related to labor and immigration law. Rape and battery are very much illegal, but domestic workers are generally too vulnerable to prosecute fully. Reforms currently under discussion would do much to alleviate some of the sources of inequality. Among those ideas sometimes discussed by government officials and parliamentarians involve easing restrictions on changing sponsors (allowing the laborer – or the new sponsor – to pay a fee rather than wait two years or obtain the consent of the existing sponsor) and still greater regulation of employment agencies operating in Kuwait. Such changes, if implemented, would probably result not simply in better working conditions for

---

[50] Reuters, March 10, 1994, based on a story that day in the *Arab Times*.

[51] See, for example, the interview with 'Abd Allah al-Faris, director-general of the General Administration for Criminal Investigation, in *al-Qabas*, January 2,1995, p. 12.

[52] The number of complaints by Filipinos was compiled by the embassy of the Philippines; complaints against Filipinos were compiled by Kuwaiti police officials and given to me by Fallah al-'Utaybi.

domestic labor but also in fewer false criminal allegations and a higher rate of prosecutions.

It should be noted that the way that criminal and civil cases can be knit together varies considerably from place to place. Arab legal systems are hardly uniform in how much they permit individuals to use the criminal law in bargaining. In Qatar, the *Shari'a* Courts have jurisdiction in murder cases (unless neither accused nor victim is Muslim), and the process is formalized in *diya* payments which the victim's family may accept or reject as they please (the amount is not subject to bargaining, however, but is fixed by the *Shari'a* judiciary). In Egypt, judges and members of the *niyaba* view their role as applying and enforcing the law and are less likely to recognize such bargaining.[53] As one member of the *niyaba* claims, "If two people hit each other a crime has occurred, and if they do not wish to pursue it, I still have to . . . I am concerned with the law. The circumstances or personalities do not bother me; I am not with the Ministry of Social Affairs."[54] Even in Egypt, however, the *niyaba* will generally need the victim's cooperation to pursue a case. As a result, it is often difficult to prevent use of the courts in bargaining among disputants.

## Courts, equality and legitimacy

More than a century ago, Egypt's political leadership embarked on an ambitious project to build centralized courts of law that would enforce newly codified law throughout the country. Since that time, legislation has been used extensively to accomplish a variety of social, political, and economic goals. More recently, almost all states of the Arab world have followed the same path, although sometimes with less enthusiasm.

In one important sense, the legal systems of Egypt and several other Arab countries are now reeling from the success of that effort. Rather than rejecting them as an alien imposition or as culturally inappropriate, Egyptians (and members of some other Arab societies) have grasped at the tools that the new legal systems have given them. Egyptian courts have been true to their mission of mediating all sorts of social relationships on the basis of codified and legislated texts, and they have been aided by the active participation of large sections of the population.

The existence of multiple fora for resolving disputes is not unique to

---

[53] However, for an analysis of how Egyptian norms regarding women do affect the application of criminal law, see Safia K. Mohsen, "Women and Criminal Justice in Egypt," in Dwyer, *Law and Islam.*

[54] Interview with Khalid 'Abd al-Ghaffar, member of the *niyaba*, Cairo, May 1992.

Egypt, nor is the willingness to "shop" for the most favorable forum.[55] The ability of socially and politically subordinate groups to use the courts has been noted elsewhere as well.[56] What seems unusual about the Egyptian case – or perhaps unnoticed in other cases – is the way that various fora are combined. It is not simply that Egyptians shop for the best forum but that they seek to use all favorable fora at once – and often to influence each other. The police, criminal courts, civil courts, direct bargaining, and family mediation are all used, often not as alternatives or consecutively but simultaneously. The concept of forum shopping, developed elsewhere, is hardly adequate to describe such strategies because it seriously understates their complexity and ingenuity and often assumes that potential litigants choose the most favorable forum. Egyptians often do not choose among fora; they choose all of them at once. Since the courts invite all comers it is not surprising that Egyptians resort to them, not as a last step but as part of a general strategy of attempting to bring pressure on the other party.

Such strategies have some effects that are not immediately obvious. Perhaps the full impact can be appreciated by a comparison to a system where the sorts of cases that fill the Egyptian courts are regarded as "garbage cases" inappropriate for courts of law. Sally Engle Merry's study of resort to courts among working-class New Englanders begins with a description of such a system:

The lower courts in the United States generally dislike handling problems between neighbors, friends, lovers, and spouses. Yet ordinary people persist in bringing such problems there. Sometimes people coping with a persistently noisy neighbor, an unfaithful lover, or a disobedient child interpret their problems as a legal one and turn to the courts for help. People come to the courts because they think the law has something to offer them: protection from a violent lover, obedience from a teenage child, punishment for a rude and inconsiderate neighbor, control over a battering husband. For women who feel vulnerable to violent men, courts offer the possibility of power.

But the court officials who handle these problems consider them out of place in the court. Most are referred to as "garbage cases," as frivolous and troublesome, and as evidence that people "use" the court. Domestic-violence cases are more likely to be considered serious but may still be categorized as garbage. Judges, lawyers, clerk-magistrates, and mediation-program staff attempt to manage and settle these personal problems as moral dilemmas while not taking them seriously as legal cases, offering lectures and social services

---

[55] See, for instance, Sally Engle Merry, "The Articulation of Legal Spheres," in Margaret Jean Hay and Marcia Wright (eds.), *African Women and the Law* (Boston University Papers on Africa, VII 1982).

[56] See, for example, James Holston, "The Misrule of Law: Land and Usurpation in Brazil," *Comparative Studies in Society and History*, 33 (4), 1991, p. 695.

rather than protection or punishment. Some plaintiffs insist that they have real problems, however, and try to persuade the court to respond in these terms.[57]

Merry describes the frustration that such people feel when they bring their cases to court and discover that they are not treated as legal cases but as appropriate only for other fora.

Courts in Egypt do intervene without reluctance in many such cases. Someone publicly insulted or harassed by a neighbor, or a wife verbally abused by her husband can go to the police or the courts and have the matter treated as serious and legal in nature. In the United States, working- and even middle-class people can feel uncomfortable in court, unfamiliar with its procedure and concerned that the legal system treats their problems as trivial and remains focused on larger issues. In Egypt the exact opposite situation occurs: those of higher social status regard the courts as disorganized, inefficient, and unruly – hardly the sort of place for respectable people to have to bring their problems. The full economic dimensions of this attitude will be examined in the next chapter. For now it is enough to note that many wealthier Egyptians express indignation when dragged into a system which they feel treats them no better than minor criminals. There are crowds, frequent delays, and endless bureaucratic procedures. One must deal with uneducated and perhaps corrupt court employees and courtrooms filled with every petty dispute imaginable. Those who can afford to avoid such a system often do so. Yet for many others, what the Egyptian courts and often the law itself offer is not delay and despair but an ally in a difficult personal matter. Even the universally acknowledged delays and inefficiencies associated with the courts in Egypt can often be useful for those seeking to delay or willing to negotiate a matter while the courts wait for a missing document.[58]

The inventiveness of Egyptians in crafting strategies combining litigation with other mechanisms and the refusal of the courts to dismiss cases that would be regarded as frivolous or inappropriate in the United States has two implications for general arguments about the social and political role of courts.

First, Egyptian courts show how law can be an equalizing force in a way that is unintended (though not necessarily regretted) by political authorities. It is not that social status, power, and wealth are suddenly

---

[55] See, for instance, Sally Engle Merry, "The Articulation of Legal Spheres," in Margaret Jean Hay and Marcia Wright (eds.), *African Women and the Law* (Boston University Papers on Africa, VII 1982)

[56] See, for example, James Holston, "The Misrule of Law: Land and Usurpation in Brazil," *Comparative Studies in Society and History* 33 (4), 1991, p. 695.

[57] Sally Engle Merry, *Getting Justice and Getting Even: Legal Consciousness among Working-Class Americans* (Chicago: University of Chicago Press, 1990), p. 1.

irrelevant when one enters an Egyptian court of law (as those subscribing to a liberal vision of law would strive for). Those who enter the courts weak will often emerge with an unfavorable result. It would be surprising to find otherwise. What is notable is not how the courts make distinctions disappear but how they can recognize them and, on occasion, compensate for them by offering tools to the weaker party. A wife who is beaten by her husband or a renter who faces eviction find that the law offers them guarantees that the courts will enforce. Some of those guarantees will not be immediately obvious by a casual glance at the law – a wife beaten by her husband seems only to be granted the right to demand a divorce from the court. What the court and the law actually offer her, however, is not simply the right of divorce but material claims (the *mahr mu'akhkhar* and the apartment) that will allow her either to pursue divorce or negotiate a more favorable relationship with her husband. Of course, the content of the law must have something to offer before the courts can be used. But what the Egyptian courts show is that the total legal status of an individual must be considered, not simply the law in the area nominally in question. Divorce law would seem to favor husbands who are allowed to divorce without cause (while wives have to show harm). But with courts that are willing to treat verbal abuse as a crime (albeit a minor one) and that treat physical abuse as a grave matter, the status of the two parties, though very different, is more equal. Even Filipino maids in Kuwait, who have none of the legal guarantees of renters or wives in Egypt, can still resort to the courts to achieve more modest goals. Their legal status may be little different from indentured servants, but they are not treated as unworthy of the courts nor are their desires (usually for reemployment rather than criminal punishment) ignored.

Second, the Egyptian case suggests that arguments about the relationship between the legal system and legitimacy are often miscast. The issue of legitimacy will be considered more fully in the conclusion, but for now it can be stated that the way Egyptians use the legal system probably does little to shape their political attitudes. Political struggles over the rule of law, described in earlier chapters, do have effects on the operation and perhaps even the legitimacy of the political system. Yet while those struggles – over the method of appointing judges or the structure of the courts – may affect the way people view the political system, such concerns have very little to do with how people view the courts in their own disputes. Courts may or may not restrict or regularize executive authority, but when a renter faces eviction, such concerns are largely irrelevant.

Most important, the argument that the legal system supports the legitimacy of a prevailing order by inducing people to view their disputes as individual problems rather than larger, even class-based phenomena, is belied by the Egyptian experience. This argument rests on the curious assumption – surprisingly widespread in the writings on law and legitimacy – that people can only approach their problems through one avenue at a time. People who bring their disputes to Egyptian courts do so not to replace other strategies but as part of them. To argue that the legal system affects the legitimacy of a prevailing order by forcing potential litigants to view and pursue their problems in certain ways misses how much litigants can resort to many fora at the same time and how instrumentalist the courts can appear. It might also understate how much potential litigants can cast and recast their problem in less than obvious ways. Far from cloaking the prevailing order with "a monument of legislation, judicial ingenuity and cant" (as Hay described eighteenth-century England), Egyptian courts offer themselves simply as tools to be used when beneficial and avoided when not.

Egyptian courts as described in this chapter seem to encourage ingenuity and initiative. But for many a purpose of law, especially civil law, is not to make people more creative but to make them more productive. In the following chapter, we consider whether the Egyptian legal system and those modeled on it provide the proper institutional framework for business and economic activity.

# 8 Business and the courts

Do courts aid or inhibit productive business activities? The perspectives on law and courts considered in chapter 1 lead us to conflicting expectations. On the one hand, some writers stress inequality and view courts as unlikely to undermine prevailing inegalitarian political and economic relationships. Such a perspective would lead us to view courts as structures furthering economic domination in the developing world. Wealthy individuals and powerful economic institutions are viewed as able to obtain far more favorable decisions from the courts than other litigants both because of the content of the law and the nature of legal procedures.

Other writers discussed in chapter 1 take a liberal view of law which leads them to stress the corrupted nature of the current legal environment in much of the developing world. Legal structures are seen as stifling entrepreneurship and privileging state over private property rights. Powerful individuals and groups benefit from prevailing structures, but this is not seen as advancing the general goal of encouraging economic development and productive initiatives.

Are courts and the law too subservient to business or too hostile? The experience of Egypt (and secondarily of the Arab states of the Gulf) suggests that both pictures are too starkly drawn. While courts are hardly oases where prevailing power relations are irrelevant, the evidence presented in this chapter, especially when viewed in conjunction with the findings presented in the previous chapter, indicate that courts are surprisingly accessible to wide sections of the population. Indeed, from the perspective of business actors, the courts are probably too responsive to non-elites. And while the Egyptian legal framework is hardly an entrepreneur's dream, in recent years the spread of arbitration has increasingly allowed some business actors to choose their own fora and sometimes their own laws, bypassing rather than reforming the indigenous legal system. In short, the courts are far less effective bastions of privilege and mercantilism than critics charge.

## Law, business, and development

Writers on law and development in the 1960s and 1970s tended to focus on the urban and rural poor; according to one participant in the "law and development" movement, many of those involved became disillusioned, eventually convinced that law could do little positive for the poor in the developing world.[1] When interest in the relationship between law and development returned in the 1980s and 1990s, attention centered on business and entrepreneurship rather than the poor. Influenced by liberal economic (and sometimes by public-choice) scholarship and the actual experience of business groups, scholars and development professionals began to argue that law could best serve economic development by enforcing contracts and property rights. Pursuit of a broader range of objectives through law (such as equity or national sovereignty) is often viewed as counterproductive and insincere.

The most powerful and detailed articulation of this perspective for Egypt came in a study commissioned by the Agency for International Development (AID), which, in the 1990s, has evinced a substantial and growing interest in the legal and institutional framework for development.[2] The AID-commissioned Bentley report describes the proper role of the government and legal system in a market-driven economy as enabling "an infinite number of transactions between and among private sector actors to take place as easily and efficiently as possible."[3] This entails establishing institutions that allow for the enforcement of contracts and access to information while holding regulation to a minimum. Specifically, with regard to the legal system, courts should be efficient and capable and must have available a body of law that is clear but not overly restrictive on private actors. The report goes so far as to advocate a new attitude in the implementation of laws and regulations. Requiring that all private actors obtain permits or provide documentation assuring compliance is tantamount to presuming everyone guilty until proven innocent. The alternative is to rely on specific reports of violations and spot inspections, and assume that all are in compliance with the law until proven otherwise. Such a change in the way laws and

[1] David M. Trubeck and Marc Galanter, "Scholars in Self-Estrangement: Some Reflections on the Crisis in Law and Development Studies in the United States," *Wisconsin Law Review*, 1974.

[2] The report set the stage for an AID project on the administration of justice in Egypt. It includes one of the most comprehensive presentations of the current Egyptian judicial structure in addition to its evaluation and recommendations for reform. See John Bentley, "Egyptian Legal and Judicial Sector Assessment: Report and Recommendations," submitted to USAID/Egypt in association with Kamel, Yehia, Abul Ela and Sakr, 4 vols., February 1994.

[3] Bentley, "Egyptian Legal and Judicial Sector Assessment," vol. II, p. 4.

regulations are viewed and enforced would aid efficiency and facilitate transactions.[4]

Rather than meeting these liberal goals, the current Egyptian legal system is portrayed as retaining its characteristics as a product of a socialist period in which the market was restricted and the legal framework for private business activity was allowed to atrophy.[5] One business leader describes Egypt's current judicial system as one which is simply unable to play any effective and expeditious role in enforcing contracts.[6]

While the Bentley report is unusually detailed in its criticisms and recommendations, it hardly stands as the lone example of business-oriented criticisms of Arab judiciaries. The view that the Arab legal systems are substantively and procedurally ineffective and even hostile to business interests is widespread among business leaders and legal practitioners in the region. The most frequent subject of criticism is the substantive content of the laws, which are generally seen as outdated, statist, or socialist in inspiration, and unclear.[7] Yet criticisms often go beyond the substantive law to the courts themselves. Business-oriented critics of Arab judiciaries complain that courts are insufficiently aware of, or responsive to, the needs of commerce and investment. In a sense they are too egalitarian; having opened their doors to a mass of small-scale lawsuits, Arab legal systems are poorly equipped to provide the legal framework necessary for efficient and productive business transactions.

### Business customers of the courts

While Egyptian courts (and Arab courts more generally) may not seem like friendly fora to business interests, creative tools have been developed to make courts more useful. In general, those active in business are able to use the courts in the same way as other litigants, and indeed are perhaps more able to bend the system to their advantage. Perhaps the best illustration of how business practices are molded to take maximum

[4] Bentley, "Egyptian Legal and Judicial Sector Assessment," vol. II, pp. 4–5.
[5] Bentley, "Egyptian Legal and Judicial Sector Assessment," vol. II, pp. 6–7.
[6] See the memo by John Bentley, November 23, 1993, on interview with Hatem N. Moustafa, Chairman, Nimos Engineering Company, Cairo, appended to Bentley, "Egyptian Legal and Judicial Sector Assessment," vol. IV.
[7] For examples of such complaints, see Delwin A. Roy, "An Examination of Legal Instrumentalism in Public Enterprise Development in the Middle East," *Georgia Journal of International and Comparative Law* 10, (2), 1980, p. 271, and the interview with ʿAbd Allah Hasan al-Jar Allah, former Kuwaiti minister of commerce and industry in *al-Watan*, June 23, 1994.

advantage of the structure of courts and their patterns of behavior is the widespread use of the postdated check.

With civil procedures working slowly and uncertainly, court fees often fixed according to the size of a dispute (and thus potentially quite significant for large cases), judges unaware of business practices, and court-employed experts overburdened and often little more aware of standard business practices than judges, few business leaders have much confidence in the civil courts. Criminal courts, by contrast, offer far speedier decisions, making them more attractive fora if a dispute can be rendered relevant to criminal law. Postdated checks have exactly that effect. Writing a check on insufficient funds is a criminal offense in Egypt and most Arab countries, and an offense that courts tend to view very seriously. A single check written on insufficient funds might easily draw a jail sentence.

It is not uncommon, therefore, to request a postdated check as a guarantee on a loan or as delayed payment for a business transaction. Rather than endure a prolonged civil suit to collect the debt, creditors need only notify criminal law authorities to begin a case. To be sure, the sanction is crude – one can threaten to have criminal courts jail a debtor but such a sentence does not obviate the need for a separate civil suit to collect the original debt. The practice of accepting postdated checks (and therefore the implied threat of criminal sanctions) is particularly widespread in small-scale business (and even personal) affairs, but it is even used in substantial business transactions. In one Qatari bank, a postdated check is the preferred form of collateral in a loan. If there are insufficient funds in the account when the check comes due, the legal staff of the bank will threaten criminal action against the debtor. This threat is sufficient to compel payment in close to half of all bad loans.[8]

Yet such strategies are hardly satisfactory solutions. The use of postdated checks does allow the threat of criminal sanctions, but such threats are often insufficient. Two disputes in Egypt illustrate the weakness of strategies involving both the civil and criminal courts. In one case, the holder of a bad check chose to file a civil suit. The debtor claimed that the signature on the check was forged – a not uncommon strategy because the typical court response is to appoint an expert to examine the signature. This can take several months (as it did in this case) and there is no penalty if the expert rules that the signature is genuine. In essence, legal procedures initiated by the creditor allowed the debtor to delay a fairly certain finding. In another case, the creditor went to the police to file a criminal complaint; the police referred the

---

[8] Interview with Fath al-Rahman 'Abd Allah al-Shaykh, assistant general manager for legal affairs, Qatar Islamic Bank, Doha, November 1994.

case to the *niyaba*. When the case got to court, the debtor was convicted *in absentia*, but the verdict did little to help the creditor because the debtor had used the delays in the case to flee to France.

Thus the complaints of business leaders that the courts do not offer the proper framework for the resolution of business disputes is hardly belied by the inventiveness of some litigants. Devices such as postdated checks are creative but makeshift solutions. And, as mentioned, business criticisms go beyond the content of the law to the structure and procedure of the courts themselves. In other words, the charge is not simply that law and public policy often give insufficient support to business activity but that the courts (sometimes because of procedures fixed by law) are unattractive fora for business disputes. Many business complaints about courts simply echo more general criticisms about delays, corruptible administrative support, and ill-defined and sometimes overly complex procedures. According to one leading Cairo lawyer, litigation is almost always inadvisable no matter how strong a case seems; in going to court "even if you win, you lose."[9]

Yet there are some specific ways in which courts present an unfriendly face specifically to business leaders. Two disparate examples can be cited. First, the progressive court fee structure in Egypt (imitated in other Arab countries, including Kuwait) makes initiation of litigation a far more expensive proposition for those involved in larger-scale disputes. In general, in a civil suit, court officials are responsible for estimating the value of the goods or services at issue in a dispute; court fees are fixed at a proportion of the value of the case. (The proportion does decline for fairly large cases, but in a significant dispute it would not be impossible for court fees to be several million Egyptian pounds.) The full fees are not due until the case is settled and then are theoretically the responsibility of the losing party. Yet even if the initiator of the lawsuit wins the case, he or she must pay the fees and then seek to recover them from the loser by further court action. Thus for small disputes, fees are small (and for certain categories of cases, such as labor disputes, forgiven altogether). For larger disputes, fees are substantial, and even a potential litigant fairly confident of his or her legal position must be willing to pay the fees and risk further litigation even if the outcome of the suit is favorable[10]

A second example of the unfriendliness of the legal system to business

---

[9] Interview with Yahya Salim, Cairo, November 1994.

[10] Bentley, "Egyptian Legal and Judicial Sector Assessment," vol. II, p. 50. For the system in Kuwait, see Ernest Alexander, "Resolution of Disputes, Arbitration and Litigation," presentation at "Seminar on Construction Claims in Kuwait: How to Deal with them," at SAS Hotel, Kuwait, January 27, 1990 (unpublished manuscript).

involves small-scale merchants rather than those involved in high-value transactions. Neighborhood vendors of basic commodities in Egypt not only have many of their operations fixed by law, but violations come under the State Security Courts and can result in jail sentences for fairly minor offenses. Those involved in the sale of basic commodities are closely monitored by the Ministry of Supply to ensure that their prices, hours of operations, and selection fall within government regulations. With many basic commodities subsidized, incentives are strong at all levels for working around the system.[11] Failure to comply with regulations has been deemed an offense not simply against proper business practices but against public security since the Second World War. One writer complained that if a supply inspector visited a neighborhood grocery asking for matches and was told by an employee that matches would not be available until the next day, the owner of the grocery could be jailed.[12] While it seems unlikely that the grocer would actually be sent to prison in such a case, supply inspectors and State Security Courts can be fairly harsh. One grocer complained that in 1991 he was fined 100 Egyptian pounds when a supply inspector discovered that a sign posting the price of eggs had fallen on the floor. A baker in the al-Sayyida Zaynab neighborhood complained that when he closed the door of his bakery a few hours early on the first day of 'Id al-Fitr in 1991 (at the end of the fasting month of Ramadan) because there had been no customers all day, supply inspectors cited him as violating fixed hours of operation. He faced a fine of 1,000 pounds (because it was his first offense); after a third offense he would be jailed. Further, he was deprived of an extra flour ration in punishment (the government had allowed bakeries extra flour in order to minimize the threat of public disturbances during and immediately after the Gulf War) and worried that he might be held accountable for selling less than the required amount. And the operator of an open-air vegetable and fruit stand in the same neighborhood, a pregnant mother of four, was sentenced to six months in jail and fined 100 pounds for overcharging in the sale of a watermelon.[13] In all cases, the merchants complained bitterly about a system that treated them as pickpockets for minor (or nonexistent) offenses. Since they had been brought before State Security Courts

---

[11] For instance, bakeries receive allotments of flour at a subsidized price. If they decrease the size of each loaf and sell the extra flour they may realize a handsome profit – or criminal charges, if they are discovered.

[12] 'Abd al-Salam Dawud, "Are We Equal before the Law?" al-Akhbar, December 7, 1985.

[13] She was accused of weighing an eight-pound watermelon at ten pounds; she claimed that the supply inspector invented the charge to exact revenge because of his long-standing animosity towards her husband. For details on how the information on these cases was gathered, see p. 188, note 3, above.

(which they regarded as military in nature), they all complained that combating the charges was futile.

The current period of limited economic liberalization has led officials to regard such complaints much more sympathetically. The parliament has begun to discuss the matter of reform of the court fee structure.[14] And many of the supply regulations have been liberalized or abandoned (especially with regard to produce pricing).

Overall, those who blame Arab socialism for the unfriendliness of the courts to business miss the historical roots of the policies and attitudes they denounce. A statist outlook on the part of Egypt's political elite that posits a public responsibility for the economic health and well-being of the citizenry began to emerge in the first half of the twentieth century and has been augmented by a determination to make the legal system effective by insuring its accessibility to the majority of the population. This outlook not only predated Arab socialism (indeed many of the elements of Arab socialism in Egypt, such as price controls, rent controls, and nationalizations, preceded the official adoption of socialist ideology by years and sometimes decades); it also has survived it (though it certainly has eroded in recent years).

Thus it is not simply an ideological hostility or lack of sympathy that makes courts seem unsuitable for many business leaders; in general, such leaders in effect complain not that the courts enforce justice unequally but that they are too egalitarian. The progressive fee structure is just a small part of the much larger problem that business leaders must use the courts on the same terms as the working and middle class. Even the greater responsiveness of senior political and legislative officials to business complaints (which has become more marked in the past two decades) is insufficient to turn the courts into friendly terrain. Merchants violating price controls feel that they are treated like petty thieves; traders wishing to enforce a contract find that they must take their place in an endless queue of litigants with seemingly petty problems. An employer brought to court by a dismissed employee finds that he or she must wait in a crowded courtroom for half a day only to find that the case is postponed.

The basis of the problem for business leaders, therefore, is not simply that substantive law is outmoded or inappropriate but that the courts themselves offer them the same uncertain, inefficient, and slow justice that they offer women seeking child support payments and renters seeking to recover excessive rent payments. What business leaders feel they need above all is an ability to settle disputes on their own terms.

---

[14] See *al-Wafd*, February 22, 1995, p. 10.

### Custom-made courts and procedures

Business leaders, especially those involved in international business, are far more able than most litigants to choose the law governing their contracts and the forum for resolving disputes. Friendliness to arbitration has varied considerably within Egypt over time, and throughout the region governments have had very different attitudes towards attempts to avoid local law and courts. The general political and economic climate has greatly affected the legal framework for arbitration in the Arab world. At the current time, the atmosphere for arbitration of all kinds is generally quite positive. Concerns over sovereignty are at an ebb, and desires are strong throughout the region to attract international trade and investment (even in some countries that formerly felt no need to court foreign business). While most focus on arbitration thus far has involved international business, there are some signs that interest in arbitration for purely domestic transactions may be increasing.

Foreign business leaders interested in trade or investment in Egypt (or the rest of the Arab world) are usually advised by lawyers to include an arbitration clause in any contract with a local actor (public or private).[15] Indeed, the existence of an arbitration clause has become standard practice in international contracts, although the content of the clause varies. Business decision-makers primarily seek to designate the forum where a dispute will be heard. Sometimes their own domestic courts are the forum of choice; other times international arbitration (such as the International Chamber of Commerce in Paris) will be designated. (Courts in the Arab world are more likely to be charged by local law to honor international arbitration than they will be required to enforce the judgments of most foreign courts.) It is also not unusual for a contract to specify the law to govern the contract (although this is generally secondary to the forum in the eyes of most international business leaders and is greeted by a wide variety of local responses). The choice of procedural law is generally governed by the location of the forum (unless specified otherwise); contracting parties are sometimes at liberty to specify the operating substantive law as well.

What is the motivation for the strong preference for arbitration – and for the desire to specify not only the forum but also the law to govern the contract? Even those who advise arbitration generally acknowledge that the strongest motivation is not past performance of the courts but unfamiliarity with their language and procedures. While a woman seeking divorce is generally quite aware of her legal standing, a potential

---

[15] The information in this section on business preferences and legal advice comes from interviews with attorneys in the United States, Egypt, and the Gulf.

foreign investor in Egypt or the Gulf is likely to be unfamiliar with local laws and business practices. Language itself is a surprisingly strong barrier because it inhibits even those foreigners willing to learn about the local environment. In addition, since the courts generally insist that documents relevant to a dispute be submitted in Arabic, this can impose substantial translation costs in a complex dispute. (An American attorney practicing in Kuwait noted that construction contracts might generate tens of thousands of relevant documents.[16]) Speed is often an important factor as well, especially given the complex and technical nature of many international transactions. Judges rarely feel comfortable rendering decisions in such disputes without reference to professional experts who can take considerable time before submitting a report. If the report itself engenders responses or further questions, litigation can seem endless. In Egypt and the Gulf, it is not unusual for a court to take several years before issuing a final decision – and the decision itself can generally be appealed. Since international arbitration is comparatively swift (consuming months rather than years), a litigant wishing a final decision quickly will thus greatly prefer arbitration as long as local courts are willing to enforce arbitrators' decisions. International arbitration is often deemed to be more predictable than local litigation. Surprisingly, the cost of litigation does not generally seem to be a factor in favoring international arbitration which itself sometimes involves considerable expense (especially attorneys' fees.)[17]

The conventional wisdom that business decision-makers place greatest value on predictability is borne out by their attitude towards arbitration and courts in the Arab world. The uncertainties connected with local courts – length of litigation, language and procedural differences, and their lack of experience – provoke greater worries than supposed shortcomings in substantive law. International traders and investors are far more likely to accept local substantive law than they are to accept local courts. It is the unfamiliar procedures of local courts and their use of Arabic more than the law they enforce that render them unattractive fora. The preference for arbitration will probably never disappear as long as the changes necessary to make local courts attractive (such as adopting English as an official language) remain impracticable.

Governments in the Arab world have harbored some suspicions about international arbitration, as have other domestic actors. International arbitration is viewed as costly and the charge is often made that it is

---

[16] Alexander, "Resolution of Disputes."

[17] Mahmud Fahmi, personal interview, Cairo, May 1992. Fahmi served on the *Majlis al-Dawla* and the state investment authority; he now works as a private attorney.

dominated by a small number of wealthy attorneys.[18] This resentment is aggravated by misgivings that international arbitration agencies are unsympathetic to governments and other litigants in the Arab world. Indeed, several unfavorable decisions (some of which seemed to denigrate Islamic law) led the Saudi government to reject any international arbitration clauses for many years.[19] Some judges in the Arab world also make clear their belief that their role is to decide cases and therefore requiring them to enforce non-judicial arbitral awards is an improper use of their authority. The extent of this opposition is sometimes overstated, however, and no Arab judiciary has ever balked at enforcing arbitration clauses (by referring disputes to arbitration and implementing arbitral awards) when specifically enjoined to do so by law.[20]

A frequent political objection to international arbitration has weakened in recent years. For many years any diminution in the authority of local courts – and certainly any attempt to make a contract subject to foreign law – was regarded by some local leaders as an infringement on national sovereignty. In a sense, this criticism dates back to the capitulations, which gave foreigners extraterritorial status, and, in Egypt, to the Mixed Courts. Not fully subject to Egyptian law, foreigners had special status and a distinct judicial system. In subsequent years, attempts to build a legal framework conducive to foreign investment were often compared to the capitulations and Mixed Court regime precisely because they offered options to international business (particularly investors) to avoid local laws and courts.[21]

While international business leaders seek predictability, political authorities have stressed the need for national control. Regional governments have generally resisted settling disputes according to foreign law more than they have resisted resort to foreign or international

---

[18] For an example of complaints of the expense of international arbitration, see the interview with Sayyid al-Shurbaji, director of the Office of Government Cases (responsible for representing official organs in litigation), "Office of Government Cases on Defending the Government," *Akhir Sa'a*, April 11, 1990, p. 20.

[19] Yahya al-Saman, "The Settlement of Foreign Investment Disputes by Means of Domestic Arbitration in Saudi Arabia," *Arab Law Quarterly*, 9 (3), 1994, p. 217.

[20] For an example of judicial suspicions of alternative dispute resolution (though not specifically international arbitration), see Hamid al-Jaraf, "For Egypt and for its Judges . . . Dangers of Transferring the American Judicial System," *al-Ahram*, February 1, 1994.

[21] See, for instance, Jeswald Salacuse, "Foreign Investment and Legislative Exemptions in Egypt: Needed Stimulus or New Capitulations," in Laurence O. Michalak and Jeswald W. Salacuse (eds.), *Social Legislation in the Contemporary Middle East* (Berkeley: Institute of International Studies, 1986); and Gamil Mohamed Hussein, "Dispute Settlement Mechanisms in Law No. 43. International Implications," *Revue Egyptienne du Droit International*, 37, 1981, p. 365.

fora. Objections to international arbitration have occurred, however. They have been far greater when they involved contracts with the government or public sector than when they involved private economic actors. Indeed, the office in Egypt responsible for representing the government in litigation put forward the argument that contracts with the government or the public sector fall within the jurisdiction of the administrative courts according to law and that any arbitration clause that seeks to avoid the jurisdiction of administrative courts is invalid.[22]

Thus the goals of local governments and of international business are not mirror opposites. The choice of forum has generally been more important to business leaders; the law governing contracts has generally been more important to local governments. The legal framework for international contracts has been a direct function of the economic and political bargaining power of the two sides. At times when governments have been more anxious to attract international investment or when they have been too weak internationally to resist pressure, they have created very favorable circumstances for arbitration. At other times they have felt able to exercise greater control over international transactions that wholly or partially take place within their territory.

The time when local governments were the weakest internationally was when their sovereignty was not yet fully established. Under the Mixed Courts in Egypt, as has been noted, an entirely separate court system existed to try cases with a mixed interest. In other parts of the Arab world, disputes involving international contracts were often solved by political bargaining rather than by litigation. The end of the Mixed Courts in Egypt brought agitation from Egyptian nationalists and business interests for legislation regulating foreign companies operating in Egypt.[23] In the Gulf, some governments felt able after independence to take a dim view of arbitration and insist on the use of local courts. Oddly, it was the great increase in oil revenues that persuaded many Gulf governments to relent; with the onset of truly large-scale projects (especially in construction) and the desire for high quality work, many governments in the Gulf felt that failure to allow international arbitration in government contracts would frighten away the sort of contractors they wished to attract.[24] In a few Gulf states, political authorities allowed even government contracts to be governed by foreign law, conceding

[22] This argument was made prior to the 1994 investment law which rejected such logic. See "Office of Government Cases on Defending the Government."

[23] See Nathan J. Brown, "The Precarious Life and Slow Death of the Mixed Courts of Egypt," *International Journal of Middle East Studies*, 25 (1), 1993.

[24] Al-Saman, "The Settlement of Foreign Investment Disputes" finds a change of attitude in Saudi Arabia in the 1970s. Ernest Alexander identifies 1979 as a turning point in the Kuwaiti attitude (personal interview, Kuwait, January 1995).

that the local legal framework was too poorly developed for complex investment and trade disputes.

In the 1970s the Egyptian government also changed its attitude because of a larger effort to attract foreign investment to the country. Political bargaining between Western countries (particularly the United States) and Egypt played a role in this shift. Investment law in Egypt was changed to encourage arbitration, and bilateral investment treaties have been negotiated with the same effect. External aid agencies have sometimes threatened to withhold grants or loans unless arbitration clauses are inserted in funded contracts.[25] The culmination of the permissive attitude towards arbitration was reached with Law 27 of 1994 which grants contracting parties almost total latitude in the choice of fora and both procedural and substantive law.[26] Contracts and arbitration agreements still may not violate public policy (making it more difficult to avoid local labor laws, for instance), though favorable local legislation on international investment has already diminished the restrictions this requirement implies. Described as a model law by its advocates, Law 27 was passed without major public controversy.[27] With the promulgation of the 1994 law, Egypt became the Arab state most supportive of arbitration – many other Arab states continue to view non-local substantive law suspiciously, and some governments are reluctant to sign contracts with international arbitration clauses (though there are few barriers to private parties doing so). Yet the regional trend towards supporting arbitration clauses and including them in both public and private international contracts is clear.

Indeed, the enthusiasm for arbitration has shown some initial signs of spreading to domestic business disputes. Arbitration was generally the

---

[25] For details on the legal changes regarding arbitration (especially relating to foreign investment) that began in the 1970s, see George E. Bushnell III, "The Development of Foreign Investment Law in Egypt and its Effect on Private Foreign Investment," *Georgia Journal of International and Comparative Law*, 10 (2), 1980, p. 301; Hala Zaki Hashem, "Legal Treatment of Foreign Investment in Egypt: A Comparative Study of Investment Law and Bilateral Investment Treaties," *Revue Egyptienne de Droit International*, 40, 1984, p. 133; and Hussein, "Dispute Settlement Mechanisms in Law No. 43" p. 365. The attitude of foreign assistance agencies is noted in "Office of Government Cases on Defending the Government."

[26] I am grateful to Dean Dilley for providing me with a copy of the law.

[27] Muhammad Abu al-ʿAynayn, vice-president of the Supreme Constitutional Court and director of the Cairo Center for the Resolution of International Investment Disputes, a major supporter of the law, described it as "the best in the world" (personal conversation, Cairo, July 1994). The only reservation I heard expressed by business lawyers regarding the law was that it remained untested. There were some misgivings that the law might take too much away from the Egyptian courts. See the comments of the director of the Office of Government Cases, in which he expresses a strong opinion on the law, then in preparation ("Office of Government Cases on Defending the Government").

preferred mechanism for settling disputes among merchants in the region at the beginning of the modern era, and in most societies arbitration systems were well established. The construction of centralized and hierarchical judicial systems and the diminution of the economic role of the private sector led these systems to atrophy (in Egypt they seem to have disappeared completely). There was sometimes interest in arbitration in specific sorts of disputes (often involving either labor or the public sector), but even where business disputants were offered arbitration systems they seem to have had little trust in them.

Recent reforms have therefore not excluded purely local disputes. The 1994 arbitration law in Egypt is friendly to arbitration in domestic as well as foreign disputes; the Kuwaiti parliament and government have recently examined domestic arbitration mechanisms. While Kuwait has allowed business disputants to resort to arbitration through either the Chamber of Commerce or the Justice Ministry, such mechanisms have been widely ignored.[28] A new law was passed to correct procedural disincentives to use arbitration (in fact, an early, though rejected, draft by the Justice Ministry would have made arbitration compulsory).[29]

It is difficult to escape the conclusion that the greatest obstacle to the use of arbitration in domestic business disputes is now not so much the legal framework – which in many countries, including Egypt, Kuwait, and Qatar is supportive – but the attitude of business decision-makers themselves. Regarding the legal system as a morass to be avoided when possible, few businesses use in-house legal counsel or regularly consult with attorneys in their operations. Thus arbitration clauses are rarely inserted in domestic contracts.[30] Resorting to arbitration once the dispute begins is often legally possible but impractical because one side generally has an interest in using the tortuous procedures of the civil courts. With the growing prominence of arbitration in international contracts and complaints of procedural delays now heard in most

---

[28] One Kuwaiti parliamentarian claimed that fewer than one-half of 1 percent of business disputes go to arbitration. Mishari al-ʿUsaymi, personal interview, Kuwait, January 1995.

[29] The text of the law is printed in *al-Qabas*, January 30, 1995 (the law was passed by parliament the next day). The proposal for compulsory arbitration was criticized by the Administration for Legal Advice and Legislation (*idarat al-fatwa wa-l-tashriʿ*) attached to the Cabinet, partly because it would have violated the constitutional right to resort to the courts (personal interview with ʿAbd al-Rusul ʿAbd al-Rida, Kuwait, director of the Administration, January 1995).

[30] Interestingly, the two model contracts for household labor mentioned in the previous chapter (one suggested by the embassy of the Philippines and the other by the Kuwaiti Office of Household Labor) do provide for mediation and non-binding arbitration.

countries in the Arab world, greater prior commitment to arbitration in domestic business disputes should be expected.

Courts in Egypt, and in the Arab world more generally, are more egalitarian structures than might be expected. Their procedures, fees, and even the laws they enforce grant middle- and working-class litigants real opportunities to defend their interests. By doing so, they become less friendly structures in the eyes of more prosperous potential litigants – not because of any procedural bias against business but because business leaders are generally more demanding in their expectations. By inviting so many to use the courts to resolve disputes, the Egyptian legal system (and the legal system of many other Arab states) has presented a forbidding face to business leaders. Courts appear to offer endless procedures and numerous indignities.

Yet while courts are more egalitarian structures than may initially appear, the legal system in which they operate is often less egalitarian. Those involved in international transactions are more able to be selective in choosing venue, procedure, and sometimes even the governing law. In other words, the legal system offers the wealthy and powerful greater opportunities for avoiding the courts or tailoring a dispute-resolution system to their individual needs. Other litigants certainly do not lack creativity in their strategies, but they have no ability to go beyond individual strategies to constructing a private legal system which issues judgments enforceable by the regular courts.

Egypt's court system, like the country's physical infrastructure, is overburdened and built to service the needs of a large and poor population. The transportation and communication systems draw frequent complaints from those who have more substantial economic interests. Many are therefore driven to find private solutions for their needs. Like Cairo buses and telephones, the courts seem designed to cater to large numbers of less prosperous citizens (though not necessarily the poor) in ways that frustrate potential litigants with business interests.

The resulting compromise is not ideal for anyone concerned, but perhaps the most obvious loser is domestic business. Less able (and perhaps thus far less interested) in constructing private arbitration systems, but equally repelled by slow (and often undignified) litigation procedures, owners of small businesses embroiled in disputes have few attractive options. The problems from such a perspective are numerous: an unsympathetic and complex bureaucracy, a legal framework with a strong statist bias, a system of courts unable to resolve disputes quickly, and a system to enforce judgments that is equally dilatory and uncertain. Those who criticize the legal system in Egypt as being unfriendly to business therefore miss the extent to which opportunities to pursue arbitration – and have arbitral awards enforced – have dramatically increased (at least for international business). And those who criticize courts as inegalitarian structures similarly miss the point that one of the chief sources of inequality is not how the courts operate but how they can be avoided.

# Conclusion

At the beginning of this study, three questions were posed concerning the social and political role of courts in the Arab world. It is now possible to advance answers to each of the questions.

First, why did Egypt's political leaders construct and maintain an independent judicial system that might seem to limit their own authority? Those accounts of legal and judicial reform in Egypt (or more generally) that stress imperialism, liberalism, or legitimation are not so much incorrect as incomplete. Imperialism did shape the course of Egyptian legal development during the late nineteenth and early twentieth centuries, if often indirectly. The timing and structure of legal reform in Egypt, however, reveal that the primary impetus was domestic. Even when imperialism played a role, legal development was often a tool that served to resist or contain imperialism rather than enforce it. Similarly, liberalism has played a role in Egyptian legal history, and the Egyptian judiciary has at times emerged as a force for liberal legality. Liberal legality in Egypt, however, has never been predicated on the idea of a minimalist state, and has generally operated within sharply defined limits. Finally, while the legal system has served to support existing political authority, the legitimating function of law has been greatly exaggerated. It is true that at times the political leadership has adopted an ideology based on the rule of law, but there is little empirical evidence that the actual institutions associated with the rule of law have generated popular support for, or acquiescence in, the political order. Such ideologies are probably better understood not as hegemonic but as aiding only in fostering coherence and unity of political vision among the political leadership. An independent judiciary, for instance, has done little to generate diffuse support for the regime, but it has been cited frequently by political leaders seeking to articulate a rationale or purpose for the regime.

The modern Egyptian legal system was born and continues to survive not because it was imposed or because it regulates relations between the state and civil society. Instead, the primary purpose of the system – in the eyes of the political leaders who have built and sustained it – is to provide support for the officially sanctioned order. The Egyptian legal and judicial system was constructed as an integral part of an effort to build a stronger, more effective, more centralized, and more intrusive state. It has been modified over the past century largely to serve that purpose (though some significant concessions to liberal legality have been made). In constructing and maintaining such a system, Egypt's political leaders relinquished some control over decisions in specific cases (though they have been more protective of extra-judicial means for politically sensitive cases). They gained far more, however, in insuring that their legislation and regulations would be enforced throughout the country and at all levels of society.

Second, why does a seemingly autonomous and dilatory system recommend itself to Arab rulers outside Egypt? The attractions of the Egyptian system for those Arab states examined here were generally the same features that appealed to Egyptian political leaders. The legal systems of the Gulf were not imposed by either the British (who preferred different models) or the Egyptians, though both Britain and Egypt exercised strong influence. Nor was there much interest on the part of the leadership, with the possible exception of Kuwait, in constructing a liberal political order based on constitutionalism and the rule of law. (In Bahrain a political opposition did possess such a vision but it was defeated in the 1950s.) Nor has the legal system fulfilled a significant legitimating function. In some states in the Gulf (most notably Qatar), reduced reliance on the *shari'a* was probably a minor liability for the regime's legitimacy. Instead, the states of the Gulf saw in the Egyptian system an opportunity to build strong and centralized court systems and to adopt comprehensive law codes. The perceived need for such institutions was probably weaker in the Arab states of the Gulf than it was in Egypt, but by independence it had proven decisive in all of them.

Third, why do so many Egyptians bring their disputes to court? Simply because the systems were constructed to make state authority operate more effectively is no reason to assume that they have that effect or only that effect. Yet the analysis here suggests that the uses that Cairenes make of the courts indicate that Egyptian courts have succeeded too well in making their presence felt. Egyptian courts are swamped with civil disputes of every conceivable variety and have become a vital tool in the survival strategies of many urban residents. Egyptian litigation techniques show that increasing reach of the state apparatus has also increased the options for individual actors in the society. The courts play a role in a wide variety of disputes, insuring that both state-mandated policies and legislation and private individuals have a powerful set of tools at their disposal. The instrumentalism displayed by the population of Cairo shows that the courts have not only successfully augmented the effectiveness of official legislation but have also created numerous opportunities for resourceful citizens. State and society are not locked in a zero-sum struggle for power and influence; the Egyptian judicial system has increased the maneuverability of both.

Popular instrumentalist views of the courts have also further attenuated the relationship between law and legitimacy. If courts were the forum of first resort, that might indicate that they are viewed as effective and part of a legitimate order. If courts were the forum of last resort, that might indicate that they (and perhaps the political structure as a whole) are viewed with suspicion. But Cairenes do not seem to take either path. Instead, courts are simply one tool among many that Cairenes use, often simultaneously and in combination, and not one that they use at the expense of other strategies. Such instrumentalism suggests that Egyptian experiences in court can hardly be expected to be a major determinant of popular attitudes to the legitimacy of the prevailing order. Use of the courts does not preclude other strategies or force Cairenes to view their disputes a particular way at the expense of others.

In Egypt, and, to a lesser extent, in other Arab states, rulers and ruled have very different but quite complementary images of courts. For rulers, courts are structures that enforce state-sanctioned policies. If they sometimes do so in inefficient or even politically annoying ways, they are still very attractive on the whole. For the ruled, courts are judged more by their usefulness than their fairness. Their procedures and rules appear as opportunities for increasing tactical mobility more than they represent fairness and justice.

The courts do seem to have some equalizing effect in Egyptian society, though this is as much because of the content of much legislation as it is because of the attractiveness of the courts. The ability of powerful economic actors to construct their own legal frameworks and dispute-resolution authorities has probably diminished this equalizing effect in recent years. It is not that courts have become less friendly to the middle class and the poor; indeed, as business leaders increasingly turn to other fora to resolve disputes, the regular courts may be in the process of becoming the exclusive preserve of those who cannot afford better.

The experience of the Arab countries examined in this study has some wider lessons for the role of courts and the rule of law. As countries of the former Soviet bloc eschew socialist legality and seek to adopt liberal models, and as Latin American and East Asian countries devote greater attention to the legal frameworks and judicial structure in support of developmental efforts, the century-long experience of Egypt and that of other Arab countries may shed some light on the likely role that courts can and will play.

First, if codified law, centralized court systems, and independent judiciaries are not universal institutions, neither can they be seen any longer solely as Western innovations. Egyptians certainly do not behave as if their judicial system is an external imposition or culturally inappropriate, and their behavior in this regard may be based on a more sound understanding of the system's nature than that held by many scholars. Importing an idea or institution is not the same as having it imperially imposed. Further, the system as it has developed has become so thoroughly a part of Egyptian society that it can be decried as alien only by those most committed to Islamicist ideologies. Even such committed activists decry not the idea of the rule of law – which they call for in the strongest possible terms – but the content of positive legislation. Thus, the effort to understand legal change in the developing world must be distanced – to a greater if not unlimited extent – from the study of imperialism.

This is not to dismiss the calls for culturally authentic law as meaningless. In much of the Arab world, the slogan of "application of the shari'a" has gained great force in recent years. Yet great as the political resonance of such appeals is at the current time, what is striking is how little the departure from shari'a models bothered those who experienced it. The issue was discussed, but generally in muted and peaceful terms. And in Egypt, when the debate over the proper sources of the law became heated and eventually violent, only a few specific legal provisions (generally criminal penalties and commercial interest) were challenged. By that time the cultural import had become thoroughly domesticated. The political appeal of the shari'a is based not simply on the promise of authenticity but also of official accountability. The application of the shari'a, in the eyes of its proponents, can deliver a kind of constitutionalism that liberal legality can only covet.[1]

Second, judicial institutions can be extremely plastic. This is true from the perspective of both executive authorities and potential litigants. The structural continuity of Egyptian courts over the past century is

---

[1] Particularly interesting in this regard are the writings of 'Abd al-Razzaq al-Sanhuri's son-in-law, Tawfiq al-Shawi. Al-Sanhuri himself sought to use the shari'a to inform Egypt's codified law; al-Shawi goes much further in his fealty to Islamic jurisprudence. See Tawfiq al-Shawi, Fiqh al-shura wa-l-istishara (al-Mansura: Dar al-wafa', 1992), especially pp. 168–76 and 192–96.

quite striking; even the reforms of the late nineteenth century that established the current system were largely evolutionary. Other Arab states have adopted Egyptian models, always consciously and often quite faithfully. With Egypt witnessing tremendous political changes over the lifetime of the current judicial system, and with the Arab world characterized by great political diversity, one might begin to suspect that Egyptian-style courts can serve many masters. This study strongly supports that suspicion. The British occupation authorities and Egypt's kings, prime ministers, and presidents have all worked largely within the framework of the judicial system established in the late nineteenth century. When executive authorities have felt the system constrained them too much, they have moved outside of it far more than they have tried to reshape it. Judges themselves have generally supported liberal legality when given the opportunity, but they have been able to operate freely under virtually every regime that has ruled Egypt. Even the one direct attempt to bring the judiciary under executive domination – the 1969 massacre of the judiciary – is notable for the minor structural changes it introduced. And even those changes that were made in 1969 were soon either reversed or themselves transformed in ways that strengthened rather than limited judicial autonomy. It is small wonder that the ruling families of the Gulf have found that the Egyptian system, while it occasionally may limit their discretion, has served to augment state capacity.

Litigants have also shown how the courts can be shaped to serve many different ends. In this process they have been aided not only by the structure and process of the judicial system but also the contents of Egypt's laws which can be friendly to working- and middle-class interests. Yet Egyptian litigiousness predates the emergency legislation of the Second World War and the laws generated by Nasserist socialism which together form the bases of many current lawsuits; Egyptians discovered how to use the courts to their own advantage almost from the beginning of the current system. Currently, Egyptians use courts and litigation in a variety of ways: as threats, bargaining chips, weapons, stalling devices, and, of course, as instruments of justice. Courts do not stand aloof from the society but have become active participants in social conflicts of all sorts. In chapter 1, the possibility was suggested that states might decrease their reliance on legal institutions as their focus moved to the economy and the provision of welfare benefits. On the contrary, however, not only has official reliance on courts continued, but popular reliance has greatly increased. Courts have not become a less important part of the state (though criminal law enforcement does absorb fewer resources).

A third and related point concerns the relationship between the legal system and the form of government. Contemporary political debate – not only in the United States but also in the Arab world and elsewhere – is often characterized by fairly loose terminology. "Democracy," "free markets," and "the rule of law" are terms used at times interchangeably or at least as mutually dependent. The Arab experience suggests a more subtle relationship between the rule of law on the one hand and democracy and markets on the other. It is true that the rule of law may be a prerequisite for democracy or markets to operate efficiently or in a sustained manner. Arbitrary rule may make democracy unstable or short-lived; a popularly elected government that is not restrained by law may quickly exceed its popular mandate and distort or destroy the procedural ground rules of democratic governance. And vague or unstable property rights may discourage the economic transactions that constitute a market economy. Thus, the rule of law may be a necessary condition for a democratic polity or a market economy. It is hardly a sufficient condition for either. To make an earlier argument more generally, the rule of law can serve different masters and certainly has done so in the Arab world.

Indeed, a system approaching the rule of law may be something that ambitious and centralized states cannot avoid. In order to insure that policies designed and desired by the central authority are implemented, technically competent and uninhibited courts may be as necessary as a complex and extensive bureaucracy. Courts independent of the bureaucratic structure can also be quite helpful in ensuring that lower officials implement centrally determined policies.[2] It is precisely for this reason that law and courts have always been seen as intimately connected with state sovereignty in the Arab world. Weak courts may give local officials excessive discretion and dilute the authority of the state; foreign-dominated courts may make bureaucrats respond to foreign governments or communities more than their own central authorities. Punctilious legalism and an independent judiciary can thus serve the purposes of very different economic and political systems.

Indeed, the usefulness of law to authoritarian regimes has led some to try hard to distinguish between "rule of law" and other law-centered ideologies, such as "rule by law" or "law-based state." The distinction is often not well articulated, but the "rule of law" is often associated with democratic legislative processes (though this association is hardly required by definition and is based on a rarely examined assumption

---

[2] This argument is expertly made in James H. Rosberg, *Roads to the Rule of Law: The Emergence of an Independent Judiciary in Contemporary Egypt*, Ph.D. dissertation, Department of Political Science, Massachusetts Institute of Technology, 1995.

that "rule of law" and democracy are mutually dependent). "Rule by
law" or a "law-based state" require that a state operate on the basis of
fixed and knowable law – which, implicitly or explicitly, must therefore
bind state authorities themselves. There is no requirement for separation
of powers or pluralism, and indeed no consideration of the process by
which law is made.[3]

This vague and elusive distinction is a product not of muddled
thinking but of muddled reality: law in authoritarian states can operate
very similarly to law in liberal democratic states. Even given a distinction
between "rule of law" and "rule by law," the institutional plasticity of
the courts discussed above makes it easy to slip back and forth between
them (as Egypt has done over the past half-century). It may be such
slipperiness that has led most writers on democratization – even those
who pay great attention to political institutions – to steer away from law
and courts.

Nevertheless, the Arab experience suggests one important distinction
between the "rule of law" and "the rule by law" that is probably
applicable elsewhere. While executive authorities respect fixed procedures in both, there is a potential difference in the extent of the
subservience of the highest executive officials to the rulings of the courts.
In normal circumstances, there is no difference. Since executive
authorities in the Arab world, as in many other countries, dominate (and
sometimes even monopolize) legislative authority, the potential risks of
subjecting themselves to the judiciary are rarely grave – executive
authorities bear primary responsibility for the content of the laws the
courts enforce. Yet in some sensitive political cases, executive authorities
may wish for tremendous discretion to abandon rules they may have
made or at least tailor their application to the exigencies of regime
survival. A judiciary that can rein in executive authority by overly faithful
(or overly liberal) implementation of the law can be inconvenient or
worse in such circumstances.

Thus it is the extent of the authority over the executive far more than
judicial independence that has been the most accurate gauge of the
extent of liberal legality in the Arab world. All other aspects of the rule of
law are quite consistent – and sometimes quite supportive – of the
desires of ambitious central authorities. Judges who are merely independent can be given legal texts that compel them to follow regime wishes in

---

[3] See, for instance, Harold J. Berman, "The Rule of Law and the Law-Based State
(*Rechtsstaat*) with Special Reference to the Soviet Union," in Donald D. Barry (ed.),
*Toward the "Rule of Law" in Russia? Political and Legal Reform in the Transition Period*
(Armonk: M. E. Sharpe, 1991); and Ronald C. Keith, "Chinese Politics and the New
Theory of 'Rule of Law,'" *The China Quarterly*, 125, 1991, p. 109.

most circumstances; such judges can be avoided when such texts are unavailable or difficult to write. Judges who are not only independent but also unavoidable can present real problems, especially if they are willing to be bold in their interpretations of legislative and constitutional texts. If rulers cannot outmaneuver, mollify, or avoid independent judges then their authority is truly circumscribed. No government in the Arab world is likely to allow such a situation to develop willingly. Only the Mixed Courts in Egypt achieved such a position and they caused a protracted political crisis in the process. Since independence, the situation has not been repeated in Egypt or elsewhere. Neither an ambitious judicial actor (such as Egypt's Supreme Constitutional Court) nor a democratic movement (such as in Kuwait's parliament) has been able to restrict executive authority in matters deemed critical by senior executive authorities.

Finally, the Arab experience indicates that the relationship between law and legitimacy is far weaker than many legal theorists have led us to expect. As discussed above, both rulers and ruled have looked to law and the courts with quite utilitarian eyes. There is little evidence that Egyptians or others in the Arab world have been swayed by the majesty of the law in their attitudes towards the political system in general or specific legislative provisions. Nor is there much evidence that Egyptian or other Arab leaders have often expected the legal system to have such an effect. There have been periods in which liberal legal language has become a more prominent part of official political statements. Egypt is currently in the midst of such a period, and other Arab states, such as Kuwait, Jordan, and Morocco, may be entering one. Even in present-day Egypt, however, such rhetoric generally refers to specific political concessions by the regime rather than an unambiguous and general commitment to the most ambitious definitions of liberal legality. And such rhetoric probably has to do more with defining the leadership's political vision for the country than it has with popular perceptions; that is, law may legitimate a ruling elite in its own eyes more than it persuades (or precludes others from persuading) a larger public audience. The use of military courts by the Egyptian government or the Israeli occupation authorities in the West Bank and Gaza has probably done little to change Egyptian or Palestinian minds about the nature of the political system, but it has allowed the governments involved to assure themselves that they rule according to the legal procedures.

It is not impossible that the legal system can play a more central role in providing legitimacy to the political order, but the price is likely to be too high for Arab regimes. If a strong and independent judiciary were able to restrict executive authority in fundamental ways, then politically aware citizens would be likely to admit that a truly liberal order had emerged. Even so, the regular work of the courts – dealing with routine litigation and crime – would be unaffected. Courts in the Arab world are likely to continue to serve those who have the power or the ingenuity to use them.

# Bibliography

NEWSPAPERS AND PERIODICALS

*Akhbar al-yawm*, weekly, Cairo
*Akhir sa'a*, weekly, Cairo
*Al-Ahali*, weekly, Cairo
*Al-Ahram*, daily, Cairo
*Al-Ahram al-iqtisadi*, weekly, Cairo
*Al-Ahrar*, weekly, Cairo
*Al-Akhbar*, daily, Cairo
*Al-Hayah*, daily, London
*Al-Jumhuriyya*, daily, Cairo
*Al-Masa'*, daily, Cairo
*Al-Muhamah*, monthly, Cairo
*Al-Muqtattaf*, monthly, Cairo
*Al-Musawwar*, weekly, Cairo
*Al-Qabas*, daily, Kuwait
*Al-Ra'y al-'amm*, daily, Kuwait
*Al-Sha'b*, biweekly, Cairo
*Al-Sharq al-awsat*, daily, London
*Al-Siyasa*, daily, Kuwait
*Al-Tali'a*, weekly, Kuwait
*Al-Wafd*, daily, Cairo
*Al-Watan*, daily, Kuwait
*Ruz al-yusuf*, weekly, Cairo
*Uktubir*, weekly, Cairo


ARCHIVAL AND UNPUBLISHED SOURCES

Alexander, Ernest. "Resolution of Disputes, Arbitration and Litigation," presentation at "Seminar on Construction Claims in Kuwait: How to Deal with them," at SAS Hotel, Kuwait, January 27, 1990.
Bentley, John. "Egyptian Legal and Judicial Sector Assessment: Report and Recommendations," submitted to USAID/Egypt in association with Kamel, Yehia, Abul Ela and Sakr, 4 vols., February 1994.
Elwan, Talaat M. *The Office of Prosecutor in Egypt*, MS thesis, Administration of Justice Department, San José State University, August 1989.
Gabr, Hatem Aly Labib. "The Interpretation of Article Two of the Egyptian

Constitution as Envisaged by the Supreme Constitutional Court," April 1994.

Great Britain. Foreign Office records
FO 141, FO 371, FO 1016, Public Record Office, Kew, England.
*Egypt No. 4 (1921) Papers Respecting Negotiations with the Egyptian Delegation.*
*Egypt No. 1 (1928). Papers Regarding Negotiations for a Treaty of Alliance with Egypt.*
*British Documents on Foreign Affairs: Reports and Papers from the Foreign Office Confidential Print,* Part I, Series B, vol. 15, University Publications of America, 1985.

Hajjar, Lisa. *Authority, Resistance and the Law: A Study of the Israeli Military Court System in the Occupied Territories,* Ph.D. dissertation, Department of Sociology, The American University, 1995.

Nosseir, Abdel Rahman. "The Supreme Constitutional Court of Egypt and the Protection of Human Rights," Chicago, 1992.

Rosberg, James H. *Roads to the Rule of Law: The Emergence of an Independent Judiciary in Contemporary Egypt,* Ph.D. dissertation, Department of Political Science, Massachusetts Institute of Technology, 1995.

Saleh, Hassan Mohammad Abdulla. *Labor, Nationalism and Imperialism in Eastern Arabia: Britain, the Shaikhs and the Gulf Oil Workers in Bahrain, Kuwait and Qatar, 1932–1956,* Ph.D. dissertation, University of Michigan, 1991.

Sherif, Adel Omar. "The Supreme Constitutional Court in the Egyptian Judicial System," Chicago, 1992.

Tabataba'i, 'Adil al-. "Mada ikhtisas majlis al-umma bi-nazar al-marasim bi-qawanin al-sadira fi halat al-hall" (The Extent of the Jurisdiction of the National Assembly in Examining Decree-Laws Issued in the Case of Dissolution), 1994 (a subsequent version was to be published in the Kuwaiti *Majallat al-muhamah*).

Tollefson, Harold Haakon. *Police and Ghaffir Reforms in Egypt, 1882–1914,* Ph.D. dissertation, Department of History, University of California, Santa Barbara, 1987.

United States. Department of State Records
National Archives: files contained within classifications 774, 783, and 883.


BOOKS AND ARTICLES

*'Abd al-Razzaq al-Sanhuri min khilal awraqihi al-shakhsiyya* ('Abd al-Razzaq al-Sanhuri through his Personal Papers), Cairo: al-Zahra' li-l-a'lam al-'arabi, 1988.

'Abd al-Raziq, Husayn. "Torture among the Niyaba, the Press and the Parliament," *al-Yasar,* 52, November 1994, pp. 4–6.

Abercrombie, Nicholas, Stephen Hill, and Bryan S. Turner. *The Dominant Ideology Thesis,* London: Allen and Unwin, 1980.

Abun-Nasr, Jamil M., Ulrich Spellenberg, and Ulrike Wanitzek (eds.). *Law, Society, and National Identity in Africa,* Hamburg: Helmut Buske Verlag, 1990.

*Al-kitab al-dhahabi li-l-mahakim al-ahliyya* (The Golden Book of the National Courts), 2 vols., Cairo: Al-matba'a al-amiriyya bi-bulaq, 1937.

Al-Sayyid (Marsot), Afaf Lutfi. *Egypt and Cromer*, London: Murray, 1968.

Altman, Andrew. *Critical Legal Studies: A Liberal Critique*, Princeton: Princeton University Press, 1990.

Anderson, Lisa. "Lawless Government and Illegal Opposition: Reflections on the Middle East," *Journal of International Affairs*, 40, 1987, pp. 219–32.

"Absolutism and the Resilience of Monarchy in the Middle East," *Political Science Quarterly*, 106 (1), 1991, pp. 1–15.

Asiri, 'Abd al-Rida 'Ali. *Al-nizam al-siyasi fi al-kuwayt* (The Political System in Kuwait), Kuwait: Matba'at al-watan, 1994.

Balfour-Paul, Glen. *The End of Empire in the Middle East: Britain's Relinquishment of Power in her Last Three Arab Dependencies*, Cambridge: Cambridge University Press, 1991.

Ballantyne, W. M. *Legal Development in Arabia*, London: Graham and Troutman, 1980.

Barry, Donald D. (ed.). *Toward the "Rule of Law" in Russia? Political and Legal Reform in the Transition Period*, Armonk: M. E. Sharpe, 1991.

Batatu, Hanna. *The Old Social Classes and the Revolutionary Movements of Iraq: A Study of Iraq's Landed and Commercial Classes and of its Communists, Ba'thists and Free Officers*, Princeton: Princeton University Press, 1978.

Bermeo, Nancy (ed.). *Liberalization and Democratization: Change in the Soviet Union and Eastern Europe*, Baltimore: Johns Hopkins University Press, 1991.

Bianchi, Robert. *Unruly Corporatism*, New York: Oxford, 1989.

Bierne, Piers, and Richard Quinney (eds.). *Marxism and Law*, New York: John Wiley and Sons, 1982.

Bishri, Tariq al-. "One Hundred Years of the Egyptian Judiciary", *Al-Quda*, 5/6, 1986, pp. 28–31.

Brinton, Jasper Yeates. *The Mixed Courts of Egypt*, revised edition, New Haven: Yale University Press, 1968.

Brown, Nathan J. *Peasant Politics in Modern Egypt*, New Haven: Yale University Press, 1990.

"Brigands and State Building: The Invention of Banditry in Modern Egypt," *Comparative Studies in Society and History*, 32 (2), 1990, pp. 258–81.

"The Precarious Life and Slow Death of the Mixed Courts of Egypt," *International Journal of Middle East Studies*, 25 (1), 1993, pp. 33–52.

"Who Abolished Corvee Labor in Egypt and Why?" *Past and Present*, 144, August 1994, pp. 116–37.

"Law and Imperialism: Egypt in Comparative Perspective," *Law and Society Review*, 29 (1), 1995pp. 103–25.

Burman, Sandra B. and Barbara E. Harrell-Bond (eds.). *The Imposition of Law*, New York: Academic Press, 1979.

Bushnell, George E. III. "The Development of Foreign Investment Law in Egypt and its Effect on Private Foreign Investment," *Georgia Journal of International and Comparative Law*, 10 (2), 1980, pp. 301–24.

Cannon, Byron. *Politics of Law and the Courts in Nineteenth Century Egypt*, Salt Lake City: University of Utah Press, 1988.

Chanock, Martin. "Writing South African Legal History: A Prospectus," *Journal of African History*, 30 (2), 1989, pp. 265–88.

Christelow, Allen C. *Muslim Law Courts and the French Colonial State in Algeria*, Princeton: Princeton University Press, 1985.

Constable, Pamela, and Artura Valenzuela. *A Nation of Enemies: Chile under Pinochet*, New York: W. W. Norton and Company, 1991.

Cromer, Earl of. *Modern Egypt*, London: Macmillan 1908.

Crystal, Jill. *Oil and Politics in the Gulf: Rulers and Merchants in Kuwait and Qatar*, Cambridge: Cambridge University Press, 1990.

Cuno, Kenneth J. *The Pasha's Peasants, Land, Society, and Economy in Lower Egypt, 1740–1858*, Cambridge: Cambridge University Press, 1992.

Davis, Eric. *Challenging Colonialism: Bank Misr and Egyptian Industrialization, 1920–1941*, Princeton: Princeton University Press, 1983.

de Soto, Hernando. *The Other Path: The Invisible Revolution in the Third World*, New York: Harper and Row, 1989.

Dwyer, Daisy Hilse (ed.). *Law and Islam in the Middle East*, New York: Bergin and Garvey Publishers, 1990.

El-Nahal, Galal H. *The Judicial Administration of Ottoman Egypt in the Seventeenth Century*, Minneapolis: Bibliotheca Islamica, 1979.

Elster, John and Rune Slagstad (eds.). *Constitutionalism and Democracy*, Cambridge: Cambridge University Press, 1988.

Engel, David M. *Code and Custom in a Thai Provincial Court*, Tucson: University of Arizona Press, 1978.

Esposito, John L. *Women in Muslim Family Law*, Syracuse: Syracuse University Press, 1982.

Finn, John E. *Constitutions in Crisis: Political Violence and the Rule of Law*, New York: Oxford University Press, 1991.

Fleuhr-Lobban, Carolyn, and Lois Bardsley-Sirois, "Obedience (Ta'a) in Muslim Marriage: Religious Interpretation and Applied Law in Egypt," *Journal of Comparative Family Studies*, 21 (1), Spring 1990, pp. 39–53.

Furnivall, J. S. *Colonial Policy and Practice: A Comparative Study of Burma and Netherlands India*, Cambridge: Cambridge University Press, 1948.

Gerber, Haim. *State, Society, and Law in Islam: Ottoman Law in Comparative Perspective*, Albany: State University of New York Press, 1994.

Ghai, Yash. "The Rule of Law, Legitimacy and Governance," *International Journal of the Sociology of Law*, 14 (1), 1986, pp. 179–208.

Ghazzali, Salah al-. *al-Haya al-dimuqratiyya fi al-kuwayt* (Democratic Life in Kuwait), Kuwait: National Union of Kuwaiti Students, 1985.

Hakim, Tawfiq al-. *Yawmiyyat na'ib fi-l-aryaf* (Diary of a Prosecutor in the Countryside), Cairo: Maktabat al-Adab, n.d., originally published 1937.

Hamzeh, A. Nizar. "Qatar: The Duality of the Legal System," *Middle Eastern Studies*, 30 (1), 1994, pp. 79–90.

Hashem, Hala Zaki. "Legal Treatment of Foreign Investment in Egypt: A Comparative Study of Investment Law and Bilateral Investment Treaties," *Revue Egyptienne de Droit International*, 40, 1984, pp. 133–66.

Hay, Margaret Jean, and Marcia Wright (eds.). *African Women and the Law*, Boston University Papers on Africa, 7, 1982.

Hay, Douglas, Peter Linebaugh, John G. Rule, E. P. Thompson, and Cal

Winslow. *Albion's Fatal Tree: Crime and Society in Eighteenth-Century England*, New York: Pantheon Books, 1975.

Heer, Nicholas (ed.), *Islamic Law and Jurisprudence*, Seattle: University of Washington Press, 1990.

Hill, Enid. *Mahkama! Studies in the Egyptian Legal System*, London: Ithaca Press, 1979.

"Al-Sanhuri and Islamic Law," *Cairo Papers in Social Science*, 10 (1), 1987, pp. 1–140.

Holston, James. "The Misrule of Law: Land and Usurpation in Brazil," *Comparative Studies in Society and History*, 33 (4), 1991, pp. 695–725.

Humud, Ibrahim Muhammad al-. "The Effects Resulting from the Parliament's Refusal of Law Number 35/1990, Issued in the Period of the Suspension of Parliamentary Life," *Majallat al-huquq*, 18 (3), 1994, pp. 551–98.

Hunter, F. Robert. *Egypt under the Khedives 1805–1879*, Pittsburgh: University of Pittsburgh Press, 1984.

"Self-Image and Historical Truth: Nubar Pasha and the Making of Modern Egypt," *Middle Eastern Studies*, 23 (3), 1987, pp. 363–75.

Hussein, Gamil Mohamed. "Dispute Settlement Mechanisms in Law No. 43. International Implications" *Revue Egyptienne du Droit International*, 37, 1981, pp. 365–79.

Hyde, Alan. "The Concept of Legitimation in the Sociology of Law," *Wisconsin Law Review*, 1983, pp. 379–426.

Imam, 'Abd Allah. *Madhbahat al-qada'* (The Massacre of the Judiciary), Cairo: Maktabat madbuli, 1976.

'Isa, Dawud Sulayman al-. "Commentary on the Judgment of the High Appeals Court, Tamyiz Section – Commercial, Issued in its Session Held November 25, 1987," *Majallat al-huquq*, 18 (3), 1994, pp. 865–90.

'Isawi, 'Ali 'Abd al-'Al al-. *Ashhar al-muhakimat fi al-ta'rikh* (The Most Famous Trials in History), Beirut: Dar al-jil, 1991.

Kairys, David (ed.). *The Politics of Law: A Progressive Critique*, New York: Pantheon Books, 1990.

Keith, Ronald C. "Chinese Politics and the New Theory of 'Rule of Law,' " *The China Quarterly*, 125, 1991, pp. 109–18.

Khanki, 'Aziz. *Al-mahakim al-mukhtalita wa-l-mahakim al-ahliyya* (The Mixed Courts and the National Courts), Cairo: Al-matabi' al-'asriyya, 1939.

Kitroeff, Alexander. *The Greeks in Egypt 1917–1937*, London: Ithaca Press, 1989.

Lawrence, Susan E. "Justice, Democracy, Litigation, and Political Participation," *Social Science Quarterly* 72, (3), 1991, pp. 464–77.

Lawyers' Committee for Human Rights. "Kuwait: Building the Rule of Law: Human Rights in Kuwait After Occupation," report dated April 1992.

"Laying the Foundations: Human Rights in Kuwait. Obstacles and Opportunities," report dated April 1993.

Lerrick, A. and Q. J. Mian. *Saudi Business and Labor Law: Its Interpretation and Application*, London: Graham and Trotman, 1982.

Lloyd, Lord. *Egypt Since Cromer*, 2 vols., London: Macmillan, 1933.

Low, Sidney. *Egypt in Transition*, New York: Macmillan, 1914.

Luciani, Giacomo (ed.). *The Arab State*, Berkeley: University of California Press, 1990.

Magavern, James, John Thomas, and Myra Stuart. "Law, Urban Development, and the Poor in Developing Countries," *Washington University Law Quarterly*, 1975, pp. 45–111.

Makhluf, Najib. *Nubar basha wama tamma 'ala yadihi* (Nubar Pasha and What He Accomplished), Cairo: Al-matba'a al-'umumiyya, 1903.

Mallat, Chibly (ed.). *Islam and Public Law: Classical and Contemporary Studies*, London: Graham and Trotman, 1993.

Mann, Kristin, and Richard Roberts (eds.). *Law in Colonial Africa*, Portsmouth: Heinemann, 1991.

Mayer, Ann Elizabeth (ed.). *Property, Social Structure and Law in the Modern Middle East*, Albany: State University of New York Press, 1985.

Merry, Sally Engle. *Getting Justice and Getting Even: Legal Consciousness among Working-Class Americans*, Chicago: University of Chicago Press, 1990.
"Law and Colonialism," *Law and Society Review*, 25 (4), 1991, pp. 889–922.

Messick, Brinkley. *The Calligraphic State: Textual Domination and History in a Muslim Society*, Berkeley: University of California Press, 1993.

Michalak, Laurence O. and Jeswald W. Salacuse (eds.). *Social Legislation in the Contemporary Middle East*, Berkeley: Institute of International Studies, 1986.

Middle East Watch. "A Victory Turned Sour: Human Rights in Kuwait Since Liberation," September 1991.
"Nowhere to Go: The Tragedy of the Remaining Palestinian Families in Kuwait," October 23, 1991.
*Behind Closed Doors: Torture and Detention in Egypt*, New York: Human Rights Watch, 1992.
"Punishing the Victim: Rape and Mistreatment of Asian Maids in Kuwait," Women's Rights Project report, August 1992.

Ministry of *Awqaf*, State of Qatar, *Al-taqrir al-ihsa'i 1411–1412 h* (Statistical Report, 1411–1412 A. H.).

Mir-Hosseini, Ziba. *Marriage on Trial: A Study of Islamic Family Law, Iran and Morocco Compared*, London: I.B. Tauris, 1993.

Mitchell, Timothy. *Colonising Egypt*, Cambridge: Cambridge University Press, 1988.

Muller, Ingo. *Hitler's Justice: The Courts of the Third Reich*, Cambridge MA: Harvard University Press, 1991.

Mwalimu, Charles. "Police, State Security Forces and Constitutionalism of Human Rights in Zambia," *Georgia Journal of International and Comparative Law*, 21 (2), 1991, pp. 217–43.

North, Douglass C. *Institutions, Institutional Change, and Economic Performance*, Cambridge: Cambridge University Press, 1990.

O'Donnell, Guillermo and Philippe C. Schmitter. *Transitions from Authoritarian Rule: Tentative Conclusions about Uncertain Democracies*, Baltimore: Johns Hopkins University Press, 1986.

Powers, David S. "Orientalism, Colonialism, and Legal History: The Attack on Muslim Family Endowments in Algeria and India," *Comparative Studies in Society and History*, 31 (3), 1989, pp. 535–71.

Przeworski, Adam. *Democracy and the Market: Political and Economic Reforms in Eastern Europe and Latin America*, New York: Cambridge University Press, 1991.

Reid, Donald M. *Lawyers and Politics in the Arab World, 1880–1960*, Minneapolis: Bibliotheca Islamica, 1981.

Rosen, Lawrence. *The Anthropology of Justice: Law as Culture in Islamic Society*, New York: Cambridge University Press, 1989.

Roy, Delwin A. "An Examination of Legal Instrumentalism in Public Enterprise Development in the Middle East," *Georgia Journal of International and Comparative Law*, 10 (2), 1980, pp. 271–300.

Roy, Delwin A. and William T. Irelan. "Law and Economics in the Evolution of Contemporary Egypt," *Middle Eastern Studies*, 25 (2), 1989, pp. 163–85.

Rudolph, Lloyd I. and Susanne Hoeber Rudolph. *The Modernity of Tradition: Political Development in India*, Chicago: University of Chicago Press, 1967.

Salih, 'Uthman 'Abd al-Malik al-. *Al-nizam al-dusturi wa-l-mu'assasat al-siyasiyya fi al-kuwayt* (The Constitutional System and Political Institutions in Kuwait), Kuwait: Kuwait Times Press, 1989.

"The Draft Law of Military Law and Punishments," *Majallat al-huquq*, March–June 1993, pp. 11–58.

Salim, Latifa Muhammad. *Al-nizam al-qada'i al-misri al-hadith* (The Modern Egyptian Judicial System), 2 vols., vol. I (1875–1914), and vol. II (1914–1952), Cairo: Markaz al-dirasat al-siyasiyya wa-l-istratijiyya bi-l-ahram, 1984.

Saman, Yahya al-. "The Settlement of Foreign Investment Disputes by Means of Domestic Arbitration in Saudi Arabia," *Arab Law Quarterly*, 9 (3), 1994, pp. 217–37.

Sammad, Mustashar Wajdi 'Abd al-. "Studies in the Exceptional Laws," *al-Quda*, (5/6), May/June 1986, pp. 20-24.

Schmidhauser, John. "Power, Legal Imperialism, and Dependency," *Law and Society Review*, 23 (5), 1989, pp. 857–78.

Shaham, Ron. "Judicial Divorce at the Wife's Initiative: The Shari'a Courts of Egypt, 1920-1955," *Islamic Law and Society*, 1 (2), 1994, pp. 217–57.

"Custom, Islamic Law, and Statutory Legislation: Marriage Registration and Minimum Age at Marriage in the Egyptian Shari'a Courts," *Islamic Law and Society*, 2 (3), 1995, pp. 258–81.

Shamari, Jasim al-. "The Political Crisis of 'Maids' between Kuwait and the Philippines," *al-Majalla*, 19 September 1993, pp. 29ff.

Shawi, Tawfiq al-. *Fiqh al-shura wa-l-istishara*, al-Mansura: Dar al-wafa', 1992.

Snyder, Francis, and Douglas Hay (eds.). *Labour, Law and Crime*, London: Tavistock Publications, 1987.

Starr, June. *Dispute and Settlement in Rural Turkey: An Ethnography of Law*, Leiden: E. J. Brill, 1978.

*Law as Metaphor: From Islamic Courts to the Palace of Justice*, Albany: State University of New York Press, 1992.

Starr, June and Jane Collier (eds.). *History and Power in the Study of Law*, Ithaca: Cornell University Press, 1989.

State of Kuwait, Ministry of Justice, *Al-kitab al-ihsa'i al-sanawi* (The Statistical Yearbook), various years.

Tabataba'i, 'Adil al-. *Al-nizam al-dusturi fi al-kuwayt* (The Constitutional System in Kuwait), Kuwait: n.p., 1994.

Taji, Muna al-. "Journalists, but They are Tried before the Supreme Military Court," *al-Sahafiyyun*, 13, May 1991, pp. 212–17.

Tate, C. Neal and Stacia L. Haynie, "Authoritarianism and the Functions of Courts: A Time Series Analysis of the Philippine Supreme Court, 1961–1987," *Law and Society Review*, 27 (4), 1993, pp. 707–40.

Tayyib, Ahmad 'Abd al-Zahir al-. "The Relationship of the *niyaba 'amma* with the Judiciary of Judgment," *al-Quda* (5/6), 1986, pp. 42–43.

Tignor, Robert. *State, Public Enterprise, and Economic Change in Egypt 1918–1952*, Princeton: Princeton University Press, 1984.

Toledano, Ehud R. "Law, Practice, and Social Reality: A Theft Case in Cairo, 1854," *Asian and African Studies*, 17, 1983, pp. 153–73.

State and Society in Mid-Nineteenth Century Egypt, Cambridge: Cambridge University Press, 1990.

Trubek, David M. and Marc Galanter. "Scholars in Self-Estrangement: Some Reflections on the Crisis in Law and Development Studies in the United States," *Wisconsin Law Review*, 1974, pp. 1062–1102.

'Ubayd, Muhammad Kamil. *Istiqlal al-qada'*, Cairo: Maktabat rijal al-qada', 1991.

'Ubaydan, Yusuf Muhammad. *Ma'alim al-nizam al-siyasi al-mu'asir fi qatar* (The Features of the Contemporary Political System in Qatar), n.p., 1984.

Vitalis, Robert. "On the Theory and Practice of Compradors: The Role of 'Abbud Pasha in the Egyptian Political Economy," *International Journal of Middle East Studies*, 22 (2), 1990, pp. 291–315.

When Capitalists Collide, Berkeley: University of California Press, 1995.

Volcansek, Mary L. "Judicial Review in Italy: A Reflection of the United States?", *Policy Studies Journal*, 19 (1), 1990, pp. 127–39.

Zemans, Frances Kahn. "Legal Mobilization: The Neglected Role of Law in the Political System," *American Political Science Review*, 77, 1983, pp. 690–703.

Ziadeh, Farhat. *Lawyers, the Rule of Law, and Liberalism in Modern Egypt*, Palo Alto: Stanford, 1968.

"Permanence and Change in Arab Legal Systems," *Arab Studies Quarterly*, 9 (1), 1987, pp. 20–34.

# Index

Printed in the United Kingdom
by Lightning Source UK Ltd.
117268UKS00001B/214-219